Computer Supported Coo

 University of Hertfordshire

Learning and Information Services
Hatfield Campus Learning Resources Centre

College Lane Hatfield Herts AL10 9AB
Renewals: Tel 01707 284673 Mon-Fri 12 noon-8pm only

This book is in heavy demand and is due back strictly by the last date stamped below. A fine will be charged for the late return of items.

 ONE WEEK LOAN

Spring

London
Berlin
Heidelberg
New York
Barcelona
Budapest
Hong Kong
Milan
Paris
Santa Clara
Singapore
Tokyo

Also in this series

Gerold Riempp
Wide Area Workflow Management: Creating Partnerships for the
21st Century
3-540-76243-4

Reza Hazemi, Stephen Hailes and Steve Wilbur (eds)
The Digital University: Reinventing the Academy
1-85233-003-1

Celia T. Romm and Fay Sudweeks (Eds)

Doing Business Electronically

A Global Perspective of Electronic Commerce

With 34 Figures

BCS

 Springer

Celia T. Romm, BA, MA, PhD
Management and Business Systems, University of Wollongong, Locked Bag 8844,
NSW 2521, Australia

Fay Sudweeks, ATCL, BA, MCogSc., PhD Cand.
Key Centre of Design Computing, Department of Architectural and Design Science,
University of Sydney, NSW 2006, Australia

Series Editors

Dan Diaper, PhD, MBCS
Head, Department of Computing, School of Design, Engineering and Computing,
Bournemouth University, Talbot Campus, Fern Barrow, Poole, Dorset BH12 5BB, UK

Colston Sanger
Shottersley Research Limited, Little Shottersley, Farnham Lane
Haslemere, Surrey GU27 1HA, UK

ISBN 3-540-76159-4 Springer-Verlag Berlin Heidelberg New York

British Library Cataloguing in Publication Data
Doing business electronically : a global perspective of
   electronic commerce. - (Computer supported cooperative work)
   1.Electronic commerce
   I.Romm, Celia T.   II.Sudweeks, Fay
   658'.05.46
ISBN 3540761594

Library of Congress Cataloging-in-Publication Data
Doing business electronically : a global perspective of electronic
   commerce / Celia T. Romm and Fay Sudweeks, eds.
       p.   cm. - - (Computer supported cooperative work)
   Includes indexes.
   ISBN 3-540-76159-4 (pbk. : alk. paper)
   1. Electronic commerce.   2. Electronic data interchange.
I. Romm, Celia T., 1954-   .   II. Sudweeks, Fay.   III. Series.
HF5548.32.D65   1998   98-9920
658'.0546- -dc21   CIP

Typesetting: Camera ready by editors
Printed and bound at the Athenæum Press Ltd., Gateshead, Tyne & Wear
34/3830-5432 Printed on acid-free paper   10772227

CONTENTS

Electronic Data Interchange (EDI)

SUMMARIES

Chapter 1. Introduction
Celia T. Romm and Fay Sudweeks

General Issues in Electronic Commerce

Chapter 2. The Impact of Electronic Commerce on Buyer Seller Relationships
Charles Steinfield, Robert Kraut and Alice Plummer

Interorganizational data networks can have two opposing effects on buyer-seller relationships. On the one hand, networks may be used to foster electronic marketplaces characterized by more ephemeral transactions between buyers and sellers. Also plausible, however, is the use of networks to strengthen existing commercial relationships and lock in partners by increasing the costs of switching to new trading partners. Our review of the literature suggests that this latter tendency toward what have been called electronic hierarchies is more prevalent. This chapter examines the theoretical rationales behind these competing effects and presents some evidence to show the conditions under which electronic marketplaces or electronic hierarchies are likely to prevail.

Chapter 3. The Link Between Information Strategy and Electronic Commerce
Albert L. Lederer, Dinesh A. Mirchandani and Kenneth Sims

The rapid growth of wide area networks in recent years has opened up a new avenue for companies to market products and services and disseminate information about them to potential customers. Two hundred and twelve companies that conduct business in such a way on an electronic shopping mall responded to an e-mail survey about the anticipated benefits that prompted them to do so. The survey also asked about three potential strategies for achieving business objectives - cost leadership, focus, and differentiation - that they may have been following. Six benefits factors - information, cost savings, competitiveness, productivity, planning and control, and new applications - emerged from this study. Competitiveness was the most important benefit and it predicted a differentiation and a focus strategy. Productivity and new applications also predicted a differentiation strategy. Cost savings predicted a cost leadership strategy. However, organizations followed differentiation and focus strategies significantly more than cost leadership. This assessment thus sheds light on the link between information strategy and electronic commerce.

Chapter 4. The Diffusion of Auctions on the Web
Stefan Klein

About 10 years ago, Malone, Benjamin and Yates claimed in their seminal article "Electronic Markets and Electronic Hierarchies" that the development of IT will lead to the diffusion of electronic markets. The theoretical part of their argument has been contested and modified. Empirical evidence has suggested that companies engage in inter-organisational network arrangements rather than turn to open markets. Lately, the emergence of the World Wide Web has confirmed a good part of Malone et al.'s argument. We will therefore summarise the move-to-the-market debate in the first part of this chapter, then turn to the diffusion of auctions on the Web in the second part and finally reconsider the scholarly arguments and look how they fit or how they can be applied to electronic auctions.

Chapter 5. Leveraging Security Policy for Competitive Business Advantage in Electronic Commerce
Neal Shaw

Network security is considered by most business people to be a nuisance; however, buyers and suppliers are increasingly concerned about network security with the proliferation of electronic commerce in today's business world. If a firm can demonstrate to its buyers and suppliers that its security policies are more effective than its competitors, then the firm has differentiated itself in the marketplace. To address this issue, this chapter proposes a framework to create competitive business advantage using security policies, and illustrates the potential of the framework by applying the principles to companies in various industries.

Commerce on the WWW

Chapter 6. The Dynamics of Establishing Organizational Web Sites: Some Puzzling Findings
Celia T. Romm and Jeanne Wong

A survey of the currently available literature on diffusion of Web technologies reveals that it is at a very early stage of development. As a result, it is difficult, if not impossible, to use existing models to describe or explain the process of establishing organizational Web sites. One of the few theoretical models that can be used as a starting point for research in this area is the Jarvenpaa and Ives model. The model consists of five propositions that describe what the authors see as the essential aspects of the diffusion of Web technology. The purpose of this chapter is to compare data collected in an Australian university to the propositions of the Jarvenpaa and Ives model. The comparison demonstrates that there is a need for a more generic model that would explain the diffusion process of Web technologies in diverse organizational and cultural contexts.

Chapter 7. Influence of Choice Context on Consumer Decision Making in Electronic Commerce
Rex Eugene Pereira

This research investigates the influence of context effects on consumer judgment and choice processes in the special case of electronic commerce. An outline of the judgment process is presented. This is used to identify the stages where context effects may occur. The literature in experimental and social psychology, behavioral decision theory and consumer research are selectively reviewed for evidence regarding context effects on judgment and decision making. The approach adopted in this chapter integrates ideas from two converging sources: the research in judgment and decision making in consumer behavior and cognitive psychology and the research in marketing issues in electronic commerce. The managerial implications of this research are answers to questions such as how best can the firm exploit this new form of transacting business to maximize its leverage in the marketplace and increase its market share? The academic contribution of this research on context effects is that it helps to reconcile two diverging research streams on judgment and choice (the economic perspective and the behavioral perspective).

Chapter 8. Electronic Public Procurement: From the International Experience to the Reality of the Mediterranean region
Bill Pergioudakis, Panagiotis Miliotis and George Doukidis

The public sector has been identified as an important area for electronic commerce applications. A number of initiatives have been introduced in order to automate the procurement cycle. In this chapter we are trying to define a two-phase model for introducing electronic procurement in the public sector, with emphasis on less-technologically-advanced countries in the Mediterranean region. Special characteristics were taken into account resulting in a step methodology for establishing a controllable environment. Major electronic procurement initiatives were also studied in order to define the requirements for a global electronic procurement service, giving special emphasis to European initiatives.

Chapter 9. ELPRO: Electronic procurement in Europe
Andrew Slade

The ELPRO project AD1003 is funded by the European Research and Development Directorate under the Telematics in Administrations program. Recent developments in Europe following the Treaty of Mastricht are leading towards the practical implementation of a single market for trade and commerce throughout the states that make up the European Community. The set of 15 states currently members of the Community are striving to create the conditions and regulatory framework necessary to allow for a truly open market including in the important area of national and local Government Procurement. This chapter presents the current results of the ELPRO project and describes the type of technology in use to provide complete procurement life-cycle support for local authorities such as City Councils or District Councils.

Electronic Data Interchange (EDI)

Chapter 10. EDI Maturity: A Business Opportunity
Dave Whiteley

Electronic Data Interchange (EDI) is accepted 'technology' in large organizations that are heavily reliant on purchases from their suppliers. EDI is an enabling technology for just-in-time manufacture and quick-response supply. EDI is normally initiated with a limited number of trading partners and on specific trade transactions, the *discovery* and *introductory* stages of EDI development. The next stage is the *integration* stage; this involves more trading partners, additional transactions in the trade cycle and the integration of EDI with the organization's business information systems. A fully *operational* EDI system requires a critical mass of electronic transactions and close co-ordination with trading partners. This integration process leads to, what has now become known as, an Inter-organizational System (IOS) and is part of the *strategic*

IS/IT infrastructure of the organization. The development of a mature EDI infrastructure so alters the nature of logistics that it sets up new ways of doing business and allows for changes in the nature of the product itself, mass-customization been a prime example. This development is the *innovation* stage of EDI maturity and it gives a new frontier of opportunity for competitive advantage.

Chapter 11. Design of Electronic Data Interchange Systems for Small/Medium Enterprises: Are our Information Technology Design Assumptions Correct?

Rob C. MacGregor, Deborah J. Bunker and Philip Waugh

There have been problem areas raised over recent years, within the literature that deals with Electronic Data Interchange (EDI) implementation in Small/Medium Enterprises (SMEs). It can be argued, however, that perhaps far more fundamental to this issue, is how Information Technology (IT) is accepted and used within SMEs. In particular, there is a need to examine whether academics and practitioners have based their opinions about the potential need for and usage of EDI on false assumptions about the way SMEs implement and use IT. This chapter begins by examining the development and advocacy of EDI, the nature of SMEs (in particular small business attitudes to the implementation and use of computer technology) and the recent findings about the use of IT and EDI in SMEs. Finally, utilizing data gathered from a recent survey of SMEs, in Australia, it is suggested that many of the premises upon which EDI systems are both designed and implemented in SMEs are based on incorrect assumptions concerning the nature, implementation and use of IT in SMEs.

Electronic Banking

Chapter 12. Paying for Goods and Services in the Information Age: Implications for Electronic Commerce

Boon Chye Lee

This chapter presents an overview of the major non-currency methods of payment and the likely impact they will have on electronic commerce. The focus is on the key characteristics which make each method more or less likely to be used in Internet transactions. Of particular interest is the development of secure payment methods that have the potential to spur the growth of electronic commerce and, in doing so, transform the way in which business is transacted.

Chapter 13. Channel Integration: A New Focus in Electronic Banking

Kristeen Gleason and Dan Heimann

Granting consumers access to financial information by telephone, PC and other access devices, challenges financial institutions to integrate new delivery technologies with existing legacy systems. The use of a high-volume transaction processing engine to centrally authorize and route transactions enables financial institutions to efficiently achieve this level of integration.

Industry Case Studies

Chapter 14. Information Systems for Electronic Banking: The Case of the Central Bank of Indonesia

Celia Romm and Farida Peranginangin

This case study describes the central bank (Bank Indonesia) of the Republic of Indonesia's electronic banking planning process. The literature reveals that the term 'electronic banking' is still not well defined. This term is often used interchangeably with 'electronic payment system' to refer to a subset of electronic commerce. It covers the electronic ways of transmitting payment data, and the settlement of payment from the payer to the payee.

Chapter 15. The Use of EDI at BHP Steel Group: An Industry Perspective

Karl Rommel

From BHP Steel's early involvement in Electronic Commerce in 1988 with the initial twelve pilot suppliers using a PC based system through to Electronic Trading Gateway Project, BHP has seen some fundamental changes in the way it conducts its business. Currently the ETG processes some 1.8 million documents per annum and is a central face for trading partners conducting business electronically.

CHAPTER 1

Introduction

CELIA ROMM
University of Wollongong

FAY SUDWEEKS
University of Sydney

The emergence of electronic commerce as a distinct area in business is seen by many researchers and executives as the most important commercial trend of our time. With the rapid adoption of networking technology by companies, the world is witnessing amazing changes in the way that business is done. Electronic commerce has been redefining all facets of business in a revolutionary manner. It is crucial to the effective functioning of organizations, especially in a world where companies have to deal with suppliers, customers, partners and their own units distributed across the world. The new business reality created by electronic commerce is no longer a projected vision of technocrats. It is a new "world order", with millions of dollars exchanged between parties daily. Electronic commerce is already playing a significant role in determining corporate strategy and in creating value. It is also already playing an important role in changing society as we know it today.

To be competitive in today's marketplace, companies need to expand commercial activities beyond national borders. The global network of electronic infrastructure has played a significant role in this expansion but the technology itself is not the factor driving the business revolution. The revolution is driven by the interaction of information technology and customer demand. Customers are not only adapting to new technologies, they are demanding more and more global competition.

The new business reality created by electronic commerce calls for appropriate research and scholarship. Instead of playing a catch-up game with this unknown monster, it is necessary that conscious and deliberate initiatives be made by academics and leaders in industry to tame it. It is also necessary that appropriate texts be created to teach students and the general public how to understand and cope with the new reality created by electronic commerce.

Doing Business Electronically addresses this goal. By providing an overview of the major areas of electronic commerce from both a scholarly and an industry perspective, this volume contributes towards closing the gap that currently exists in this area. Some of the questions that the authors address are:

- how do companies cope with issues of integrity and security?

- with real time electronic transactions, what are the implications for new and existing financial institutions?
- how do we preserve intellectual property rights in a global, information-intense market?
- how can companies achieve effective performance by streamlining information flows?
- how can networked communities benefit from global collaborative systems?
- what do the high tech offerings of multimedia technology imply for next generation marketing?
- how should academic researchers and corporate managers address these issues?

Doing Business Electronically is primarily intended as a textbook for graduate level students taking courses in electronic commerce. Courses in this area are currently being introduced in many schools of business around the world, at both undergraduate and graduate levels. This book can stand alone or supplement a more introductory textbook in electronic commerce.

As a collection of research work in electronic commerce, *Doing Business Electronically* can also be used as a support text for courses in marketing, business strategy, management of information systems, organizational change, project management, product innovation, and international management. All of these - and more - are areas where there is a growing awareness of the key role of electronic commerce in business. In fact, one of the major advantages of this book is that it can be used by lecturers to expand the applicability of an undergraduate text to graduate students by exposing them to the electronic commerce implications of their discipline.

Doing Business Electronically will also appeal to anyone who owns or has access to a computer. It can be of interest to vendors who wish to sell on the World Wide Web. It could also be of interest to managers who are developing their companies' electronic commerce strategies, establishing their organizations' WWW sites, or responding to customers who prefer to communicate with the company electronically.

The collection of readings on electronic commerce in this book covers the general issues, major technologies, and processes that are associated with electronic commerce. In addition to scholarly work by leading researchers, two cases by industry executives are included. The geographic distribution of the contributors gives a transnational perspective on electronic commerce. Contributors represent Australia, Denmark, Greece, Malaysia, United Kingdom and the USA.

The book consists of five sections: General Issues in Electronic Commerce; Commerce on the World Wide Web; Electronic Data Interchange; Electronic Banking; and Industry Case Studies.

1.1. General Issues in Electronic Commerce

This section introduces a range of general issues associated with electronic commerce. Charles Steinfield, Robert Kraut and Alice Chan open the section by introducing a key issue in electronic commerce; that is, its complex effect on buyer-seller relationships. Their chapter discusses two opposing possibilities: (i) that data networks may "free" the market by enabling more ephemeral transactions between buyers and sellers; and (ii) that they will restrict or even "enslave" players by locking them into existing relationships from which it is technologically difficult to escape. The chapter reviews the literature in this area suggesting conditions under which the second scenario is more likely to occur.

Al Lederer, Dinesh Mirchandani, and Kenneth Sims, continue the theme of changes to buyer-seller relationships in Chapter 3 by exploring the specific expectations that sellers have of the electronic marketplace. Based on a survey of over two hundred companies that conduct their business in an electronic shopping mall, the authors conclude that competitiveness is the major benefit that companies expect to gain as a result of their electronic commerce activities and that this expected benefit predicts their differentiation and focus strategy.

In Chapter 4, Stefan Klein takes a global perspective of the dilemma raised by Steinfield, Kraut and Chan; that is, whether electronic commerce leads to a more open or a more constrained market. Using auctions on the web as its focus, it concludes that their emergence does, indeed, lead to a more open market but only under specific conditions.

The issue of security, as a crucial element in buyer-seller relationships in electronic markets, is discussed by Neal Shaw in Chapter 5. Shaw proposes a framework for using security policies, demonstrating how it could be used to achieve competitive advantage in different segments of the electronic commerce market.

1.2. Commerce on the WWW

This section introduces a range of issues associated with commerce on the World Wide Web (WWW or the Web). In Chapter 6, Celia Romm and Jeanne Wong discuss the strategy of establishing organizational web sites. An Australian case study is used as a basis for proposing a generic model for conceptualizing the process of organizational Web site development.

Another strategic issue related to business on the Web is the importance of understanding cultural factors that influence the purchasing behavior of consumers who are shopping at electronic malls. Most important among these factors, according to Rex Pereira in Chapter 7, is information about cultural factors that affect consumers' involvement in the buying decision, customers' perceived risk, customers' income and credit, and customers' mode of learning.

In Chapter 8, Bill Pergioudakis, Panagiotis Miliotis, and George Doukidis take a unique perspective on Web commerce by looking at the electronic procurement of the public sector in the Mediterranean region. They outline a two-phase model for introducing electronic procurement, with particular emphasis on related European initiatives in this area. Also focusing on European electronic procurement activities, Andrew Slade uses the case study ELPRO (Electronic Procurement in Europe) in Chapter 9. The author investigates how to provide electronic means of placing contracts from very large public bodies with suppliers across the world.

1.3. Electronic Data Interchange

This section discusses a range of issues associated with electronic data interchange (EDI). This technology is described in Chapter 10, with a range of real life examples from different industries in which this technology has been implemented. The author, Dave Whiteley, then proceeds to outline an *EDI Maturity Model* which formalizes the process of implementing EDI in organizations and incorporates it with a re-engineering of the company's supply chain.

The second reading in this section, Chapter 11 by Rob MacGregor, Deborah Bunker and Philip Waugh, focuses the discussion of EDI on small business. The major assertion made by the authors is that many premises upon which EDI systems are designed and implemented in small businesses are based on incorrect assumptions concerning the nature, implementation, and use of this technology in small business. The authors call for a realization that EDI can be an "enslavement" technology of small firms by larger ones and consequent reluctance on the part of small firms to use this technology for this reason.

1.4. Electronic Banking

This section focuses on electronic banking as a major subcategory of electronic commerce. Chapter 12, by Boon Lee, focuses on payment methods, particularly those with a potential application to electronic commerce. Following a review of recent trends in the use of noncurrency payment methods in developed countries, the chapter focuses on the implications from these emerging technologies for the future development of electronic banking.

Kristeen Heimann and Dan Glasson, in Chapter 13, build on the theoretical issues raised by Lee by taking a more practical approach. The major rebuttal of the Heimann and Glasson chapter is to outline the major challenges and ideal solutions for electronic banking. The authors' conclusion is that, in order to meet its objectives, an electronic banking system needs to be available around the clock, flexible, secure, and high performing at both high and low peak times.

1.5. Industry Case Studies

The last section of the book introduces two electronic commerce case studies. The first case study by Celia Romm and Farida Peranginangin, in Chapter 14, describes the electronic banking planning process of the central bank of the Republic of Indonesia. The case study, written by an executive of the bank, reviews the planning process of this major electronic commerce system, comparing it to models of IT planning in the public and private sector.

Chapter 15, the second case study in this section, describes in detail the introduction of electronic commerce applications to one of Australia's largest companies. Karl Rommel, Head of Electronic Commerce at BHP Ltd, discusses the range of electronic commerce technologies used by the company, the process of implementing them, and some of the outcomes, both positive and negative, that have resulted from these initiatives.

CHAPTER 2

The Impact of Interorganizational Networks on Buyer-Seller Relationships

CHARLES STEINFIELD
Michigan State University

ROBERT KRAUT
Carnegie Mellon University

ALICE CHAN
Cornell University

2.1. Introduction

During the past decade, organizational theorists, business consultants, and telecommunications managers and vendors have directed our attention to the strategic role that information can play in the competitive strategy of firms (see, for example, Bradley, Hausman and Nolan, 1993; Keen, 1988; Porter and Millar 1985). Throughout the 1980s, widely discussed case examples demonstrated how the use of telecommunications networks to link firms to their suppliers and distribution chains conveyed important first mover advantages to such firms as American Hospital Supply and McKesson. The reported benefits to the firms deploying such interorganizational networks included: increased efficiency of order processing; reduced costs due to just-in-time inventory management; locking in trading partners because of the difficulties competitors faced once a network was in place; and greater ability to customize products and services based upon information arising from the transactions carried by the network (Cash and Konsynski, 1985; Johnson and Vitale, 1988).

In the past, these networks were typically put into place by a dominant firm in a value chain, and were built upon proprietary applications running over private networks. Chrysler, for example, required its parts suppliers to participate in its Electronic Data Interchange (EDI) network. Hence, it should not be surprising that they were often implemented with the most important existing trading partners. In fact, on the upstream side, a typical goal for such applications as EDI was to reduce

Reprint from *Journal of Computer Mediated Communication* 1(3): http://www.ascusc.org/jcmc/
© 1995, Annenberg School of Communication, University of Southern California. Used with permission.

the total number of suppliers and enhance the quality and efficiency of the overall purchasing function (Kekre and Mudhopadhyay, 1992).

The increasing standardization of such applications as EDI, as well as the availability of lower cost public network infrastructures, has convinced several researchers that interorganizational networks will not only proliferate, but will be applied in qualitatively different ways. In particular, as the barriers to participating in such electronic transactions diminish, some researchers now believe that the conditions are ripe for the establishment of electronic marketplaces. Rather than having networks only link existing trading partners in a tightly coupled arrangement, such new electronic markets could conceivably include larger numbers of buyers and sellers (Malone, Yates and Benjamin, 1987; Wildman and Guerin-Calvert, 1991).

The popular press is inundated with reports of the ongoing commercialization of the Internet, and the rush of firms to establish a presence in this new virtual marketplace (e.g. *Business Week*, 1994). Because this is a near ubiquitous and public infrastructure, built upon a common set of standards, it has the characteristics that many feel would be necessary for the growth of electronic marketplaces. In much the same way, years before, France established the Teletel infrastructure that permitted firms to establish linkages to their trading partners at a lower cost than if they used private networks. Although not meant for high volume transactions (e.g. Teletel required the establishment of a dial-up connection for each transaction) it could easily permit smaller trading partners to share data and automate transactions with each other (Steinfield and Caby, 1993).

The purpose of this chapter is to examine the prevailing theoretical expectations for the effect of networks on interorganizational relationships, and develop propositions that are relevant for the new infrastructure environment characterized by public and ubiquitous data networks like the Internet. Our conclusions are based upon a critical review of previous literature on interorganizational networks, and a re-examination of empirical studies that specifically look at the uses of public and ubiquitous networks.

The chapter is organized into the following sections. Section II provides a review of the literature examining the likely impacts of interorganizational networks on the ways that firms coordinate with each other. Here we show that the prevailing logic, adapted from Malone, Yates and Benjamin (1987), is that a reduction in coordination costs enabled by information technology is likely to produce large changes in the ways that firms select and maintain relationships with trading partners. Malone and colleagues emphasize that networks can facilitate tighter coupling through the integration of production across firms as well as reduced search costs that might encourage relations that are more market-like across firms. However, their essential argument, that reduced coordination costs afforded by networks will lead to more market-like arrangements, is somewhat ambiguous, since improved coordination is necessary for both types of outcomes. Hence, their analysis makes it difficult to hypothesize about the ultimate effects of interorganizational networks on the relations between firms. We explicitly focus on two variables not well developed in the previous literature: the relative openness of the network infrastructure, which has its effects by reducing the costs of adding new parties to an interorganizational network, and the locus of control of the electronic network service, which influences the kinds of incentives participants face vis-a-vis the addition of new buyers or sellers.

Section III then examines the empirical evidence to date, in particular by examining survey research and case studies where firms did, in fact, use public (hence relatively open in our view) data infrastructures as a platform for interorganizational networks. We show that the reduced cost of adding new subscribers does appear to alter the ways in which interorganizational networks are used, but not necessarily in a fashion consistent with the expectations of Malone et al. (1987). We further show that the locus of the control of an electronic network service does appear to explain different structural outcomes. Taken together, both the theoretical arguments and the empirical evidence lead us to believe that firms will use interorganizational networks to build tight relationships with their trading partners, rather than to select suppliers on a transaction by transaction basis from a large pool. We further believe that for electronic marketplaces to emerge, where there are both multiple buyers and multiple sellers and the network performs search and product/service matching functions, some form of third party market maker is needed.

Finally, Section IV discusses the limitations of the empirical work to date, noting that it lacks measurement of the processes by which networks are hypothesized to have their effects on interorganizational relations. In particular, without specific measurements on the costs and benefits of network usage for acquiring goods in an electronic marketplace vs. usage for more tightly integrated production that implies foregoing the advantages of the market as a coordination mechanism, we cannot fully explain the prevalence of electronic hierarchies in the empirical studies. We suggest alternative explanations based upon such variables as the existence of interpersonal relationships among members of a firm, and the degree of trust between firms. Without further empirical investigation, our conclusions remain speculative.

2.2. Electronic Interorganizational Networks and Organizational Forms

2.2.1. OUT-SOURCING VERSUS IN-HOUSE PRODUCTION

The production of almost any complex product consists of acquiring various raw materials and other components and crafting them, with each step presumably adding value as the product wends its way towards its ultimate consumer. The value chain consists of the movement of the components through various stages of production and distribution as they are transformed into final products (Porter, 1980). To make and sell a news magazine, for example, one must integrate reporting, writing, editing, photographs, typography, layout, paper, printing, subscription services, mailing labels, and physical distribution. A firm must decide to produce each of these goods or services in-house or to out-source it. For example, most news magazines do not own either their own paper mills or printing presses, but they do hire editors as salaried employees. They may instruct employee-reporters to write a story or they may commission one from a stringer or other freelancer. Photographs may come from their own photographers or be purchased from a stock house. Explaining whether a firm would produce a good or service in-house or buy it on the open market has been a traditional question in economics and organizational sociology.

Most economists believe that were it not for the costs of coordination, markets would generally be more efficient mechanisms for production than hierarchies. By being able to sell to many customers in a market, a producer could acquire more experience, level the load of production across many customers, and capitalize on economies of scale, all of which generally lead to more efficient production. Similarly, in a market, customers can shop around for the best combination of price, quality, or other desirable attributes and, because they have choices, are not held hostage to the opportunistic behavior of any single supplier. Competition among suppliers would also lead to efficiencies.

The rub is that when purchasing goods and services on the open market, costs of coordination can be high. Economists point to the extra costs that out-sourcing imposes on coordinating the economic transactions themselves. In particular, when out-sourcing, firms have additional costs as they search for appropriate suppliers, specify contracts, enforce the contracts, and handle financial settlement (Williamson, 1975). For example, customers can have difficulty specifying what they want and searching through the many alternatives to find the best suppliers and best wares, and suppliers incur costs in advertising the availability of their goods and services to potential customers (Malone et al., 1987). Once an economic transaction has been agreed upon and goods produced, the customer needs to insure that suppliers are meeting the terms of the contract, for example, by continuing to supply high quality goods according to an agreed-upon schedule. Monitoring through various quality-control programs is expensive. Once the goods have been delivered, the customer needs to receive an invoice and producers need to be paid. Arranging billing and payment between large numbers of customers and suppliers can be expensive.

Williamson argues firms exist precisely to reduce the costs of negotiating, monitoring and executing transactions that are necessary when acquiring goods and services in the open market[1]. His term *transaction costs* refers to these costs.[2] He distinguishes between markets and hierarchies in terms of the economic location of production. The term *hierarchy* is used to refer to the case of in-house production, with economic decisions made by managerial fiat, while the term *market* refers to cases of out-sourcing, where the acquisition of goods is subject to the laws of supply and demand.

Williamson further explains a firm's choice of in-house (hierarchy) vs. out-sourcing (market) in order to obtain some good by examining factors that can influence both opportunistic behavior of other firms and the costs of search in the

---

[1]However, see Granovetter (1985) for an argument that merely producing goods and services in-house provides no guarantee against the opportunism that Williamson sees as the basic reason for the existence of firms. Theorists still need to explain why economic agents, be they employees or contractors, act in a firm's best interest.

[2]The phrase transaction costs is to be preferred to Malone et al.'s phrase coordination costs. As we shall see below, both the costs of coordinating economic transactions and the costs of coordinating production may both increase with out-sourcing.

marketplace. A variety of forms of *asset specificity* can make a firm vulnerable to opportunism. When the assets required to produce a good are specific, they are only of value to the firm needing them.[3] If provided by another firm, this firm may behave opportunistically (i.e. extract a higher price than necessary) since it realizes the buyer is dependent and cannot easily obtain the asset elsewhere. Under these conditions, a firm is more likely to choose hierarchy as a form of governance.

Complexity of product information has also been related to opportunism and search costs (Malone et al., 1987). When a good is highly complex, it may be harder for a buying firm to know whether the selling firm is engaging in opportunistic behavior. Moreover, it may be harder to communicate the good's features in the marketplace with enough precision to enable adequate matching of needs. Hence, this feature too should encourage a firm to produce the required good in-house.

In addition to the cost of coordinating the economic transactions, out-sourcing often leads to higher costs of coordinating production itself. Because external suppliers of raw materials or services are likely to be further away than an in-house supplier, the difficulties of coordination across space are likely to be higher. In addition, because external suppliers are likely to have worked with a firm for a shorter duration than in-house suppliers, the external suppliers will have lost some advantages due to learning. In the case of a news magazine, for example, it may be more difficult for editors and photographers to decide which one in a set of photographs is appropriate for an article and to determine how to crop it, if the photographer is located far away. By working with the same photographer over an extended period, the editor is likely to have learned the photographer's tastes and vocabulary, making editorial direction and decision making easier.

Malone and colleagues (1987) argue that the use of electronic communication links between firms can reduce both the costs of coordinating economic transactions and the costs of coordinating production. Coordination of both sorts consists of communicating information and processing it. Because modern information technology lowers the costs of both communication and information processing, Malone and his colleagues hypothesize that "the result of reducing coordination costs without changing anything else should be an increase in the proportion of economic activity coordinated by markets" (p. 489). That is, they expect that these lowered coordination costs would encourage more out-sourcing by enabling firms to buy goods and services less expensively than to produce them in-house (Malone, 1987; Malone et al., 1987, 1989). To the extent that the cost of communication and information processing are reduced, the cost disadvantage of out-sourcing a production process is also reduced. Returning to our magazine example, if an editor could as easily identify and vet a distant, freelance photographer as a nearby

---

[3]Four forms of asset specificity that have been discussed are site, physical, human, and time (Malone et al., 1987). Site specificity means that the factor of production, e.g. raw materials, is only available in a particular location. Physical asset specificity means that the factor of production cannot be used for anything else, and is therefore only useful for the one firm. Human asset specificity means that particular skills are needed in order to produce the factor of production. Finally time specificity means that the factor of production is only useful at a particular point in time; that is, it is perishable.

employee and could as easily share information with the freelancer, the editor would benefit from out-sourcing photography. If, for example, the editor could easily search through photo archives over the World Wide Web (or Web), or share new photographs with a freelancer through multimedia electronic mail or through screen sharing software, the costs of working with external sources of photography would be reduced, but the advantages of having a larger pool of photographs or photographers would remain.

Empirical tests of the hypothesis that greater use of interorganizational networks leads to greater out-sourcing are only starting. Consistent with this hypothesis is evidence at the industry level that increases in investment in information technology were associated with a decline in average firm size and rise in the number of firms (Brynjolffson, Malone, Gurbaxani and Kambil, 1993). Kambil (1991) shows that industries investing more of their capital stock in information technology also contract out more of the value of the goods and services they produced to external suppliers (i.e. a higher buy/make ratio in production), with a two-year lag. Limitations in the data, however, mean that the analyses are only suggestive. For example, analyses conducted at the industry level (2-digit SIC codes) do not necessarily speak to the way particular firms deploy information technology. Moreover using general information technology as the independent variable obscures the unique role that interorganizational networks might play.

2.2.2. ELECTRONIC MARKETS VERSUS ELECTRONIC HIERARCHIES

Malone et al. (1987) make an additional prediction about the effects of inter-organizational data networks that has not yet been tested. They argue that even when production is out-sourced, networks will encourage market-like rather than hierarchy-like control of production processes. When one considers markets and hierarchies as control mechanisms rather than as locations of production, the distinction between them is continuous rather than dichotomous. Control here refers to the means by which the behavior of employees or trading partner firms is *governed* (hence the term *governance* is often applied), and opportunistic behavior avoided. Even when out-sourcing, firms can have more or less hierarchical relationships with an economic partner. Under a *hierarchical* mechanism, value chain activities are controlled and directed by management decisions either within a single firm or across several interacting firms. Managerial decisions rather than selection in the open market set product and service attributes. A buyer does not choose from among many potential sellers, but instead procures goods and services from a predetermined supplier. There are many different forms of hierarchical control, including partnerships, alliances, or simply stable, long term buyer-supplier relationships. If a single firm serves as the sole supplier to many buyers, the former's relationship with each of the latter is considered hierarchical. Similarly, long term relationships in which trading partners adopt common values, operate on the basis of trust rather than contract, and make accommodations to each other also represent hierarchical relationships.[4]

In contrast, when a *market* mechanism is at work, the flow of materials and services through the value chain is coordinated by a decentralized price system. Relationships among firms can be short-lived, since price and net value received on a transaction by transaction basis determine the exchange of economic resources. The availability of goods and services varying in price, quantity produced, quality standards, delivery schedules and other attributes is not determined by explicit managerial direction in a dominant supplier or buyer firm or a cluster of them. Assuming perfect market information, buyers purchase from whichever supplier can offer the best combination of these attributes.

Again, consider the editor of a news magazine looking for a photograph to run with a story about eastern Europe. If the editor sent an employee to take the pictures, this would clearly be an example of a hierarchical relationship, as the term is used by Williamson. If the editor searched through several stock houses to select an already existing photograph, this would be an example of a market-based purchase. However, if the editor gave the photography assignment to a freelance photographer with whom he had worked extensively in the past and who received a substantial portion of his income from the news magazine, most observers would agree that the relationship between news magazine and photographer is hierarchical, even though the editor out-sourced the photography.

According to Malone et al. (1987), interorganizational electronic networks can improve coordination between firms in two contrasting ways. By using electronic networks to reduce the costs of searching for appropriate goods and services, firms can achieve an *electronic brokerage* effect. Examples of using electronic interorganizational electronic networks to reduce search costs include the NASDAQ system which creates an electronic market for over-the-counter stocks, the EasySabre airline reservation system, which allows consumers to search for and compare ticket prices and availability before ordering, on-line multiple listing services which help real estate agents and customers to narrow down the houses they visit, and CommerceNet which allows firms in Silicon Valley to order computer supplies on the Web. These services all connect different buyers and sellers through a shared information resource (like a centrally maintained database or the decentralized Web) and provide some tools for searching the data. They help the buyers to quickly, conveniently and inexpensively evaluate the offerings of various suppliers. The electronic brokerage effect can increase the number of alternatives as well as the quality of the alternative ultimately selected, while decreasing the cost of the selection process.

---

[4]Hierarchy is a misleading word to use in this case, since it implies authority relations. Where long term relations are based upon trust, we use hierarchy only to suggest that the trading partners are tightly coupled rather than linked only by ephemeral market-like transactions. Others use terms like value-added partnerships or networked organizations, and suggest that these are qualitatively different forms of organization than either market or hierarchy (Johnston and Lawrence, 1988; Powell, 1990).

By using electronic networks to reduce the costs of tightly integrating a particular buyer and seller, firms can achieve an *electronic integration* effect. An example would be an electronic data interchange system that connects a retailer's point of sale terminals to a supplier's delivery system, decreasing the likelihood of the retailer going out of stock on popular goods (Weber, 1995). Another example is the integration of CAD/CAM systems between a computer chip design firm and a silicon foundry, that allows the designers of a chip to monitor the manufacturing process and to have more flexibility in changing their designs (Hart and Estrin, 1991). This effect is manifested when technology is used not only to facilitate communication but also to tightly couple processes at the interface between stages of the value chain.

Malone et al. hypothesize that using electronic interorganizational networks for these different effects will have consequences for the control mechanisms regulating firms' transactions with their trading partners. To the extent that firms use electronic networks for their electronic brokerage effects (i.e. to lower search costs), they will tend to develop electronic market relationships with their trading partners. Since the technology makes it easy for firms to search through many possible suppliers, firms will use these networks to develop a relatively large pool of suppliers, with relatively little loyalty over different transactions to particular suppliers. On the other hand, to the extent that firms deploy electronic networks for their electronic integration effect (i.e. to tightly couple with trading partners), they will tend to develop long-term, hierarchical relationships with their trading partners.

Malone et al. (1987; 1989) propose that over time electronic brokerage effects will dominate electronic integration effects, as competition, regulation and improving public infrastructure draw additional firms onto networks and as search costs drop more rapidly than integration costs. Therefore, they claim that one of the major effects of interorganizational networks would be a shift from hierarchical to market relationships. "Some of the initial providers of electronic markets have attempted ... to capture customers in a system biased towards a particular supplier. We believe that, in the long run, the significant additional benefits to buyers possible from the electronic brokerage effect will drive almost all electronic markets toward being unbiased channels for products from many suppliers." (Malone et al, 1987, p. 492.)

Malone et al. base their predictions about the dominance of electronic markets on the relative benefits they anticipate firms will receive from electronic brokerage and electronic integration. Invariably, these benefits do not favor electronic brokerage over integration. Which one they favor is likely to be a complex function of the attributes of the products being exchanged, the information networks being used, and the business environment in which the networks are deployed. In addition, whether firms deploy electronic networks for brokerage or integration itself is also likely to be influenced by the pre-existing relationships among particular suppliers and buyers, and these starting conditions will therefore shape whether market or hierarchical relationships develop over the long term. The following section briefly discusses some product attributes, network infrastructure, business environment and interfirm relationships that are likely to influence how interorganizational electronic networks are deployed.

Product attributes. The value of external networks for product search increases as geographic, temporal, or cognitive constraints make product location and selection difficult. Thus, use of information networks should lead to more market-like relationships between buyers and sellers, when there are large numbers of potential suppliers, when suppliers are geographically separated, when there are many comparable products in the industry, and when prices or products change rapidly.

As Malone et al. (1987) note, products low in complexity are easier to describe and search for than products higher in complexity. Therefore, they hypothesize that electronic markets are more likely to develop among firms exchanging simpler products. Product complexity is partially an intrinsic characteristic of the product, but can be the outcome of prior attempts to apply information technology. For example Malone et al. would expect to see an electronic market develop for books, because books can be easily searched for through various information retrieval techniques (e.g. Salton and McGill, 1979) and because prior applications of information technology have led to the construction of the ten digit ISBN number, which for some purposes completely describes a book. On the other hand, an electronic market for photographs, for which no conventional product descriptors or search techniques exist, would be less likely to develop.

Product complexity may interact with network attributes. Text descriptions may limit the complexity of product descriptions on low-bandwidth telecommunications networks, while graphical browsing may allow richer product descriptions on high bandwidth networks.

When product search is difficult, networks can provide additional value to the extent to which they facilitate searches. Thus one would expect that network facilities such as directory services, which make locating a large number of potential suppliers easier, and intelligent comparison programs would lead to more market-like relationships between suppliers and buyers.

Network infrastructure. The nature of the network infrastructure can directly influence the type of relationships developed among firms. The *openness* of a network is perhaps the most important network attribute to consider. Networks are more open to the extent they allow easy communication with a new customer, supplier or other entity over the network. Networks become more open if they use public protocols already adopted by major equipment and software providers, if many individuals and firms already use the networks, and if the financial and behavioral costs of acquiring, deploying, and using the hardware and software needed to communicate over the network are low. The telephone network in the United States is a prime example of an open network. Over ninety percent of individuals and almost all businesses have a telephone service. The open protocols governing telephone interconnections means that interconnection is easy, and because of economies of scale and various subsidies, the costs of both terminals (i.e. phones) and monthly service is relatively cheap. The Teletel network in France and the Internet/Web network in the United States are examples of open data networks. Using any of these networks, the cost to a customer to search for potential suppliers (via an 800 number call or a search service on the Web) is low. Conversely, the cost for a supplier of adding an additional customer is also very low.

It is generally the case that large firms most aggressively take advantage of innovations (Moch and Morse, 1977), including interorganizational electronic networks (Streeter, Kraut and Lucas, 1996). One consequence of the low cost of open networks, however, is that the advantages of both electronic brokerage and electronic integration may be extended to small firms and even individuals.

Open telecommunications networks are a prerequisite for market-like relationships between suppliers and buyers. Both multiple suppliers and multiple buyers need to be joined, and this can happen only if standards or other network attributes permit interconnection by multiple parties, without substantial network-specific investment on the part of either buyers or sellers. Thus, one would expect more market-like relationships between buyers and sellers when the communication networks they use are more open. While open telecommunication networks are a prerequisite for electronic markets, they do not guarantee it. Simply by encrypting some data or by allowing only individuals with passwords to access a service, one can convert an open application to a proprietary one.

Business environment and network control. We have argued that open networks are a prerequisite for using external networks to achieve electronic markets. But whether firms will agree to subscribe to industry-wide standards, to have competitors join trading consortia, or to make their data and other internal processes open to a large number of outsiders depends in part on the entities that control the networks and on the industry structure. Networks run by third parties, who are neither buyers nor sellers on the network, are more likely to lead to market-like relationships between buyers and sellers. Since the third party's return is based on the volume of network transactions, the network provider has little reason to exclude either buyer or seller. On the other hand, on a seller controlled network, sellers will be motivated to exclude other sellers in order to retain customer loyalty (e.g. American Hospital Supply). Similarly, on a buyer-controlled network, the buyer may be motivated to exclude other buyers to capture the benefits of the efficiency that the network provides (e.g. General Motors' EDI system). Moreover, under some circumstances, buyers may wish to exclude some sellers to reduce their search costs and to convince a restricted number of sellers to engage in relationship-specific investments (Bakos and Brynjolffson, 1992).

Network control will have its effects primarily when the power relationships among potential sellers, among potential buyers, and between buyers and sellers are unequal. If one seller dominates a market, then the seller will perceive opening their networks as threatening its market share. On the other hand, if no seller has dominant market share, then the network externalities associated with increasing the size of the market overall are likely to prevail. In particular, since having a mass of small and roughly equal sellers on the network would encourage additional buyers to use the network, these opportunities to increase the customer base would encourage sellers to tolerate other sellers on the network. Similarly, if no one buyer has enough power to dominate an industry or dominate a network of suppliers, then the benefits of network externalities will overwhelm the disadvantages of sharing efficiency gains (e.g. mass market customers). These benefits include both the increased numbers of suppliers to choose from, and the cost reduction in using the network resulting from economies of scale, greater reliability and ease of use of the network, and so forth.

Network control and the business context will also influence the evolution of services on a network. In a seller-initiated network, when one seller dominates a market, not only will any efforts to open the network to other sellers be resisted, but a service evolution strategy that progressively locks in buyers by raising switching costs will be followed. To implement this strategy, the supplier may provide the buyer with value-added information such as purchase histories or other useful management information. Such a service evolution strategy will further result in more tightly coupled hierarchical relations between the seller and its buyers. If buyers are very numerous, network services will increasingly be used both to reduce sellers' share of transaction costs and to enhance revenue. The seller's costs can be reduced by imposing on the buyer both labor costs (e.g. having buyers key in orders) and capital and communications costs (e.g. using buyers' terminals and requiring them to pay their own telecommunications charges) for the seller's. The more numerous (i.e. mass market) the buyers, the greater will be the tendency to derive revenue directly from network service provision itself, mostly by charging communications and information service usage fees to buyers. However, in cases where networks become highly successful, sellers may choose to allow in competitors on a fee basis, as in the SABRE system of American Airlines. In cases where no one seller is dominant, and buyers are numerous, seller-provided network services will mainly focus on increasing the share of basic transactions that are conducted electronically. To the degree that an electronic market develops, new services providing a richer set of functions will be offered, often for a fee. However, these features will not be as custom tailored to the needs of any particular buyer as in the case of a seller network that is attempting to lock in buyers.

2.3. Empirical Investigations of Electronic Networks and Interorganizational Relationships

The previous section reviewed many of the predictions that a transaction cost perspective would make about the impact of interorganizational electronic networks on relationships among firms, and suggested some technological and business-environment issues that must be considered in specifying predictions. While Malone and colleagues (1987) predicted that in the steady state, greater use of interorganizational networks would lead to more market-like relationships among firms, the empirical evidence reviewed below does not support this expectation. It is not clear whether this failure of prediction results from (1) insufficient openness of the telecommunications networks, (2) business environments in which interorganizational networks have been first deployed, or (3) a mis-specification of the electronic brokerage versus integration gains afforded by the networks. To date, the empirical evidence has been too gross to identify the mechanisms through which the use of interorganizational networks is affecting the relationships among buyers and sellers.

Most research on interorganizational networks has used case studies of specific private network-based systems to examine the conditions under which firms use external data networks and the strategic advantages they seek to achieve. Well known examples include McKesson's use of their network to link to independent pharmacies and American Hospital Supply's use of their network to take orders from hospitals (Keen, 1988; Malone and Rockart, 1993). In both of these cases, the systems were interorganizational, but were not open to other suppliers. The networks and the application were proprietary and under the control of the supplier, with private networks used to provide the infrastructure. The networks were primarily put into place with existing trading partners, and were not accessible by those not included in the system. Particularly in the case of McKesson, which extended the applications supported by their system from simple order entry to include such value-added services as insurance claims processing for pharmacists, the use of the network bound customers more tightly to the supplying firm and enhanced an already existing hierarchical relationship.

A multi-organization study by Brousseau (1990) also concluded that the modal use of business-to-business external networks has been to support electronic hierarchies, not electronic markets. Brousseau reviewed 26 interorganizational networks, finding that most were used to reduce production or distribution costs and served to reinforce already existing hierarchical relationships among firms. Only in two - the petroleum business and textiles - was the use of interorganizational networks associated with buyers gaining advantage by having more suppliers from which to choose. Taken collectively, previous case study research illustrates that interfirm networks are often used to support electronic hierarchies, rather than electronic marketplaces.

One hypothesis explaining the prevalence of electronic hierarchies is that the high cost of extending private networks to trading partners encourages linkages only when a meaningful volume of transactions is expected to occur. The firm controlling the network application is further encouraged to add new types of transactions to fully load the network, justifying the dedicated capacity to each trading partner. We would thus anticipate that where data networks are proprietary and fragmented, as in the United States before the explosive growth of the Internet, electronic hierarchies would be more common than electronic marketplaces. This further suggests that when public and ubiquitous data networks are available, the same constraints on connecting low volume trading partners, or potential partners for whom anticipated volume is uncertain, do not exist. Under such conditions, electronic marketplaces, where more fleeting trading relationships can economically be supported by network-based transactions, should be more likely. It is useful, then, to explore the outcome of earlier experiences with ubiquitous data networks, in order to better understand the dynamics of electronic commerce on the Internet and other future electronic commerce platforms.

2.3.1. OPEN NETWORKS AS A PLATFORM FOR ELECTRONIC COMMERCE

Before the opening of the Internet to commercial and non-academic traffic, public data networks in the United States were mainly offered by on-line information service providers such as CompuServe. At one point CompuServe even marketed a business information service, enabling firms to use CompuServe's extensive network for electronic mail and the provision of company data to employees and others to whom a company wished to provide access.

Outside of the United States, one of the oldest examples of a truly ubiquitous, open, public data network is the Teletel network created by France Telecom starting in 1982 (Lucas, Levecq, Kraut and Streeter, 1995). Teletel consists of the widespread deployment of the Minitel data terminal, an electronic telephone directory, and almost 25,000 other information and communication services and business applications, used by businesses and residential consumers. In 1995, there were over 6.5 million Minitel terminals in France with a growth rate of approximately 10% per year. About 20% of French households have Minitels and about 80% of businesses have at least one Minitel. Altogether about 40% of the non-retired French population had access to Teletel either at work or at home in 1992 (France Telecom, 1992). It thus has the basic characteristics to function as an electronic commerce platform, and has supported the emergence of an entirely new electronic information services industry in France, despite the comparatively low penetration of home computers.

Case studies conducted on firms using the Teletel and other broadly available electronic service networks as business networking platforms (i.e. where the network infrastructure itself is not under the control of the firm offering the application) illustrate the motivations of suppliers when they develop applications for electronic commerce. Steinfield, working with several collaborators has conducted qualitative case studies of the way firms in the United States and France use interorganizational videotex networks (Steinfield and Caby, 1993; Steinfield, Caby and Vialle, 1993). These studies have documented the ways in which the openness provided by the network in large measure determines the kinds of applications that can be deployed, but not the motivation for deploying them. Unlike internal data networks, which are primarily used to cut operational costs, external networks allow firms to create new differentiating services or revenue-producing products. The ability to use networks for revenue production increases as the networks become more ubiquitous. Surprisingly, however, the modal use of even open networks is to develop hierarchical, long-term relationships among firms. The low cost of the open networks allows these hierarchical relationships to extend to even tiny business partners. It is primarily, however, when the open networks extend to the end consumer that these networks are used to support electronic markets.

The case of a large US manufacturer illustrates the use of an external network with a limited subscriber base to offer EDI-like capabilities, resulting in cost savings plus an ability to differentiate its service from those of other manufacturers (Steinfield and Caby, 1993). This manufacturer initially used CompuServe to communicate with its mobile sales force. Once its independent dealers saw sales people communicating by electronic mail, they requested access to the system, and soon two thirds of the seventy or so dealers had accounts. The marketing staff, realizing that they now had an electronic link to their immediate customer base, deployed applications that provided product and sales-support information directly to dealers. Essentially, private company data was made accessible to dealers. The system was expanded to facilitate completion of transactions as well, enabling dealers to order new trucks on-line. Advantages to dealers included fewer errors in ordering, the ability to check on delivery dates, and a more rapid response from marketing and sales support personnel. In line with our propositions, the service, developed and under the control of the manufacturer, was clearly used to strengthen pre-existing ties to the dealers, rather than to permit currently unaffiliated dealers to order products. Hence, the ubiquity was merely among a "closed user group" rather than among the set of all truck dealers. As suggested by such authors as Cash and Konsynski (1985), the network raised switching costs, rather than lowering them, despite the fact that CompuServe's network was widely available and could have easily supported "switched" services (i.e. a dealer dialing up another "service").

Once networks become more ubiquitous, companies can use them to create revenue-producing products, new lines of business, and even new markets. A central point is that with these widely available data networks, service providers can assume a large potential customer base, with whom it pays to have transactions even on an infrequent and casual basis. In France, the Teletel videotex system provides such ubiquity. But, even so, it does not transform business trading relationships into electronic marketplaces. On the other hand, case studies again illustrate the role that such networks play in enabling suppliers to reinforce existing trading relationships, capture new business, and increase the costs their customers incur if they wish to switch to new suppliers.

Steinfield, Caby and Vialle (1993) describe a large, multinational, electrical appliance and consumer electronics manufacturer that used Teletel for EDI-like connections to approximately 10,000 separate retailers and independent repair people throughout France. The after-sales service subsidiary of this manufacturer provided replacement parts and training to its widely dispersed customer base. The Teletel system permitted electronic transactions even with the smallest trading partners. By permitting on-line ordering, coupled with courier service for rapid delivery, the firm was able to eliminate regional parts warehouses, and reduce the average time for repairing defective appliances from two weeks to two days. These savings occurred because repair people used to wait until they had a sufficient need for parts before driving to a regional warehouse. After the system was implemented, they essentially used the equivalent of a "just-in-time" stocking practice for replacement parts. Moving to a centralized warehouse near Paris reduced the need for replicated inventories, and extra personnel around the country and created substantial savings. Moreover, repair people were further bound to the supplying firm after the introduction of a revenue producing expert system-based training application. Technicians connected to the expert system which proceeded to ask a series of questions designed to diagnose the fault and indicate the repairs needed. This "just-in-time" training service meant that repair people did not need expensive and lengthy in-person training, a difficult task given the short life cycle of new electronics products. They were charged a fee for connecting to the service, but it clearly helped to further promote their dependence on the supplying firm. The expert system also accumulated data on repair problems and provided feedback to the design and manufacturing divisions of the company in order to help detect and correct potential structural flaws in their products. As in the earlier examples, a primary motivation for this service was to prevent repair people from obtaining parts and services from other suppliers. Ubiquity merely made it possible for a supplier to manage relationships with a very large set of buyers, but did not drive the supplier to open their service to other suppliers.

Other case examples from Steinfield et al. (1993) show similar patterns of use of electronic service networks. In one, a clothing manufacturer specializing in men's suits used the Teletel network to link to boutiques and other clothing retailers. They created an application that allows a sales person to input a customer's measurements electronically using their Minitel terminal. The measurements are sent to a computer-controlled cutting machine at the factory, and the equivalent of a custom-made suit is then produced. Hence, retailers could offer a specialty product heretofore only available from tailors, with more rapid turnaround. At the same time, of course, the application was designed to offer retailers a wide range of standard-sized suits produced by this manufacturer. The custom-made suit application helped to attract retailers into a trading relationship, which then was broadened to include many other product lines. This application, as the others noted above, did not offer boutiques any possibility of acquiring products or services from other clothing manufacturers.

Were there examples of electronic marketplaces on the Teletel system? Indeed there were, although case study techniques do not tell us anything about their prevalence. Perhaps the most famous electronic marketplace using the Teletel network is the service created by Lamy, a French firm that publishes various industry reference guides (Steinfield et al., 1993). Lamy originally published the government tariff regulations for the French trucking industry. They then used the Teletel network to provide an application that assisted truckers in calculating the appropriate tariffs for carrying freight between French destinations. After the deregulation of the trucking industry tariffs in France, Lamy used their relationship with truckers to offer a new service that created a spot market in the industry. Freight forwarders subscribed to the service, entitling them to post offers in real time for any immediate hauling needs they had. Truckers could then dial up the service at any time, input their originating and destination points and available capacity, and receive all matching offers. Truckers then contacted the freight forwarder to arrange to transport the goods. In this way, truckers could fill up excess capacity that remained during a normally scheduled trip, or fill up their trucks for a return trip home. France's trucking industry became the most efficient in Europe following the implementation of this service.

Lamy essentially played the role of the market-maker in this example. They were not themselves in the freight-forwarding or transport business, but brought the two together to create a real time exchange. The usage was impressive - with France's 25,000 independent truckers regularly searching the database for a small fee. Posted offers arrived constantly; an informant reported during the interview for the case study, that dozens of offers arrived in a period of several minutes. Lamy extracted a fee for their market-making service, however, based on the pay-per-call charges to truckers and the subscription fees to freight forwarders. Their incentive was to attract as many freight forwarders and truckers as possible. Therefore, as proposed above, an electronic marketplace emerged only with the help of a third party player who functioned as an exchange.

One quantitative study of interorganizational networks in France and the United States provides more compelling evidence that even open networks are typically used to support hierarchical relationships among firms (Streeter, Kraut, Lucas and Caby, 1996). Their survey of over 600 firms in the two countries compared France, with its nationally interconnected and relatively ubiquitous Teletel network, to the United States, with its collection of private data networks, most of which were inaccessible to the general public.[5] The research showed that firms that extensively used data networks connecting them to trading partners were more efficient in order processing. Results also showed that compared to small firms, larger firms (i.e. ones with greater sales and more employees) are more likely to use the data networks for a wide variety of corporate communications, even in France. The survey measured use of any form of data network, not just the Teletel. However, among firms in France that used Teletel for their business applications, the association of firm size and network use disappeared. This result suggests that ubiquity makes the benefits of networking available even to smaller firms.

Both in France and the United States firms seemed to use the interorganizational data networks to bind customer and supplier firms. In support of this, the survey found that the more firms used external data networks of any sort, the more stable and long-lived were their trading relationships with their customers and the more frequent were their transactions with them. So, even though the Teletel network made connections to low volume trading partners financially practical, it did not transform the relationships among trading partners into electronic marketplaces with short-lived relationships among firms. Rather, the quantitative evidence suggests that open networks reinforced existing trading patterns. One important exception to this pattern was that while the electronic hierarchy structure was prevalent with business trading partners, firms using Teletel were more likely to pursue a mass market strategy with the general public.

2.4. Discussion and Conclusions

Our review of the empirical literature shows that both electronic hierarchies and markets have been observed in practice, but the former are, in fact, more commonly observed in business to business networks. In general, the more extensively firms used interorganizational networks, the more hierarchical were their relationships with trading partners, even when using highly open and ubiquitous public data network infrastructures. The relative openness of the network did not appear to predispose firms to relate to their business trading partners on a transaction-by-transaction basis, although the reduced cost of adding new partners did appear to make it easier for electronic service providers to include trading partners that generate low volumes of transactions. Opening the network even extended to individual customers. The case study findings also were consistent with our expectation that third party market makers, who provide such brokerage services as product search, comparison, and evaluation, are likely to be necessary for real electronic marketplaces to evolve.

Although the survey and case study findings presented are broadly consistent with the expectations developed earlier in the chapter, they cannot distinguish

---

[5]The survey was conducted in 1992, before the explosive growth in the United States of the Web and commercial on-line services.

between two competing explanations for the prevalence of electronic hierarchies over markets. If the need for third parties to set up an exchange was the only reason, then why are there not many more examples like Lamy?

The economic explanation for the prevalence of electronic hierarchies is that the benefits derived from heightened integration of production activities outweighs the advantages the network might afford in finding new sources of supply. The survey and case studies tell us little about the specific costs firms incur in their transactions - - costs of search and advertising, trade execution, settlement, monitoring, or service after the trade. We do not know if other suppliers were available, and if there was sufficient variability in price, quality, or service to make the search for new suppliers worthwhile. We do not know if acquired goods were standard, and therefore obtainable elsewhere, or customized, and asset specific. To see where electronic networks provide benefit, and whether that benefit is greater in reducing search costs (hence encouraging electronic markets) or integration costs (hence encouraging electronic hierarchies), the unit of analysis must be shifted to the level of the transaction itself. Only then can the costs and benefits of using a network in support of transactions with external trading partners be examined, and a comparison of electronic search versus integration be made.

Such an approach will also permit us to contrast the above economic explanation with one based more on sociological factors. The empirical relationship frequently observed between the use of external data networks and electronic hierarchies may result from firms opening their networks only to those with whom they already have a long history of successful commercial transactions, emphasizing the importance of interpersonal relations and organizational trust (see Zucker, 1986).[6] Mansell and Jenkins (1992) have found that even in industries with EDI standards, participation was generally confined to pre-existing business relationships. Granovetter (1985) has provided a compelling argument for expecting social relationships to form the basis for much economic activity. This view is consistent with the recent competitive strategy and organization theory literature that emphasizes cooperative relations among firms in a value chain, network, or cluster (Johnston and Lawrence, 1988; Powell, 1990). By empirically examining transactions among firms, noting which are electronic and what the relational characteristics of the trading partners are, this source of explanation can be tested.

Given these limitations, and the directions for future research, does our review have some implications for the future of electronic commerce on the Internet? The Internet permits information rich communication, is open, is based on a set of common standards, and is increasingly ubiquitous. With the soaring popularity of the Internet, which is considered by many industry observers to be the most viable national (and global) information infrastructure, the U.S. may soon have the open, ubiquitous network ideal for electronically mediated commercial transactions.

---

[6]This is not to say that there are no economic reasons for basing trading patterns on trust and pre-existing relations. It may well be that the reduced costs of monitoring to control for opportunistic behavior among firms that trust each other provide savings over arms-length relations that require extensive contractual control.

Fledgling attempts at creating electronic marketplaces at the business-to-business level are in evidence, such as CommerceNet. Many electronic shopping malls have appeared as well, although these seem to be targeting the end consumer rather than the upstream business market.

Our review suggests that network attributes - in particular, openness - are important, but do not operate in a vacuum. Other factors, such as the locus of control of the electronic service application and the business environment, are likely to interact with the use of the Internet to promote both hierarchical and market-like structures. Given the Teletel experiences, we should see many supplier organizations developing Internet applications that promote electronic transactions and information flows among trading partners. If previous trends continue, at the business-to-business level, these will most likely map onto existing trading relationships, capitalizing on the benefits of electronic integration. The logistics of dealing with more trading partners at this intermediate level will likely preclude market-like arrangements. However, as with Teletel, many firms will exploit the reach of the network to find new customers, and will be encouraged to move to a mass market strategy if they are not already doing so. Our review suggests, however, that true electronic markets, permitting the easy comparison and acquisition of products and services across many suppliers on a spot market basis, will be less common, and dependent upon market making intermediaries. The directory, search, and intelligent agent services appearing now on the Web are evidence of this need (Sarkar, Butler and Steinfield, 1995).

2.5. References

Bakos, J. Y. and Brynjolffson, E.: 1992. When quality matters: Information technology and buyer-supplier relationships, Unpublished manuscript, University of California, Irvine, CA.

Bradley, S., Hausman, J. and Nolan, R. (eds): 1993, *Globalization, Technology and Competition: The Fusion of Computers and Telecommunications in the 1990s*, Harvard University School Press, Boston, MA.

Brousseau, E.: 1990, Information technologies and inter-firm relationships: The spread of interorganizational telematics systems and its impact on economic structure, Presented to the *International Telecommunications Society*, Venice, June.

Brynjolffson, E., Malone, T., Gurbaxani, V. and Kambil, A.: 1993, Does information technology lead to smaller firms? Unpublished manuscript, Massachusetts Institute of Technology, Cambridge, MA.

Business Week: 1994, The Internet: How it will change the way you do business, *Business Week*, November 14, 80-88.

Cash, J. I. and Konsynski, B. R.: 1985, IS redraws competitive boundaries, *Harvard Business Review*, March-April, 134-142.

France Telecom: 1992, *Minitel Strategy*, Author, Paris.

Granovetter, M.: 1985, Economic action and social structure: The problem of embeddedness, *American Journal of Sociology*, 91(3), 481-510.

Hart, P. and Estrin, D.: 1991, Interorganizational networks, computer integration, and shifts in interdependence: The case of the semiconductor industry, *ACM Transactions on Information Systems,* 9(4), 370-398.

Johnston, H. R. and Vitale, M. R.: 1988, Creating competitive advantage with interorganizational information systems, *MIS Quarterly,* 153-165.

Johnston, R. and Lawrence, P.: 1988, Beyond vertical integration: The rise of the value-adding partnership, *Harvard Business Review,* July-August, 94-101.

Kambil, A.: 1991, Information technology and vertical integration: Evidence from the manufacturing sector, *in* M. Guerin-Calvert and S. Wildman (eds), *Electronic Services Networks: A Business and Public Policy Challenge,* Praeger, NY, pp. 22-23.

Keen, P.: 1988, *Competing in Time: Using Telecommunications for Competitive Advantage,* Ballinger Press, Cambridge, MA.

Kekre, S. and Mudhopadhyay, T.: 1992, Impact of electronic data interchange technology on quality improvement and inventory reduction programs: A field study, *International Journal of Production Economics,* 28, 265-282.

Lucas, H., Levecq, H., Kraut, R. and Streeter, L.: 1995, France's grass-roots data net, *IEEE Spectrum,* November, 71-77.

Malone, T.: 1987, Modeling coordination in organizations and markets, *Management Science,* 33, 1317-1332.

Malone, T., Yates, J. and Benjamin, R.: 1987, Electronic markets and electronic hierarchies: effects of information technology on market structure and corporate strategies, *Communications of the ACM,* 30(6), 484-497.

Malone, T., Yates, J. and Benjamin, R.: 1989, The logic of electronic markets, *Harvard Business Review,* May-June, 166-171.

Mansell, R. and Jenkins, M.: 1992, Electronic trading networks: EDI and beyond, *Conference Proceedings, IDATE 91,* Montpellier, France, November.

Moch, M. and Morse, E.: 1977, Size, centralization and organizational adoption of innovations, *American Sociological Review,* 42, 716-725.

Porter, M. E. and Millar, V. E.: 1985, How information gives you competitive advantage. *Harvard Business Review,* July-August, 149-160.

Porter, M. E.: 1980, *Competitive strategy: Techniques for analyzing industries and competitors,* The Free Press, New York.

Powell, W.: 1990, Neither market nor hierarchy: Networked forms of organization, *in* B. Staw and L. Cummings (eds), *Research in Organizational Behavior,* 12, 295-336.

Salton, G. and McGill, M. J.: 1979, *Introduction to Modern Information Retrieval,* McGraw-Hill, NY.

Sarkar, M. B., Butler, B. and Steinfield, C.: 1995, Intermediaries and cybermediaries: A continuing role for mediating players in the electronic marketplace, Journal of Computer Mediated Communication, 1(3): http://www.ascusc.org/jcmc/.

Steinfield, C. and Caby, L.: 1993, Strategic organizational applications of videotex among varying network configurations, *Telematics and Informatics,* 10(2), 119-129.

Steinfield, C., Caby, L. and Vialle, P.: 1992, Exploring the role of videotex in the international strategy of the firm, Paper presented to the *Telecommunications Policy Research Conference,* Solomons Island, Md, September.

Streeter, L. A., Kraut, R. E., Lucas, H. C. and Caby, L.: 1996, How open data networks influence business performance and market structure, *Communications of the ACM,* 39, 62-73.

Weber, J.: 1995, Just get it to the stores on time, *Business Week,* March 6, 66-67

Wildman, S. and Guerin-Calvert, M.: 1991, Electronic services networks: Functions, structures, and public policy, *in* M. Guerin-Calvert and S. Wildman (eds), *Electronic Services Networks: A Business and Public Policy Challenge*, Praeger, NY, pp. 3-21.

Williamson, O.: 1975, *Markets and Hierarchies: Analysis and Antitrust Implications,* Free Press, NY.

Zucker, L.: 1986, Production of trust: Institutional sources of economic structure: 1840-1920, *in* B. Staw and L. Cummings (eds), *Research in Organizational Behavior*, Vol. 8, JAI Press, Greenwich, CT, pp. 53-111.

CHAPTER 3

The Link between Information Strategy and Electronic Commerce

ALBERT L. LEDERER
University of Kentucky

DINESH A. MIRCHANDANI
University of Kentucky

KENNETH SIMS
Cumberland College

3.1. Introduction

Electronic commerce is emerging as an increasingly important way for organizations to reach potential customers. In effect, it moves the workplace to the customer's site. Its low cost increases its attractiveness. It is now beginning and will probably continue to have a dramatic impact on business into the 21st century (Hornback, 1995).

However, electronic commerce presents many challenges to the organizations that implement it. For example, they must provide both meaning and quality to a variety of users in different contexts (Madnick, 1995). Also, as with other information systems, they must link it to their business strategy (King, 1988). In fact, electronic commerce can be seen as a means to implement competitive strategies in large corporations, small businesses, and startup companies (Applegate, Holsapple, Kalakota, Radermacher and Whinston, 1996). For example, it can allow a company to improve productivity, increase cash flows, decrease inventory, and enhance customer relations (Boynton, 1994). However, empirical research has yet to confirm that organizations view it in this manner.

The research described in this chapter sought to investigate the link between the benefits organizations seek from electronic commerce and their intention to use electronic commerce to carry out specifically recognized business strategies by surveying companies that use it. An extensive literature review has found no similar survey. However, such a study can help researchers understand the benefits of information technology sought by organizations in implementing electronic commerce. It can also help them comprehend the use of strategic applications in

Reprint from *Journal of Organizational Computing and Electronic Commerce* 7(1), 17-34

general. It can help practitioners see the potential of electronic commerce in their own firms.

3.2. Background

Electronic commerce has emerged as a term describing a variety of market transactions that are enabled by information technology (Applegate, McFarlan and McKenney, 1996). It thus represents the subset of telecommunications services that connect interorganizational systems. It provides the ability to share a wide range of communiqués and data easily with trading partners (Adams, 1994). This broad view includes public email networks such as MCI Mail, CompuServe, and the Internet as well as groupware programs, such as Lotus Notes and WordPerfect Office (Adams, 1994). Electronic data interchange (EDI), bar coding, fax, imaging, and smart cards are a few of the technologies in the growing list of tools that make up electronic commerce (Spence, 1994).

This study, however, examines strictly one specific aspect of electronic commerce; that is, marketing on the Internet. The Internet has become the de facto electronic highway (Stewart, 1993). "[T]he Net is pushing itself into the realm of everyday experience. As a result of almost three years of unrelenting press coverage and exponential growth, the Internet is now part of mundane reality ... [It] is currently growing faster than television, radio, or the printing press ever did" (Strangelove, 1995). The ability to market on the Internet has arrived only gradually, as advances in PC and telecommunications technology have improved access (Day, 1994). An attraction to companies for doing business on the Internet is that "screens around the world are shop windows - globalism comes with the lack of physical territory" (Anonymous, 1994) at very low cost (Dodge, 1995).

However, the Internet presents a special challenge to marketers because it differs substantially from all previous advertising media. Every other medium familiar to advertisers has restricted the amount of information that could be sent and the feedback that could be received. The Net, as an advertising medium, allows the company to provide more, not less, information (Strangelove, 1995). Thus, the information highway brings together electronic business practices to the advantage of individual organizations striving to increase their competitiveness.

These organizations typically use a planning process to select new information systems to help them do so. This process - which produces an information strategy - may propose and compare the potential, anticipated benefits of many information systems. Managers refer to some of these as strategic information systems because they are aligned with their corporate strategies (Applegate et al., 1996; Clemons, 1991; Ives and Learmonth, 1984; Runge and Earl, 1988).

Some evidence suggests that companies consider their Internet efforts to be such systems (Dodge, 1995). However, generally the evidence to the deliberate planning of a strategic information system has not always been persuasive (Powell, 1992). For electronic commerce to be an integral part of an organization's information strategy, it is important to understand the anticipated benefits that prompt an organization to implement it.

Via an extensive literature review (Lederer and Mirani, 1995), researchers have identified 33 potential, anticipated benefits of information systems. Table 1 lists each with its original references. The table also shows statistics that will be discussed later. Because the list is intended to be comprehensive, the benefits of electronic commerce are probably subsumed in it. Moreover, one would expect these benefits to be linked to the business strategy with which the organization intends to align electronic commerce.

Table 1. Importance of each benefit.

Benefit	Mean	Std. Dev.
Enhance competitiveness or create strategic advantage (Anonymous, 1990; Janulaitis, 1984; Lay, 1985; McGugan, 1987; Parker and Benson, 1987; Sullivan-Trainor, 1989; Sullivan-Trainor, 1991)	5.34	1.80
Enable easier access to information (Orli and Tom, 1987; Rivard and Kaiser, 1989)	5.24	1.98
Provide new products or services to customers (Sullivan-Trainor, 1989)	4.88	2.16
Increase the flexibility of information requests (Orli and Tom, 1987; King and Schrems, 1978)	4.68	2.10
Improve customer relations (Orli and Tom, 1987; Rivard and Kaiser, 1989)	4.66	2.09
Enhance the credibility and prestige of the organization (Orli and Tom, 1987)	4.57	2.05
Provide better products or services to customers (Anonymous, 1990; Parker and Benson, 1987; Sullivan-Trainor, 1989)	4.49	2.25
Increase volume of information output (Rivard and Kaiser, 1989)	4.46	2.32
Align well with stated organizational goals (Parker and Benson, 1987)	4.24	2.09
Enable the organization to respond more quickly to change (added during pilot in Lederer and Mirani, 1995)	4.23	2.31
Enable faster retrieval or delivery of information or reports (Sullivan-Trainor, 1989; Rivard and Kaiser, 1989)	4.21	2.41
Help establish useful linkages with other organizations (Parker and Benson, 1987)	4.19	2.08
Save money by reducing communication costs (Smith, 1983)	4.09	2.29
Change the way the organization conducts business (Parker and Benson, 1987; Sullivan-Trainor, 1989)	4.01	2.17
Increase return on financial assets (added during pilot in Lederer and Mirani, 1995)	3.93	2.24
Enhance employee productivity or business efficiency (McGugan, 1987, Sullivan-Trainor, 1989; Sullivan-Trainor, 1991; Rivard and	3.90	2.17

Kaiser, 1989; King and Schrems, 1978; Smith, 1983)		
Speed up transactions or shorten product cycles (Anonymous, 1990; Parker and Benson, 1987; Orli and Tom, 1987)	3.84	2.25
Improve the accuracy or reliability of information (Orli and Tom, 1987; Rivard and Kaiser, 1989; King and Schrems, 1978; Vaid-Raizada, 1983)	3.70	2.15
Present information in a more concise manner or better format (Rivard and Kaiser, 1989)	3.55	2.22
Enable the organization to catch up with competitors (Parker and Benson, 1987)	3.26	2.25
Allow previously infeasible applications to be implemented (Sullivan-Trainor, 1991; Orli and Tom, 1987)	3.06	2.16
Improve management information for strategic planning (Parker and Benson, 1987; King and Schrems, 1978)	3.05	2.06
Improve information for management control (Parker and Benson, 1987; Orli and Tom, 1987; King and Schrems, 1978)	2.89	2.14
Improve information for operational control (Parker and Benson, 1987)	2.79	2.11
Allow other applications to be developed faster (Smith, 1983)	2.78	2.04
Provide the ability to perform maintenance faster (added during pilot in Lederer and Mirani, 1995)	2.47	2.02
Save money by avoiding the need to increase the work force (Smith, 1983)	2.46	2.08
Save money by reducing travel costs (Smith, 1983)	2.31	1.93
Save money by reducing the work force (Parker and Benson, 1987; Sullivan-Trainor, 1989; Orli and Tom, 1987, Rivard and Kaiser, 1989)	2.25	1.96
Save money by reducing system modification or enhancement cost (Smith, 1983; Vaid-Raizada, 1983)	2.24	1.78
Save money by reducing hardware use (Orli and Tom, 1987)	1.85	1.49
Provide greater data or software security (Vaid-Raizada, 1983)	1.82	1.51
Facilitate organizational adherence to government regulations (added during pilot in Lederer and Mirani, 1995)	1.52	1.24

Porter (1980) has identified three such strategies - cost leadership, differentiation, and focus - which have repeatedly influenced business performance and that managers manipulate. Cost leadership means providing a standardized product at very low per-unit costs for many price-sensitive buyers (Porter, 1980; Porter, 1985). Differentiation means providing outputs that are considered unique industry-wide and serves many relatively price-insensitive buyers. Focus means providing products that fulfill the needs of just a few buyers in an industry. The field of strategic management has received this typology well (Dess and Davis, 1982; Galbraith and Schendel, 1983; Hambrick, 1983; Wright, 1984).

Porter's presentation suggests that firms can choose any of the generic strategies. However, the size of a firm, its access to resources, and its industry may limit its choices (Wright, 1987). Thus, larger firms in an industry may primarily compete with cost leadership or differentiation while smaller ones can only use focus (Wright, 1987). Typically, however, firms use a mixed strategy where they emphasize certain of Porter's strategies (Hambrick, 1983; Miller and Friesen, 1986; Dess and Davis, 1984).

This research expects a company's anticipated benefits from electronic commerce to predict its information strategy in terms of Porter's generic competitive strategies. The existence of a relationship would confirm a link between information strategy and electronic commerce. It would also help explain why organizations implement electronic commerce. Thus the study sought to answer the following, specific research questions:

- Do organizations implement electronic commerce to support general business strategies and if so, which strategies do they seek to support?
- What benefits do companies anticipate from their implementation of electronic commerce?
- Do anticipated benefits predict particular strategies?

3.3. Methodology

3.3.1. INSTRUMENT DEVELOPMENT

The survey instrument had the following major sections:

- Three questions asking the extent to which the organization planned to use electronic commerce to achieve each of Porter's generic competitive strategies. A 1-7 ratings scale allowed the respondent to indicate that extent. These items appeared in order to help answer the first research question about the strategies organizations seek to support.
- The list of 33 benefits from Table 1. Respondents chose from a 1-7 (1 being very little and 7 being very much) Likert-type scale to indicate how much importance each of the 33 benefits held in implementing the entry at a World Wide Web site called the Internet Mall. A 34th question allowed them to enter a benefit and rating they considered in addition to the benefits from Table 1. These items are present to answer the second research question about the benefits organizations seek. Along with the three strategy questions, they also help answer the third research question about whether anticipated benefits predict strategies.
- Two general questions about the company's view of the importance of electronic access for customers. The questions asked about the importance of such access to present and future business strategies. Respondents chose from a 1 to 7 scale. These questions were asked to assess the importance of the research topic.
- Questions for demographic purposes about the organizations' and subjects' characteristics.

Three local area companies who have entries on a local provider's commercial World Wide Web page participated in a pilot of the survey instrument. The first two pilot subjects provided useful comments about the contents and introduction to the survey. The third pilot did not result in any changes.

To conclude the pilot, fifteen companies with a listing on the Internet Mall were randomly selected and emailed copies of the survey. (The method for obtaining their email addresses is described below.) This tested the delivery and reply technique and also provided some preliminary information about an expected response rate. No changes were made to the survey as a result of this emailing.

3.3.2. SUBJECTS

The study focused on one of the noteworthy cyberspace shopping centers, the Internet Mall (Ellsworth, 1995). The Internet Mall offers a company a display location for its products on one of the mall's many "floors." The company can thus provide information about the products or permit customers to order them. These entries contain email addresses or hypertext links to locations where the "cybercustomer" can find more information.

The Internet Mall began as a distributed list of 34 companies in February 1994. It was the first public listing of commercial entities on the network. As of February 1996, over 6,500 firms were listed on the Mall pages (up from about 1,200 when this research project started) and approximately 6,200 people accessed them each day (Taylor, 1996).

Of the 1,200 entries, the researchers obtained 846 unique email addresses. To do so, they used Netscape Navigator to download the document source for each Internet Mall entry from the Internet. A computer program searched each downloaded document source and extracted company names and electronic email addresses. This procedure found 846 companies with unique email addresses. Another computer program inserted the company name in an electronic copy of the survey and mailed it to the corresponding email address.

Subjects were asked to respond via email within seven days of receipt. The mean duration until a response was 1.8 days. After seven days, a second emailing of the survey with a reminder went to the non-respondents. The mean duration for responses to this message was 4.8 days. Completed surveys came from 212 subjects for a response rate of 25%. Thirty-five (4%) of those surveyed responded that they did not wish to participate.

3.3.3. DEMOGRAPHICS

As Figures 1 and 2 show, respondents were generally highly experienced, having worked for their current employer in a variety of positions such as accounting, finance, marketing, sales, production, human resources, and information systems. On average, they directly supervised about 10 employees and had an average of 6 years of experience with their current employer. Most of the respondents had at least a 4-year college degree and over 40% had attended some graduate school.

Their organizations represented a variety of business interests as seen in Figure3. (The total percentage in Figure 3 exceeds 100% because some organizations had multiple categories.) These organizations were not large; on average, they employed about 30 persons.

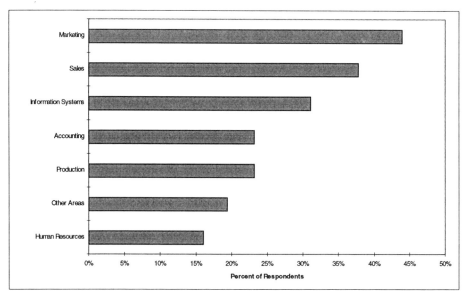

Figure 1. Respondents' work experience by functional area.

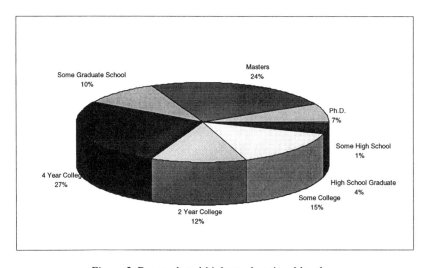

Figure 2. Respondents' highest educational level.

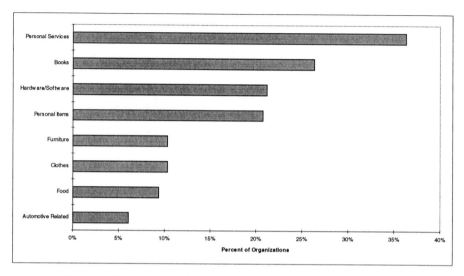

Figure 3: Types of products and services of respondents' organizations.

Figure 4 shows that a majority of the respondents sold their products or services over the Internet. Many also sold their products over such commercial networks as America On-Line, CompuServe, Prodigy, and GENIE.

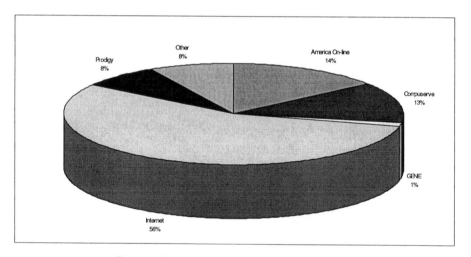

Figure 4. Networks of respondents' organizations.

Most of the surveyed organizations, however, did not solely prefer to market over electronic networks. Instead they opted for more traditional means of marketing such as door-to-door sales, phone orders, and fax as seen in Figure 5.

The fact that marketing on the Internet may finally have arrived is reflected in the number of information requests from customers that each respondent organization received in the first three months of 1995. However, as Figure 6 indicates, most of these information requests did not appear to translate directly into sales. Perhaps the apparently low sales are disappointing. Probably respondents expect them to rise or they expect the information requests to translate into sales through other media.

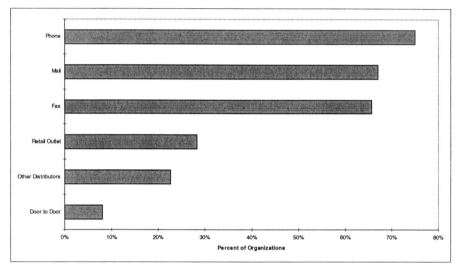

Figure 5. Other channels for customer orders.

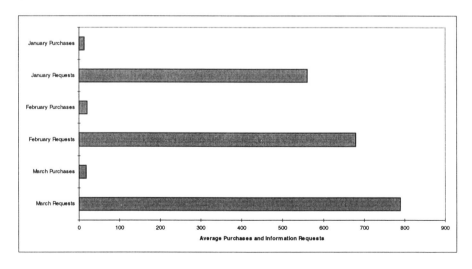

Figure 6. Monthly purchases and information requests.

3.4. Data Analysis

Respondents viewed electronic commerce as growing in importance in their business strategy. On a 1 to 7 scale, they rated its current importance in their organization's business strategy at 4.40. On the same scale, they rated its future importance at 5.58. Probably in absolute terms, these numbers are not particularly great. Nevertheless, a paired t-test indicated that the difference between the two means is significant (t=11.12, p ≤ .001). This difference is reported here to show the participants' optimism about electronic commerce and thus the importance of understanding it.

RQ1: Do organizations implement electronic commerce to support general business strategies and if so, which strategies do they seek to support?

In response to the items asking the extent to which the organization planned to use electronic commerce to achieve each of Porter's generic strategies, subjects rated focus at 5.58, differentiation at 5.53, and cost leadership at 4.21. Paired t- tests showed that the focus and differentiation ratings were significantly higher than the cost leadership rating (p ≤ .001). In other words, the research participants indicated they use electronic commerce more diligently to market products to particular buyers and make the products appear distinct from those of their competitors than they use it to deliver products and services at the lowest possible costs. Such findings begin to provide insight into why organizations are implementing electronic commerce.

RQ2: What benefits do companies anticipate from their implementation of electronic commerce?

Table 1 reports the findings from the 33 benefit questions. The highest respondent ratings were for the "Enhance competitiveness or create strategic advantage" and "Enable easier access to information." In fact, each of these two benefits was significantly higher than all of the others in Table 2 (t=3.12, p ≤ .01 for the former and t=2.37, p ≤ .05 for the latter). Such findings suggest that competition is at the heart of the decision to implement electronic commerce and that its implementers want to use the ease of electronic access to information to increase their competitiveness.

Table 2. Factor analysis.

	Loadings for Factor					
	1	*2*	*3*	*4*	*5*	*6*
Factor 1: Information (∝ =.89)						
Increase the flexibility of information requests	.738	.053	.339	.205	-.010	.111
Improve the accuracy or reliability of information	.728	.222	.131	-.042	.286	.010
Present information in a more concise manner or better format	.712	.175	.153	.179	.049	.352

Enable easier access to information	.702	.059	.217	.233	.103	.026
Increase the volume of information output	.652	.044	.147	.250	.176	.078
Enable faster retrieval or delivery of information or reports	.630	.233	.140	.187	.069	.300
Improve customer relations	.623	.044	.404	.212	.173	-.025
*Improve information for operational control	.478	.309	-.141	.287	.399	.432
*Enable the organization to respond more quickly to change	.428	.219	.315	.281	.361	.212
Factor 2: Cost Savings (∝ = .89)						
Save money by reducing the work force	.034	.808	.036	.195	-.008	.166
Save money by reducing travel costs	.099	.792	.171	.092	.037	.013
Save money by reducing system modification or enhancement cost	.157	.759	.147	.010	.243	.140
Save money by avoiding the need to increase the work force	.027	.749	.043	.325	.029	.219
Save money by reducing hardware use	.271	.664	.062	-.050	.210	.249
*Save money by reducing communication costs	.242	.489	.237	.392	.126	.001
Factor 3: Competitiveness (∝ = .82)						
Provide new products or services to customers	.331	.133	.707	.068	.062	.241
Enhance competitiveness or create strategic advantage	.175	.167	.639	.316	.284	.070
Provide better products or services to customers	.445	.152	.593	.047	.158	.080
Enhance the credibility and prestige of the organization	.355	.130	.554	.207	.328	.038
*Change the way the organization conducts business	.171	.223	.491	.441	.037	.357

Factor 4: Productivity (∝ = .77)						
Enhance employee productivity or business efficiency	.278	.241	.297	.697	.043	.108
Increase return on financial assets	.300	.188	.043	.656	.200	.094
Speed up transactions or shorten product cycles	.446	.154	.117	.554	.221	.109
*Align well with stated organizational goals	.145	-.004	.242	.467	.411	.087
Factor 5: Planning and Control (∝ = .78)						
Help establish useful linkages with other organizations	.114	-.016	.275	.253	.628	.112
Improve management information for strategic planning	.214	.249	.127	.282	.611	.392
Enable the organization to catch up with competitors	.186	.432	.299	-.113	.592	.014
Improve information for management control	.435	.354	-.090	.249	.520	.317
Factor 6: New Applications (∝ = .82)						
Allow previously infeasible applications to be implemented	.107	.225	.292	.079	.100	.796
Allow other applications to be developed faster	.247	.321	.086	.133	.299	.695
Eigenvalue	12.21	2.63	1.36	1.31	1.17	1.01
% of Total Variance Explained	40.7	8.8	4.5	4.4	3.9	3.4
Cumulative Variance Explained	40.7	49.5	54.0	58.4	62.3	65.7

*Item omitted because loading did not exceed .500

Participants rated most of the cost savings items somewhat low, indicating that they do not yet see improved cash flows and reduced inventory (Boynton, 1994) as benefits of their electronic commerce efforts. Probably, they have not yet linked their customer ordering features to their back-office functions (e.g., order entry).

Probably, they are not planning to eliminate other means of advertising (e.g., catalogs) in favor of an electronic form in the near future. Predictably, the highest rated "Save money..." was related to the cost of communications. The other five "Save money..." questions had averages of less than 2.50. Thus the analysis of individual benefits provides an interesting perspective.

On the other hand, factor analysis serves as a useful means of reducing such a large number of items to a more manageable number. It can thus make key themes visible (Nunnally, 1978). It reveals, in effect, the items that belong together. That is, it shows which ones measure the same theme and how much they do so. A factor is thus a construct assumed to underlie a group of items or an individual one. A factor loading can be seen as the correlation between the item and a factor. Eigenvalues represent the amount of variance accounted for by given factors. Cronbach's alpha reliability coefficient measures the extent to which the items that load on a factor correlate with one another.

Prior to factor analysis, the researchers screened the data (Churchill, 1979). They retained benefits only if they correlated with a global measure of importance in the decision to implement the firm's electronic entry. Three benefits (facilitate organizational adherence to governmental regulations, provide the ability to perform maintenance faster, and provide greater data or software security) did not correlate significantly ($p \leq .05$) and were dropped from further analysis.

The factor analysis revealed six factors among the 30 remaining benefits. Table 2 shows the factor loadings. Items with loadings greater than .5 were retained. Thus, of the 30 remaining benefit items, five were dropped because they did not load above .5 on any factor. Table 2 indicates them with an asterisk. Cronbach's alpha reliability coefficients are shown in the table.

Table 2 also contains labels that the researchers applied to the factors. In general, most of the factors are very meaningful sets of items and the labels synthesizing the benefits were easily identifiable. One factor, named information, focused on how the organization's entry improved the presentation of information. Another factor, cost savings, included benefits that reduce or contain the organization's operating costs. One factor called competitiveness included four of the seven most important benefits in Table 1. It concerned improving the competitive advantage of the organization with new and better products and services. Another factor, named productivity, included faster transaction processing and improved employees' productivity. Probably the fifth factor, planning and control, was the least focused although its items were related to management's planning and control functions. The final factor, new applications, dealt with the creation of new information systems.

RQ3: Do anticipated benefits predict particular strategies?

Multiple regression analysis shows the relationship among variables in the form of an equation. If an exact relationship does not exist, regression analysis chooses the "best" equation to describe the relationship. Regression coefficients are the coefficients of the explanatory variables in this equation. A measure of how well a multiple regression equation fits the data is provided by the coefficient of determination, R^2, which represents the proportion of variation in the dependent variable explained by the regression. The F statistic provides an additional measure of how well the multiple regression equation fits the data. Non-significance of the F-statistic implies that the explanatory variables in the regression equation are of little or no use in explaining the variation of the dependent variable. Multivariate multiple regression considers more than one dependent variable.

Multivariate multiple regression tested the relationship between the subjects' anticipated benefits and the three strategies. Table 3 shows the results of the regression including the individual regression coefficients for each of the three strategies. It also shows the mean of the importance of each factor.

The significance of the Pillai's F value of 5.107 (p ≤ .001) validates the use of the individual univariate regression procedures (Barker and Barker, 1984). In general, the F statistics in Table 3 indicate that the anticipated benefits of electronic commerce predicted the organizations' intended strategies.

Table 3. Multivariate tests of significance.

Factor (Mean Importance)	Regression Coefficients		
	Focus	Differentiation	Cost Leadership
1: Information (4.35)	.158	-.089	.211
2: Cost Savings (2.21)	.065	.130	.271[**]
3: Competitiveness (4.81)	.237[*]	.262[*]	-.122
4: Productivity (3.87)	.114	.281[**]	.101
5: Planning & Control (3.34)	-.064	.096	-.026
6: New Applications (2.91)	.018	-.232[*]	.056
R^2	.205	.224	.181
F	7.166[**]	8.046[**]	6.135[**]
[*]p ≤ .05. [**]p ≤ .01.			

The regression analyses yielded five statistically significant relationships between the six benefits factors and three strategies. The cost savings factor predicted the cost leader ship strategy. The competitiveness factor predicted the focus and differentiation strategies. The productivity and new applications factors predicted the differentiation strategy.

3.5. Discussion

This research examines the link between information strategy and the use of electronic commerce to market products and services and disseminates information about them. It suggests that organizations implement such electronic commerce in order to enable them to differentiate their products and services from their competitors' and to focus on particular customers. Presumably managers feel that electronic commerce either makes their products and services inherently different from those of their competitors or that it at least makes them appear different. Moreover, their focus is likely to be on potential customers who are technologically savvy and affluent enough to have access to their entry. In any case, the significantly higher ratings of differentiation and focus strategies than cost leadership strategy suggests the electronic commerce application is deliberate and planned.

Of the six benefits factors, only two - competitiveness and information - have means above 4.00, the midpoint on the 1 to 7 scale. Combined with the low importance of the cost leadership strategy, this suggests that organizations are emphasizing increased sales more heavily than reduced costs.

The most important anticipated benefit factor is competitiveness (with a mean of 4.81). Not surprisingly, this factor - providing new and better products and services as well as enhancing the organization's competitiveness, credibility, and prestige - predicts both the differentiation and focus strategies. This suggests that respondents feel that electronic commerce is actually helping them to improve their products and services or to develop new ones as well as to market to their customers better.

Two less important benefits also predicted differentiation. First, the link between the productivity benefit and differentiation probably suggests some recognition that electronic commerce can support such back-office functions as order entry and catalog distribution. Interestingly, this benefit does not predict a cost leadership strategy and hence the observer may conclude that organizations perceive the benefits of increased productivity in terms of customer service rather than cost leadership.

Second, the inverse relationship between the new application's benefit and differentiation strategy may indicate that the organization's time and effort devoted to developing electronic commerce may reduce its resources for other new applications.

Besides predicting differentiation and focus strategies, one benefit factor, namely cost savings, predicted cost leadership. However, the cost savings benefit was the least important benefit. Perhaps organizations in some cases do seek such benefits from electronic commerce. However, it appears likely that they have not yet begun to tap its cost savings benefits significantly.

3.6. Implications for Researchers

This study helps researchers understand the relationship between the benefits organizations seek from an information technology and the strategies they attempt to accomplish with the technology. The findings in this research suggest that the implementers of electronic commerce are at least to some extent seriously planning how they will reap the advantages of the new technology. In other words, its implementation is not a random experiment or a mindless rush to a new technology.

The study also makes a contribution by demonstrating the use of email to administer a research instrument. This approach (in this case a somewhat recursive use of the Internet to study the Internet) will probably be used much more extensively in research on other subjects in the future. The response rate and the quick turn-around time here suggest that email can prove a valuable tool to researchers.

At the same time, while helping us to understand why organizations implement electronic commerce, the research raises more questions about the decision to do so.

For example, this study concentrated on the link between information strategy and electronic commerce as seen by those responsible for electronic commerce. It might also be reasonable to investigate whether those responsible for business strategy have the same views. Because the organizations in this study were fairly small, perhaps those are the same individuals but in many cases they may not have been.

This study investigated the benefits that were anticipated and the strategies that were intended. In doing so, it suggests the need to investigate whether the benefits were actually achieved and the strategies realized.

This study identified 212 organizations that had implemented their electronic entry. One might legitimately ask how these organizations differ from the numerous others that have not yet done so. In other words, what motivates early implementers and why does it not motivate others?

Perhaps the most interesting finding of this research is that companies perceive competitive advantage and not cost leadership as a benefit of electronic commerce. Possibly organizations are concerned about data security and have not begun accepting financial transactions, an activity that would probably provide monetary savings. Other reasons may explain this surprising finding and future research should investigate them.

Finally, perhaps simply by investigating electronic commerce empirically, the study raises broader research questions about it. For example, how can organizations identify their electronic commerce needs? How can they most effectively and efficiently acquire or develop electronic commerce applications? How should the human interfaces for electronic commerce be designed to benefit the organization best and help it execute its strategies?

3.7. Implications for Managers

This research can be useful to managers who wish to gain the greatest value from electronic commerce. First, the research identifies a potential checklist of 33 general benefits of information systems. Managers can evaluate each benefit by asking if they want electronic commerce to provide it in their organization. If they do, they can further consider how electronic commerce might do so for their firms.

They can also consider more carefully the anticipated benefits that have prompted other organizations to implement electronic commerce (i.e. in particular, those with higher means in Table 1). Managers should recognize that their competitors are implementing electronic commerce with such benefits in mind. This might inspire those organizations that have not yet done so to implement electronic commerce now. Perhaps more importantly, managers might try to ascertain specifically how their competitors are achieving these particular benefits and thus how they might do so too.

On the other hand, current interest in electronic commerce had not translated into extensive sales at the time of this study. This suggests that companies perhaps should now implement electronic commerce with the view that it will be more important to their future strategies rather than their immediate ones. In fact, implementing electronic commerce today may be more a defense against competitors than an aggressive move to compete. Indeed, implementers should probably have little reluctance to invest in electronic commerce based largely on the fear that if they fail to take advantage of it, their competitors still will.

Managers should also recognize that their competitors are not yet using electronic commerce to realize benefits related to monetary savings (i.e. these were among the least important benefits in Table 1) or to execute a cost leadership strategy. Perhaps today electronic commerce is used primarily to inform customers about products and services. Nevertheless, it seems reasonable that electronic commerce has an important role in controlling costs in ordering, billing, shipping, and other back-office functions. Thus managers should probably begin to think about how they can use electronic commerce to gain monetary savings benefits by feeding transactions into existing order entry systems as well as inventory, shipping, billing, and other related subsystems.

Perhaps it is ironic that the most important benefit item - enhance competitiveness or create strategic advantage - may suffer from the greatest weakness. That is, most of the benefits in this study are very often achievable. And while it is clearly possible to use an emerging technology such as electronic commerce to achieve the competitive advantage, sustaining such an advantage can prove very difficult. Perhaps its early implementers - the respondents in this study - have targeted the most difficult benefit as their most important. Perhaps they are overly sanguine.

3.8. Conclusion

This research investigated the link between information strategy and electronic commerce by asking three questions. It found that organizations implement electronic commerce to support differentiation and focus strategies rather than cost leadership. It found that they seek benefits associated with increased competitiveness and better information rather than those associated with improved productivity, planning and control, new applications, and cost savings. Finally, it found that the increased competitiveness benefit predicted differentiation and focus strategies. In doing so, it lays the groundwork for further research and improved practice regarding the link between information strategy and electronic commerce.

3.9. References

Anonymous: 1990, Evaluating technology's payback, *IBM Directions*, 4(3), 29-31.

Anonymous: 1994, Net profits, *Economist*, 332(7871), July 9, 83-85.

Adams, E. J.: 1994, Better connected, *World Trade*, September, 98-100.

Applegate, L. M., Holsapple, C. W., Kalakota, R., Radermacher, F. and Whinston, A. B.: 1996, Electronic commerce: Building blocks of new business opportunity, *Journal of Organizational Computing and Electronic Commerce*, 6(1), 1-10.

Applegate, L. M., McFarlan, F. W. and McKenney, J. L.: 1996, *Corporate Information Systems Management: Text and Cases*, Richard D. Irwin, Homewood, IL.

Barker, H. R. and Barker, B. M.: 1984, *Multivariate Analysis of Variance (MANOVA): A Practical Guide to its Use in Scientific Decision Making*, University of Alabama Press, University, Ala.

Boynton, A. G.: 1994, Electronic commerce 'focusing on success', *Chain Store Age Executive*, January, 126.

Clemons, E.: 1991, Evaluation of strategic investment in information technology, *Communications of the ACM*, 34(1), 22-36.

Churchill, G.: 1979, A paradigm for developing better measures of marketing constructs, *Journal of Marketing Research*, 16 (February), 64-73.

Day, J.: 1994, Brave new cyberworld, *Bank Systems and Technology*, September, 62-66.

Dess, G. and Davis, P.: 1982, An empirical examination of Porter's generic strategies, *National Academy of Management Proceedings*, August, 7-11.

Dess, G. and Davis, P.: 1984, Porter's generic strategies as determinants of strategic group membership and organizational performance, *Academy of Management Journal*, 27, 467-488.

Dodge, J.: 1995, The Net harbors some search snags, *PC Week*, May 22.

Ellsworth, J. H.: 1995, Boom town, *Internet World*, June, 33-35.

Galbraith, C. and Schendel, D.: 1983, An empirical analysis of strategy types, *Strategic Management Journal*, 4, 153-173.

Hambrick, D. C.: 1983, An empirical typology of mature industrial product environments, *Academy of Management Journal*, 26, 213-230.

Hornback, R.: 1995, Electronic commerce in the 21st century, *Journal of Systems Management*, May/June, 28-33.

Janulaitis, V. M.: 1984, Are the risks worth taking? *Computerworld*, In Depth, August 13, 18(33), 13-22.

Ives, B. and Learmonth, G.: 1984, The information system as a competitive weapon, *Communications of the ACM*, 27(12), 1193-1201.

King, J. L. and Schrems, E. L.: 1978, Cost-benefit analysis in information systems development and operation, *Computing Surveys*, 10(1), 19-34.

King, W. R.: 1988, How effective is your information systems planning?, *Long Range Planning*, 21(5), 103-112.

Lay, P. M. W.: 1985, Beware of the cost benefit model for IS project evaluation, *Journal of Systems Management*, 36(6), 30-35.

Lederer, A. L. and Mirani, R.: 1995, Anticipating the benefits of proposed information systems, *Journal of Information Technology*, 10, 159-169.

Madnick, S. E.: 1995, Integrating information from global systems: Dealing with the "On- and Off-Ramps" of the information superhighway, *Journal of Organizational Computing*, 5(2), 69-82.

McGugan, I.: 1987, Competitive advantages vs. tyrannosaurs techie, *Computing Canada*, April 30, 13(9), 18, 20.

Miller, D. and Friesen, P. H.: 1986, Porter's generic strategies and performance: An empirical examination with American data, *Organization Studies*, 7, 37-56.

Nunnally, J. C.: 1978, *Psychometric Research*, McGraw-Hill, New York.

Orli, R. J. and Tom, J. C.: 1987, If it's worth more than it costs, buy it! *Journal of Information Systems Management*, Summer, 4(3), 85-89.

Parker, M. M. and Benson, R. J.: 1987, Information economics: An introduction, *Datamation*, December 1, 33(23), 86-96.

Porter, M.: 1980, *Competitive Strategy: Techniques for Analyzing Industries and Companies,* Free Press, New York.

Porter, M.: 1985, *Competitive Advantage: Creating and Sustaining Superior Performance,* Free Press, New York.

Powell, P.: 1992, Information technology and business strategy: A synthesis of the case for reverse causality, *Proceedings of the Thirteenth International Conference on Information Systems,* Dallas, Texas, 71-80.

Rivard, E. and Kaiser, K.: 1989, The benefit of quality IS, *Datamation,* January 15, 35(2), 53-58.

Runge, D. and Earl, M.: 1988, Gaining competitive advantage from telecommunications, *in* M. Earl (ed.), *Information Management: The Strategic Dimension,* Oxford University Press, Oxford.

Smith, R. D.: 1983, Measuring the intangible benefits of computer-based information systems, *Journal of Systems Management,* 33(9), 22-27.

Spence, M. A.: 1994, Electronic commerce is the first beneficiary of the information highway, *CAM Magazine,* June, 6.

Stewart, T. A.: 1993, Boom time on the new frontier, *Fortune,* Autumn, 128(7), 153-161.

Strangelove, M.: 1995, The walls come down, *Internet World,* May, 40-44.

Sullivan-Trainor, M. L.: 1989, The push for proof of information systems payoff, *Computerworld,* April 3, 23(14), 55-61.

Sullivan-Trainor, M. L.: 1991, End of IS budgets as we know them? *Computerworld,* December 24, 1990/January 1, 1991, 24(52,53), 15.

Taylor, D.: 1996, About the Internet Mall, *http://www.mecklerweb.com/imall/about.htm,* January 31.

Vaid-Raizada, V. K.: 1983, Incorporation of intangibles in computer selection decisions, *Journal of Systems Management,* 33(11), 30-36.

Wright, P.: 1984, MNC-Third world business unit performance: application of strategic elements, *Strategic Management Journal,* 5(3), 231-240.

Wright, P.: 1987, Research notes and communications: A refinement of Porter's strategies, *Strategic Management Journal,* 8, 93-101.

CHAPTER 4

The Diffusion of Auctions on the Web

STEFAN KLEIN
University of Münster

4.1. The Proposition: From Electronic Hierarchies to Electronic Markets

> ... the result of reducing coordination costs without changing anything else should be an increase in the proportion of economic activity coordinated by markets. (Malone, Yates and Benjamin, 1987, 591)

In an influential article, written under the auspices of MIT's *Management in the 1990s* Research Program, Malone et al. (1987) hypothesize the influence of emerging information and communication technologies on the execution and coordination of economic transactions. Their claim is that information technology (IT) will increasingly be used to coordinate economic activities and will consequently increase the share of market coordination over hierarchical coordination. Their argument is based on the transaction cost theory that compares coordination costs of different governance structures, such as markets and hierarchies. As IT reduces coordination (and information) costs, market transactions become more attractive. In greater detail, they focus on asset specificity and complexity of product description as transaction features that determine the choice of coordination mechanisms. If both are high, hierarchical coordination is most efficient; if both are low, market coordination is preferable.

Malone et al. argue for two trajectories towards electronic markets, one is based on biased information systems which have become economically feasible through the emergence of IT, the second is based on an electronic hierarchy where standardization opens the system up for competitive pressure. There are different starting points as far as the functional scope and organizational setting of the systems are concerned; however, competitive pressure and to some degree governmental regulations sustain the shift towards electronic markets in both cases.

4.2. The Rebuttal: Move to the Middle

> This hypothesis states that the lower cost and better monitoring capability of IT and the lower relationship specificity of IT investments will cause firms to

> engage in a greater degree of outsourcing; moreover, this increased
> outsourcing will be from a reduced set of suppliers with whom the firm has
> long-term cooperative relationships. (Clemons and Reddi 1993, 809)

The 'shift to the market' hypothesis has been challenged by Clemons and Reddi
(1993, 810), who - again based on transaction cost theorizing and a limited amount
of empirical evidence - propose the 'move to the middle' hypothesis. The move to
the middle is a double move: away from the hierarchical vertically integrated organization to a higher degree of outsourcing, and at the same time away from faceless
market relations towards a situation where the firm relies on a few cooperative partners. The first part of the move towards outsourcing is based on reasoning similar to
Malone et al. (1987): IT lowers transaction costs, the costs of coordination and
monitoring and the relationship specificity of IT investments, and hence makes
outsourcing an advantageous option. The role of IT in this process is to at least
partly offset exogenous factors that usually increase transaction costs, such as relationship-specific investments, small numbers bargaining, demand uncertainty etc.
The second part of the argument, however, gives reasons why companies increasingly choose long-term cooperative relationships instead of market relationships:
long-term relationships provide higher incentives to invest in IT and in the requisite
organizational adaptations and learning processes (Seidmann and Wang 1992). At
the same time, long-term relationships provide some protection against the risks of
opportunistic behavior and especially the loss of critical resources (Clemons and
Row, 1992, 646-648).

In order to explain which conditions favor a 'move to the middle' as opposed to
a 'move to the market', Clemons and Reddi (1994) proposed a model of three variables that affect the price and the transaction risk. These variables are (a) product
complexity and the variability of product prices over time and among suppliers, (b)
the reducing relationship-specificity, and (c) the increasing cost-effectiveness of IT.
If both price and transaction risks are low, a partnership solution is most likely; if the
transaction risk is low but the price risk is high, market transactions are more efficient.

An increasing number of suppliers can be taken as an indicator of the move-to-
the-market. However, empirical findings show, on the contrary, that firms in many
industries are reducing the number of their suppliers. Bakos and Brynjolfsson's
(1992) explanation is that although overall coordination costs are decreasing, this
effect is often offset by an increasing demand for quality. As quality and non-
contractible actions of suppliers become more important, the buyer has to provide
incentives for the supplier to invest in underlying relationship specific assets. A
limited number of suppliers is such an incentive as it increases the bargaining power
of the supplier and reduces the risk of buyer defection. Their argument is that the
importance of non-contractible issues in a supplier-buyer relationship determines the
optimal number of suppliers. The buyer relinquishes part of his power in order to
create an incentive for the supplier to invest in the relationship. It is a balancing act
of control over gains from investments and quality improvements. Non-contractible
properties of the relation are dealt with through contracts concerning the exclusive-
ness of the relation and a barter of power concerning the division of revenues. What
we see is a growing reliance on (specific) institutional arrangements to provide the

right balance of interests in the area of non-contractible and intangible aspects of inter-firm relationships.

4.3. The Synthesis: 'Anything Goes' and Mixed-Mode Hypothesis

> In essence, Information Systems enable organizations to do what they want much more efficiently and flexibly ... It is therefore suggested that in practice the outcome will be a mixed mode of operation in which elements of both markets and hierarchies are evident simultaneously. (Holland and Lockett 1994, 409)

In contrast to a dominating economic rationale, Holland and Lockett (1994) emphasize the strategic dimension of governance decisions. They propose what may be described as the 'anything goes' hypothesis, stating that whatever governance form a firm chooses, IT can be used to accentuate the effects of the chosen governance structure and to improve its efficiency. In hierarchical relationships IOS are designed to foster the organizational integration, in market relationships IOS reduce information and transaction costs and facilitate the ease of switching among several suppl-iers.

In response to the primarily transaction cost-oriented approaches, Holland and Lockett (1994) have developed an extended theoretical framework and have included business marketing, manufacturing strategy and organizational behavior literature. Based on these literatures and in contrast to the prevailing contextual determinism, they develop a research framework for coordination strategy and propose the 'mixed mode hypothesis': firms develop different forms of market and hierarchical relationships that are maintained simultaneously. The interrelations and interdependencies of governance structure, asset specificity, market complexity and coordination strategy are analyzed in order to explain interorganizational arrangements. Holland and Lockett (1994, 410-413) use five cases to illustrate different examples of vertical relationships on a continuum from a high level of organizational integration and hierarchy to fragmented business relationships and a market system of trade. All but the market system example shows a combination of hierarchical and market arrangements. These mixed-mode arrangements combine the benefits of markets, such as high incentives to lower costs and improve quality, with the benefits of hierarchies, namely the efficient integration of operations.

The move-to-the-market debate is characterized by two major developments:

- The theoretical scope has been extended beyond transaction cost theorizing. Organization theory and political economy (Bensaou, 1993), resource dependence theory and network theory (Reekers and Smithson, 1994), and business marketing, manufacturing strategy and organizational behavior (Holland and Lockett 1994), have been taken into consideration and led to conceptually richer arguments.

- Throughout the debate, the initial question "What is the impact of IT on governance structures?" has been rephrased as "What is the strategic rationale for the selection and possibly combination of coordination mechanisms?".

As electronic auctions on the Web provide new evidence for the diffusion of electronic market mechanisms, we take a closer look into types of auctions, the underlying strategic rationale and the impact of the Web on their emergence and diffusion.

4.4. The Emergence of Auctions on the Web

> Auction markets provide centralized procedures for the exposure of purchase
> and sale orders to all market participants simultaneously. (Lee, 1996, 398)

Auctions are formalized trading procedures in which the trading partners' interaction is governed by specific trading rules. In many cases an (electronic) auctioneer is functioning as an intermediary. Electronic auctions are a special case of automated negotiations (Beam and Segev 1997). The auction patterns vary with the trade objects and trade rules. They cover extremes, such as auctions for commodities like financial products, metals or agricultural products on the one side, and auctions for unique items of art on the other.

Since the diffusion of the Web has gained momentum and the number of Web users is rising steeply, a proliferation of electronic markets, in particular electronic auctions, can be observed. *AuctionNet,*[1] *NETIS auctionweb,*[2] *The Internet Auction List,*[3] *Bid Find WWW Auction Search,*[4] *The Auction Hunter,*[5] are examples of Web sites with listings of numerous, altogether hundreds of auctions.

> More than 150 auction sites are now open on the Web, selling everything
> from industrial machinery to rare stamps. Airlines such as Cathay Pacific and
> American have auctioned spare seats on their Web sites. AuctionWeb, which
> is a mixture of a classified-ad service and an auction room for people selling
> everything from rare Barbie dolls to barbecue grills, conducted 330,000 auc-
> tions on-line in the first quarter of this year alone. Onsale, the largest on-line
> auction service and one of the few profitable ones, sells $6m worth of com-
> puter equipment and electronic goods a month. Last month it became the first
> on-line auction firm to hit the stockmarket, going public at a valuation of
> nearly $100m. (Economist, 1997)

4.5. Types of Auctions and Motives of Participants

As the trade objects and contexts for auctions are very diverse, we have tried to cluster some of the main types and motives for auctions (for different mechanisms of price determination see Reck, 1993, 1994, 1997).

---

[1] http://www.auction.net

[2] http://www.auctionweb.com/online/

[3] http://www.usaweb.com/auction..html/

[4] http://www.bidfind.com

[5] http://www.auctiionhunter.com

4.5.1. AUCTIONS AS COORDINATION MECHANISM

Auctions are increasingly used as an efficient coordination mechanism for establishing equilibrium (price). Examples are an automated auction among software agents to control air conditioning at Xerox (Markoff, 1996), power auctions (Singh et al., 1997) or in the future auctions for the allocation of telecommunication bandwidths. In these auctions there is little or no human intervention during the trading.

4.5.2. AUCTIONS AS A SOCIAL MECHANISM TO DETERMINE A PRICE

For objects that are not traded on traditional markets, that may be unique or rare items, or that are offered randomly or at long intervals, an auction creates a marketplace attracting potential buyers, often experts. By offering numerous special items at one time and by attracting a good amount of attention, these auctions provide the requisite exposure of purchase and sale orders and hence liquidity of the market in which a price can be determined. Typical examples of this pattern are auctions of art or rare items as well as auctions of communication frequencies (Lewyn, 1994; Cramton, 1995) or Web banner advertising space (*E.Commerce Today*,[6] 11 April 1997).

4.5.3. AUCTIONS AS EFFICIENT ALLOCATION MECHANISMS

For the allocation of limited resources, auctions are used to (dynamically) establish a price that reflects the scarcity of the resource and the preferences of the bidders. Klausz et al. (1998) have shown in an experimental setting that auctions lead to a more efficient capacity utilization of congested IT resources.

For consumer items that are difficult to market via the established distribution channels, such as:

- products with a limited shelf life or last minute products like seats in a scheduled flight,
- overstocked products that shall be separated from the new product series,
- discontinued or reconditioned items,

the auction is a separate distribution channel, targeted at a wide audience that might be prepared to accept the product restrictions in return for a significant discount. The auctioneer attempts to provide sufficient breadth and depth of the market in order to continually attract interested buyers that have a high likelihood of finding something and sellers that have a high likelihood of clearing their stocks if they set the price low enough. A typical example of this type of auction is Onsale (Economist, 1997).

4.5.4. AUCTIONS AS A HIGHLY VISIBLE DISTRIBUTION MECHANISM

The fourth type of auction is similar to the third as items are auctioned off as a kind of special offer. In this case, however, the set-up of the auction is different. Typically

---

[6] *E.Commerce Today* (http://www.adbot.com), the Newsweekly of Internet-Based Electronic Commerce and Business Strategy, is an electronic information service published by V-Networks, Inc.

one supplier auctions off a limited contingent of items and uses the auction primarily as a mechanism for gaining attention and attracting those customers that are bargain hunters or have a preference for the gambling dimension of the auction process. The airline seat auctions by Cathay Pacific, American Airline and Lufthansa fall into this category. A special case is auctions in which the trading objects are donated and the auction return is dedicated for charitable purposes.

The motivation and possible gains for the respective players vary with the different auction types. Table 1 gives a summary of the main motives:

Table 1. Motives of the participants in different auction types.

Auction type / Role	*Coordination mechanism*	*Price discovery*	*Allocation mechanism*	*Distribution mechanism*
Buyer	short term acquisition of resources, e.g., for demand peaks, auction as a mechanism to achieve an equilibrium	often experts/ professional collectors trying to acquire rare items at a reasonable price	preference compatible access to scarce or congested resources, bargain hunting, gambling motive	bargain hunting, gambling motive possible side motive: charity
Supplier	short term allocation of resources, load balance	exposing items for sale to a sufficient breadth of demand, hope for a high price	clearance of inventory, efficient capacity utilization	attention, PR, direct sales channel, possible side motive: charity
Intermediary	often electronic auction without auctioneer	achieve high breadth and depth of the auctions, high trading volume result in high returns, competitive advantage over other auctions	achieve high breadth and depth of the auctions, high trading volume result in high returns, competitive advantage over other auctions	limited role because of 1:n supplier-buyer relation, service provider for the supplier side

4.6. A Framework for Auctions

While we have started to explain the diversity of auctions and motives for the further diffusion of auction mechanisms, we would now like to focus on the constituting elements of (electronic) auctions (Figure 1) and argue briefly how the Web is changing the conditions of auctions.

4.6.1. AUCTIONEER

The auctioneer provides the institutional setting for the auction, that is, for the different transaction phases of the trading process: information exchange, price determination, trade execution and settlement. While some traditional auctioneers are entering the field of electronic auctioning, we also see a majority of new entrants.

Some of them are affiliated with the suppliers of the trading goods; some emphasize their role as intermediaries who provide trading platforms for a variety of products and vendors.

4.6.2. ACCESS RULES FOR BUYERS AND SUPPLIERS

Among the main institutional design parameters are the access rules for buyers and suppliers. In particular, electronic auctions depend on their reputation, for example, whether the trading goods are available and of the promised quality, and whether trades are executed without friction. While there is a basic distinction between expert auctions and those for the general public, individual auctions vary in respect of control mechanisms, required advance payments, or other credible commitments of the participants.

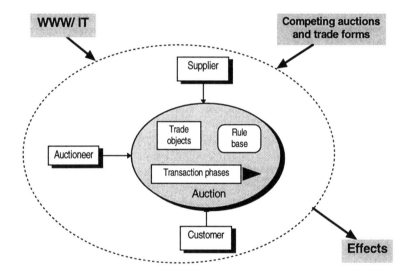

Figure 1. The constituting elements of auctions.

4.6.3. TRADE OBJECTS

The variety of potential objects traded on auctions can be distinguished as three broad categories:

- For commodities, auctions improve the market transparency and facilitate ad-hoc price determination.
- For perishable products in a wider market sense, such as airline seats or over-stocked products, auctions attract potential buyers and they are distinct channels that allow vendors to maintain a different price level from traditional sales channels.
- For scarce or rare products, such as pieces of fine art, collectors items or communication frequencies, auctions are institutionalized procedures for

price determination. By bringing together potential buyers and sellers they create a marketplace and make current levels of supply and demand more transparent.

4.6.4. TRADE OBJECT DESCRIPTIONS

Electronic markets initially have been developed for commodities and products with standardized product descriptions. The progress of technology allows to considerably extend this range into objects that require more complex product descriptions. In addition, samples can be provided or experts can be involved to evaluate products and probably communicate with potential buyers electronically.

4.6.5. TRADE RULES

Numerous rules have been developed that govern the trading process, in particular the exposure of bids and offers and the trade execution. Reck (1997) has specified a set of generic rules and indicated how these may be used to design new types of auctions.

4.6.6. EXECUTION PROCESS

A wider set of rules governs the exchange and logistics of goods and payments. These rules complement the actual rules for the price determination process (Heck et al., 1997). The enforcement of these rules is meant to guarantee the correct execution of trades and is of the utmost importance in an electronic environment.

4.6.7. THE IMPACT OF THE WEB

While most of the motives for auctions are independent of the underlying technology, we have scrutinized how the Web influences the constituting elements of auctions. The Web as a "global hypermedia computer-mediated environment" (Hoffmann and Novak, 1995) represents the result of IT achievements in numerous areas: advanced client-server architectures, low-cost, widely diffused hypermedia clients, low-cost communication infrastructure, platform independent software, and so forth. These features have an impact on the diffusion of auctions:

- The communication infrastructure with millions of potential trading partners facilitates the global visibility of offerings. Even highly specialized items for selective customer groups can thus be marketed efficiently.
- Standardized mechanisms for hypermedia representation of trade objects have increased the manageable and economically feasible complexity of electronic product descriptions.
- The development and diffusion of standardized search mechanisms and event-driven notification of bidders as well as mechanisms for secure payments encourage customers to opt for Web auctions with electronic trade execution.

Table 2. Summary of impact areas.

Parameter	Impact of the Web
Auctioneer	Lower entry barriers, opportunity for direct sales
Access rules	Customizable, theoretically millions of potential customers can be reached
Trading objects	Focused product segments can be auctioned off, the technology extends the complexity of the product description
Trading rules	The trading rules reflect the lack of a guaranteed service
Settlement	For digital products the entire trading cycle can be handled on the Web, for physical products the trading process and the physical logistics of the trade objects can be separated, leading to a reduction of costs.

4.6.8. COMPETING AUCTIONS

As the number of auctions, especially on the Web, is mushrooming, the amount of competition among auctions for comparable trade objects is rising. While this is beneficial in terms of general attention, it might limit the liquidity of less popular auctions. Further research is needed in order to determine what the critical success factors for individual auctions are. Likely candidates for success factors are as diverse as the reputation of an auction, trading rules, the level of commissions and fees or the expected liquidity of the market.

4.6.9. EFFECTS

The different motives we have described are clearly pointing towards intended effects from the perspectives of various players. However, it is not only difficult to identify causal relationships between, for example, trading rules and effects, but there are also numerous potential side effects. A major concern of the suppliers is that it will be difficult to isolate auctions from other sales and distribution channels because customers will adapt their buying behavior. As a result, an increasing price pressure, not only on the auctioned products but also as a side effect on those products that have not been singled out for auctions, is feared. Given the dynamics of the underlying product markets and the individual market places where the respective products are traded, it is difficult to assess what the effects of auctions will be.

4.7. The Impact of the Web on the Diffusion of Auctions

While most of the motives for auctions are independent of the underlying technology, we have scrutinized how the Web influences the constituting elements of auctions as depicted in Figure 1. However, the distinction between the effects of electronic auctions in general and of Web-enabled auctions is sometimes blurred.

Figure 2 depicts hypothesized causal interrelationships between different areas of impact.

Figure 2. Causal network.

4.7.1. IMPACT OF THE WEB

The main determinants of the Web affect the cost calculations of the participants and the transaction processes:

- reduced communication costs for the participants,
- reduced information and search costs for the customers,
- extended complexity of the trade object description,
- separation of the trading process and physical logistics of the trade objects.

As a result, the costs for participating in an auction are decreasing.

4.7.2. PRIMARY EFFECTS

Primary effects of these changes are:

- lower entry barriers for auctioneers, suppliers and customers,

- higher and faster transparency of the offerings,
- lower costs for setting-up and running auctions, consequently lower transactions fees and commissions can be charged,
- lower costs for the logistics of the trade object as a result of the separation between trading process and physical logistics.

However the flip side of increased electronic trading is:

- higher risks of undetected faults and poor quality of trading items, and
- higher contractual hazards.

Part of the reduced information cost is offset by the extension of the search space that the Web facilitates. While the cost of searching for items on a global scale has been prohibitive for most buyers in the past, it has become a feasible option as a result of the diffusion of the Web and related search mechanisms.

4.7.3. SECONDARY EFFECTS

The above-mentioned factors and primary effects influence the major success factors of auctions:

- efficiency of price determination and trade execution,
- liquidity of the auction,
- trade volume, and
- achieved price level.

While technology directly affects the cost calculations of the participants, its effects are also reflected in the institutional rules that govern auctions:

- market access for suppliers and buyers,
- trading rules, mechanisms of price determination and transparency,
- rules for trade executions, and
- trading fees and commission.

These rules have an impact on the liquidity of the market and the efficiency of the price determination as well as, indirectly, on trading volume and price level. An assessment of the immediate effects has to take a number of additional aspects into consideration, such as competing auctions or trade forms, trade objects, the situation of the market or the participants' behavior.

The trust of participants is built (or destroyed) as a result of the participants' ongoing experience with the trading process. On a systemic level, the institutional rules as well as the reputation of the auctioneer influence the level of the perceived risk (Laat, 1993; Loose and Sydow, 1994). The level of transaction fees and commissions determine the risk of bypassing (see Weber, 1994).

4.8. The Move-to-the-Market Hypothesis Reconsidered

We have argued that empirical evidence suggests an extension of market mechanisms and we have tried to show how features of the Web are related to accelerated diffusion of electronic auctions. We would now like to come back to the academic discourse about the impact of IT on governance structures and relate our findings about Web auctions to the respective arguments.

4.9. From Electronic Hierarchies to Electronic Markets?

A number of the effects that Malone et al. (1987) have predicted, can be substantiated in relation to Web auctions.

1. Communication Effect

Communication costs have been significantly reduced and the communication intensity has mushroomed.

2. Brokerage Effect

> The introduction of the electronic auction can shift brokered or dealer markets into auction markets. ... The electronic auction substantially reduces coordination costs by allowing transactions to take place without middlemen. (Lee, 1996, 401)

Not only have traditional markets been complemented by electronic markets, but numerous new markets have emerged. While some of the middlemen have been replaced, new cybermediaries have also come forth.

3. Decreasing Asset Specificity and Time Specificity

While Malone et al. argue that IT is reducing the asset specificity of production technology, the proliferation of the Internet and Internet-related standards and protocols (TCP/IP, Internet services, HTTP, VRML, Java etc.) have considerably lowered the asset specificity of IT investments and engendered the rise of new IT market segments. This trend however might be reversed in the future as the variety and complexity of Internet-related technology is rising quickly.

Malone et al. (19987) have added time specificity as a further type of asset specificity. Contrary to their prediction that high time specificity leads to hierarchical coordination, electronic auctions are examples of coordination mechanisms targeted at time specific products such as last minute flights.

4. Rising Complexity of the Product Description

Most significant progress has been made in extending the complexity of product descriptions while lowering their cost at the same time.

To sum up, a number of Malone et al.'s predictions have been confirmed and the empirical evidence underscores the general line of their argument. However, the described development also provides fresh evidence for the concerns of those researchers who have voiced rebuttals against Malone et al.'s claim.

4.10. Move to the Middle

While we have focused on electronic markets and auctions in our analysis, Internet market research emphasizes, not surprisingly, the salience of solutions for supply chain integration and closed user groups, so called Extranets, that thrive on the Internet. But even if we focus on markets, the analysis of reasons for closer relationships among business partners contributes to the understanding of the desig success of Web auctions. So we are shifting the perspective from the question ' ....ı is the most efficient governance structure?" to the question "What can we learn from the governance structure debate about success factors of auctions?".

4.10.1. QUALITY AND TRUST

Non-contractible issues, such as quality and trust, are crucial issues for Web auctions, however they can be facilitated by a strict institutional regime and auctioneers' trust building measures. When quality is a concern, a third party, the auctioneer, has to provide safeguards and control mechanisms to ensure the quality of the trade objects and reduce the hazards of the trade execution (Bakos and Brynjolfsson, 1992). The requirements of trust are applied to the selection of the auctioneer and the governance structure of the auction. That is, we are distinguishing two types of relationships: the primary trade relationship between buyer and seller, and the service provision relationship between the auctioneer and the respective trading partners. The loose relationship among trading partners is complemented by a trustworthy relationship between trading partners and auctioneer. However, a good reputation of the auction and (system) trust in the effectiveness of the institutional rules and the trade system may be functional substitutes for the personal trust that results from a relationship.

In a centralized market, the trading partners outsource the provision of safeguards for a flawless trade execution to the auctioneer and they build a fairly stable relationship with the auctioneer for that purpose.

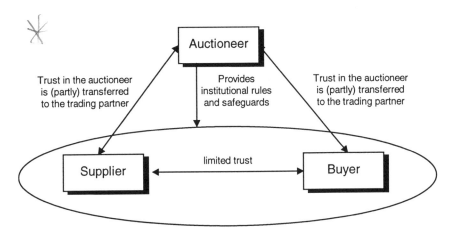

Figure 3. Triangular trust relationship.

4.10.2. SMALL NUMBER OF SUPPLIERS

Applying Bakos and Brynjolfsson's (1992) argument to the development of auctions would suggest that trading partners will trade, despite a rising number of auctions, only with a small number of auctioneers.

Heck and Ribbers (1996, Heck, Damme, Kleijnen and Ribbers, 1997) have shown that the institutional arrangements of the auctions, in particular the rule for trade object representation and examination, and the interests of stakeholders, warrant a careful analysis as success factors of electronic auctions.

4.11. Mixed-Mode Hypothesis: Strategic Positioning of Web Auctions

Holland and Lockett (1994) have emphasized the strategic rationale of governance decisions and have given a number of illustrative examples and cases of sequentially combined governance structures. The evidence of Web auctions enables us to extend their argument in favor of concurrently combined governance structures. As oil wholesalers in the past have combined procurement from spot markets and within stable contractual relationships, companies are using Web auctions for the sale of returns and overstocks while using, at the same time, traditional sales and distribution channels.

4.11.1. SEGMENTATION

The different types of auctions that we have distinguished suggest a careful positioning of the auction mechanism by the suppliers, often complementing market or customer segments or other sales and distribution channels. Some examples are:
- last minute offerings in tourism,
- relatively good used cars, as the complexity of the product description rises exponentially with the age or deterioration of cars (Lee, 1997),
- special offers or stock-offers in the apparel business,
- offers that are restricted to traditional markets such as East African flowers (Heck and Ribbers, 1996).

4.11.2. IMAGE BUILDING

The high attention that Web auctions have drawn in the past enabled suppliers to use them to carefully (re-)cast their image. While, for example, the airlines have not fundamentally changed their pricing strategies, they have at least suggested a more flexible approach to pricing and have auctioned off limited contingents of tickets or offered tickets at lower prices for direct sale on the Web.

4.12. Conclusions

Web auctions and electronic markets in general have recently emerged at a rapid rate. Technological progress and the proliferation of global hypermedia communication infrastructures have enabled numerous players to expand the use of the advantages of auction mechanisms in a computer-mediated environment:
- The Web has provided low-cost access to a global market space and at the same time highly focused customer groups.

- The wide availability of standardized software clients for access to auctions, in most cases just Web browsers, has extended the group of potential participants.
- Cost-efficient communication infrastructures and low-cost market-engines have enabled auctioneers to set up auctions quickly and with limited investments.
- Expert examination and hypermedia representation of trade objects facilitate the separation of trade process and physical logistics of the trade items, thus lowering the transaction costs even further.

A simple conceptual analysis of this development against the background of the move-to-the-market debate has highlighted some of the success factors for electronic auctions as well as arguments for their strategic positioning:

H 1: If product branding and customer attention is a concern, especially in markets with a strong position of trade intermediaries, auctions provide the opportunity to raise or re-emphasize customer attention.

H 2: Auctions provide allocation efficiency for specific product segments that can be isolated to a certain degree such as last-minute offerings, returns, over-stocks etc. At the same time traditional distribution channels and trade forms are maintained.

H 3: Companies deploy electronic market mechanisms in combination with other coordination mechanisms.

H 4: The Web enables suppliers and auctioneers to approach a global audience with very specific interests and needs, thus generating the requisite liquidity even for specialized market segments.

H 5: Recent technological progress enables players not only to extend traditional market mechanisms into the electronic realm but also to use auctions in new application areas where no market mechanisms have previously been employed.

4.13. References

Bakos, J. Y. and Brynjolfsson, E.: 1992, Why information technology hasn't increased the optimal number of suppliers, *WP 3472-92*, Sloan School of Management, October.

Beam, C. and Segev, A: 1997, Automated negotiations: A survey of the state of the art, *WI* 39(3), 263-268

Bensaou, B. M.: 1993, Interorganizational cooperation - The role of information technology: An empirical comparison of US and Japanese supplier relations, *in* J. I. DeGross, R. P. Bostrom and D. Robey (eds), *Proceedings of the 14th ICIS*, Orlando, FL, pp. 117-127.

Clemons, E. K. and Reddi, S. P.: 1993, Some propositions regarding the role of information technology in the organization of economic activity, *in* J. F. Nunamaker and R. H. Sprague (eds), *Proceedings 26th HICSS, Vol. IV: Collaboration Technology and Organizational Systems and Technology*, IEEE Computer Society Press, Los Alamitos, CA, pp. 809-818.

Clemons, E. K. and Reddi, S. P.: 1994, The impact of IT on the degree of outsourcing, the number of suppliers, and the duration of contracts, *in* J. F. Nunamaker and R. H. Sprague (eds), *Proceedings 27th HICSS, Vol. IV: Collaboration Technology, Organizational Systems and Technology*, IEEE Computer Society Press, Los Alamitos, CA, pp. 855-864.

Clemons, E. K. and Row, M. C.: 1992, Information technology and industrial cooperation, *in* J. F. Nunamaker and R. H. Sprague (eds), *Proceedings 25th HICSS, Vol. IV: Information Systems*, IEEE Computer Society Press, Los Alamitos, CA, pp. 644-653.

Cramton, P. C.: 1995, Money out of thin air: The nationwide narrowband PCS auction, *Journal of Economics and Management Strategy*, 4(2), 267-343.

Economist: 1997, *On-line Auctions*, 31 May - 6 June.

Heck, E. van, Damme, E. van, Klejinen, J. and Ribbers, P.: 1997, New entrants and the role of information technology - case study: The teleflower auction in The Netherlands, *in* J. F. Nunamaker and R. H. Sprague (eds), *Proceedings 30th HICSS, Vol. IV: Information Systems - Organizational Systems and Technology*, IEEE Computer Society Press, Los Alamitos, CA.

Heck, E. van and Ribbers, P. M. A.: 1996, Effects of electronic markets: An analysis of four cases in the Dutch flower and transport industries, *in* J. F. Nunamaker and R. H. Sprague (eds), *Proceedings 29th HICSS, Vol. IV: Information Systems - Organizational Systems and Technology*, IEEE Computer Society Press, Los Alamitos, CA, pp. 407-416.

Hoffmann, D. L. and Novak, T. P.: 1995, Marketing in hypermedia computer-mediated environments: Conceptual foundations, *Working Paper No. 1*, Research Program on Marketing in CME, Vanderbilt, January.

Holland, C. P. and Lockett, G.: 1994, Strategic choice and interorganizational information systems, *in* J. F. Nunamaker and R. H. Sprague (eds), *Proceedings 27th HICSS, Vol. IV: Collaboration Technology, Organizational Systems and Technology*, IEEE Computer Society Press, Los Alamitos, CA, pp. 405-413.

Klausz, F. J. and Croson, D. C. and Croson, R. T. A.: 1998, An experimental auction to allocate congested IT resources, *in* H. J. Watson (ed.), *Proceedings 31st HICSS, Vol. VI*, IEEE Computer Society Press, Los Alamitos, CA, pp. 363-373.

Laat, P. de: 1993, Technological alliances - securing trust by mutual commitments, *in* M. Ebers (ed.), *Proceedings ESF-Conference on Forms of InterOrganizational Networks: Structures and Processes*, Berlin, pp. 435-464.

Lee, H. G.: 1996, Electronic brokerage and electronic auction: The impact of IT on market structures, *in* J. F. Nunamaker and R. H. Sprague (eds), *Proceedings 29th HICSS, Vol. IV: Information Systems - Organizational Systems and Technology*, IEEE Computer Society Press, Los Alamitos, CA, pp. 397-406.

Lee, H. G.: 1997, Electronic market intermediary: transforming technical feasibility into institutional reality, *in* J. F. Nunamaker and R. H. Sprague (eds), *Proceedings 30th HICSS, Vol. IV: Information Systems - Organizational Systems and Technology*, IEEE Computer Society Press, Los Alamitos, CA.

Lewyn, M.: 1994a, What price air?, *BW*, 14 March, pp. 54-55.

Loose, A. and Sydow, J.: 1994, Vertrauen und Ökonomie in Netzwerkbeziehungen - Strukturationstheoretische Betrachtungen, *in* J. Sydow and A. Windeler (Hg.): *Management interorganisationaler Beziehungen*, Westdeutscher Verlag, Opladen, pp. 160-193.

Malone, T., Yates, J. and Benjamin, R.: 1987, Electronic markets and electronic hierarchies: effects of information technology on market structure and corporate strategies, *Communications of the ACM*, 30(6), 484-497.

Markoff, J.: 1996, Can Xerox auction off hot air?, *The New York Times*, 24 June, D5.

Reck, M.: 1993, Formally specifying an automated trade execution system, *Journal for Systems Software*, 21, 245-252.

Reck, M.: 1994, *Types of Electronic Auctions,* in W. Schertler, B. Schmid, A. M. Tjoa and H. Werthner (eds), *Information and Communications Technologies in Tourism,* Springer-Verlag, Vienna, pp. 236-243.

Reck, M.: 1997, Trading-process characteristics of electronic auctions, *International Journal of Electronic Markets*, 7(4), 17-23.

Reekers, N. and Smithson, S.: 1994, EDI and interorganizational coordination in the European automotive industry, *Proceedings SISnet Conference*, Barcelona, Spain.

Seidmann, A. and Wang, E.: 1992, electronic data interchange: Competitive externalities and strategic implementation policies, *Computer and Information Systems Working Paper CIS 92-03*, William E. Simon Graduate School of Business Administration, University of Rochester, May.

Singh, H., Hao, S. and Papalexopoulos, A.: 1997, Power auctions and network constraints, *in* J. F. Nunamaker and R. H. Sprague (eds), *Proceedings 30th HICSS, Vol. IV: Information Systems - Organizational Systems and Technology*, IEEE Computer Society Press, Los Alamitos, CA.

Weber, B. W.: 1994, Transparency and bypass in electronic financial markets, *in* J. F. Nunamaker and R. H. Sprague (eds), *Proceedings 27th HICSS, Vol. IV: Collaboration Technology, Organizational Systems and Technology*, IEEE Computer Society Press, Los Alamitos, CA, pp. 865-874.

CHAPTER 5

Leveraging Security Policy for Competitive Business Advantage in Electronic Commerce

NEAL G. SHAW
Texas Tech University

5.1. Introduction

Electronic commerce is slowly changing the way companies do business; however, firms are becoming increasingly apprehensive about doing business electronically because of security concerns (Bhimani, 1996). Horror stories about hackers, thefts of sensitive financial data, and insecure systems have built psychological barriers that many businesses and executives have yet to overcome (Ahuja, 1997).

Most business executives view computer security as a nuisance that must be handled with extreme caution. Numerous articles and books have been written detailing various computer security attacks and how to prevent them (Ahuja, 1997). On the other hand, an issue that has not been adequately addressed in either academic or practitioner literature is the possibility that security can actually be used as a differentiating factor between competitors. If leveraged properly, computer security can be used as a selling point for a company that does business electronically. Buyers and suppliers will be more willing to do business with a company that has effective security policies than with a company that does not have proper security controls.

This chapter combines the Porter and Millar (1985) competitive forces model and the Bhimani (1996) Internet security model to develop a comprehensive framework for security policy to create competitive business advantage in electronic commerce. We first review some relevant background literature in the fields of business advantage, electronic commerce, and security, and then we develop the framework.

5.2. Background and Motivation

Electronic commerce is a relatively new field, and thus the body of literature related specifically to EC is quite small compared to that of other, more established fields (Yadav and Shaw, 1997). On the other hand, much research has been dedicated to competitive advantage and also to computer security. This chapter will draw from the literature of these more established areas and apply the work to the more recent area of electronic commerce.

A recent EC framework proposed by Applegate et al. (1996) regulated the issues of security and authentication to the common business services infrastructure. In an extension of this framework, Shaw and Yadav (1997) include individual layers for security and authentication. They also include a top layer for business goals and requirements for EC within an organization. Creating competitive advantage is one such requirement that could fall into this layer of their framework. Various authors have noted that security is a necessary component of any electronic commerce system (Bhimani, 1996; Ahuja, 1997; Shaw and Yadav, 1997). Thus there is sufficient precedent from the literature for this chapter to apply principles of computer security and competitive advantage to electronic commerce.

Computer security is an extremely broad topic and can thus be defined in various ways. This chapter will define security as the protection and authentication of computer data (Bhimani, 1996), in transit or stationary, as well as the confidentiality of sensitive information via human organizational sources (Ives and Cheney, 1987). According to Bhimani (1996) there are the following five fundamental security requirements:

1. *confidentiality* - all communications for a transaction are available only to the parties involved in the transaction and to no one else,
2. *authentication* - all parties involved in a transaction should be able to verify that the other parties are in fact who they claim to be,
3. *data integrity* - data sent as part of a transaction should not be allowed to be changed by unauthorized parties while in transit or while stored on a machine,
4. *non-repudiation* - all transactions must be recorded and logged so that neither party can deny having been involved in a particular transaction,
5. *selective application of services* - some parts of a transaction may need to be concealed while other parts of the same transaction do not.

These five requirements for secure transactions on the Internet serve as the basis for our framework for security policy. These components are generalized so that they apply to many situations, and they certainly apply to electronic commerce transactions. Electronic tools are gradually replacing traditional businesses practices (Liddy, 1996), so firms must consider requirements such as these for success in today's marketplace.

Competitive advantage can be thought of as turning the balance of power between a firm and its competitors in favor of the firm (Laudon and Laudon, 1997). Porter (1980) describes two primary ways to create competitive advantage within an industry:

1. *lowering cost* - implementing new strategies or redefining processes to enable the firm to produce the same product as competitors at a lower cost, thus creating an advantage,
2. *enhancing differentiation* - focusing on an aspect of the company's product that sets it apart from competitors.

Although one could likely make a case for the cost benefits of computer security as well, this chapter will focus on creating competitive advantage by enhancing differentiation from competitors. The framework will show how a company can use its security policy to produce a product that will be differentiated from competitors.

The framework will also be based upon Porter and Millar's (1985) five forces model for competition in an industry, in which they describe the following five forces that shape the nature of competition within an industry:

1. *threat of new entrants* - the threat that new competitors might enter into the industry and change the structure of the existing competition,
2. *threat of substitutes* - the threat that new products might have the potential to replace a firm's products,
3. *rivalry among existing competitors* - the level of the threat posed by the rivalry among the existing competitors in the industry,
4. *power of buyers* - the power of the buyers of the products from an industry to shape the nature of the competition,
5. *power of suppliers* - the power of the firms that supply raw materials and intermediary products to an industry to affect the nature of the competition in the industry.

Again it is likely that all five forces of Porter and Millar's model can be affected by a firm's electronic commerce security policy. This chapter, however, will only consider the power of buyers and the power of suppliers since these are the two forces that will be most directly impacted by computer security.

To create competitive advantage, a firm must present its position in computer security as an advantage because technology cannot create an advantage without proper support from the enterprise (Hopper, 1990). Therefore in the changing marketplace of today, firms must present their security services as significant enhancements to the value chain (Rayport and Sviokla, 1995; Clemons and McFarlan, 1986) in order to produce a competitive advantage.

5.3. A Comprehensive Framework for Leveraging Electronic Commerce Security Policy to Create Competitive Business Advantage

With the increasing competition in all areas of today's global marketplace, companies are increasingly trying to find an advantage over competitors. In the relatively new area of electronic commerce, businesses are putting forth an even greater effort to find a differentiating factor to leverage for competitive advantage because of intense competition for early market share. Possibly the most important factor slowing widespread growth of electronic commerce is the fear of security breaches (Ahuja, 1997). Thus it seems likely that firms have an opportunity to use computer security to create competitive business advantage within their industries. Figure 1 shows a framework for an organization to leverage its security policies to enhance differentiation of services against competitors. The framework is in the form of structured guidelines divided into three main groups: confidentiality, verification, and selectivity, based on Bhimani's model. Each group is then divided into subgroups based on the power of buyers and the power of suppliers from Porter and Millar's five forces model. At the subgroup level, several guidelines are listed that will help a firm create competitive differentiation of services. It is important to remember that Bhimani (1996) has already argued that all of these services must be present in any transaction; this chapter argues that these particular services are the most fundamental points on which to base competitive differentiation in order to create competitive advantage. A detailed description of each of the groups and subgroups is given below.

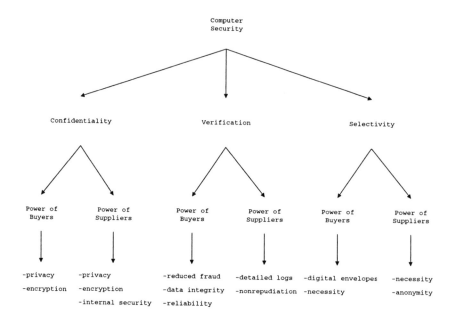

Figure 1. A comprehensive framework for leveraging security policy for competitive business advantage in electronic commerce.

The first factor in the model, confidentiality, is analogous to the confidentiality component of the Bhimani model. This category refers to the aspects of computer security that deal with the privacy and confidentiality of data. As Ives and Cheney (1987) point out, however, not all compromised data is stolen via computer means. In fact much confidential data about a company's computer system is stolen via the spoken word. Thus we use confidentiality to refer to the privacy of information not only stored on a computer but also the computer knowledge retained by the employees of a firm. A company can leverage confidentiality of data to influence buyers because buyers want to keep information private. Credit card numbers, checking account numbers, transaction details, etc. are all examples of information that should be kept hidden from view in an EC transaction. For the same reason, suppliers can be influenced. That is, suppliers want transactions to remain confidential to prevent disclosure of sensitive information.

The second factor, verification, refers to three issues of Bhimani's model, authentication, data integrity, and non-repudiation. In an EC transaction, authentication must be present because we must be able to verify that the party on the other end of the transaction is who it claims to be. Consumers and firms alike can be defrauded if authentication rules are not in place to verify the parties in a transaction. Data integrity is critical as well so that data cannot be altered with proper authorization. Again, a company or consumer can easily become the victim of fraud if someone were to modify part of a transaction; that is, the dollar amount, quantity, etc. In addition, neither party should be able to deny having participated in a transaction (Bhimani, 1996). Non-repudiation features are added to a robust security policy to ensure that neither buyers nor suppliers are defrauded by repudiation of transactions. Verification can be used as a selling point to buyers to ease their fears of fraud and thus increase their willingness to participate in EC (Ahuja, 1997). Suppliers are likely to be pleased with the presence of detailed logs and transaction records so that they will be assured that no one can deny having participated in a transaction.

The third and final factor in the framework, selectivity, refers to Bhimani's fifth component - selective application of services. If a company's security policy has selectivity, then there exists the ability to apply security measures to specific parts of a transaction, but not to all parts. In short, this feature means that a buyer or supplier should have access to only the parts of the transaction that are absolutely necessary. For example, a supplier does not need to know the bank account number of the buyer for the transaction to occur. The financial information, such as bank account number, should be sent directly to the financial institution. Similarly, a buyer should not have access to extraneous information about the supplier that is not necessary for the transaction to occur.

5.4. Illustration of the Comprehensive Framework

To show the practical applications of the comprehensive framework for leveraging security policy to create competitive advantage in electronic commerce, we will apply the framework to two companies in different industries:

1. *McKesson Drug Company* - to demonstrate the power of buyers,
2. *Open Market, Inc.* - to demonstrate the need for selectivity.

The following paragraphs will illustrate the potential for each of these companies to use the proposed framework.

McKesson's order entry and inventory management system, Economost, is one of the most often cited examples of a strategic information system (Clemons and Row, 1988). Economost is an electronic system that automates order entry for McKesson's customers. Employees at pharmacies can browse the shelves and electronically place orders through Economost that will arrive overnight. Thus the entire cycle - ordering, billing, etc. - is processed electronically. One of the keys to the success of Economost is the wide acceptance that it has earned throughout the pharmaceutical industry (Clemons and Row, 1988). There was a time, however, when it was not clear as to whether or not the industry would accept such a revolutionary electronic tool. Understandably, many local pharmacies were reluctant to join the Economost system because of fears of theft of sensitive financial data, proprietary information, etc. The framework presented in this chapter could have been applied by McKesson to convince the pharmacies that its systems were secure. If McKesson had demonstrated to its buyers that its system were secure in three aspects: confidentiality, verification, and security, it is likely that the barriers to the introduction of Economost could have been lowered significantly.

Open Market is a relatively new firm designed to sell products and services for the global electronic marketplace (Applegate and Gogan, 1996). In other words, Open Market is an electronic commerce company. The company saw an opportunity to develop and sell secure systems that would allow merchants to place goods for sale on the Internet and give consumers the opportunity to buy them on the Internet as well. Open Market has an opportunity to create a competitive advantage in the intensely competitive electronic commerce market. If, for example, Open Market were to develop and market a system targeted to be the first to have completely selective application of secure mechanisms, the firm could create product differentiation. The third factor in the model, selective application of services, is also the component of Bhimani's (1996) model that is the least widespread in commercially available products. Thus Open Market, or another competitor, has a significant opportunity to enhance product differentiation by providing selectivity in security mechanisms.

5.5. Conclusions and Future Research

This chapter has proposed a comprehensive framework for leveraging security policy to create competitive business advantage in electronic commerce. The framework has implications for practitioners and researchers alike. For practitioners, the framework serves three functions:

1. a model to help devise a security policy that can create competitive business advantage (points on which to sell the company's services),
2. a basis on which to evaluate existing security policies,
3. a basis on which to evaluate other companies for proposals and solicitations.

Various kinds of research are possible using the framework as a guide. Case studies of EC companies and empirical validation are two areas that should be addressed. As an illustration of research issues that warrant investigation, consider the following research questions:

1. How can we quantify the effects of EC security policy?
2. How will emerging technologies affect security and its business impact?
3. Will empirical studies validate the model and its applications?
4. Is there a significant difference between the actual value of computer security and the perceived value of computer security?

5.6. Acknowledgements

The author would like to thank Mary B. Burns as well as the editors for their insightful comments on earlier versions of this manuscript.

5.7. References

Addonizio, M. L. and Balaguer, N. S.: 1992, Chrysler Corporation: JIT and EDI (A), *HBS Case No. 9-191-146*, Harvard Business School.

Ahuja, V.: 1997, *Secure Commerce on the Internet*, AP Professional, Boston.

Applegate, L. M., et al.: 1996, Electronic commerce: Building blocks of new business opportunity, *Journal of Organizational Computing and Electronic Commerce*, 6(1), 1-10.

Applegate, L. M. and Gogan, J. L.: 1996, Open Market, Inc., *HBS Case No. 9-195-205*, Harvard Business School.

Bhimani, A.: 1996, Securing the commercial Internet, *Communications of the ACM* 39(6), 29-35.

Clemons, E. K. and McFarlan, F. W.: 1986, Telecom: Hook up or lose out, *Harvard Business Review*, 91-97.

Clemons, E. K. and Row, M.: 1988, McKesson Drug Company: A case study of Economost - A Strategic Information System, *Journal of Management Information Systems,* 5(1), 38-50.

Hopper, M. D.: 1990, Rattling SABRE - New ways to compete on information, *Harvard Business Review,* 118-125.

Ives, B., and Cheney, P. H.: 1987, Loose lips, *Information Strategy: The Executive's Journal* 3(4), 19-24.

Laudon, K. C. and Laudon, J. L.: 1997, *Essentials of Management Information Systems*, Prentice-Hall, New Jersey.

Liddy, C.: 1996, Commercial security on the Internet, *Internet Research: Electronic Networking Applications and Policy*, 6(2/3), 75-78.

Porter, M. E. and Millar, V. E.: 1985, How information gives you competitive advantage, *Harvard Business Review,* 149-160.

Porter, M. E.: 1980, *Competitive Strategy*, Free Press, New York.

Rayport, J. F. and Sviokla, J. J.: 1995, Exploiting the virtual value chain, *Harvard Business Review,* 75-97.

Shaw, N. G. and Yadav, S. B.: 1997, Characteristics of system requirements for electronic commerce, *Proceedings 3rd Americas Conference on Information Systems*, Indianapolis.

Yadav, S. B., and Shaw, N. G.: 1997, A comprehensive framework for understanding electronic commerce, *Proceedings 8th International Conference of the Information Resources Management Association*, Vancouver, BC, Canada.

CHAPTER 6

The Dynamics of Establishing Organizational Web Sites

Some Puzzling Findings

CELIA T. ROMM AND JEANNE WONG
University of Wollongong

6.1. Introduction

Recent publications herald Web technology as a revolutionary or transformational technology, i.e. one with the potential to dramatically change the way that organizations conduct their business (Bickel, 1996; Kalakota and Whinston, 1996; Rayport and Sviokla, 1995). Some of the areas that are seen as most likely to undergo radical change as a result of the introduction of Web technologies to business organizations are: (i) informational structures; (ii) management strategies; (iii) distribution channels; and (iv) product mix.

A survey of the literature on Web technologies reveals that, even though it is growing at a high rate, much of it is still dedicated to the technical aspects of the diffusion process, such as how to connect to the Internet (LeJeune and Duntemann, 1995) and how to use Web browsers (Brown et al, 1995; Krol, 1994; Pitter and Minato, 1996). Other areas within the growing body of research on Web technologies include the study of marketing implications of the Web (Savola, Westenbroek and Heck, 1995), and design issues (Emery, 1996; Sterne, 1995).

Most importantly for our purposes, there are only a handful of studies that actually describe the process of diffusion of organizational Web technology within organizations. One of the pioneering studies in this area was recently conducted by Jarvenpaa and Ives (1996). In their research, the authors not only described in detail how two organizations in the US developed their Web technology capabilities, but also made a series of propositions on how this process can be theoretically conceptualized.

The objective of this chapter is to use the Jarvenpaa and Ives (1996) study as a starting point for a more general model capable of describing the diffusion of Web technologies in organizations. To achieve this goal, this chapter goes through the following steps. First, based on the Jarvenpaa and Ives (1996) model, five propositions that have been identified by these authors as relevant to the diffusion of Web technologies in organizations are outlined. Second, based on data collected in Australia, the degree to which the Jarvenpaa and Ives propositions can be

generalized across industries and cultures is assessed. Third, given that there is a gap
between the Jarvenpaa and Ives propositions and the Australian case, an alternative
approach, the Establishing Organizational Web Sites (EOWS) model, is presented.
The chapter is concluded with a discussion of directions for future research and
methodological implications from the EOWS model.

6.2. Literature Review

Before we consider the Jarvenpaa and Ives (1996) paper, a few words about the
diffusion of information technology innovations in general are in order. McFarlan
and McKenney (1982) were among the first to suggest that during the diffusion of
new information technologies, the creative functions of implementation should be
separated from the control functions. Furthermore, they suggested that organizational
structures should be modified to support the different aspects of the diffusion
process. Thus, while a more flexible, organic structure where management controls
are loose and informal was recommended for the earlier, more creative stages of
technology diffusion, rigid, mechanistic organizational structures and procedures
were seen as appropriate for the later, more controlled stages of the diffusion
process.

Following the McFarlan and McKenney directive, Cash, McFarlan and
McKenney (1983) advocated the creation of special groups within the information
technology function or appointing special "idea champions" as intermediaries
between users and information technology. These individuals or special groups were
expected to identify new technologies that had the potential to address users' needs,
and, then, support the development and diffusion of such technologies within the
organization. Cash and McLeod (1985) suggested in another paper that strategic
planning processes led by top management might help identify promising
technologies and then provide funds for piloting them in the organization prior to an
organizational-wide implementation.

In contrast to these directives, other researchers, most particularly those
borrowing models from the literature on organizational radical change (Gersick,
1991; Beers, Eisenstat and Spector, 1990) maintained that the diffusion of informational technologies that are "revolutionary" in nature, cannot be initiated by the
upholders of the status quo. These theorists claimed that there are cognitive, motiva-
tional and organizational reasons why those who are in positions of power would be
unable to lead changes that undermine revolutionary change. Instead, they advocated
the importance of "idea champions" (Schon, 1963; Howell and Higgins, 1990) as
vehicles of spontaneous, non-organizationally sanctioned innovation and change.

A variety of issues were mentioned by researchers as reasons for the fact that
radical change *cannot* be led by those in power. These include:

1. People's past experience and education dictate the alternatives that they
    consider. People in positions of power are constrained by their personal
    experiences. Given that these people are often older than the idea champion

of new technologies, they might be less inclined to support them (Dearborn and Simon, 1958).
2. Revolutionary change involves a loss of what is familiar and comfortable. Given the fact that radical change may influence the distribution of power within an organization, elevating the change champions at the expense of others, it may be resented by those likely to lose power, namely, those in current positions of power (Markus, 1981, 1983).
3. Current organizational policies and obligations constrain the behavior of current stakeholders. Another way of stating this argument is to argue that as individuals and groups become more skilled in their activities, they have a tendency to routinize their modes of behavior and become less inclined to change them (March and Simon, 1958).

The obvious conflict between the above arguments - that some of them advocate top management involvement as a pre-requisite to a project success while others claim that radical change cannot be led by top management - was the theoretical starting point for the Jarvenpaa and Ives (1996) study. Their study is one of the pioneering attempts to systematically analyze the process of Web technologies diffusion in organizations. Based on two in-depth case studies conducted in two computer companies in the US, Jarvenpaa and Ives made five propositions that reflect their understanding of what the diffusion of Web technologies in organizations is about.

The first proposition in the Jarvenpaa and Ives model is that the introduction of Web technologies is likely to occur with only peripheral involvement of the information technology function. This assertion was supported by the fact that in both organizations studied by the authors members of the informational technology unit were either peripherally involved or took a traditional control orientation which centered around formalizing, and safeguarding the existing information systems resource.

The second proposition in the Jarvenpaa and Ives model is that the introduction of Web technologies is likely to occur with minimal if any involvement by top management. This assertion was supported by the fact that in both organizations studied by the authors top management was very minimally involved, particularly at the early stages of the diffusion process. In both organizations Web technology was diffused for months and used extensively by a large number of organizational members before members of top management (in both cases the company CEO) expressed support for the project publicly.

The third proposition in the Jarvenpaa and Ives model is that the introduction of Web technologies is likely to be accomplished by an ad-hoc, cross-functional group that has no formal organizational responsibility for promoting the technologies. This assertion was supported by the fact that in both organizations studied by the authors ad-hoc groups, mostly from the R&D and Marketing Communication areas were established as informal champions of Web technology. In both cases, these groups invested significant efforts in demonstrating the profit potential of the new technologies, giving presentations to external CIO's, and fostering attention from the external press to the importance of Web technologies.

The fourth proposition in the Jarvenpaa and Ives model is that a performance crisis can be used to stimulate the introduction of Web technologies to an organization, but that a crisis is not necessary for this change to occur. The assertion was supported by the fact that one of the two organizations studied by the authors experienced a performance crisis shortly after the Web technologies project had started. It was thanks to this crisis that the CEO and other top managers began to see Web technologies as part of a solution that could benefit the company.

The fifth proposition in the Jarvenpaa and Ives model is that the introduction of Web technologies to an organization can be triggered or supported by "staged events", some of which could be deliberately *manufactured* by the leaders of the project. This assertion was supported by the data collected by the authors in that in both organizations, the project leaders took advantage of real or imagined deadlines to push the project forward. While in one organization the deadlines were largely manufactured by the leaders, in the other they were triggered by a real threat from the competition when it was revealed that it was about to launch its own Web page.

In the following sections the above propositions are considered as they apply to case data collected in Australia. The discussion attempts to reconcile the differences between the American and the Australian experience by proposing the EOWS model.

6.3. Case Study

Data for this study were collected by the authors at an Australian University referred to here as UOA (the name of the University as well as the names of all characters in the case have been withheld to protect their anonymity - the names that are used are pseudonyms). Data was collected over a period of two years.

The major source of data for this study was interviews, which were conducted with twenty members of the University. An additional source of information was a variety of hard copy documents supplied to the researchers by the interviewees. During data analysis, data from all sources pertinent to a particular event were analyzed and the interpretations of all interviewees for that event compared. A decision as to the meaning of the event for the various individuals involved was reached only when it was supported by the data from all sources and when it was agreed on by the researchers.

1. Interviews

In-depth interviews with twenty members of UOA were the most important source of data for this study. During data collection, a semi-structured interview schedule, consisting of a series of open-ended topics was utilized. The questions gauged interviewees' memories of the events, as well as their interpretation of the meaning of the events. Even though the interview schedule was semi-structured, an attempt was made to cover the *same* topics in all interviews. Issues on which interviewees disagreed received special attention. When such issues were identified, they were included in subsequent interviews, with a special attempt made to reach consensus among the interviewees over these issues. In addition to gathering personal details (such as background information, career data, and future plans), interviewees were asked to describe the quality of their work life while the case events took place, relationships with other members of the organization, and areas of responsibility. The interviews lasted on average about ninety minutes, and were all taped, transcribed and analyzed by the authors.

A content analysis scheme was used for the interview data. The scheme included a categorization of major themes in the interviews, with particular emphasis on issues relating to the details of the implementation events and the interpretation of these events by the interviewees.

Interviews were conducted over a period of two years (1995 to 1996), which roughly corresponded to the duration of the case events. On average, two interviews were held with each interviewee, bringing the number of interviews to forty. Members of three major groups were interviewed:

1. *Academic Staff.* There were 10 interviewees from the academic staff; four Professors (including two Department Chairs and one Dean); three Associate Professors; and three Assistant Professors. The academic sample was derived from six different departments from all major divisions at UOA. All academics selected as interviewees had direct or indirect knowledge of the events on which the case focused. To make sure that information about the case events was as complete as possible, all members of the University Campus Wide Information Systems (CWIS) committee (see following sections for more details) were interviewed.

2. *Administrative Staff.* Five interviews were conducted with individuals who were categorized as "administrative staff". From top management, the Provost and the Personal Assistant to the President were interviewed. Two secretaries were also interviewed. Each of the secretaries was from a different department within UOA strongly associated with the Web technology project.

3. Five interviewees were members of the Information Technology Department (ITD): the Head of the Department, the Head of User Services, the secretary of the CWIS committee and the past and present coordinators of the Web project support unit were interviewed.

2. Textual Analysis

A variety of documents were collected at various stages of the implementation project. These included promotional materials, training transparencies, and minutes of relevant meetings. Textual analysis also included in-depth study of the organizational chart, hard and soft copy correspondence, newspaper clippings, and progress reports. A major source of data for the textual analysis was email messages. Over 100 email messages pertaining to the project were made available to the author by the key players in the case. The email messages were analyzed using a specially constructed qualitative content analysis scheme. The scheme involved a thematic categorization of the issues discussed on email by the various players in the case.

3. Case Data

UOA is a medium-sized University, with over 1000 staff members and over 13,000 students. The University is centrally located within a densely populated, highly industrialized metropolitan area. UOA has a reputation for being one of the most technologically advanced academic institutions in the country, investing substantial resources in experimental, emerging technologies. The diffusion of Web technologies at UOA followed a highly successful email implementation, which started in 1988 and was completed in 1992, shortly before the case events started. In the following sections we describe the diffusion of Web technologies at UOA in terms of four phases, spanning the years 1993-1996.

1993: Sporadic Diffusion of Web Technologies

Following the success of the email diffusion in the years prior to 1993, many staff members at UOA were using early Internet technologies. The majority of users were academics. They were using a variety of search engines such as Mosaic, Archie and Gopher, to support their research and networking initiatives with colleagues in other academic institutions.

In mid 1993, the Head of the Information Technology Unit (ITU), Mr Adam Neil, was becoming aware of the need to identify one UNIX based, multi-platform (compatible with both Macs and PCs) to support the file servers around the university. In the search for the one technology that would be most suitable for UOA, Mr Neil instructed his subordinates to consider and test several options, including, Gopher, WAIS, Apple Share and Mandarin. Despite the search effort, by the end of 1993, a decision as to the best technology to support Internet servers on campus had *not* been made.

1994: The CWIS Committee

The first months of 1994 marked a dramatic change in the development of the Web technologies project. The change started when Professor Mark Lind, UOA Provost for Research and the Chair of UOA Computer Planning Policy committee (CPPC), announced during the committee's first meeting for the year that the President of UOA had authorized him to suggest to the committee the launching of a Campus Wide Information Systems (CWIS) project. A CWIS steering committee, to be created as a sub-committee of the CPPC, was to supervise a project that would result in the creation of an integrative multi-platform Web based intranet for UOA. By the end of the meeting, the Computer Planning committee appointed Mr Anthony Moore, one of Mr Neil's deputies and the Head of the Administration Information System (AIS) unit, as Chair of the newly established CWIS committee.

Following the decision of the CPPC, Mr Neil instructed a team of experts within ITU to renew the search for a technology that could support Internet servers around the campus. By this time (mid 1994), Web technologies became popular in the industry. They were seen by the members of the ITU search team as much more exciting than the options that they considered in 1993. Most importantly, Web technologies were seen as the most appropriate solution to UOA's multi-platform problem. Following this line of reasoning, the group decided to recommend the Web as the anchor for the University information infrastructure. In line with this recommendation, contact was established with several Web technologies vendors. Within a few weeks, a contract was signed with Netscape, with Netscape Enterprise, the company's more advanced product, becoming the basis for UOA's Web technologies infrastructure.

By the end of 1994 the newly established CWIS committee held its first meeting. The meeting was attended by five individuals. Three of the committee members were from ITU (including Mr Neil and Mr Moore). The remaining two members included Mr Jack Ford, the Head of UOA Department of External Relations, and Professor Jeffrey Wood, Chair of the Department of MIS. The major decision made by the committee during its first meeting was to allocate $40,000 as a salary to a person appointed as coordinator of the Web technologies project. It was agreed that the person hired as coordinator of the Web technologies project would also be the secretary of the CWIS committee.

Within a month after the committee's meeting took place, Mr James Cooper took office as the new coordinator of the Web technologies project. Mr Cooper had extensive experience as a manager in the IS industry. He had been working with Web technologies for years, including several years' experience as a private consultant in this area. By appointing him as coordinator of the project, the members of the CWIS committee had clearly expressed a commitment to Web technologies.

1995: Launching the Web Project

Mr Cooper interpreted his role as coordinator of the Web technologies project in several ways. First, as secretary of the CWIS committee, he decided to make the committee more representative of the University community. To achieve this goal he decided to approach three additional academics and invite them to join the committee. The new members included Professor Jane Peel, the Chair of Computer Science, Professor Susan Brown, the Chair of Art History, and Professor Gill Grant, the Chair of Psychology. The addition of the three professors not only changed the committee in terms of disciplinary representation (with less representation to IT people and more to members of other units within the University), but also made the committee significantly more balanced in terms of gender.

Another decision taken by Mr Cooper was to focus the committee's work around the establishment of a new Web site. Even though the University already had a one-page Web site, it was felt that a much more sophisticated site was needed. During the remainder of 1995, discussions over the content of the Web site became the main issues of concern for the CWIS committee. The debates focused on the following issues:

The design question

While the administrative members of staff on the committee were adamant that the first page of the Web site should highlight issues relating to Foreign Students, who represented a major source of income for the University, the academic insisted that such a design would be discriminatory to other sub-groups within the student body, i.e. blacks and females. It was finally resolved that all students would appear on the top of the list as one group.

The standards issue

While the representative of the IT group and the External Affairs group within the committee were strong advocates of one set of standards, the academic members of the committee saw the attempt to impose such standards as "stifling of academic creativity". After long debates, it was finally agreed that the various departments within the University would be allowed to use whatever design tools, color scheme, or structure they chose. The only proviso was that all departments would put the University logo at the bottom of their "official" Web pages.

The control debate

Here the committee was divided between the more technically oriented members who felt that the ultimate control of the Web site should be with ITU, and the academic members of the committee who felt that departments should not be pestered by the IT group about updating their Web pages. The final decision of the committee was that ITU would make its expertise available to departments who would choose to approach it for training and advice. However, it would not police the Web site and would not impose deadlines for updating individual Web pages.

By the end of 1995 the CWIS committee had met four more times (bringing the total number of meetings for that year to five). Toward the end of the year, the format for the University Web site (the first page) was agreed on. Mr Cooper was instructed to construct individual pages for the different units within the University. In particular, he was to lead the very difficult and time-consuming project of getting most of the central administration documents on the Web - a project that was expected to continue for at least another year.

1996: Consolidation of the Web Project

The CWIS committee continued to hold meetings during 1996 but not at the same frequency as during 1995. During 1996 only two meetings were held and these were attended by less than two thirds of the members of the committee.

During 1996 several members of the committee started to be disillusioned with the project. Several of the academic members complained that the promise to create a "paper free organization" was not forthcoming. Indeed, many of the central administration departments who were supposed to convert their hard copy documents to electronic databases and make them available to users on the University's Web server, did not meet this goal, claiming that other responsibilities left them no time to perform this extra job. Other members of the committee were concerned about issues of data security. Thus, several of the academic members of the committee who were initially enthusiastic about the prospect of using the Web to send theses to external referees, started to worry that the Web was not secure enough for this purpose. Other members of the committee raised concerns about access to University databases by unauthorized personnel, most specifically, students.

By the end of 1996, Mr Cooper, the project coordinator, was starting to realize that many departments within the University were simply not joining the Web technology bandwagon. Despite pressures from ITU, and continuing investment in training and promotion efforts, it was clear that the project was not going to be completed by the end of 1996 as was expected. This prompted Mr Cooper to ask for additional resources that would allow him to establish a special development group to assist units that were unable to meet the deadline. The proposal did not win the support of the majority of the CWIS committee members, many of whom claimed that the project leaders should concentrate on the "quality" of the University Web site rather than on its "quantity". The unanimous decision of the committee, was, however, that if Mr Cooper felt that additional resources were necessary, he should attempt to secure them through his superiors at the ITU.

Five months later, when 1996 drew to a close, Mr Cooper finally managed to secure the necessary resources to finish the project. By this time, the majority of the departments at UOA had their own Web pages and so the money was to be invested in the development of Web-based databases to support Administration services on the Web server.

Interestingly, and despite the technical success of the Web technologies project, the views of the UOA members about it were highly polarized. While many academics (including the academic members of the CWIS committee) said that they were manipulated by the IT group into being a rubber stamp to IT's secret agenda, the IT people (including the IT members of the committee) blamed the "academics" for what they saw as "the less than optimal outcome of the project".

6.4. Discussion

What can we learn from the data in the case study? Despite the fact that the case study took place in a university, an organization with a unique culture that differs significantly from other industries, the differences between our findings and those of the Jarvenpaa and Ives (1996) study are striking. In contrast to the propositions of the Jarvenpaa and Ives model, in UOA, the Web technologies project was very much led by the information technology unit, with a high degree of involvement by top management. Furthermore, in our case study, the Web technology project was not triggered by a performance crisis, nor was it punctuated by event based crises manufactured by the project team.

Put differently, it appears that the Australian case lacked almost all the characteristics that led Jarvenpaa and Ives to label the Web technologies projects in their sample "transformational", "radical" or "revolutionary". In our case, the project was a reflection of the continuing commitment of UOA's top management to technological innovation. It was also a natural continuation of other projects initiated by the IT function prior to the case events. In view of the fact that both the IT group and other members of top management were directly involved in the project from the start, it is difficult to claim that it posed a threat to the organizational power distribution or changed it in a significant way, as suggested by the label of "transformational", "radical", or revolutionary.

How can we explain the disparity between the Jarvenpaa and Ives propositions and our case? Several answers can be given to this question, each pointing to a different direction for an extension of the Jarvenpaa and Ives framework.

The first possible explanation relates to the fact that the data for the Jarvenpaa case studies was collected in organizations, which represented a different *industry* than the Australian case. The Jarvenpaa and Ives case studies were based on data collected in two computer companies, while the Australian case centered on the diffusion of Web technologies in a university. It can be argued that the two industries differ not only in their organizational structure and work processes, but, more importantly, in their organizational culture, leading to totally different strategies for diffusing Web technologies. This possibility calls for an integration of the variable of "industry" in any model that attempts to theoretically conceptualize the process of establishing organizational Web sites.

Another possible explanation for the disparity between the Australian case and the Jarvenpaa and Ives findings might be related to the fact that the data for the Jarvenpaa and Ives study was collected in the US, while the data for our case was collected in Australia. Prior research on national cultures (Hofstede, 1980, 1994a; and 1994b) tells us that national culture is a major variable determining relationships within organizations. Even though the American and Australian cultures are assumed by Hofstede to be quite similar, some significant differences between them do exist. In particular, the Australian culture is significantly higher than the American culture on uncertainty avoidance (Australians are more risk avert). The Australian culture is also significantly lower on power distance (power differentials between managers and employees are highlighted more in the US than in Australia). Based on these differences, it can be argued that relative to American organizations, Australian organizations would value participative decision making (lower power distance score), while at the same time, discouraging risk taking (higher uncertainty avoidance score). This would explain the more participative and yet highly centralized management of the Web technologies project in our case relative to the two American cases studied by Jarvenpaa and Ives.

The importance of national culture as a determinant of diffusion process of Web technologies calls for an integration of the variable of "culture" in any model that attempts to theoretically conceptualize the process of establishing organizational Web sites.

Finally, the disparity between the Jarvenpaa and Ives findings and our case can be explained by issues that are idiosyncratic to the organizations observed. This explanation calls for an in-depth analysis of the decision making patterns typical to organizations undertaking Web technologies projects, including the motivations of the various players, the politics of the process, and the influence strategies that are deemed legitimate by the organizational culture.

To conclude this discussion, we would like to present the EOWS model. Figure 1 presents a pictorial depiction of the model. As indicated in this figure, the model perceives the process of diffusion of Web technologies in organizations as a seven-step process, consisting of need, conception, investigation, bargain, acceptance, delivery, and review. The basic model in supplemented with the variables of "industry" and "culture", which are seen as modifying its basic components.

What is the meaning of the various components of the model? In the following sections, we will define and explain the content of the seven steps of the model with specific examples from Web technologies projects.

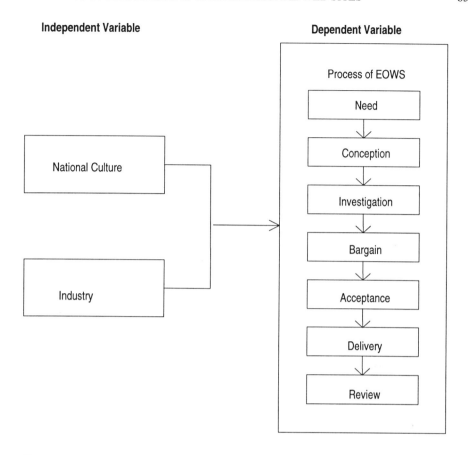

Figure 1. National culture and industry as the determinants of the establishing Organizational Web Sites (EOWS) process.

1. Need
The Need stage is the most important step of in the EOWS process. It involves the identification of needs to be satisfied through the Web technologies project.

2. Conception
The focus of the Conception stage is on how the need, identified in the first stage should be satisfied. At the conception stage, the WWW technology is introduced and the people who are exposed to this technology consider its ability to satisfy their needs.

3. Investigation
If the use of WWW technology is considered a means to satisfy the re-defined need, an investigation into the possibility of wide scale diffusion will be carried out. Depending on the aforementioned factors in the Conception stage, two types of investigation can be initiated: informal investigation (not supported by top management) and formal investigation (supported and most probably resourced by top management).

4. Bargain

The Bargain stage may take two distinct directions. First, the committee members may debate the practicability and validity of the report findings, which will eventually involve amendments to the report. Second, the committee members may debate the actual strategy of the implementation process. This could involve the sharing of responsibility for the individual components of the project, the scrambling of resources to finance the various stages of the implementation, and the fight for a better promotion of the project within the organization.

5. Acceptance (Rejection/Re-Investigation)

The emergence of this stage concludes the process of bargaining, even though it may not reflect a state of satisfaction for all committee members. If the WWW technology is officially accepted, resources will be allocated to support its implementation. If the use of WWW technology is rejected or re-investigation is required, this will have little or no impact on the allocation of resources.

6. Delivery

This stage is characterized by actualizing all the ideas that have been collected in the former stages and turning them into deliverables. These deliverables include the development of an organizational Web site and the production of organizational Web pages.

7. Review

After the official launch of the organizational Web site, certain mechanisms are likely to be set up in order to encourage feedback from users internal and external to the organization. The availability of feedback mechanisms will facilitate the quality control and the inflow of new suggestions.

6.5. Conclusion

The discussion in the previous sections suggests several possible directions for future research.

First, the seven steps in the basic model which are seen here as linear, may in some instances be circular, i.e. sub-processes that take the organization members "backward" or "forward" may occur. For example, it is possible that organizations that are at the Investigation stage may sometimes regress back to the Conception or even Need stages. It is also possible that as the process progresses new needs that have not been identified at the beginning of the process may emerge, leading to a continual repetition of the process.

Second, the inclusion of "industry" and "culture" as variables that modify the basic seven steps of the model call for a variety of empirical investigations into the specific ways in which these variables do, indeed, modify the process. Such investigations should include in-depth studies of the process of diffusion of Web technologies in private and public sector organizations and in cultures that are not necessarily English speaking nor technologically advanced.

Finally, the EOWS model calls for an in-depth socio-political analysis of the decision making patterns typical of organizations undertaking Web technologies projects. Such analyses will involve a careful study of the power and politics of the Web technologies project, with particular emphasis on the players, their motivations, and their influence strategies.

The introduction of a Web technologies project to an organization is a far more complex process than is commonly assumed. The decision process that leads to the creation of an organizational Web site involves aspects that go far beyond the technology that supports the site. The Web site is the organization's business card. It promotes the company's image externally with potential customers, competitors and partners. If the site is used as the anchor for an organizational intranet, then, it is also the carrier of the company's internal image, with its employees.

Given the key role that a Web site can play in an organization it is no wonder that the decisions that pertain to its creation and maintenance, as indicated in our case, are highly political, reflecting the interplay of different stakeholders within the organization.

The politics of the decision making process leading to the creation of an organizational Web server or Web site is, thus, a promising area for future research. The politics of the decision making process surrounding the creation of a Web site can explain why even within the same industry and even within the same national culture (the two cases in the Jarvenpaa and Ives study) diffusion strategy can still differ markedly. When a comparison is made between organizations in different industries and cultures (our case) an understanding of the internal politics of the project can augment the explanatory power of the other two variables.

6.6. References

Beers, M., Eisenstat, R. A. and Spector, B.: 1990, Why change programs don't produce change, *Harvard Business Review*, 68(6), 158-166.

Bickel, R.: 1996, Building Intranets: Internal webs give companies a new solution to an old problem, *Internet World*, pp. 72-76.

Brown, M. and Associates: 1995, *Using Netscape 2, Special Edition*, Que Corporation, Indianapolis.

Cash, J. I., McFarlan, F. W. and McKenney, J. L.: 1983, *Corporate Information Systems Management: The Issues Facing Senior Executives*, Irwin, Homewood, Illinois.

Cash, J. I. and McLeod, P. L.: 1985, Managing the introduction of information systems technology in strategically dependent companies, *Journal of Management Information Systems*, 1(4), 5-23.

Dearborn, D. C. and Simon, H. A.: 1958, Selective Perceptions: A note on the departmental identification of executives, *Sociometry*, 21, 140-144.

Emery, V.: 1996, How to grow your business on the Internet, Coriolis Group, Inc., Arizona.

Gersick, C. J. G.: 1991, Revolutionary change theories: A multilevel exploration of the punctuated equilibrium paradigm, *Academy of Management Review*, 16(1), 10-36.

Hofstede, G.: 1980, *Culture's Consequences: International Differences in Work-Related Values*, Sage Publications, California.

Hofstede, G.: 1994, Management scientists are human, *Management Science*, 40(1), 4-13.

Hofstede, G.: 1994, The business of international business is culture, *International Business Review*, 3(1), 1-14.

Howell, J. M. and Higgins, C. A.: 1990, Champions of technological innovation, *Administrative Science Quarterly*, 35(2), 317-341.

Jarvenpaa, S. L. and Ives, B.: 1996, Introducing transformational information technologies: The case of the World Wide Web technology, *International Journal of Electronic Commerce*, 1(1), 95-126.

Kalakota, R. and Whinston, A. B.: 1996, *Frontiers of Electronic Commerce*, Addison-Wesley, Reading, Massachusetts.

Krol, E.: 1994, *The Whole Internet: User's Guide and Catalogue, 2nd Edition*, O'Reilly and Associates, Inc., California.

LeJeune, U. A. and Duntemann, J.: 1995, *Netscape and HTML Explorer*, Coriolis Group Inc., Arizona.

March, J. G. and Simon, H.: 1958, *Organizations*, John Wiley, New York.

Markus, M. L.: 1981, *Implementation Politics - Top Management Support and IS Involvement, Systems, Objectives, Solutions*, pp. 203-215.

Markus, M. L.: 1983, Power, politics, and MIS implementation, *Communications of the ACM*, 26(6), 430-444.

McFarlan, F. W. and McKenney, J. L.: 1982, The information archipelago: Maps and bridges, *Harvard Business Review*, September/October, 109-119.

Pitter, K. and Minato, R.: 1996, *Every Student's Guide to the World Wide Web*, McGraw-Hill, New York.

Rayport, J. F. and Sviokla, J. J.: 1995, Exploiting the virtual value chain, *Harvard Business Review*, 73(6), 75-85.

Savola, T. Westenbroek, A. and Heck, J.: 1995, *Using HTML, Special Edition*, Que Corporation, Indianapolis.

Schon, D. A.: 1963, Champions for radical new inventions, *Harvard Business Review*, 41(2), 77-86.

Sterne, J.: 1995, *World Wide Web Marketing: Integrating the Web into Your Marketing Strategy*, John Wiley, New York.

CHAPTER 7

Influence of Choice Context on Consumer Decision Making in Electronic Commerce

REX EUGENE PEREIRA
University of Texas at Austin

7.1. Introduction

> One must learn by doing the thing, for though you think you know it - you have
> no certainty, until you try. (Sopholes 400 BC)

How do consumers browsing the electronic shopping malls on the Web make their
purchasing decisions? This question is of crucial interest to advertisers and
marketing managers given that the volume of business transactions on the Web is
projected to grow to more than US$100 billion by the year 2000 (Hoffman and
Novak 1996a). The Web has the potential to revolutionize global marketing. Small
firms could set up a Web site at a relatively low cost and leverage this Web presence
to reach millions of customers worldwide and compete with large multinational firms
globally. The Web offers significant advantages over traditional marketing channels
by providing marketers with the ability to transact business with their customers
effortlessly, regardless of the fact that they may be in different locations and in
different time zones. For products such as software and information-based products,
the Web could serve not only as the medium of communication and transaction of
business, but also as the medium of delivery of the product to the user.

The critical issue is whether the Web offers significant advantages over
traditional marketing channels such as retail malls, home shopping via television and
direct mail. The Web could potentially be used by companies for a variety of
purposes. These range from providing product information and information about the
company, collecting data and conducting market research, providing customer
support and service in a cost-effective manner, providing a means of internal
communication within the company, and conducting business transactions with their
customers. Many software companies and information systems departments of other
companies are using the Web to facilitate distribution of software and upgrades to
their users in a cost-effective manner. For example, Microsoft saves millions of
dollars by making the upgrades to its software available to be downloaded via the
Web using any browser instead of having to ship these upgrades individually to each
user. These tasks could be performed in a very cost-effective manner using the Web

as the vehicle of delivery and could result in huge cash savings to the company and improve the profitability of the company. Furthermore, the greater the number of users on the Web, the larger will be the customer base which these companies are able to access; hence the larger will be their motivation to provide better services through the Web. This will increase the benefit that each user will obtain by using the Web.

The approach adopted in this chapter integrates ideas from two converging sources: the research in judgment and decision making in consumer behavior and cognitive psychology (Samuelson and Zeckhauser 1988; Simonson and Tversky 1992), and the research in marketing issues in electronic commerce (Jarvenpaa and Todd 1998; Kalakota and Whinston 1996; Hoffman, Kalsbeek and Novak 1996; Hoffman and Novak 1996; Hoffman, Novak and Chatterjee 1996; Gupta 1995; Quelch and Klein 1996; Armstrong and Hagel 1996).

7.2. Prior Research on Choice Context and Electronic Commerce

7.2.1. RESEARCH ON MARKETING ISSUES IN ELECTRONIC COMMERCE

Prior research on marketing issues in electronic commerce has focused on the demographic profile of the potential consumers who may use the Web for shopping purposes. Jarvenpaa and Todd (1998) examine the factors that influence consumer perceptions and attitudes towards shopping on the Web. They identify four categories of factors that may influence consumer attitudes towards shopping in virtual malls: product perceptions, shopping experience, customer service, and perceived risk. Hoffman, Novak and Chatterjee (1996) propose a framework to categorize the commercial development of the Web. They identify two broad categories of Web sites as Destination Sites (which include Online Storefronts, Internet Presence Sites and Content Sites) and Web Traffic Control Sites (which include Shopping Malls, Incentive Sites and Search Agents). They discuss the impact of the Web on marketing communications and the barriers to the adoption of the Web. Quelch and Klein (1996) analyze the potential of the Web as a vehicle for marketing purposes from a variety of perspectives and discuss the implications of using the Web as a marketing vehicle, the potential challenges which have to be met and the issues which have to be resolved. The challenges to be met are the inadequate technology infrastructure and the need to reorganize the organizational structure. The issues to be resolved mainly pertain to legal, regulatory and policy issues.

Armstrong and Hagel (1996) introduce the notion of Web users as a community. The implication of the emergence of these electronic communities, from the marketing perspective, is that it provides marketers with the opportunity to cross-sell products and services of many providers within their community, since the buying needs of consumers within a particular community will be highly correlated with each other. Markus (1987) hypothesizes that interactive technologies such as the Web follow an "all-or-none" framework. That is, the utility that each user derives from the use of the network is positively correlated to the number of other users on the network. Given the rapid growth in the number of users of the Web in the past three years, many people feel that this technology has already achieved "critical mass" and is here to stay and change the way we live our lives, much like the telephone.

7.2.2. LITERATURE ON CONTEXT EFFECTS ON CONSUMER CHOICE

Simonson and Tversky (1992) found that consumer choice is influenced by the context in which the decision is made. Consumer decision making involves many different types of judgments. Consumers' judgments of a particular stimulus are usually made in the presence of other stimuli. These other stimuli that are present define the "context" of the decision. Judgments of a stimulus are affected not only by the attributes of the stimulus itself, but also by the other stimuli which accompany it in the judgment context. This chapter deals largely with "context effects" in judgment and choice. Context effects refer to instances in which the judgment process or its outcome is due to other stimuli in the set of available options. The study of context effects assumes that the choice probability of an alternative is not only a function of its attributes, but is also based on other alternatives being considered.

7.3. Model of the Consumers' Decision-Making Process

The way in which context effects occur in judgment and decision-making tasks is illustrated in the model in Figure 1. Consumers' overt judgments could be influenced by choice context in at least three potential ways. First, context may influence which aspects of a stimulus are selected for processing. Context could influence the selection of aspects for processing in two ways. It could bias attentional focus on certain external information or cause selective retrieval of information from long term memory, influencing the contents of short term memory. Alternatively, it could influence how information in short-term memory is combined to make a judgment or a choice. Second, context may influence the scale values (i.e., the subjective, encoded representations of the stimulus cues). That is, context may influence the category judgments by changing the response language that consumers use to report their subjective judgments. Finally, context may influence the judgment function that translates private evaluations to overt ratings. Context may also influence the order in which features are examined in processing rules such as "elimination by aspects" (Tversky 1972).

7.4. Theoretical Development of the Hypotheses

The hypotheses generated in this section examine the effects which the introduction of a new alternative (electronic shopping malls) into the choice set will have on the use of the previously existing alternative choices (retail malls, direct mail catalogs).

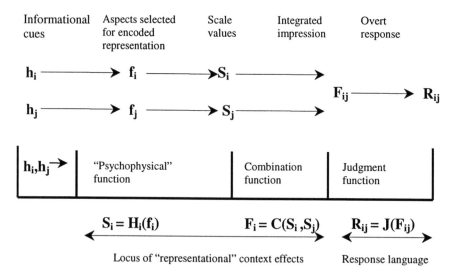

Figure 1. A model of choice context effects on judgment and decision making.

7.4.1. HYPOTHESIS 1

Hypothesis 1 examines the role of prior knowledge and experience on the influence of context effects in consumer judgment processes. Experience in performing the task plays an important role in the decision-making process of people. If the subject is experienced in performing a particular task then, even though the subject may not be explicitly cued with regard to the characteristics of the task situation, the subject may unconsciously retrieve cues from past experiences in performing the task, which will reduce the unfamiliarity of the task situation. For example, subjects who have used the Web previously to perform tasks such as shopping will not need to be explicitly cued with regard to the characteristics of the domain. However, if they have no previous experience in performing this task, then the task is very unfamiliar to them, especially in a relatively complex task such as using a computer to shop on the Web. In this case, the cueing of the subjects would make a big difference in their perception of the shopping experience on the Web. Thus we see that prior experience at shopping on the Web influences the awareness of context-dependent attributes which in this case are the information search costs, the price of the goods and the quality of the goods and services. This lack of experience in performing the task can be compensated for by making the subject perform an explicit rating scale treatment of the context dependent attributes prior to making his judgment. In this manner the consumer is made explicitly aware of the context dependent attributes.

Hypothesis 1. If the consumer lacks experience in shopping on the Web, then the context effects of a representational nature will influence the purchase judgment only if the consumer is made aware of the context-dependent attributes of the alternatives prior to making the purchase decision.

This awareness could be achieved by cueing the subject about the context dependent attributes by administering a rating scale treatment in which the consumer would rate the alternative choices on the context-dependent attributes and then make his judgment. What this implies is that if the consumer did not make the rating scale judgment prior to the purchase judgment, then the size of the context effects of a representational nature would be negligible, especially if we are dealing with innovative new technologies such as electronic commerce and the Web. This is in contrast to what we would expect from standard choice behavior. We would normally expect the effect size of the context effects of a representational nature to be strong enough to show a significant effect irrespective of whether the subjects have received prior treatment on a rating scale. This means that the process of making the pre-purchase judgment makes them aware of the difference in the context-dependent attributes of the alternatives. In order to observe the context effects on consumer judgment, we require that the consumer should have knowledge not only of the alternatives under consideration, but also of all the other alternatives in the choice set. Thus, if the subjects are not aware of the context-dependent attributes of the alternatives, then the context effects will be nullified and we will not be able to observe these effects.

7.4.2. HYPOTHESIS 2

Hypothesis 2 is an extension of work done by Mellers and Birnbaum (1982a) who found that in judgments of multi-dimensional stimuli, where the stimuli were in the same modality or in equivalent units, context produced no systematic reversals in the rank orders of the stimuli. However, reversals did occur in judgments that involved cross-modality comparisons or combinations (Mellers and Birnbaum 1982b). Context would normally have no impact on the psychological representation of information (i.e., the scale value) of stimulus information along a given dimension. However, novel and innovative technologies and tasks, such as shopping at electronic shopping malls, may require subjects to integrate dimensions that cannot be readily compared because (a) one or more of the informational dimensions is described in unfamiliar units, or (b) the integration task requires the subject to make trade-offs that are unfamiliar. In such cases, it is as though an additional processing stage is interposed between evaluation of the scale values of informational inputs and integration of the information. Thus, in multi-dimensional judgments that require the subjects to make unfamiliar tradeoffs, context can influence the effective scale values of the inputs (Mellers and Birnbam 1982b).

> **Hypothesis 2.** If the consumers are familiar with the task (experienced in shopping at the electronic shopping malls using Web browsers) but are not fully aware of the alternatives, then the context effects will be nullified.

7.4.3. HYPOTHESIS 3

Hypothesis 3 is based on the theory related to the asymmetric dominance of alternatives when the newly introduced alternative asymmetrically dominates the previous choice set. The dominated alternative increases the choice proportions of the alternative that dominates such a placement. If we generalize this to the Web domain, we have to deal with questions regarding the wisdom of not setting up a Web site for an electronic shopping mall. Even though this alternative may be inferior to the traditional marketing channels (such as retail malls and direct mail catalogs) it could still be useful because of its ability to influence positively the evaluation and sales through these alternative marketing channels. This issue, in fact, addresses the issue of regularity of the choice probabilities. In other words, the assumption of regularity of choice probabilities is violated by adding an asymmetrically dominated alternative to the choice set. Regularity is a property that is assumed by virtually all models of probabilistic choice (Tversky 1972). This property asserts that the probability of choosing a from choice set {a, b} must be greater than or equal to the probability of choosing a from a choice set {a, b, c}. However, if c was asymmetrically dominated (i.e., dominated by a but not by b), the addition of c to the choice set actually increased the probability that a would be chosen. Since the alternative c, in such cases, is more similar to a than to b, and since previous theorizing (Tversky 1972) postulated that new options should attract choices at the expense of similar alternatives, this is particularly surprising.

This hypothesis thus postulates that when an asymmetrically dominated alternative is added to the choice set, it increases the choice shares of the alternative that dominates it. This is referred to as an "attraction effect", where the likelihood of purchasing an alternative increases in the presence of another alternative. This effect is not accounted for in most choice models, and emphasizes the importance of basic research to develop a more comprehensive theory of the choice process. This attraction effect is in fact a subset of a more general problem where the likelihood of purchasing an item in a choice set is influenced by the other members of the choice set.

Hypothesis 3. Suppose the consumer is offered the same products through the traditional marketing channels such as the retail malls or the direct mail catalogs as well as the electronic shopping malls. However, the prices posted for the same products at the electronic shopping malls is considerably higher than that for the corresponding products at the retail malls but lower than that of direct mail catalogs. In this case, the consumer may not purchase any merchandise through the electronic shopping malls (since it is the dominated alternative) but he will probably purchase much more merchandise than expected at the retail malls since he will perceive that he is getting a bargain at this outlet.

The understanding of this hypothesis is best enhanced by using a simple representation of the choice set in the context of beer. Two alternatives constitute a core set, labeled as a competitor and the target, with neither of the alternatives dominating the other. The target alternative is the alternative whose market share is of interest in the research. Both the competitor and the target are described on two attributes, price and quality as ($2.20,70) and ($1.80,50) respectively. All other attributes are assumed to be irrelevant to the choice, either because they are not important or because the alternatives are identical on those attributes. The preferences on both the attributes are monotonically increasing. What would happen if this core set were expanded to include an asymmetrically dominated alternative? An example of an asymmetrically dominated alternative would be a product described as ($1.80,40), that is, having the same price as the target, but of a lower quality. This alternative is unlikely to be chosen, and is therefore termed as a "decoy" or the "new alternative". This increases the range on the attribute that the target is weaker, and such a placement strategy is called a "range increasing strategy". Another example of an asymmetrically dominated alternative is ($2.20,50), that is, higher priced than the target, but of the same quality. This increases the frequency of the target's stronger attribute, and is referred to as a "frequency increasing new alternative". This effect is illustrated in Figure 2.

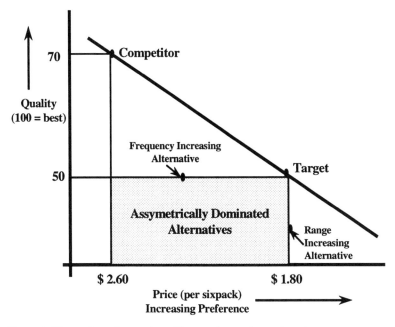

Figure 2. Illustration of attraction effects and new alternative placement strategies.

There are a number of reasons why these findings from attraction effects are important. Attraction effects violate assumptions made in modeling choice, such as regularity and proportionality. Generalizability to the marketplace raises questions about the conventional wisdom of not marketing an inferior product, its usefulness being to influence positively the evaluation and purchase of other alternatives. There are other ways in which these effects are significant.

There are several, possibly interacting reasons why a new alternative might be expected to increase the share of the target at the expense of the competitor. These reasons include perceptual framing of the decision problem, the evaluation process used and the choice situation.

The perceptual framing of the decision problem could cause the attraction effects via several mechanisms. Range effects would alleviate the target's deficit on its weaker attribute. Consequently this extension will increase the preference for the target vis-à-vis the competitor. Frequency effects could also cause the attraction effects. Increasing the frequency of alternatives along the dimension on which the target is superior might increase the weight of the dimension. This would result in spreading the psychological distance of the target over the competitor. Scaling effects could cause attraction effects because the addition of new alternatives affects the means and variances of the attributes. If judgments are comparative, then the choice context will affect the perceived relative value of the alternative. Popularity of the new alternative could contribute to the attraction effect in that all alternatives are considered viable. Attention is drawn to the new alternative/target combination as being a more popular choice set because of proximity.

The evaluation process used in the choice decision could cause the attraction effects via several mechanisms. Simplification of the choice task could cause the attraction effects because the hypothesized cost of thinking would be less for the dominated pairs than the non-dominated pairs. The choice process used could contribute to the attraction effects because selection involves a series of paired comparisons. Each pair is evaluated on an attribute by attribute basis. An initial pairing of the new alternative with the competitor would eliminate the competitor, thereby increasing the target's probability of being chosen. Sequential elimination could cause attraction effects. The choice rule is to eliminate the worst alternative on an attribute (Bettman 1979). This is consistent with risk averse behavior.

The choice situation or choice context could cause attraction effects in several ways. The major cause of the attraction effects would be due to the familiarity and meaningfulness of the attributes. Attraction effects could be caused because the underlying meanings of attributes are not easy to understand, or because subjects do not have experience with the product.

The major extension of the research on attraction effects is to untangle the reasons for its occurrence. Understanding these reasons would help to model this phenomenon, so that it can then be incorporated into a comprehensive theory of choice, instead of being cited as an exception to existing theories. The work on context effects on judgment and choice cite the change in the meaning of an attribute as a possible reason for the attraction effects. An important research gap identified by these streams is the need for a simple model to capture the change in the meaning of an attribute. Such a model would provide a framework within which different new alternative positions could be systematically varied, and the effects studied. One new alternative strategy that has not been tested is when an alternative superior to the target is introduced. The managerial implications of testing this against the usual new alternative positions is in testing the effects of introducing a "better" as opposed to an "inferior" alternative. Even if both products (which have an equal probability of purchase) are not conceived simultaneously, a firm introducing an improved product into the market may choose to continue marketing the inferior product so displaced. Neither Huber and Puto (1983) or Huber, Payne and Puto (1982) address such sequencing or deal with the question of whether a properly positioned inferior product added to an existing market would have the same effect on a firm as a superior product added to an existing market.

In addition to testing an underlying model of shift in the meaning of an attribute, what is also required is some other measures besides choice. As was pointed out in the earlier discussion, measures of choice may mask any systematic shifts in evaluation, because only the most preferred alternative is chosen. What is missing is any measure of how much this is preferred over the other alternatives in the choice set. The answer is not the collection of judgment type measures, as these may not be similar to the process through which choice is made. What are needed are measures that are similar to choice but could co-vary with the choice process. One such measure is the degree of satisfaction with the choice made. While satisfaction is defined as a post-consumption evaluation that the chosen alternative is consistent with the prior beliefs, the proposed use of this variable is to measure the degree of preference of the chosen alternative vis-à-vis the other alternatives in the choice set. We would expect that if, in one set, the preferred alternative is much better than the others, the degree of satisfaction would be higher than in another set where the difference is not as marked.

While the shift in meaning could be one possible explanation of the process, other reasons also need to be tested. One of the reasons cited for expecting attraction effects is that the new alternative makes the pairwise comparison between the target and the new alternative much easier than other pairwise comparisons. The efficacy of this reason could be tested by sequentially introducing new alternatives better than the target into the choice set. If deletion is taking place, then these new alternatives should lead to a greater proportion of respondents dropping the competitor. A major limitation of the past work on attraction effects has been that judgments and choice are made in contexts where the respondent is assumed to be fully aware of the alternatives in the choice set. Given this type of situation, the relevant factors to examine become familiarity, meaningfulness of the attributes, and combination rules for dissimilar attributes. An obvious and important extension is the study of choice or judgments made in the search situation where the respondents are not familiar with all the alternatives in the marketplace.

7.4.4. HYPOTHESIS 4

A number of reasons positing why attraction effects occur have been offered. These were discussed earlier. Ratneshwar, Stewart and Shocker (1987) failed to fully account for these effects after controlling for meaningfulness of the attributes, and familiarity of the choice situation, the two common reasons cited for context effects in the literature. Based on the protocol analysis, and a judgment task, Ratneshwar, Stewart and Shocker (1987) cite relative attribute variation as a possible reason for these effects. While the results based on past research support the models of comparative valuation, a major limitation of this work is that all the new alternative positions studied have been for "inferior" alternatives. A common marketing strategy of introducing a "superior" new alternative has not been tested.

Hypothesis 4. The departure from regularity will be proportional to the shift in the relative utilities of the existing alternative.

The underlying explanation is that the shift in the utilities is caused by the perceptual valuation of the attributes. Shifts in perceptions are influenced by the changes in the mean, range or variance of the attributes, caused by the introduction of a new alternative in the choice set. Hypothesis 4 is a strong test for the relative attribute valuation as an explanation for attraction effects. It tests not only for the direction of these effects, but also for the relative magnitude between two new alternative strategies.

7.4.5. HYPOTHESIS 5

Tests of the relative attribute valuation (shift in meaning) hypothesis should be linked to measures that reflect an underlying change across the two choice situations. Discrete choice measures only measure which alternative is preferred and not by how much. One measure that can be used to measure the strength of preference is the level of satisfaction with the choice made. We can expect that changes in the level of satisfaction (a judgment type measure) should be related to the new alternative placement strategies.

Hypothesis 5. Increase (decrease) in levels of satisfaction with choice will be proportional to the increase (decrease) in the valuation of the best alternative.

Hypotheses 4 and 5 both test the validity of comparative attribute valuation. These hypotheses do not focus on the differences between the three models of comparative attribute valuation.

7.4.6. HYPOTHESIS 6

One of the competing reasons for "attraction effects" is based on changes in the cost of thinking (Shugan 1980). The new alternative positions used in past research matched one of the attribute levels for an existing alternative (that is, were asymmetrically dominated). If pairwise comparison underlies the choice process, then the comparison between this new alternative and the target becomes easier (as there is no variance in one of the attributes used in this pairwise comparison). In contrast, the pairwise comparison between the core products would involve a higher "thinking cost". If this process explanation underlies the "attraction effects", it is logical to expect that, between two choice sets, one of which contains an asymmetrically dominated alternative, the deletion of the "target" alternative from the choice set would be higher than when the alternative is not asymmetrically dominated. Empirical evidence for this explanation is mixed. Ratneshwar, Stewart and Shocker (1986) report that their results, using verbal protocols, do not support this reason. Klein and Yadav (1989), on the other hand, show that choice sets containing asymmetrically dominated alternatives result in a larger number of these alternatives being deleted. If this explanation is correct then we should expect that the deletion of the "target", when the new alternative is asymmetrically dominated, should be higher than when the new alternative is not asymmetrically dominated (that is, "inferior"), leading to hypothesis 6.

Hypothesis 6. The introduction of a new asymmetrically dominated alternative to the core set should cause a higher deletion of the "target" in comparison to the introduction of an inferior new alternative.

Effectively, this hypothesis is an indirect support for the attribute valuation model, as it helps to rule out a competing explanation that the attraction effects are caused by a change in the processing rule.

7.5. Conclusions and Proposed Extensions to the Research

7.5.1. MANAGERIAL IMPLICATIONS OF THIS RESEARCH

This research has several important implications for the design of marketing strategy by firms. In the near future the Web is going to become an important channel for marketing given the rapid increase in Web use which is projected to occur over the next few years. The Web has got the potential to evolve from merely being a channel of advertising and communication to being a channel through which all the phases of the purchasing process are completed. For some products like information products and software the Web may even become the channel of distribution. Given this evolving technology and its impact on the marketing process, it is critical that marketers gain a thorough understanding of the issues involved in the decision-making process of the consumer and the factors that will increase the propensity of the consumer to make purchases from the electronic shopping malls.

The managerial implications of this research on context effects are answers to questions such as: How best can the firm exploit this new form of transacting business to maximize its leverage in the marketplace and increase its market share? How should the firm position its products in the electronic marketplace? Should it position its products as superior in attributes (implying a higher quality to price trade-off) or inferior in attributes as opposed to the conventional channels (the retail malls and the direct mail catalogs)? We will obtain significant prescriptions for the design of marketing strategy with regard to how the new alternative should be positioned. How can marketers exploit the context effects? Suppose a retail chain sets up an electronic mall on the Web and sets the prices for the products sold through the electronic mall considerably higher than the prices for the corresponding products sold through their retail outlets and direct mail catalogs. They may not experience any sales through the electronic mall, but they will probably experience a spurt in the sales of their products through the retail outlets and direct mail catalogs because the consumers will be under the impression that they are getting a bargain at these outlets.

The research on context effects adds to the insights about competitiveness among alternatives in the marketplace. The managerial implications of the research on context effects are answers to questions such as: If a new alternative is to be introduced in the market, would it help to continue with the existing alternative? For a new product strategy, would it be better to position a superior alternative or add an inferior alternative? Understanding of context effects would allow firms to influence the search process as well as the evaluation of alternatives. One marketing strategy may be aimed at gaining inclusion in the search set. Others may be aimed at increasing the chances of getting selected. Furthermore, context effects can aid in assessing the potential impact of new products on existing alternatives. Research on stagewise contextual decisions is quite critical in the marketing context. In a variety of choice situations, consumers simultaneously assimilate information and make a decision to either continue the information search for new alternatives or to choose an existing alternative. This effect is likely to occur when an alternative is purchased infrequently and consumers are not likely to have information on existing alternatives or when alternatives change frequently due to competitive actions (such as in the airlines industry). Under these situations, buyers are likely to have weak priors on attributes and the evaluation of alternatives would necessarily involve developing benchmarks or frameworks to assess how good or bad an alternative is on the attributes/features. Information search in these situations plays the role of reducing risk (Stigler 1961) or enhancing the degree of comfort in making a choice from among the existing alternatives. These aspects of search and context behavior cannot be captured by the traditional (linear-additive) multi-attribute models of choice.

Traditionally, given the two alternative situations, new product strategies evolve around capitalizing on the substitution effects. These strategies would recommend new product introduction so as to maximize the impact of this new alternative on the share of the competitor. The attribute space for the new alternatives would be in the proximity of the competitor's stronger attribute. In a number of choice situations, this attribute space may not be the only desirable area that should be explored. In many markets the competitor's stronger attribute is likely to be due to a competitive advantage that may not be easy to copy. Even if a new product is launched close to the competitor, this "me-too" product may have serious problems due to credibility claims because of the order of entry. In contrast the work on context effects draws attention to the attribute space in the proximity of the alternative of interest (target). New alternatives are positioned to enhance the share of this alternative. Past research on attraction effects partitions the attribute space in the proximity of the target into frequency enhancing (along the target's stronger attribute) and range increasing strategies (along the target's weaker attribute). The model of relative attribute valuation, in contrast, allows the computation of context effects at any point of the attribute space. The optimal position for a new product is likely to change dramatically depending upon the other brands being considered. Such an optimal positioning should take into account the relative effect that other brands are likely to have on the brand of interest. The purpose of this research is to develop a framework that would help in deriving and testing propositions about context effects in the realm of electronic commerce.

This research emphasizes the importance of being selected early in the search. Customers only evaluate a few alternatives before making a choice, and inclusion in the choice set is a necessary qualification for being selected. The implications of this research are applicable to industries where frequent changes in the product take place, and the customer has to engage in a search and evaluation process to generate the alternatives for each choice situation (such as the purchase of cars, airline tickets, or apartment rentals).

7.5.2. ACADEMIC CONTRIBUTION OF THIS RESEARCH

The major theoretical contribution of this chapter is in providing a framework for examining context effects on consumer judgment and choice. Past research has used a variety of labels such as "frequency increasing", "range increasing" and "asymmetrically dominated decoys" to test different new alternative strategies. The simple models of relative attribute valuation provide a framework that incorporates all these strategies. While the focus of past research has been to test the effect of these strategies on the choice proportions of the "target", this framework allows us to study the joint effect on both the "target" and the "competitor".

The academic contribution of this research on context effects is that it helps to reconcile two diverging research streams on judgment and choice. The economic perspective of rational decision making involves extensive deliberation and a complete evaluation of the important attributes. It results in an optimal choice. The normative framework of the economic man postulates optimality of search, evaluation and choice. The behavioral perspective of decision making is that decisions are largely heuristic in nature, are generally made in the context of incomplete information and usually result in sub-optimal outcomes. In this case the decision maker is treated as an overwhelmed satisficer, attempting to react to the choice environment by using some heuristic for search, evaluation and choice. This research on context effects provides the middle ground and seeks to reconcile these two opposing stereotypes of decision making.

Past research has largely explored "customer centered" uncertainty such as experience with the choice task, meaningfulness of the attributes, changes in the choice rule and limitations in information processing. Such a view is consistent with work on probabilistic multi-dimensional scaling. Consider the contexts in which attraction effects might be most salient. If defined as a movement of preferences towards a new alternative, the effect is likely to be most salient when information about the offered set is needed to make the decision. It will occur within product classes for which one has very little information, or in which the meaning of the attributes is unclear. An attraction effect should be most salient in choosing between attribute based products within classes for which the attitude towards the alternatives are relatively fluid. This suggests that attraction effects will be more important in emerging markets such as the electronic commerce environment or in segments where customers are in the process of forming brand preferences.

7.5.3. PROPOSED EXTENSIONS TO THIS RESEARCH

Most of the research done in this area to date examines the effects of choice context in static choice settings. The manipulations use a fixed set of alternatives about which judgment (preference measures) or choice data is collected. We need to extend this framework to examine the context effects in a dynamic setting where we could observe the effects of choice context on the search patterns of the subjects. It would be interesting and informative to do research which would link the context effects to the depth of search and to the type of search. This could be done by allowing the subjects to browse through the electronic shopping malls in search of a pre-specified product.

The study of context effects is an important domain for consumer researchers in view of the growing interest in situational influences on consumer judgment and choice. We need to do more work on how context governs attention and memory retrieval processes that determine which aspects of a stimulus would be processed. Probably the most urgent area which needs to be investigated is the context effects on the processing agenda; for example, the order in which dimensions are processed in choice strategies such as "elimination by aspects" (Tversky 1972).

7.6. References

Armstrong, A. and Hagel, J.: 1996, The real value of online communities, *Harvard Business Review*, 135-141.

Bettman, J. R.: 1979, *An Information Processing Theory of Consumer Choice,* Addison-Wesley, Reading, Massachusetts.

Birnbaum, M. H.: 1974, Using contextual effects to derive psychophysical scales, *Perceptions and Pschophysics,* 15(1), 89-96.

Chakravarti, D. and Lynch, J. C.: 1983, A framework for exploring context effects on consumer judgment and choice, *in* R. P. Bagozzi and A. M. Tybout, *Advances in Consumer Research,* Association for Consumer Research, Ann Arbor, 10: 289-297.

Dandekar, A. G. and Pereira, R. E: 1992, Computer assisted instruction, *Communications of the Computer Society of India,* 16(2), 9-14.

Dandekar, A. G. and Pereira, R. E.: 1995, Adaptive beam-forming for the OTH-B Radar, *Journal of the Institute of Engineers (I) - Electronics and Telecommunications,* 76(September), 33–39.

Engel, J. F., Blackwell, R. D. and Miniard, P. W.: 1986, *Consumer Behavior,* 5th edn, Dryden, Hinsdale.

Hoffman, D. L., Kalsbeek, W. D. and Novak, T. P.: 1996, Internet and Internet use in the US, *Communications of the ACM,* 39(12), 36-46.

Hoffman, D. L. and Novak, T. P.: 1996, Marketing in hypermedia computer-mediated environments: Conceptual foundations, *Journal of Marketing,* 60(3), 50-68.

Hoffman, D. L., Novak, T. and Chatterjee, P.: 1996, Commercial scenarios for the Web: Opportunities and challenges, *Project 2000 Working Paper,* Owen Graduate School of Management.

Hogarth, R.: 1983, *Judgment and Choice,* John Wiley, New York.

Huber, J., Payne, J. and Puto, C.: 1982, Adding asymmetrically dominated alternatives: violation of the regularity and similarity hypothesis, *Journal of Consumer Research,* 9, 90-98.

Huber, J. and Puto, C.: 1983, Market boundaries and product choice: Illustrating attraction and substitution effects, *Journal of Consumer Research,* 10, 31-44.

Huber, J., Holbrook, M. B. and Kahn, B.: 1986, Effects of competitive context and of additional information on price sensitivity, *Journal of Marketing Research,* 23, 250-260.

Jarvenpaa, S. L., and Todd, P. A.: 1998, Consumer reactions to electronic shopping on the Internet, *Journal of Electronic Commerce,* forthcoming.

Kahneman, D. and Tversky, A.: 1979, Prospect theory: An analysis of decisions under risk, *Econometrica,* 47, 263-281.

Kahneman, D. and Tversky, A.: 1982, The simulation heuristic, *Judgment Under Uncertainty: Heuristics and Biases*, Cambridge University Press, Cambridge.

Kahneman, D. and Tversky, A.: 1984, Choices, values and frames, *American Psychologist,* 39, 341-350.

Kalakota, R. and Whinston, A. B.: 1996, *Frontiers of Electronic Commerce,* Addison-Wesley, Reading, MA.

Klein, N. M. and Yadav, M. S.: 1989, Context effects on effort and accuracy in choice: An enquiry into adaptive decision making, *Journal of Consumer Research*, 15, 411-421.

Mellers, B. A. and Birnbaum, M. H.: 1982a, Contextual effects in social judgment, *Journal of Experimental and Social Psychology*, 8(3), 491-511.

Mellers, B. A. and Birnbaum, M.H.: 1982b, Loci of Contextual Effects in Judgment, *Journal of Experimental Psychology : Human Perceptions and Performance*, 8 (4): 582-601.

Ofir, C. and Lynch, J. G.: 1984, Context effects on judgment under uncertainty, *Journal of Consumer Research*, 11, 688-679.

Payne, J. W.: 1982, Contingent decision behavior, *Psychological Bulletin*, 92(2), 382-402.

Pereira, R. E.: 1997, Organizational impact of component based systems development, *in* G. Wojtkowski, W. Wojtkowski, S. Wrycza, and J. Zupancic, (eds), *Systems Development Methods for the Next Century*, Plenum, New York, pp. 241-257.

Pereira, R. E.: 1998, An economic evaluation of alternative mechanisms for regulating the information superhighway, *International Journal of Electronic Commerce*, forthcoming.

Pereira, R. E. and Dandekar, A. G.: 1993, A heuristic model for computer based training, *Communications of the Computer Society of India*, 17(1), 16-18.

Pereira, R. E., Kang, S. and Whinston, A. B.: 1997a, Influence of choice context on consumer decision making in global electronic commerce, *Proceedings 3rd Americas Conference on Information Systems (ACIS'97)*, pp. 224-226.

Pereira, R. E., Kang, S. and Whinston, A. B: 1997b, Impact of object oriented systems development on IS-end user relationships, *Proceedings 3rd Americas Conference on Information Systems (ACIS'97)*, pp. 765-767.

Quelch, J. A. and Klein, L.: 1996, The Internet and international marketing, *Sloan Management Review*, Spring, 60-75.

Ratneshwar, S., Shocker, A. D. and Stewart, D. W.: 1987, Toward understanding the attraction effect: The implications of product stimulus meaningfulness and familiarity, *Journal of Consumer Research*, 13, 520-533.

Samuelson, W. and Zeckhauser, R.: 1988, Status quo bias in decision making, *Journal of Risk and Uncertainty*, 1, 7-59.

Shaw, T. and Pereira, R. E.: 1997, The sources of power between information systems developers and end users: A resource dependence perspective, *in* G. Wojtkowski, W. Wojtkowski, S. Wrycza, and J. Zupancic, (eds), *Systems Development Methods for the Next Century*, Plenum, New York, pp. 463-471.

Simonson, I. and Tversky, A.: 1992, Choice in context: Tradeoff contrast and extremeness aversion, *Journal of Marketing Research*, 29: 281-295.

Stigler, G.: 1961, The economics of information, *Journal of Political Economy*, 69, 213-225.

Tversky, A.: 1972, Elimination by aspects: A theory of choice, *Psychological Review*, 79, 281-299.

Tversky, A. and Kahneman, D.: 1974, Judgment under uncertainty: Heuristics and biases, *Science*, 185, 1124-1131.

CHAPTER 8

Electronic Public Procurement

From the International Experience to the Reality of the Mediterranean Region

VASILIOS PERGIOUDAKIS, PANAGIOTIS MILIOTIS AND
GEORGIOS DOUKIDIS
Athens University of Economics and Business

8.1. Introduction

Public procurement refers to the acquisition of goods and services by any governmental department, agency, organ or other unit, or any subdivision thereof. Public procurement is a superset of private procurement. All issues related to private procurement procedures still apply, while there are other specific rules that have to be followed, imposed by the government of each country. More specifically, less developed and under developed countries are facing major problems concerning the appliance of control mechanisms and the dissemination of information. Large sums of money are lost every year in specific procurement contracts while employees find it difficult to handle large volumes of paper and apply sophisticated evaluation criteria for introducing scales of economy.

In the past few years, a number of initiatives have been introduced in order to facilitate parts or the whole of the procurement cycle, whether in the private or public sector. Their major objective was to introduce information technology (IT) into traditional bureaucratic procedures while establishing advanced telecommunication networks among the partners involved to facilitate information exchange, based on electronic commerce technologies. All efforts aimed at establishing an electronic environment that would support public authorities and private companies, especially SMEs, in accessing procurement information and exchanging all papers related to a procurement activity (Blili, 1994).

In this chapter we investigate these initiatives in the area of procurement with respect to the special user requirements in Mediterranean countries, also taking into consideration the special features that characterize a developing environment, in order to propose a framework for introducing electronic procurement in the Mediterranean region. In the second section, we describe a typical public procurement life cycle. In the third section, major deficiencies related to these procedures are depicted. In the fourth section, major initiatives based on the introduction of electronic commerce technologies are presented, with emphasis on European Union (EU) funded projects. Finally we propose a two-phase framework for establishing electronic procurement in the Mediterranean region: the first phase relates to less technologically advanced countries' requirements, and the second introduces a fully automated electronic environment based on the experience and infrastructure of the first phase.

8.2. Current Practices in Public Procurement: The Paper-Based Environment

Public procurement is a significant economic activity for all countries. Usually two distinct kinds of players participate in the public procurement procedure:

1. *Public Organizations* (procuring entities), which publish their intention to procure goods or services under certain rules and restrictions imposed by the Government of each country.
2. *Suppliers* (usually privately owned businesses, mostly of small and medium size), which respond to calls for bids, indicating their intention to sell; suppliers have to bid either individually or as a consortium; that is, in collaboration with other suppliers for a particular bid.

In addition, countries that belong to the EU are obliged to follow specific rules on public procurement, a fact that complicates the procedures involved even more. Thus EU countries have to follow specific regulations imposed by the EU concerning publication of Calls for Tender in European journals (Official Journal of European Commission - OJEC), for the dissemination of information in all EU countries, and standardization for the establishment of an open market with equal rights, especially for SMEs (Pergioudakis et al., 1997a; Pergioudakis et al., 1997b).

In general terms, a typical public procurement life cycle, with minor exceptions, can be decomposed into three processes.

8.2.1. TENDERING

The tendering process involves the announcement (on the procurer's side) of its intention to acquire certain goods or services, and the submission of bids (on the supplier's side) regarding this announcement. Specifically, the tendering process involves the following steps (Pergioudakis et al., 1997a; Pergioudakis et al., 1997b; Intrasoft SA, 1996):

1. *Call for Tender*
   The administration (as the procuring entity) lets potential suppliers know of its intention to acquire a certain product or products. This announcement may be open and public, or restricted to a group of potential suppliers. For small acquisitions under a certain amount of money, an open announcement may be bypassed. A Call for Tender is usually a "one to many" distribution activity. Information is exchanged in order to assist potential suppliers in preparing

their bids in a more comprehensive manner, or to form consortia in order to submit their bids mutually.

2. *Tender*

Following the Call for Tender, interested suppliers will respond by submitting a bid prior to the deadline for the submission of tenders. The procuring entity may provide the supplier or contractor with a receipt showing the date and time at which the tender was received, depending on the governmental rules that apply in each country. This is a "one to one" information exchange phase. It is basically one way, although it may eventually require some bi-directional exchange to clarify bids. Access to the supplier's material is needed, such as product catalogues, descriptions of products (technical specifications), and price catalogues.

3. *Notice of Award*

After the submission of bids, a supplier has to be chosen. During the evaluation procedure, the procuring entity may ask suppliers or contractors for clarifications of their tenders in order to assist in the examination, evaluation and comparison of tenders. A set of evaluation criteria is then used in order to identify the successful tender. These criteria may include the financial state and liability of the supplier, the quality of products or services, the work plan, and so forth. The result of the evaluation procedure is announced to all bidders (and the EU in the case of an EU country). Furthermore, information relating to the examination, clarification, evaluation and comparison of tenders is not disclosed to suppliers or contractors or to any other person not officially involved in the examination, except in special cases (e.g., related to national security issues, depending on the regional regulations of each country).

8.2.2. CONTRACTING

The solicitation documents may require the supplier or contractor whose tender has been accepted to sign a written procurement contract conforming to the tender. In such cases, the procuring entity and the supplier or contractor sign the procurement contract within a reasonable period of time after the notice of acceptance is dispatched. The procurement contract comes into force when the contract is signed by the supplier or contractor and by the procuring entity. Before this time, the procuring entity may engage in negotiations with suppliers or contractors that have submitted acceptable proposals, seeking or permitting revisions of such proposals, provided that the opportunity to participate in negotiations is extended to all such suppliers or contractors.

8.2.3. TRADING

The trading procedures in the public procurement life cycle are similar to those that take place in an ordinary procurement life cycle. The procedure can be decomposed into the following actions:

- *Acquisition.* This activity goes through the traditional exchanges and may refer to invoicing, payment and delivery activities.
- *After sales support.* Following the delivery of goods, a set of activities may be required in order to fulfil the terms of the contract such as documentation and maintenance.

All these procedures may involve special activities that relate to national regulations applied to public procurement. Furthermore, tenders in EU countries should be translated into all 11 official EU languages and make reference to European standards or pre-standards (European Commission, 1995).

8.3. Problems with Current Practices

Traditional manual procedures, such as public procurement, are facing many deficiencies, especially in less developed environments that are characterized by old-fashioned bureaucratic procedures, corruption, and so forth. These problems are related to the following issues (Yap et al., 1994; Murphy, 1993; Schnitt, 1993; Land, 1990; Doukidis et al., 1995; Evert, 1992; Blili et al., 1994; Gurbaxani et al., 1991):

1. *Complicated Procedures and Extended Relationships*
   It is clear that business practices in public authorities are much more complicated than those in the private sector. We should also note that the decision-making process is rather complex and often depends on various levels of hierarchy from the initial decision to the final contract assignment (signature of the authorized person). This also results in payment delays. In the case of public procurement, it is quite common that specific employees do not have the qualifications needed to make a decision related to purchasing activities; that is, to evaluate a bid. Furthermore, standard evaluation criteria are often not available to employees to pre-qualify suppliers and evaluate bids, in order to apply an efficient purchase management procedure. That fact results in many contracts for the same product, work or service, sometimes from the same supplier with different values. Another issue here is that the network of existing and potential partners of the public sector is very extended. This fact seems to further complicate the whole environment since no trade relationship with the public sector is a fixed one. In other words, there are many suppliers who could submit a more cost-effective bid for the authority. Another deficiency here is that most tenders are effectively closed in order to support certain relationships. Most of them have a certain value that is often larger than the value of the product or service to be purchased.

2. *Excessive State Intervention*
   Public organizations are generally subject to a certain degree of political control from outside the organization. The wide extent of the public sector, combined with shifts in policy and ideology, means that large sections of the economy are natural targets for the prevailing political culture. In addition to explicit policy changes, these organizations are also subject to politically inspired instability regarding the state-controlled appointment of senior

managers. In this way, political accountability can dominate accountability to such organizations' suppliers, customers and staff.

3. *Bureaucratic Dysfunctionalities*
   The dysfunctional formalization of administrative procedures, the bureaucratic rationality of 'acting according to the rules', and an inflexible system of control are common in public administration but they are especially strong in traditional bureaucracies. They typically constrain innovative thinking and decision making, thus perpetuating the dysfunctionality and preventing them from utilizing innovative technologies like electronic commerce. Efforts are being made to reform such bureaucracies in less developed countries but much remains to be done.

4. *Absence of Clear National IT Policy*
   Smaller, less technologically advanced countries typically have not established a national IT policy due mainly to their small IT market and the severity of their other problems (financial, political, social) as well as a lack of local expertise. Thus IT is normally attributed a low priority which does not promote either the growth of the IT market or the use of IT in private and public enterprises. In addition, the IT infrastructure is also limited and less advanced.

5. *Large Volume of Paper*
   A lot of paper transactions are involved in the procurement process. Less developed countries seem to have a quite large public sector resulting in a total deficiency in the functionality of the sector. Paper transactions involve time consuming, expensive, slow and unsatisfactory activities, especially when no standard forms are available.

6. *Lack of Flexible Centralized Control*
   Purchase management is quite a difficult operation especially when there are no flexible centralized control mechanisms. This leads to unsystematic purchases that do not meet the real needs of the procuring organization. Furthermore, the extremely distributed nature of public administration results in the lack of a single face to industry. State intervention also promotes this insufficiency.

7. *Lack of Information Quality*
   Each public authority and each supplier has its own format for tender and bidding forms. This lack of standards results in information of inadequate quality that has to be processed either for evaluation or for publication (market awareness).

8. *Resistance to Change*
   It should be pointed out that people are quite resistant to change especially when IT is involved. Public employees are much more resistant than those in private companies, due to the low productivity level (information systems are expected to support work) and the state intervention in job arrangements. It is clear that public organizations play a catalytic role in the adoption and

successful implementation of electronic commerce, especially in the case of procurement. EU directives point out this urgent need for electronic commerce adoption in the public sector.

Specific problems have arisen quite frequently in the past, especially in EU countries, where the information in tender notices submitted to the EU for publication is of inadequate quality or incomplete. These mistakes or omissions have resulted in notices being of an insufficient standard to satisfy either the needs of the users or the formal requirements of EU directives. In addition, specific European legislation exists (Pergioudakis et al., 1997a; Pergioudakis et al., 1997b; Greek Ministry of Development, 1996), concerning:

1. *Publications*
   Contracting entities must send notices of their intended purchases of supplies, works and services to the Office for Official Publications of the EC (EUR-OP) for publication in the Official Journal of the EC.

2. *Translation*
   EUR-OP has to ensure that notices, when received, are translated and published in eleven languages in Supplement S to the Official Journal of the European Community and in the database TED (Tenders Electronic Daily), within strict time limits.

3. *European Standards*
   Contracting authorities at EU level and within the EU member states are obliged to make reference to European standards or pre-standards.

8.4. International Initiatives for the Automation of Public Procurement

8.4.1. THE EUROPEAN EXPERIENCE

The EU identified deficiencies in the current system many years ago. The need for an improvement in the European public procurement life cycle has grown out of a number of concerns. The most pressing of these was that the publication system in use was finding it increasingly difficult to deal effectively with the volume of notices that needed to be processed. January 1995 saw a 45% increase in the number of tenders published compared to January 1994 (Pergioudakis et al., 1997a; Pergioudakis et al., 1997b; Intrasoft SA, 1995). The accession of Sweden, Finland and Austria added significantly to the number of notices to be published. With the possibility of the future Association of Central and Eastern European countries looking increasingly likely, and the new public procurement markets opened to EU suppliers in the USA and Japan, it was essential that a new mechanism was put in place to deal with this significant increase in activity (Pergioudakis et al., 1997).

In order to improve the information flow and the quality of information, the CEC/DG XV has taken various actions and conducted studies to identify the needs and interests of different participants in the overall information exchange that underlies public procurement. The aim was to identify areas in which it would be possible to enhance the performance of the system at low cost and without imposing additional burdens on participants. Furthermore, in order to check the technical feasibility, the usefulness, the commercial potential, as well as the true costs and benefits involved according to the conclusions of the actions taken so far by the Commission and guidelines given by the Member States, the Commission decided to execute a series of pilot projects. The system of information exchange, established for these purposes acquired the acronym SIMAP (Systems d'Informations pour les MArches Publics). The purpose of the project (Intrasoft SA, 1995; Intrasoft SA, 1996) was:

- to provide a mechanism for public administrations which allows them to submit for publication information on public procurement opportunities;

- to provide the means for disseminating that information to potential suppliers throughout the Community; and

- to create a real and open internal market for all operators, equal opportunities for access and a greater ability to participate in the whole procurement life cycle at affordable cost.

Currently, all member states, with the exception of Belgium and Italy, are participating in the SIMAP pilot project. Norway and Iceland, as EEA members, are also participating, and Switzerland has expressed interest.

The realization of SIMAP is split into three components:

- the "notification" and "diffusion" function: the "notification" function aims to provide telematic means for information flows from contracting authorities to the Commission and the Publication Office and its purpose is to enhance the quality of the procurement notices; the "diffusion" function aims to set up a system to disseminate the collected notices and other valuable information to economic players involved in the public procurement process;

- a set of information tools to improve the monitoring of the European public procurement market;

- a set of studies and standardization works to define the requirements and options for pan-European electronic tendering and the role that SIMAP could play in different scenarios.

SIMAP established two intermediaries between a contracting entity and the EUR-OP:

- The DEPs (Data Entry Points) constitute the entry points for notice submission. It can be either an individual contracting entity fulfilling solely its own needs; a contracting entity offering its data entry services to other contracting authorities as well as carrying out its own data entry; a body officially appointed for this purpose by member state national authorities.

- The SCU (SIMAP Central Unit) is assigned to the collection and validation of the notices received from the DEPs and the subsequent transfer of this information in a suitable format to the EUR-OP.

During the implementation of the SIMAP Pilot Project, three notice types have been identified and mapped into forms: the Prior Information Notice (or Periodic Notice), the Contract Notice, and the Notice of Contract Award, based on the same EDI message (CONITT).

Currently SIMAP is realizing an extension of the initial pilot phase (100 users) to include more than 1,000 users in EU countries. In parallel, two major research projects in the field of public procurement have been launched under the Telematics program (Pergioudakis et al., 1997):

- TAPPE (Telematics for Administrations: Public Procurement in Europe), a project partially funded by the EU. Based on SIMAP's outcome, TAPPE aims to automate all steps of the European public procurement environment, and also to provide private companies with access to procurement opportunities, while implementing some improvements to existing infrastructure established by SIMAP. TAPPE demonstrators will use the special features of the Internet in order to provide a friendly, open, easy to handle and cost effective service.

- ELPRO (Electronic Public Procurement System in Europe). ELPRO has established an 'Electronic Procurement Network', aimed at providing information and transaction services to public authorities and companies regularly submitting tenders. Technologies used include EDI and WWW interfaces.

Both initiatives are targeting the full automation of the European public procurement life cycle and aim to meet the requirements of both procurers and suppliers to this end. The extent to which this will be achieved is a topic that shall be further exploited as a result of the pilot projects that will take place in the future.

An interesting case for the dissemination of public procurement information, which is already functioning in Europe, is EPIN (European Procurement Information Network). EPIN is a business development tool that provides access to a database of contract notices from public bodies and utilities in Europe, USA and GATT countries. In addition, EPIN provides its subscribers with access to company details via the EPIN Industrial Park. Subscribers can use this information to create qualified supplier lists and to select suppliers for tender lists.

EPIN consists of a WWW Server residing in Dublin, which has links to a number of procurement information services. For an annual/quarterly subscription, suppliers and customers receive a user name and password that enable them to:

- access all public procurement notices from the electricity, gas, water, transportation, telecommunications, local and central government authorities from across Europe, the USA and the GATT Countries.

- input their company profile and post it to EPIN Central.

The EPIN package comprises two different data sources within the application:

- *EPIN Leads.* This application allows users to query the contract notice database and search for leads of interest to their company stored in the EPIN Central database. The EPIN Central database contains all Contract Notices published in the Supplement to the Official Journal of the European Communities (all notices that appear in TED).

- *EPIN Industrial Park.* This permits suppliers to input their company profile and upload it to EPIN central. The company profile includes information on the products and services a company supplies as well as a brief company description and contact information. If any of the information becomes out of date, it can be updated. This information is used to generate a unique home page for each EPIN subscriber. The home pages of each subscriber can be browsed using a key word search interface. The information in the Industrial Park is an on-line company brochure and, when used with e-mail, can provide a valuable contact point for a company on the Internet.

4.2. THE INTERNATIONAL EXPERIENCE

Two of the most widely known initiatives at international level are already operating in the USA. The first is a private sector initiative, targeting industrial and commercial organizations as users; the second includes a large number of public organizations involved in the procurement process.

General Electric Information Services (GEIS), in an attempt to reduce its purchasing costs, studied the traditional contracting process and identified activities that do not add value to the whole cycle. They developed an open system called TPN (Trading Process Network) (Cafiero, 1996). TPN is a service that facilitates the business-to-business buying and selling of industrial goods and services. It consists of two modules:

- TPNPost module, which allows for structured electronic bidding, and

- TPNMart module, which allows for end-user buyers to search and place orders from a private catalog.

The service gives the opportunity to categorise products, submit Calls for Tender, identify sources, accept and evaluate bids, notify participants, browse catalogues and release orders. The technologies used to implement the system include:

- a database that contains all Requests for Quotes (RFQs) from buyers,

- electronic catalogs, which contain product and supplier-information to be used by potential buyers in the supplier selection stage, and

- the Web, for a user-friendly interface between the system and end-users.

Suppliers register with the system by filling a prequalification form, available on GEIS's Internet home page. Potential buyers download the list of suppliers from the supplier database and select the ones meeting their particular requirements. Once the selection is completed, the buyer uploads the RFQs and the supplier list. Based on the buyer's selection, the suppliers are notified via fax of the upcoming project that they have been invited to bid on. The suppliers can search the database and download selected RFQs. Furthermore, they can fill out their response and submit their quotes. Following this procedure, the buyer can evaluate their responses, and invite the suppliers for additional rounds before he makes his final selection. The system provides additional support services, such as a dedicated 800 number, implementation and support services, training and technical support. In order to participate in the system, potential suppliers need, among other things, a Netscape browser, Adobe Reader and specific application software provided to them by GEIS. This same application software is installed on the buyer's side.

The second effort to automate the procurement cycle was initiated by the US Department of Defense (DoD) as a result of the US Federal Acquisition Streamlining Act of 1994 (FECAT, 1994; US DoD, 1996). The technology mainly used in this case was Electronic Data Interchange (EDI). The systems infrastructure consists of gateways, EC Processing Nodes (ECPNs) and Value-Added Networks (VANs) (Cockburn, 1996). Each gateway consists of hardware and software that provide EDI translation services, archiving, security and environment management for converting non-standard business application systems data into a standard EDI format to be sent to government business systems.

There are two ECPNs that provide communications connectivity between VANs and gateways to support the exchange of EDI transactions between government procurement agencies and private sector suppliers. Information from a government agency is sent to the supporting gateway. After EDI-translation and archiving by the gateway, the information is transmitted to one of the two ECPNs, which then transfers it to VANs that have been previously certified and connected to the system. VANs distribute the EDI message to potential suppliers.

In the case of a bid, the reverse order is followed. In order for a supplier to participate in the system, the supplier must have a computer, modem, connection to a certified VAN, and an EDI software package. The supplier is also obliged to pass the so-called "compliance testing process", which is a testing exchange of EDI messages with the ECPNs and the DoD's test facility. Once the process is successfully completed, the test facility informs the central contractor registration center, which validates and registers the supplier as DoD's trading partner. From this point forward, all information between a trading partner and the DoD's procuring agencies is exchanged via EDI: requests for quotations, responses to requests for quotations, purchase orders, purchase order acknowledgments, ship notices, invoices, payment orders and award notices.

A lot of other electronic commerce applications in the field of procurement have been considered in our research, such as the Canadian Open Bidding System (by ISM Information Systems Management Corporation), the Mexico Procurement Update System, and the Hong Kong Government Supplies Department (GSD) Procurement Service. All these cases clearly prove that electronic commerce technologies can be used to provide sufficient infrastructure for the elimination of certain deficiencies in the private as well as the public procurement process. However, electronic commerce adoption implies that certain technological infrastructure should exist in the relevant markets while procedures should firstly be simplified and controlled. All these issues are addressed in the following section.

8.5. Towards a Mediterranean Electronic Public Procurement Environment

Taking into consideration the international initiatives for electronic procurement, the special characteristics of less developed environments such as the Mediterranean region, and specific electronic commerce issues related to public procurement, we have developed a two-phase approach to the establishment of a broad and open electronic procurement service. Both phases can be considered as part of an evolutionary course for the successful adoption of electronic commerce.

- During the *first phase*, public authorities should be examined from a business perspective resulting in a specific regulatory framework to simplify and streamline procedures and finally facilitate the adoption of electronic commerce. Countries that do not have the necessary infrastructure for establishing electronic commerce applications and have extensively complicated procedures characterized by a lack of control and auditing should deploy this phase first. Information technology should play a leading role in storing electronically the procurement cases, in the final decision, and in establishing control mechanisms to public authorities' crosschecking capabilities.

- The *second phase* involves the adoption of electronic commerce from a more technical perspective, based on the streamlining of procedures that will result from the first phase and the control mechanisms already established. Developed countries, characterized by mature electronic commerce users and simplified procedures, will introduce additional electronic catalog services for information retrieval on products and services, and for the certification and authentication of users. Secondly, electronic commerce technologies will play a vital role in establishing standard communication channels among all involved partners. This phase is a three-step course.

8.5.1. PUBLIC PROCUREMENT: THE RE-ENGINEERING PHASE

As already mentioned, public activities are quite often characterized by complicated procedures. Evaluation of process efficiency is based on traditional methods and governmental priorities while controls often happen in the background. Such environments are met in less developed countries where regulation frameworks take into account only the provision of public services while the total efficiency of the governmental mechanism is placed in the background.

The application of electronic commerce technologies in such environments will result in automated procedures with no users, while traditional procedures will again take over. Electronic commerce can prove to be a strategic tool for increasing the efficiency of public authorities but when adopted with no preliminary preparatory phases it will only result in a loss of money. Business process re-engineering (Schnitt, 1993; EWOS, 1995; Venkatraman, 1991; Swatman et al., 1993; 1994; Brenner et al., 1996) should not only be a result of adopting electronic commerce, but should also happen before. It eliminates those factors that will create obstacles to future development and provides the necessary business models that will facilitate the adoption of the new electronic services. The proposed framework for introducing a stable environment for public procurement is depicted in Figure 1.

Step 1. Streamlining of Procedures. In this phase, all procedures involved in the public procurement environment are analyzed and streamlined. This should start from the highest levels of hierarchy inside a public authority. First, the decision process should be certified, based on standard criteria. It is common for employees, even though they have to follow standard procedures for accomplishing their work, to define their own standards to avoid more work. A typical example is that many people sign on behalf of others inside a public authority. The question here is which processes should be streamlined and consequently simplified. Streamlining of procedures will allow for control mechanisms to be applied.

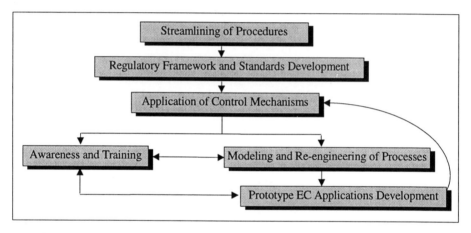

Figure 1. Steps for public procurement facilitation in less developed environments.

Step 2. Regulatory Framework and Standards Development. A regulatory framework for controlling purchases and contract assignment on the one hand and for giving access to all suppliers (especially SMEs) on the other, should also be applied in order to stabilize the procurement activities. Standards, where possible, should also be developed; that is, bidding form (tender). Much work on that issue is being undertaken by the EU. The important issue here is that each EU country should conform to EU standards while also defining its own standards for internal control of purchase activities. Due to the increasing number of suppliers seeking the opportunity to compete on an equal footing, and the increasing demand of public organizations to achieve value for money purchasing, a framework for pre-qualifying and evaluating suppliers should be defined. Criteria for evaluating bids or the supplier performance before or after the award of a contract should also be developed. Categories of criteria can be developed in order to evaluate different kinds of bids (supplies or works) and relationship models should be built to weigh criteria in specific tenders.

Step 3: Application of Control Mechanisms. Having developed standard evaluation and tracking methods for controlling and auditing the performance of suppliers and procurers, specific information systems (mainly decision support tools) should be developed in order to manage the complexity of information and assist purchasing departments to draw up supplier bid lists, enabling the purchasing decision to be simplified. These systems will also encourage structured and formalized procedures in procurement and can be made contract specific.

Step 4. Awareness and Training. The introduction of information systems for storing incoming and outgoing information, such as bidding, will allow for the further development of electronic commerce applications for automating the communication process. Nevertheless, people are still not aware of what electronic commerce is and what its benefits are, especially inside public organizations. The adoption of electronic commerce tools, such as the international initiatives that were already presented, without preparing the people to use them, will result in limited and inadequate use of expensive tools. Electronic commerce will not exploit its full benefits.

Step 5. Modeling and Re-engineering of Processes. In parallel, procedures that relate to procurement activities should be investigated with regard to business modeling and re-engineering. It is quite frequent to hear that electronic commerce results in, or helps with, the re-engineering of your business. We believe that for full exploitation of electronic commerce benefits, processes should be re-engineered before its appliance. It is not sensible to apply electronic commerce technologies to traditional processes in order to re-engineer them with regard to the efficient flow of information or advanced decision support, for example. No proof exists to justify that processes should be done this way, especially under the aspect of the Information Society. It is clear that with the appliance of specific control mechanisms, even before the adoption of electronic commerce, certain procedures could be eliminated.

Step 6. Prototype Electronic Commerce Applications Development. After the BPR investigation, prototype electronic procurement systems should be developed or used (if they already exist), such as SIMAP, ELPRO or TAPPE, in order to help users get familiar with the technology. Prototype systems prepare users for advanced electronic services.

8.5.2. PUBLIC PROCUREMENT: THE ELECTRONIC COMMERCE PHASE

In order to provide procurers and suppliers with advanced services and guidance regarding procurement information and opportunities, software tools and multimedia storage mechanisms should be developed, and communication channels should be established for the exchange of standard information, mainly under the aspect of the Internet evolution. This will allow easier browsing and retrieval of procurement information and facilitate the traditional paper-based environment. Standard procedures for public procurement should also be supported in order to establish an open market with equal rights, particularly for SMEs (Zimmerman, 1996; Murphy, 1993; Blili, 1994; Gurbaxani, 1991). In this case, there are already developed and tested solutions (in some cases), in both the European and International experience. More analytically, the following services should be offered in an advanced electronic procurement environment.

Resources of Information

To allow access to information for procurement opportunities in an open market, advanced information services should be provided. Standard storage mechanisms should be deployed in order to host relevant information and further facilitate information provision and sharing. The services included here are:

- supplier assistance and guidance to procurement opportunities for bid preparation,
- inventory of company profiles (suppliers and procurers) for consortia forming,
- inventory of product catalogues with technical specifications and multimedia-enhanced services,
- inventory of possible sources and databases containing information related to public procurement,
- information on qualification of products and services (based on the efficient purchase management tools of the previous phase),
- legal assistance regarding public procurement,
- assistance in calls for tender in the multi-lingual environment of the public procurement European market (especially for EU countries),
- information on commerce, strategy, competitiveness and local specifications to give essential information to businesses to prepare sound proposals,
- evaluation of existing and potential resources in a domain (per country, per industrial sector) for finding partners and evaluating the competitiveness of potential bids,
- codification of procurement information for easier browsing and retrieval by suppliers.

The Web and the Internet can provide partners with an inexpensive and user-friendly platform for information administration either for purchasing or for the promotion of products and services.

Certification and Authentication

To ensure security and availability in electronic commerce transactions, directory services are required to (Kalakota et al., 1996; Zimmerman, 1996):

- support identification and registration of users,
- get partner addresses (e-mail, EDI etc.),
- get basic business information,
- ascertain business capabilities,
- get financial information from other institutions,
- know availability of technological opportunities (transmission means, support of EDI, security means),

- get public keys of parties for confidentiality (encryption),
- get public keys (and credentials) for authentication (sender and recipient).

Certification and authentication services are considered carefully when the Internet is used as an electronic commerce platform. On the other hand, many applications for securing the Internet and establishing an open environment for public and private key management, are continually being developed (Cockburn, 1996; Kalakota et al., 1996; Zimmerman, 1996).

Electronic Communication and Exchange of Information

The introduction of EDI and generally standard electronic commerce technologies requires user maturity and an advanced, stable technological infrastructure. In order to facilitate the whole procurement cycle, it is necessary to introduce communication channels among partners, based on existing internal systems and user requirements. Basically the services needed for this purpose are electronic tendering, electronic contracting and electronic trading. A fully supportive and automated electronic procurement environment is depicted in Figure 2.

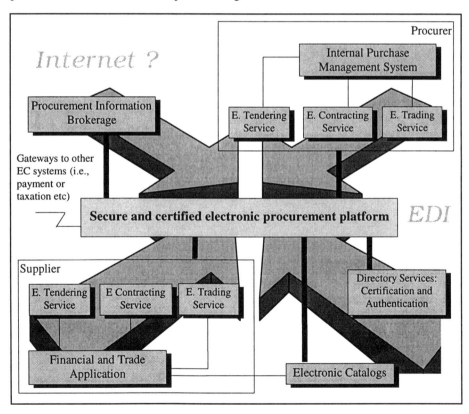

Figure 2. An automated electronic procurement environment.

Electronic Tendering

It is clear that all major international initiatives in electronic procurement deal with this phase of procurement, as it is the most important one. Electronic tendering includes: Electronic Announcement of Calls for Tender, Electronic Receipt of Calls for Tender, Electronic Submission of Bids and Electronic Announcement of Tender Award. From this viewpoint, the evaluation of bids could be facilitated further due to the fact that all information will be in electronic format and will be gathered in minimal time (EDI messaging). All such systems should cooperate with the internal application systems for controlling and auditing and finally offer a communication mechanism for the exchange of standardized information. Specific EDI messages have been developed for this purpose such as CONITT (invitation for tender) and CONTEN (bidding message). A global solution should take into account all major initiatives in this field, especially those under the auspices of the EU, in order to fulfill all user requirements across Europe and the Mediterranean region.

Electronic Contracting

Certified applications should be developed or further extended in order to provide procurers and suppliers with an efficient and secure communication channel for exchanging standard information on contracts. The contract handling systems should interconnect and cooperate with the information resources provided and the evaluation systems developed for administration and control of purchases, in each site. Exchange of information should be based on already established standards (EDIFACT: CONEST message).

Electronic Trading

Based on the experience of national electronic procurement systems and private electronic trading cases, an electronic system should be established to assist procurers and suppliers to communicate in a faster and more efficient manner, exchanging standard EDI messages. This issue is partially solved, due to the existence of electronic commerce systems for traditional trading processes (i.e., ordering, invoicing etc.) in the private sector which facilitates information exchange among trading partners (suppliers and customers). On the other hand, more research work is needed to define integration guidelines with existing applications from a business perspective, especially in the procurer site, and to streamline all procedures (tendering, contracting and trading) in an integrated service, taking into account the special characteristics of each public procurement environment.

8.6. Conclusion and Further Research

In this chapter we have identified some deficiencies in the public procurement life cycle, taking into account the needs of less developed countries such as the Mediterranean region and all features that are provided by the major initiatives in the field of electronic procurement. It is clear that a lot of re-engineering work has to be done especially concerning how the public sector works and how it should work under the aspect of the Information Society.

Our observations can be summarized as follows:

- Re-engineering is needed before the application of IT, especially when traditional procedures involve many deficiencies. It should be pointed out that we would not need standard electronic exchange tools for invoicing if invoices did not exist. Is it clear why companies use invoices and what is the added value of this form? Taxation.

- Mediterranean countries should follow a two-phase plan for introducing electronic procurement services. Streamlining and standardization of procedures should be the first step while advanced electronic services provision should follow.

- The Internet can be used for the electronic procurement platform because it combines broadness, cost efficiency, user friendliness and, most importantly, common information access. Of course there are many issues that still need to be addressed.

- EDI is needed in the final phase in order to simplify and standardize the information exchange for automating data processing and publication.

Finally, in the past few years we have seen the development of a multiplicity of sectorial, regional and national electronic public procurement systems. Bringing these systems together in one worldwide standard system would guarantee open access for all to a user-friendly and standard procedure (Pergioudakis et al., 1996).

8.7. References

Blili, S. and Raymond, L.: 1994, Information technology: Threats and opportunities for small and medium sized enterprises, *International Journal of Information Management*, 13(1), 127-137.

Brenner, W. and Hamm, V.: 1996, The role of information technology in reengineering procurement processes, *Proceedings 4th European Conference on Information Systems*.

Cafiero, W.: 1996, Electronic commerce on the Internet - for real!, Paper presented at the *First Electronic Commerce World 1996 Conference*, Columbus, Ohio, USA.

Cockburn, C. and Wilson, T.: 1996, Business use of the World Wide Web, *International Journal of Information Management*, 16(2), 83-102.

Doukidis, G. and Smithson, S.: 1995, *Information Systems in the National Context*, Ashgate Publishing, Avebury, UK.

European Commission: 1995, *Public Procurement Group: EPHOS Scope Specification for PPG review*. DG III.

European Commission: 1995, *Public Procurement In Europe: The Directives.*

Evert, M.: 1992, *Basic Principles for the use of IT in the Public Sector*, Athens.

EWOS: 1995, Transforming European procurement for the Information Age, *Proceedings European Workshop for Open Systems*, Brussels.

Federal Electronic Commerce Acquisition Team: 1994, *Streamlining Procurement through Electronic Commerce*. Virginia.

120   DOING BUSINESS ELECTRONICALLY

Greek Ministry of Development: 1996, *Public Procurement Directives In Greece*, Athens.

Gurbaxani, V. and Whang, S.: 1991, The impact of Information Systems on organizations and markets, *Communications of the ACM*, 34(1), 59-73.

Intarsoft SA: 1995, SIMAP *Deliverable 1.3.1: User Requirements*, INTRASOFT SA, Athens.

Intrasoft SA: 1995, SIMAP *Deliverable 1.4.1: Functional Specification*, INTRASOFT SA, Athens.

Intrasoft SA: 1996, TAPPE *Deliverable 4.1: Detailed Work Plan compiling the relevant outcome from SIMAP*, INTRASOFT SA, Athens.

Kalakota, R. and Whinston, A.: 1996, *Frontiers of Electronic Commerce*, Addison-Wesley, Reading, MA.

Land, F.: 1990, Viewpoint: The government role in relation to Information Technology, *International Journal of Information Management*, 10, 5-13.

Murphy, D.: 1993, *Electronic Commerce: A Government Procurement Perspective*. Procurement Automation Institute, Arlington USA.

Pergioudakis, V., Doukidis, G. and Pappas, J.: 1997a, Public procurement in Europe: Towards an integrated electronic commerce environment, *Proceedings 7th MINI Euro Conference on Electronic Commerce*, Bruge, Belgium

Pergioudakis, V., Doukidis, G. and Pappas, J.: 1997b, Defining an architecture for electronic public procurement in Europe, *Proceedings 10th International Electronic Commerce Conference*, Bled, Slovenia.

Schnitt, D.: 1993, Re-engineering the organization using information technology, *Journal of Systems Management*, 14(22), 41-42.

Swatman, P. and Swatman, P.: 1993, Business process redesign using EDI - An Australian success story, *Proceedings 6th International EDI Conference*, Bled, Slovenia.

Swatman, P. and Swatman, P. and Fowler, D.: 1994, A model of EDI integration and strategic business re-engineering, *Journal of Strategic Information Systems*, 3(1), 41-60.

US Department of Defense: 1996, *Introduction to Department of Defense Electronic Commerce: A handbook for business*, Electronic Commerce Office.

Venkatraman, N.: 1991, *IT - Induced Business Reconfiguration*, Oxford.

Yap, C., Soh, C. and Raman, K.: 1994, Effect of government incentives on computerization in small business, *The European Journal of Information Systems*, 3(3), 191-206.

Zimmerman, J.: 1996, *Doing Business with the Government using EDI*, Van Nostrand Reinhold.

CHAPTER 9

ELPRO: Electronic Procurement in Europe

ANDREW SLADE
University of Sunderland

9.1. Public Procurement in Europe

The prosperity of member states and of the European Union as a whole depends on
the competitiveness of their economies and the success of their enterprises in local,
regional, national and world markets. The scope and complexity of these markets is
growing at a fast rate for two reasons: the liberalization of trade at national,
European and world-wide levels; markets are being opened up in response to the
European Single Market and to the Government Agreement on Tariffs and Trade
(GATT); the increasing fragmentation of large organizations, particularly in the
public sector, and an increasing tendency for them to divide into purchasers and
suppliers, with competition among suppliers. In the United Kingdom, government
legislation enforces competition in public services.

At present, about 150,000 procuring entities make about 150 calls for tenders
each day in Europe. The number is expected to grow to around 1000 per day in the
next two years. The ability of administrations, procuring entities and suppliers to
meet the demands of increasing international competition is severely hampered by
limitations in the means currently available to initiate, develop, manage and respond
to projects that are subjected to competitive processes. Competitiveness in its turn
depends on efficient procurement systems and efficient information flows in these
systems, and there are actual and potential hindrances to the achievement of these.

In an age of rapidly growing use of electronic communications, the search for
solutions to these difficulties points to the necessity for a comprehensive electronic
procurement system. The ELPRO project has been established to develop such a
system. ELPRO aims to provide an electronic procurement system which will meet
the needs of procuring entities (purchasers) and suppliers in the field of the public
procurement of goods, works and services both now and in the future.

9.1.1. THE REQUIREMENTS OF USERS

ELPRO addresses the needs of three overlapping user groups: administrations
including both the European Commission and Member states; procuring entities in
the public, utilities and private sectors and suppliers and potential suppliers in
particular SMEs (small and medium sized enterprises)

Administrations

The primary needs of administrations derive from three sources. Firstly there is a legal requirement for all states signatory to the GATT World Trade Organization accords to comply with international trade laws on the dissemination of complete, correct and timely tender information world-wide on equal terms, a requirement which in Europe it is the responsibility of European Commission to implement.

Secondly the European Commission has always viewed its public procurement regime not only as a means of complying with the GATT but also as a lever and demonstrator to encourage the liberalization of the private sector procurement field and complete the creation of a single European market. The Commission has a clear need to realise this objective by encouraging increasing private sector participation in open procurement throughout Europe. The third requirement for administrations is more political in nature and is to secure the economic health and welfare of their administrative area, and to provide support to the creation of employment opportunities in their regions. This political imperative is clearly stated in both the EC white paper "Growth Competitiveness and Employment", European Commission 1993 and in the Bangemann Report, Bangemann 1994,as well as in the policies and activities of government at all levels.

Procuring Entities

Procuring entities in both the public and private sector will seek to avoid electronic procurement unless they are confident that Europe, their member state, their local area or their firm has a competitive edge in using these systems. There is a need for an electronic procurement system that demonstrably enhances their competitive edge and at the same time provides the cheapest or most economically advantageous procurements possible within the legislative framework.

Increasingly, many member states are exposing to the market services that have been previously carried out directly by state employees. There is a need in these circumstances for the enhancement of selection, evaluation and award processes and contract transfer arrangements. Procuring entities, both public sector organizations subject to procurement legislation and private sector firms not directly subject to GATT rules, need open electronic procurement systems developed which maximize the benefits of open competition (in terms of sharper prices and increased innovation) without overburdening them with either bureaucracy or a volume of tender responses with which they cannot cope.

Suppliers

In the pre-TELEMATICS age, imperfections in paper information flows occurred because of physical delays in time and space. In the electronic age the imperfections are due more to differences in access to and ability to analyze electronic information. These differences are in part geographical - one of the reasons for the whole TELEMATICS program is to help reduce the five to ten year advantage which the US and Japan are perceived to have over Europe as a whole. However the differentials within regions and economic sectors are infinitely greater. The key need is to improve the ability of European suppliers - and particularly SMEs in under-developed sectors - to access and analyze procurement information.

Since the information supplied by procuring entities is rarely perfect in the first instance, there is a fall-back requirement for an effective means for suppliers to obtain clarification from the responsible technical and administrative people in procuring entities on the terms of the procurement.

Piloting the User's Requirements

There are several drivers for the position in Europe regarding electronic procurement, viz:

- political push for the establishment of a single European market,
- legal push for bodies governed by international trade laws to transfer procurement information to the world markets,
- efficiency push for this to be done using TELEMATICS,
- political pull for the above to be achieved in ways which enable the regions of Europe to support their local industry and which benefit European firms, in particular SMEs.

These factors have led to the development of pilot systems that can be used to investigate the extent to which current technology can be used to support the procurement process and handle the many requirements outlined above. The remainder of this chapter will examine the requirements for electronic procurement in more details and describe one solution to the problems posed. Before describing the solutions adopted it is important that the reader has an understanding of the processes involved, accordingly the next section will describe the nature of public procurement in Europe.

9.2. Public Procurement

The effective analysis of and development of pan-European tools for procurement depends first on a common understanding of procurement procedures. Procurement is complex, with many facets and interpretations, but it is possible to reduce this to common elements. Figure 1 is a conceptual chart of the procurement procedure, and its relevance to legal requirements and the outside world. It is followed by a brief description of the procurement process as it is understood by purchasers and suppliers in member states.

9.2.1. METHODS OF PUBLIC PROCUREMENT

Public procurements are for a wide variety of goods, works and services. Contracts may be large or small, short term or long term, or on-going from year to year. They may be for a closely specified procurement, or they may be more general, as in the case of call-off contracts (which are agreements to purchase if the need arises). Public procurements are carried out in these contexts and for all of them there is a series of stages for the procurer:

- concept,
- preparation,
- pre-tender: either entry to a Standing/Pre-qualified list (for future invitation to tender for a range of potential contracts), or selection for a specific short list for invitation to tender; selection carried out against a range of criteria,
- tender,
- post-tender,
- contract performance,
- contract payments.

Some procurements are relatively simple and may not include all these stages. The pre-tender and tender stages may be run as one stage. Figure 2. below gives details of the stages of the procurement process.

		Conceptualization (in which a project is originated)		
		Preparation (in which a project is discussed with others and agreed and documentation is prepared)		
		Pre-Tender (in which a procurement is formalized and expressions of interest obtained from the outside world)		
RELEVANT TO THE OUTSIDE WORLD		**Tender** (in which invitation to tender are issued, received, evaluated and the tender awarded)		RELEVANT TO COMPLIANCE WITH EUROPEAN AND INTERNATIONAL LAW
		Post Tender (in which detailed contract negotiations are carried out)		
		Contract Performance (in which the contract is performed in consultation with the procurer)		
		Contract Payments (which involves ordering, invoicing and payment under the contract)		

Figure 1. Legal issues.

The Directives of the European Community

EC Public Procurement Directives regulate procedures for selection and award in public procurements. These Directives are consistent with the GATT (but the detail of the Directives may be amended in the light of GATT). The Directives must be implemented by member states by integration with their own legislation and apply to contracts above certain value thresholds. These thresholds are determined by the EC and apply to all contracts with an absolute value in excess of the thresholds, to contracts with a value over 48 months in excess of the thresholds if for a contract longer in duration than 48 months, including ongoing contracts, to contracts for goods, works and to contracts for some services.

The EC public procurement rules contain time limits for certain stages in the process; these time limits may vary according to type of procurement and type of procuring entity. Contracts below the thresholds are subject to national laws, including time limits for certain stages the procedures and regulations of individual procuring entities Each member state has its own laws and regulations relating to procurement. Procuring entities usually have their own regulations, codes of practice etc. Procurers must determine the basis on which the contract will be awarded: lowest price or 'most economically advantageous tender' (which includes consideration of quality as well as price). In the case of the latter, the procuring entity must determine what the detailed criteria are. For selection of tenderers or selection of entrants to a Standing/Pre-qualified list, selection is carried out on the basis of 'fitness' to carry out the contract; the procuring entity determines (within legal boundaries) what it will take into account.

Procurement Procedures

Procedures take three forms:

- *open procedure*: expressions of interest are invited which include tender submissions; the procurer must consider all tenders
- *restricted procedure*: a two stage procedure, in which expressions of interest are invited and a certain number are invited to tender
- *negotiated procedure*: expressions of interest are invited, and the procurer selects a restricted number with whom to negotiate the terms of the contract and the price to be paid.

These procedures are in general terms common to all types of procurement, though they may be applied in different ways. Contracts may be administered from previously assembled lists of potential contractors. These lists may be used for procurements not subject to full EC public procurement directives and for contracts where the procurer is a utility. Figure 2 details the procedures employed by each party to the procurement.

9.3. Model Procurement Systems

The model procurement system implies that procurers have a unified system which could in principle be entirely electronic and internally consistent and complete and which could therefore be exported to and replicated in suppliers' establishments in its entirety. Suppliers could complete the documentation and reply electronically as appropriate. Such a transfer of information would appear thus:

Integrated Electronic Total Procurement System	Supplied in total to	Supplier

Stage	Procurer	Suppliers
CONCEPT	Originates project (internal systems); outline proposals, committee/board agreement	
PREPARATION	*Develops the details of the procurement:* publication of PIN in OJEC if appropriate drafts specification, referring to catalogues and other library information as appropriate identifies model/specimen contract documents sets timetables, with reference to statutory requirements decides procedures and application of EC/national legislation and organization's own procedures/regulations determines criteria for selection and award decides whether to draw tender list from Standing/Approved/Pre-qualified List or to advertise specific procurement if specific advertisement, decides how information on potential contractors will be gathered: through an expression of interest questionnaire, or through listing information required in the advertisement/contract notice may consult potential suppliers *Prepares documentation as appropriate:* Specification Contract conditions and other contract documents Advertisements/contract notices Expression of Interest Questionnaire	*Seek possible tendering opportunities:* identify forthcoming procurements of interest through analysis of PIN notices/seek information on procedures for joining Standing/Approved/Pre-qualified Lists seek information on qualifications required by procurer *For individual procure-ments:* identify possible sub-contracting opportunities seek possible partners respond to calls for consultation *Apply to join Standing/Approved/ Prequalified Lists* seek information on qualifications required by procurer request application/ expression of interest questionnaire complete and return questionnaire/supply required information
PRE-TENDER *Expression of Interest*	*Advertises contract:* publication of notice in OJEC if required local/national advertisements *Issues Expression of Interest questionnaires (if used)* on receipt of requests from potential suppliers *Also issues instructions for tendering if open procedure is used* *Receives completed Expressions of Interest* (information supplied either in form of pre-issued questionnaire or direct response to advertisement/notice with information required) *Proceeds to evaluation for award of contract (see below) if Expressions of Interest also include tender (open procedure)*	*Identify advertisements/ contract notices which are of interest:* seek information on qualifications required by procurer identify possible sub-contracting opportunities seek possible partners respond to calls for consultation *Requests questionnaire if this method is used by procurer* *Returns completed questionnaire/ collected information to procurer by closing date OR Returns completed questionnaires/ required information together with tender if open procedure is being used*

PRE-TENDER
Selection
	Assesses applications against pre-determined
	criteria to select either:
	those qualified to enter
	    Standing/Approved/Pre-qualified List
	those who will be invited to tender for a
	    specific contract
	OR
	Selects from a Standing/Approved/Pre-
	qualified List those who will be invited to
	tender for a specific contract
	May seek clarification/further information
	from applicants
	Finalises contract documents, Invitation to
	Tender and Instructions to Tenderers
		Respond to requests from
		procurer for further
		information/ clarification

TENDER
Invitation to
tender
	Issues formal Invitations to Tender to those
	selected
	Receives and responds to requests for
	clarification and for associated and
	additional information during the tender
	period
	Notifies those not selected for Invitation to
	Tender (unless using Standing etc. List)
		Those selected (and no
		others) receive Invitation to
		Tender
		Seek and select potential
		  sub-contractors, and/or
		  partners
		Seek clarification and
		  associated and additional
		  information from procurer
		Prepare tender submissions

TENDER *Award of contract*	*Receives formal tender submissions by due* *date* Evaluates these against pre-determined criteria Seeks and receives clarification/further details from tenderers if necessary Identifies successful contractor Informs successful contractor; awards contract Notifies unsuccessful tenderers	*Submits tender in the form* *required by due date* *May receive requests from* *procurer for clarification/* *further details; if so,* *responds to these requests* *Receives notification that* *tender is successful or* *unsuccessful*
POST TENDER	*Undertakes detailed negotiations with* *successful tenderer on details of the contract* *as appropriate* *Notifies OJEC of award of contract, if* *appropriate*	*Participates in post-tender* *negotiations with procurer*
CONTRACT **PERFORM-** **ANCE**	*Monitors performance of contract by* *contractor*	*Carries out contract in* *accordance with contract* *documents; supplies* *monitoring information to* *procurer*
CONTRACT **PAYMENTS**	*Certifies work for payment* *OR* *issues defaults/penalties/claims for non-* *performance* *As appropriate, makes payment on receipt of* *invoice from contractor*	*Invoices procurer at agreed* *intervals for work completed*

Figure 2. Detailed procedures for procurement.

This model may be possible to implement in practice in structurally simple procurements in markets in which both the procurer and all potential suppliers have common telematic infrastructures and there are no external references to other systems or information sources. In reality, some procurements are structurally simple, others are very complex. In simple procurements there is little penetration of formal standardization in such fields meaning that tender documents can be self contained without reference to external documents, and such contracts are often expressed in an informal, qualitative form, with one person administering the whole process. In complex procurements, the reverse is the case. Two types of deviation from a perfect procurement model are set out below. Both are indicative of procurement processes in the real world.

9.3.1. HORIZONTAL SEGREGATION

In complex contracts work is often segregated horizontally, with the result that no one person either controls or knows the content of the totality of the contract. This is perhaps most manifest in major construction contracts. Figure 3 illustrates a scenario in this field from the procurers' point of view, indicating the electronic commerce tools that may be most appropriate at each stage.

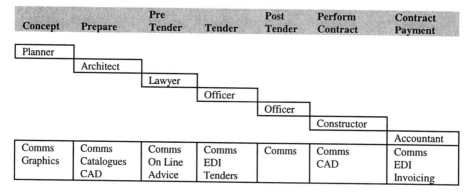

Concept	Prepare	Pre Tender	Tender	Post Tender	Perform Contract	Contract Payment
Planner						
	Architect					
		Lawyer				
			Officer			
				Officer		
					Constructor	
						Accountant
Comms Graphics	Comms Catalogues CAD	Comms On Line Advice	Comms EDI Tenders	Comms	Comms CAD	Comms EDI Invoicing

Figure 3. Procurers' viewpoint.

In many cases, the work indicated above is carried out in isolation and hard copies only are passed between stages. The common exception to this is the exchange of electronic copies between people in the same or linked professions within the same organization, for example between the architect and the construction supervisor.

Even where common telematic tools are used, there is no guarantee that the communications systems used are consistent even within a single organization. Different and sometimes incompatible mail systems may be used within a single procurement. Similar horizontal segregation can also occur on the supplier side.

9.3.2. VERTICAL SEGREGATION

Even without horizontal segregation across departments, there are general vertical breaks in telematic integrity in many procurement systems. This does not mean that it is impossible to develop mutually beneficial electronic procurement systems. Figure 4 indicates how a procurement system can develop on the basis of partial and/or discretionary links between disjointed or stand-alone applications used by procurers and suppliers.

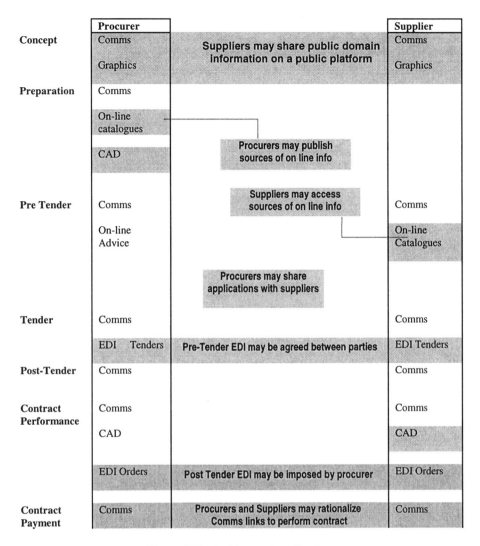

Figure 4. Vertical integration of tools.

9.3.3. DEVIATION FROM MODEL: BUSINESS AND TECHNOLOGY ISSUES

Business Constraints

It is not only structural or procedural faults that result in deviation from the ideal procurement model. Despite the increasing prevalence of Internet based business information services there are still many services which are offered at present only on other channels. As electronic security and on-line payment systems are developed on the Internet many services will undoubtedly be either transferred or replicated on the Internet, but it is likely that multiple systems will coexist for some time to come.

Technology Constraints

The very nature of public procurement may also militate against the development of harmonized procurement systems as between purchasers and suppliers. It is not possible under the public procurement laws of Europe and GATT to develop long-term partnerships with suppliers and work towards an integrated supply chain in the way that, for example, became common in the motor industry and which led to the development of harmonized procurement based on EDI systems such as ODETTE. The fact that contracts must be subjected to competitive tendering on a regular basis means that it may not be worthwhile a supplier adopting a purchaser's procurement information and EDI links if that would mean changing existing systems, particularly if the contract is of low value or short duration.

This position is improving all the time as standardization and harmonization of both the EDI and communication fields moves forward, but at present valid business and technological reasons still exist for deviations from model procurement systems.

9.3.4. PUBLIC PROCUREMENT: WIDER PERSPECTIVES

Fair and Free Trade

Developments in trade throughout the world are leading to an explosion of procurement opportunities which cross national boundaries. These developments include the removal of barriers in order to promote international trade on a fair and free basis, and legislative regulation of competitive processes to ensure that competition takes place on a proper basis. Both these developments are key to the need for an efficient and effective electronic procurement system such as ELPRO is designed to be.

Over the past fifty years the United Nations and other international bodies have been working towards fair and free terms of trade as a cornerstone of a peaceful and prosperous world. Both the Rio Earth Summit on sustainable development and the Uruguay round of the GATT agreed the importance of an accelerated progress towards fair and free terms of trade. The establishment of the World Trade Organization has consolidated this progress, and significant steps are now being made in this field across the world. In terms of public procurement, the Marrakech Government Purchasing Agreement, which came into force on 1 January 1996, substantially widened the scope of the former GATT GPA, extended the scope of the GPA to local and regional authorities as well as national bodies, to works and services as well as goods, and also required the establishment of direct and timely remedies for aggrieved contractors.

Fair and free trade implies ever-increasing competition. Like any other part of the world, the European Union has a duty to do all it can to secure the maximum benefits for its citizens within an increasingly competitive world. The primary instruments for developing conditions under which European industry and commerce can compete with the world have been:
- establishment of the Single European Market,
- harmonization of laws and standards,
- liberalization of public sector markets within Europe.

However, the consequences of the liberalization of markets to achieve either global or European objectives can be disadvantageous for local economies. At the regional and local level, and particularly in economically disadvantaged regions, the implementation of the public procurement directives must be accompanied by effective local measures to assist local firms to take best advantage of the single market.

9.3.5. RECOMMENDATIONS OF THE EUROPEAN COMMISSION

Single Market Issues

At the European level the effective working of the single European Market becomes the paramount issue. The European Commission's analysis of regional and social aspects of public procurement in the context of the single European market were published in the Commission Communication of 22 September 1989 COM (89) 400 final, Commission 1989.

As part of the background, the Commission set out the expected economic benefits of the achievement of a single market. Public procurement accounted for some 15% of Community GDP. They estimated that in the medium to long term, economies rising to as much as 0.5% of GDP would arise as a result of liberalizing the public procurement market. However, the Commission was concerned at the potential negative impact of the liberalization of trade on local economies, particularly in disadvantaged areas:

> There may however be a risk that the opportunities created by the opening-up of public procurement will not be seized, because of the historic legacy of protectionism, technological backwardness, low productivity, failure to organize markets, and poor exporting skills.

The Effect on Local Economies

The European Commission has suggested action to support the ability of local economies to participate in wider markets, particularly in terms of the participation of SMEs. This action includes:

- Informing SMEs better about public procurement markets.
- Development of databanks permitting those contracting authorities that wish to do so to publish, efficiently and at low cost, contracts below the thresholds in the directive and so make them available to SMEs.
- Incorporation in such databanks of information on potential SME suppliers, indicating their field of activity, previous experience, information on quality assurance and so on.
- Organizing procurement fairs.
- Better training of managers of SMEs.
- Improved access to larger contracts: division of larger contracts into lots, and allowing SMEs to tender for single lots alongside firms tendering for many or all lots. The Commission recognized the potential for this strategy to work against the search for economies of scale, and say that the SMEs chances of winning depend on having compensating competitive advantages, for example greater flexibility or lower overheads.

- An active subcontracting policy. The Commission recognized that subcontracts are an important means of improving access by SMEs to large contracts. They suggest an number of technical improvements, including clarifying the extent to which the directive allow sub-contracting facilitating the development of new relationships between prime contractors and subcontractors by making more information available, particularly as regards the indication by the tenderer, when he submits his tender, of his intention to subcontract and through the publication of such information when notice is given of the award of a contract.
- Mutual guarantees of fair and effective performance, including fair and efficient payment systems.
- Association of enterprises: the Commission believe that contracting authorities could assess associations of SMEs to undertake work based on their combined technical and financial capacity. This would be technically more complex than most existing analyses carried out by most procurers in most fields.

9.3.6. IMPLICATIONS FOR PROCUREMENT SYSTEMS

For most purposes, European procurement regime may be regarded as a more detailed version of the Government Purchasing Agreement, and there are no additional features required to accord with the GPA. The primary implication is in the potential for procurement systems to provide direct links into and support for requirements made of national governments under the GPA. A secondary implication is the nation states could find a procurement system offering low-cost international provision and multi-lingual support a useful mechanism to assist developing countries under the GPA requirements.

At the European/local level public procurement systems must link closely with generic information systems aimed at both regional economies generally and at individual companies. The Commission's recommendations were written in 1989, and referred to physical services, many of which are or can now be carried out at the virtual level using telematics.

9.4. Changing User Needs: Developments in Procurement

There are number of current and possible future developments in the procurement field which have a potential high level of significance for electronic procurement systems. The services directives includes a two level application of the EC procurement regime, under which those services which the Commission believed when drafting the directive were in fields in which appropriate conditions for transnational trade had not been achieved and are subject to a procurement regime based on the application of non-discriminatory specifications and the reporting of awards only for an interim period.

The Services Directive includes an internal commitment to the review of this class of services with a view to subjecting them to the full procurement regime. Some of these services, in particular personal services such as heath and social care, education and cultural services, currently represent huge areas of expenditure in all member states, and their transfer to the full procurement regime would add significantly to the volume of tenders administered under the regime. Although market conditions may have been immature when the directives were originally drafted, much experience has now been gained in the development of markets in many of these fields, and it seems likely that a significant number of services will be regarded as capable of being procured under the EC regime. Although often conceptually complex, such services are often amenable to structurally simple and self contained procurement regimes.

The services directive also contained an obligation to review - by 1996 - whether the in-house performance of services adversely affects the achievement of a single European market. It is self-evident that in principle this is the case. If work is carried out in-house it is not offered to the market and it is impossible for European firms to tender for the work and grow. This, together with pressure on member states to reduce state expenditure to meet the Maastricht criteria for monetary union, indicates that there may be significant pressure and support for the privatization - or at least the compulsory competitive tendering - of public sector services. The types of work most likely to be subject to such developments are works contracts, manual services such as waste disposal, refuse collection and ground maintenance, infrastructure maintenance and professional services such as information technology and construction-related professional services.

The two key implication of such a development would be a significant increase in the volume of structurally complex procurements, and if in-house providers are allowed to tender for work offered to the market, a need to develop tendering procedures with appropriate "Chinese walls" built in to ensure fairness and transparency.

Out-sourcing of staff is a related development to privatization and compulsory competitive tendering, but with a different impetus and different implications. Out-sourcing is increasingly common in both the public and private sector, as Figure 5 shows, and can occur in both highly skilled areas in which organizations find it difficult to recruit suitably qualified and experienced staff, and in low-skilled areas which organizations believe to be peripheral to their core activities and an unwelcome drain on scarce management resources. The development of teleworking is providing an important stimulus to out-sourcing.

Out-sourcing can be viewed as the change from an employment contract to a procurement contract. The freedom of movement of people, though enshrined in EC law alongside the freedom of goods and services and capital, is less strongly protected than other factors of production. Under the procedures on the free movement of workers, for example, there are procedures to restrict movement to areas of high unemployment or experiencing severe structural economic change, a concept which has no parallel in respect of other factors of production (goods, works, services or capital). Out-sourcing is likely to result in more transnational working as a result. Out-sourcing is likely to involve the conceptually complex but structurally simple type of contract. The ordering, invoicing and payment systems could be linked with or even be part of proprietary teleworking packages, and final payment could well be to a personal bank account.

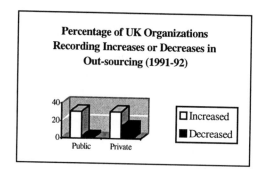

Figure 5. Growth of out-sourcing in public bodies.

Joint ventures between the public and private sector are becoming increasingly common. Unlike the possible developments mentioned above, joint ventures (and particularly those in which the private sector bear the majority of risk) are likely to result in a single public sector procurement awarding a concession to a consortium of private sector partners who would then award some, most or all of the actual goods, works and service contacts under private sector rules.

The original contract could be highly complex in financial, technical, and aesthetic terms, and is likely to involve trans-national partnerships. Within the venture, there may be contracts which are still majority funded by the public sector and which must be administered under the EC regime. If these are interlined with private sector elements of the overall project, it is likely that all connected procurements would at some level or another have to be linked to that in the public sector to ensure consistency in terms of standards etc.

9.4.1. THE FUTURE

Current developments in the procurement field are likely to add substantially to the volume of tenders administered through the EC procurement regime. Many of the new tenders are in fields particularly suited to electronic tendering. Further developments indicate a requirement for tendering systems to be able to deal effectively with both in-house tenders, and to integrate with teleworking systems. The next section describes in outline the ELPRO system and its application to the problems outlined above. Interested readers can consult the ELPRO development team at Sunderland University to obtain further information regarding details including how to assist the team in evaluating the system in practice.

9.5. ELPRO System Architecture

9.5.1. ELPRO DESIGN - KEY CONCEPTS

Kernel

The subscriber, user and project database is protected by a kernel software layer. This layer performs authentication and checks access rights. All servers, gateways and other applications are built upon this kernel which guarantees that problems with software outside the kernel should not affect system security. The only exception may be administrative programs, using ODBC access. In this case, database security will prevent modification of project relevant data and only allow modification of user and subscriber tables.

Servers

Servers interact with users in a request-response manner, e.g., with the ELPRO client or a Web browser. There are usually many server processes or threads running in parallel.

Gateways

Gateways connect ELPRO to other computer systems, e.g. e-mail, TED, OJEC. E-mail will require a listener(in) and a talker process(out), TED a batch import process, OJEC a batch export process.

Client(s)

Clients connect to the ELPRO system over a network using private or standard protocols. Several types of clients are discussed. "The client" always refers to the ELPRO specific client, connecting via the ROP protocol. In future versions it may be that several versions of the client are needed. For example some local authorities are requesting that the model for ELPRO be extended to cover the whole range of purchasing activities they have. This will require a much more extensive and comprehensive catalogue facility than that envisaged in ELPRO. We shall allow for this in the system design by providing all necessary kernel/server facilities and providing different modes of access via special purpose clients.

Administration

Administration is concerned with PROVIDER tasks, not tasks done by an "administrative" user. Administration has to handle subscriber and user registration. HELPDESK functionality should allow limited access to project and document files to support users without electronic access.

   Many administrative functions are implemented in the ELPRO client, and it can be used with the appropriate privileges/roles/titles registered in the user profile, this avoids the need for a separate administration program. This will also allow for remote support between different service providers in different countries.

9.5.2. DISTRIBUTION OF TASKS

ELPRO follows a client-server three tier approach for distribution of the different tasks. Figure 6 summarizes the levels and technologies. The three levels can be distributed on different computers to handle a large number of users. The protocols between presentation systems and applications are stateless, so a pool of application processes can handle many simultaneous users and keep their state information in, for example, shared memory or on disk.

Level	HTML	ELPRO	Mail
Presentation	WWW Browser	ELPRO Client	mail clients and backbone
Protocol	HTTP	ROP	SMTP, X400, ...
Application	WWW Server and Gateway	ELPRO Server	mail gateways
Database	database		

Figure 6. Client-Server architecture.

Networking Overview

Table 1 gives an overview of the local and remote clients to the ELPRO server and also indicate some of the considerations that the project had in assessing the suitability of technologies.

Table 1. Technologies available.

Client	Protocol	Alternative	Problem areas
TED import	Telnet	x.25, ISDN. ftp (if available)	structure and import of project information correlation with existing information
Official Journal	ftp	fax	SGML syntax of exported information
WWW browser	http/html		login and logout security authentication not based on operating system connection to database on different computer dynamic (WWW-)pages no doubling of information (WEB and Database)
ELPRO client	tcp/ip, sockets	rpc, corba, sql/odbc	session handling and stateless protocol multistep transactions encryption, authentication connection to database upload, download of documents (large data)
Electronic mail Gateway	SMTP	X.400 MAPI	different document types project context authentication and encryption mail gateways
FAX	via email		incoming fax handled manually
EDI	EDIFACT	ftp	EDIFACT document types and profiles
Provider connectivity, Admin	telnet	snmp	general access, administration security
Provider connectivity, Database Sync	ftp		exchanging of bulk data format of data
Billing data export	file		export billing data to invoice system format of data

9.6. ELPRO in Practice and Further Work

The ELPRO project is in its demonstration phase where many public authorities across Europe are using the system in earnest to help evaluate its effectiveness in practice. It is anticipated that the evaluation will provide information about the nature of the service offered, the acceptability of the way of working imposed by the system, and other factors related to the business of conducting public procurement. It is becoming clear that systems of this type will be the norm rather than the exception in the near future.

Once the demonstration phase has ended, the European Union's Research and Development Program will move into a new and exciting phase with the introduction of the Fifth Framework Program. This will address many of the issues raised in this chapter particularly the effects on citizens of the adoption of electronic commerce and related technologies by governmental authorities. In the next 4 years the European Union will spend in excess of 3363 million ECU (approximately 3695 million US dollars at today's prices), on the development of the information society in Europe. This does not include any funds for the development of new technology for underpinning the systems of the future that will be available from other sources within the Fifth Framework Program. The effort will be on 'creating a user-friendly information society' and the individual action lines are:

- systems and services for the citizen,
- new working methods and electronic trade,
- multimedia contents and tools,
- essential technologies and infrastructures.

It can be seen from this that Europe and its constituent states are committed to the development of electronic means of doing business both for the private and the public domain and it is confidently expected that the benefits in terms of better services and greater economic effectiveness will flow from this effort.

9.7. Acknowledgements

The first part of this chapter has drawn extensively on the work done during the early part of the ELPRO project and the author wishes to acknowledge the contribution made to this paper by the partners of the ELPRO project, in particular Mick Riley of the City of Newcastle Council for his work on the Requirements analysis of the ELPRO system. ELPRO is a shared cost research action supported by the Administrations Section of DG12 and the TELEMATICS Research program under project number AD1003.

9.8. References

Bangemann, M. 1993: European Commission, DG XIII, 'Europe and the Global Information Society': Recommendations to the European Council. Brussels, 26 May 1994. http://www.ispo.cec.be/infosoc/backg/bangeman.html

Growth, Competitiveness, Employment. The Commission White Paper on the challenges and ways forward into the 21st century. COM(93) 700, 1993, ISBN 92-77-62698-4

ELPRO 1996. ELPRO Requirements Specification, Deliverable 3.1 of Project AD1003. University of Sunderland, Sunderland UK. 31 May 1996

Commission 1989. European Commission Paper on Procurement in Europe, Brussels. COM (89) 400 final.

CHAPTER 10

EDI Maturity: A Business Opportunity

DAVE WHITELEY
Manchester Metropolitan University

10.1. Introduction

Electronic Data Interchange (EDI) is one of the three principal 'technologies' of electronic commerce. It shares the field with electronic markets, such as airline booking systems, and with the more informal area of consumer electronic commerce that is typified by much of the commercial activity on the Internet. These three over-lapping areas of electronic commerce are represented diagramatically in Figure 1.

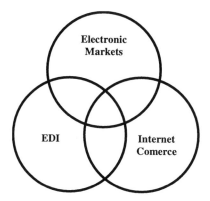

Figure 1. The three categories of electronic commerce.

Each of these three areas of electronic commerce has a distinctive role to play. The role of EDI is in the area of regular repeat transactions between commercial organizations; the obvious examples are vehicle manufacturers ordering components and supermarkets replenishing their stocks of produce. In these organizations, and in many similar trading arrangements, a supply contract is agreed and then followed up by standardized orders on a regular basis until, at some stage, the contract is discontinued, renewed or placed with an alternative supplier. EDI is not often used for the pre-sale/contract element of the trade cycle. The role of EDI is order exchange and, potentially, all exchanges in the execution and settlement phases of the trade cycle (Figure 2).

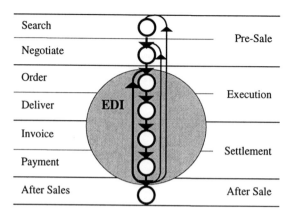

Figure 2. EDI and the trade cycle.

EDI is a formal system. It requires that:

- identities of the products and organizations involved in the trade exchange be unambiguously codified;
- trade exchange be translated and formatted in accordance with an EDI standard;
- business systems of both trading partners interface with EDI software (not always the case but, if it is not done, many of the benefits of EDI are lost);
- organizations set up a data exchange system (normally using a post and forward network), and;
- above all, trading partners work closely together to make the system work and to derive full benefit from the system.

As indicated above this formality is appropriate to the execution and settlement phases of repeat transactions but not normally to the pre-sale or any after-sale trade exchanges.

EDI is now the normal way of doing business for many organizations and trade sectors. EDI is gradually expanding into new trade sectors and organizations that use EDI are enhancing their systems to include more exchanges in the trade cycle. The development of EDI within an organization and a trade sector gives opportunities for efficiency gains and for re-engineering the supply chain. It also gives the opportunity to change the nature of the product that is offered by the organization. The opportunities offered by an EDI system are further examined in this chapter, as is the possibility of integrating business to business EDI systems with business to consumer electronic commerce systems.

10.2. EDI Maturity Model

The development of EDI within an organization or a trade sector goes through a number of stages. Saxena and Wagenaar (1995) suggest a three stage EDI maturity model as a part of a three-way analysis of EDI development in organizations, trade sectors and nations. This chapter further develops the concept of EDI maturity with a six-stage maturity model (Figure 3), and links it to the opportunities for competitive advantage (see also Whiteley, 1996).

Figure 3. EDI Maturity Model.

The stages of EDI development as represented in the model are:

1. *Discovery Stage*

   The first stage in EDI development is the *discovery stage*. Discovery can be by an organization choosing to adopt EDI to gain competitive advantage or to solve an administrative problem. Sometimes it arises from the realization that competitors are adopting EDI and that being left behind will result in competitive disadvantage. For most organizations discovery has come in the form of a 'request' from a significant customer organization that is converting its trade transactions to EDI - such 'requests' are not necessarily negotiable (Bray, 1992; Whiteley 1994).

2. *Introductory Stage*

   Organizations setting out on the EDI path generally start with a pilot scheme. Initiators of EDI trading networks will choose one or two trading partners with which to pilot a single message (transaction) type. Organizations that are forced into EDI trading by an insistent partner start electronic trading in a similar way. This stage can be termed the *introductory stage*. This stage requires investment - there are direct costs in computer hardware and software but, at least as significant, will be the time commitment in establishing the parameters of the electronic trading relationship. This stage, on its own, does not result in any cost saving or efficiency gain.

3. *Integration Stage*

   Having found out about EDI and having gained some practical experience the system can be developed further. Very probably the introductory system was a freestanding system with transactions being manually transcribed from the

EDI system to the main business system (or visa-versa depending on the selected message type). There is little benefit in an EDI system if, for example, orders have to be printed and then typed back into the order processing system. The next stage therefore is to interface the EDI software with the business application so that EDI messages can be transferred electronically and automatically between the two systems. This stage is referred to as the *integration stage*. The work involved in this stage is very variable but often expensive. To establish the service EDI software can be bought 'off the shelf'. Integrating the EDI software and the business system will often require writing a tailor-made interface system. The EDI software will provide interface file formatting facilities but is not likely to be able to match the validation and integrity checks that a business system would normally apply to input data. Integration is an essential stage for the large user of EDI. Many small organizations, often forced into EDI by a large trading partner, never achieve integration:

> Consultants at Sema estimate that 80 per cent of their EDI customers are still printing out the information they receive by EDI and re-keying it. (Bray, 1992)

4. Operational Stage

Integration realises the EDI benefits of saving time and avoiding transcription errors. Real business benefits only come when a significant number of trading partners and/or commonly used trade transactions are converted to EDI. Reaching a 'critical mass' in the volume of electronic trading gives cost savings - the staff dealing with manual transactions can be redeployed. The conversion of the major part of the trade cycle, both in volume of trading partners and in numbers of message types is the *operational stage*. Different organizations have placed differing emphasis on the completion of the operation stage. Retailers have been keen to convert all their suppliers to EDI orders but there has been less emphasis on electronic invoicing and payment (see, e.g., BhS, 1994). The vehicle assemblers however tend to be more advanced in implementing other message types, see for example the Rover Cars case study (Baker, 1991). Completing the electronic trade cycle speeds up business transactions and gives the opportunity to look at the organization of that trade cycle and the supply chain. A fuller picture of the operational use of EDI is given in Section 4.

5. Strategic Stage

There are savings to be made by simply replacing paper documents by their electronic equivalent. The real opportunities come from making changes to established business practice. These opportunities only arise when significant progress is made in the operational stage - the implementation of these changes is the *strategic stage*. Possible areas of change and examples of where such changes have taken place are:

- The sequence of trade documents can be revised. Document matching is a considerable problem in order processing. Customers have to match deliveries to the orders, and invoices to the deliveries; suppliers have to match payments to invoices, each process made more complex by disparate document types, part deliveries (i.e. less than the full amount ordered) and incorrectly recorded codes. EDI makes the process easier - at the very least codes should be correct and in the proper place. EDI also gives the opportunity to re-engineer the trade document cycle, The Ford Motor Company, for instance, has introduced 'self billing' for delivered components thus omitting one stage of the matching process (for themselves if not their suppliers).

- EDI can give dramatic time savings. The time between formulating a replenishment demand and the order being processed by the supplier can be as short as is required - for all orders not just rushed orders. This has facilitated the reduction or elimination of stock holding (by the customer organization at least) and is a part of the development of just-in-time (JIT) manufacture and quick response supply. Examples of this abound. Rover's use of JIT is documented in Baker (1991). Retailers have also used EDI for quick response supply, eliminating stock holding in the stores or their own warehouses.

The establishment of electronic trading relations can involve considerable discussion and cooperation (although it can also be a case of '*EDI or die*' - here is what we do - now you fit in). This is part of a pattern, in some trade sectors, of closer cooperation between customer and suppliers that involves cooperation in design, production and a long-term trading relationship. This can be reinforced by the electronic interchange of production plans or EPOS data. BhS (a large UK clothing retailer), for example, link EPOS data and EDI orders; they say of their suppliers "by knowing the sales of his product, he can be more pro-active in his dealings with BhS" (BhS, 1994).

6. *Innovation Stage*

The establishment of an operational EDI infrastructure and the change of operational procedures that it facilitates also give the possibility of changing the nature of the product or the provision of new services. These developments are termed the *innovation stage* in the model and it is contended that they open up new possibilities for competitive advantage. Examples of such developments are only just emerging as the early users of EDI achieve maturity in their systems. Examples of the innovative use of EDI and the possibilities of competitive advantage are discussed in Section 5.

10.3. EDI and Competitive Advantage

EDI goes back a long way. Some authors have traced its origins back to the Berlin Airlift of 1948 (e.g., Swatman and Swatman, 1992) but EDI, as we know it today, with formal EDI standards and the use of value added data services (VADS) dates back to the 1980s.

The 1980s was also the period when concepts of competitive advantage were popularized. Porter published his model of competitive rivalry (1980) and subsequently the model of the generic supply chain (1985). The two classic case studies of competitive advantage were that of the use of electronic markets in SABRE airline booking systems and the use of EDI (or EDI-like systems) by American Hospital Supply (AHS) (latterly Baxter Health Care). Both of these systems were dependent on information and communication technologies (ICTs) and these technologies were seen as the enablers of competitive edge strategic information systems (Johnson and Vital, 1988; Earl, 1989).

The use of ICTs to gain competitive advantage requires a degree of surprise - an ambush effect. AHS's online ordering system was introduced before its competitors thought of such a service and was then further developed with the provision of 'value added services', in order to maintain competitive advantage. A similar example is Brun Passot (Jelassi, 1994), a French office supply company, that developed online ordering and EDI Systems when its competitors had no comparable offerings. Interestingly, both companies were offering electronic trading links to customer organizations (as opposed to suppliers) and operated in fragmented markets where competitors did not necessarily make extensive use of IT (and possibly did not have the resources and expertise needed to make available such facilities). In the case of AHS, their EDI development preceded a period of restructuring in the market and the emergence of a much smaller number of larger suppliers. Jelassi (1994) hints that similar developments might be expected in the currently fragmented French office supply sector. These cases seem to tie up with the often overlooked assertion of Porter: 'the power of technology as a competitive variable lies in its ability to alter competition through changing industry structure'.

The cases of AHS and Brun Passot have not proved to be typical. The most notable EDI trading communities have been between large customer organizations and their supplier network; the hub and spoke pattern of electronic trading (Bray, 1992; Whiteley, 1994). The development of such an EDI infrastructure tends to be a semi-public undertaking. The use of EDI requires the cooperation of trading partners and many of these trading partners are suppliers to competitor organizations. These EDI developments are usually quickly copied by competitor organizations and hence there becomes a pattern of competitive efficiency gains across most or all the major players in a market segment (in some instances internationally and in some cases on a national basis). A recent case of copycat developments, although not strictly in the EDI arena, has been the tracking facilities made available in the express packet industry. In this case Federal Express made tracking information available through a Web site in November 1994 to be followed after six months by UPS with a similar service. The third major player in the industry, DHL, had technical problems in providing a matching facility and trailed in over a year later (Bloch et al., 1996). The outcome is that no one organization gains a significant competitive advantage (although there are cases of competitive disadvantage where one or two players in the market do not keep up with the ICT and electronic trading norms for their market sector).

The potency of EDI as a tool for gaining competitive advantage was questioned as early as 1990. According to Benjamin et al. (1990):

Implicit in the early writings on EDI has been the assumption that these systems hold great potential for providing strategic advantage. One of our conclusions, however, is that EDI applications, rather than being a competitive weapon, are increasingly a necessary way of doing business ....

EDI developers do continue to claim competitive advantage but, in general and in reality, they are doing no more than taking part in the competitive drive for low cost and service efficiency within their trade sector.

10.4. The Operational Use of EDI

The operational use of EDI implies the use of electronic trading with the majority of trading partners, a significant volume of trade transactions and that the EDI interfaces are integrated into the order processing, stock control and/or production planning business systems.

10.4.1. OPERATION OF EXECUTION PHASE TRANSACTIONS

The execution phase of the trade cycle is concerned with the logistics of having *the right goods, in the right place, at the right time* (and at the right price). The basic exchanges of the order and delivery note can be augmented by further exchanges, for example planning information and order confirmation (Figure 4).

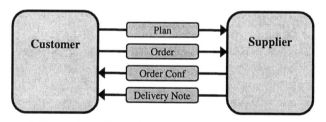

Figure 4. Electronic exchanges in the execution phase of the trade cycle.

For suppliers to respond quickly to orders they must either keep adequate stock (an overhead their just-in-time customers are reducing or eliminating) or they must have a good idea of what orders to expect. This need is addressed by sending EPOS data in the retail trade and production plans/forecasts in manufacture. These exchanges help the supplier to anticipate the requirements of their customers, plan their production and place orders on their suppliers.

The order, when it comes, will be against a pre-determined contract. In retail, the *call-off* order specifies the quantity required and where and when it is to be delivered (to the retailer's distribution centre or direct to the store). In manufacture, the order is commonly called a schedule (the contract is the order), again it specifies the quantities and delivery times but possibly also a sequence of packing to match the requirements of the production line:

In the automotive industry, car assembly plants will give only a few hours notice of the number and type of seats or wiring harnesses required. This notice is given

when the manufacture of the body shell for those seats and harness has already
started. (Blacker, 1993)

In some cases, for selected components, the delivery times are less than an hour.

Failure to meet the order can mean spaces on the shelf in the shop or the halting
of the production line. The order confirmation exchange indicates that the order has
been received and processed but also details any supply problems so that the
customer can attempt to adjust plans to meet the situation.

The delivery note exchange confirms the dispatch, or imminent dispatch, of the
goods. It is the final confirmation of availability and it can also cut down on the
clerical work associated with the customer's goods-inwards. An electronic delivery
note is separate from the goods and hence does not serve the normal purpose of
confirming delivery. Very often it will be supplemented by bar code labels on the
consignment that, when scanned, connect the physical delivery with the electronic
delivery note. For some systems the order exchange will include bar-code
requirements from the customer that assist in the automated sorting and storage of
goods in the customer's distribution centre.

The restructuring of the supply chain, including the use of EDI, can make
dramatic changes in operational efficiency. In 1995, Tesco (UK supermarket group)
reported:

> ... it [EDI] has also played its part in cutting stocks, transforming a level of four
> weeks' supply turning 13 times a year onto just over two weeks supply with 36
> turnarounds. Over the past 10 years ... lead times have dropped from 10 days to
> three. (Computing, 1995a)

10.4.2. OPERATION OF SETTLEMENT PHASE TRANSACTIONS

The use of EDI in the settlement phase of the trade cycle has the purpose of reducing
paperwork, eliminating queries and cutting out errors. The basic exchanges are the
invoice and the payment, with an itemized payment advice, an important component
of the latter exchange (Figure 5).

Electronic invoices cannot be said to be lost in the post, but the big advantages of
EDI invoices are standardization and accuracy. The EDI invoice contains the exact
codes the customer used in the original order and the supplier used in the delivery
note. Provided the customer has integrated EDI into its business systems matching
the invoice to the order and delivery is exact and automatic and it can take care of
split orders and partial deliveries.

Figure 5. Electronic exchanges in the settlement phase of the trade cycle.

The EDI invoice should eliminate document-matching problems for the customer and the electronic payment, with an itemized advice, should do the same for the supplier. The EDI payment advice maps onto the unpaid invoice data and makes it clear which items have been paid for and which are still outstanding.

The use of EDI in the settlement phase can dramatically reduce queries, speed up payments and reduce the work involved in reconciling documentation. Rover Cars report:

> ... before EDI reconciliation took as long as two to three months. With EDI and self-billing, 92% of the invoices are right first time. (Computing, 1995a)

The use of EDI for ordering often encourages smaller and more frequent orders and hence increases the necessity to automate the invoice reconciliation process. Some organizations use EDI only for the settlement phase. Companies in the catering trade, for example, give their local manager/chef discretion in selecting and purchasing supplies but then handle and account for all invoices centrally, using EDI, to make the processing load manageable.

10.5. EDI and Innovation

Organizations and trade sectors where EDI is the normal way of doing business have been able to alter the efficiency of their supply chain out of all recognition over the last ten or so years. These changes are also allowing them to change the nature of the service they offer to their customers, the trebling of the range of products offered by the supermarkets was an early example of this.

In manufacture, EDI coupled with just-in-time logistics and changes in production techniques have greatly reduced the production planning cycle time. At Rover Cars the time from production planning to completion of a vehicle has been reduced from seven weeks to two (Computing, 1992). At the dealer end of the car business the problem has always been to marry up the customer's requirement for model, colour, options, etc. with available stock - often resulting in a not entirely satisfactory compromise. Rover are now bringing the consumer and production side of the business together. The customer can, using a workstation in the showroom, specify their exact requirements and the order can be transmitted electronically into the production planning process. Rover now produce all cars for the UK domestic market to customer specifications. The customer gets the car he or she wants and Rover have sold off a large car compound at the Longbridge factory to a supermarket chain (itself a leading EDI user) (Computing, 1995b; Palframan, 1995; Coopers and Lybrand, 1996). Similar examples are Raleigh who will build their top of the range mountain bicycles to a customer specification and Levi Jeans who, if you are female and live in the US, will produce, from the factory, a made to measure pair of jeans (Bloch et al., 1996).

In the retail trade the use of EPOS data, coupled with just-in-time supply, has the potential to dramatically increase the responsiveness of the retailer, and the supply chain, to market conditions. This is the case in the fashion trade where early intelligence on the styles and colours that are selling can help ensure that the goods the consumer wants are the ones on the racks. The same is also the case in the 'best seller' book trade. Timely market intelligence can allow reprints of successful blockbusters to be rushed out before the stock disappears and the public interest is lost. The point is illustrated by a quote from a speech by Eddi Bell, chairperson of Harper Collins at the 1992 BIC Symposium:

> With EPOS and EDI working together on our behalf, we could have had the reprint out three weeks earlier; no bookshop need ever have been out of stock - and we could probably have doubled our sales during this early 'hot' period.

The converse is that the same market information could dramatically reduce the half cf all printed books that are remaindered or pulped.

10.6. Conclusions

EDI has been adopted with enthusiasm in a limited number of trade sectors - principally sectors where the major players are heavily reliant on the efficient operation of their supply chain. The use of EDI has enabled just-in-time manufacture and quick-response supply. For mature users of EDI the changes in logistics, efficiency and, in some cases, service provision have been dramatic.

The use of EDI, except in a limited number of well-documented cases, has not produced strategic competitive advantage; in most sectors EDI developments by one player have been quickly copied by competitors.

The development of a mature EDI infrastructure allows for innovation. Innovations are taking place in the areas of mass customization and responsiveness to market intelligence. The Rover example links consumer electronic commerce with inter-organizational electronic commerce (i.e. EDI) to develop a new way of doing business with potential competitive advantage (and with possible implications for the future of the franchised main dealer network). A further example of successful consumer electronic commerce are the on-line bookshops that use the book trade EDI systems for their supply chain operations. Organizations entering the consumer electronic commerce market will need a supply chain that can respond efficiently:

> ... if an [consumer] order can be placed electronically in a split second, it will be unacceptable that processing and delivery take several days. (Raman, 1996)

and for an operation of any complexity that will, in all probability, mean EDI.

The potential exists for organizations with mature EDI infrastructures to use that capability imaginatively to create competitive advantage. There is the potential, of course, for competitors to copy but, to pre-qualify for the contest, they must have a similarly mature EDI infrastructure. Some competitors will be disqualified from the race, a mature, efficient and electronically coordinated supply chain is a long-term investment.

10.7. References

Benjamin, R., de Long, D. and Morton, M.: 1990, Electronic Data Interchange: How much competitive advantage?, *Long Range Planning*, 23(1), 29-40.

BhS: 1994, *The Role of Computers within BhS*, BhS, London.

Baker, C.: 1991, EDI in business, *Accountancy*, April.

Blacker, K.: 1993, The basics of EDI in manufacturing, *Electronic Trader*, III(IX), 12-14.

Bloch, M., Pigneur, Y. and Segev, A.: 1996, Leveraging electronic commerce for competitive advantage: A business value framework, *Ninth International Conference on EDI-IOS*, Bled, Slovenia.

Bray, P.: 1992, Web or wheel, *Which Computer*, January, pp. 50-58.

Computing: 1992, Eyes for the road, *Computing*, 20 February, p. 32.

Computing: 1995a, The focus: Electronic Data Interchange, *Computing*, 26 January, pp. 37-44.

Computing: 1995b, Rover will never make a car that nobody wants (Microsoft advert), *Computing*, 20 April, p. 32.

Coopers and Lybrand: 1996, *Logistics for Competitive Advantage: A European Perspective* (Book and Videos), ProActive Communications, Huntingdon.

Earl, M.: 1989, *Management Strategies for Information Technology*, Prentice Hall, New York.

Jelassi, T.: 1994, Binding the customer through IT, *Competing through Information Technology*, Prentice Hall, Hemel Hempstead, pp. 84-106.

Johnson, R. and Vitale, M.: 1988, Creating competitive advantage with interorganizational information systems, *MIS Quarterly*, June, 153-165.

Palframan, D.: 1995, Concurrent Affairs, *Computing*, 2 June, p. 32.

Porter, M.: 1980, *Competitive Strategy: Techniques for Analysing Industries and Competitors*, Free Press, New York.

Porter, M.: 1985 *Competitive Advantage: Creating and Sustaining Superior Performance*, Free Press, New York.

Raman, D.: 1996, EDI: The backbone for business on the Net, *Electronic Commerce and Communications*, 4, 18-21.

Saxena, K. and Wagenaar, R.: 1995, Critical success factors of EDI technology transfer: A conceptual framework, *Third European Conference on Information Systems*, Athens.

Swatman, P. and Swatman, P.: 1992, EDI system integration: A definition and literature survey, *The Information Society*, 8, 169-205.

Whiteley, D.: 1994, Hubs, Spokes and SMEs: Patterns of electronic trading and the participation of small and medium-sized enterprises (SMEs) in EDI networks, *5th World Congress of EDI Users, Research Forum*, Brighton.

Whiteley, D.: 1996, EDI Maturity and the competitive edge, *Logistics Information Management*, 9(4).

CHAPTER 11

Design of Electronic Data Interchange Systems for Small/Medium Enterprises

Are our Information Technology Design Assumptions Correct?

ROB MACGREGOR, DEBORAH BUNKER AND PHILIP WAUGH
University of Wollongong

11.1. The Development of Electronic Data Interchange (EDI)

Three decades ago, Electronic Data Interchange (EDI) was developed as a business tool for reducing paperwork which, it was found, seriously affected the efficiency of many businesses. The design assumptions were based on the views that much of the routine business information that passes between organizations is highly structured and standard. These assumptions were the result of the structured and standardized methods and approaches to the design and use of IT within organizations, both small and large (Alter, 1996). The movement of information, it was thought, was merely mechanical, requiring minimal decision making and thus could be handled by a machine rather than the human being (EDI World Institute 1995; Tsai, Richards and Kappelman, 1995).

Early advocates of EDI stressed that its benefits included: elimination of re-keying of errors; faster trading cycles; better customer response; reduced inventory levels; reduced information and storage and more efficient use of information (Tsai et al., 1995; Harvey, 1992). More recently, the EDI World Institute (1995) suggested that the benefits of EDI to small/medium enterprises (SMEs) include: improving the bottom line; working faster and better within the organization; gaining strategic advantage; strengthening customer relations and preparing for the future in business.

Yet, despite both the longevity and the continuing development of EDI, it has failed to live up to the promises, especially in SME implementations. Chatfield and Alston (1997) state that while electronic commerce technologies are being quickly adopted by Australian organizations the use of EDI in SMEs is lagging behind. In their case study of the organization Combined Rural Traders (CRT), they cite the following barriers to the adoption of a financial EDI system:

- resistance to paper-less transactions,
- distrust of EDI technologies and systems due to a bad experience implementing an internal financial system,

- supplier fear of increased levels of inventory and business risk as EDI changed CRT's business processes,
- Australian banks' lack of interest in CRT's EDI initiative,
- lack of technology and solution providers' (third party hardware and software) support for CRT,
- telecommunications providers' slow response in provision of technical information for CRT's cost estimates for the project.

A number of reasons for general EDI failure in organizations are given in the literature. Anson (1995) suggests that EDI is difficult to implement, adding that only a very small percentage of companies use EDI and of those, most use it less than other technologies. This is supported by a recent Roy Morgan Research survey in Australia (1995). Higgins (1995) suggests that a fundamental drawback with EDI is the question of security, while Barker (1995) suggests that for EDI to be considered seriously by small business, it needs to be cheaper to acquire and develop, presented as a technology which can carry out functions other than the transmission of purchase orders, and acceptable in a court of law.

It is interesting to note that while there are many advocates for the use of EDI as an interorganizational tool (Zack, 1994; Pletsch, 1994; Huttig, 1994; Evans-Correia, 1994; Udo and Pickett, 1994; Tuunainen and Saarinen, 1997), most accept that those problems raised by Barker (1995) and Higgins (1995) are still yet to be solved.

11.2. What is a Small/Medium Enterprise (SME)?

The nature of SMEs has been the topic of both governmental committee findings as well as research initiatives. Brigham and Smith (1967) found that SMEs tended to be more risky than their larger counterparts. This view is supported by later studies (Walker, 1975; Delone, 1988). Cochran (1981) found that small business tended to be subject to higher failure rates while Rotch (1987) suggested that small businesses had inadequate records of transactions. Perhaps most important in any discussion concerning SMEs is the view given by Barnett and Mackness (1983), that small firms are not miniature versions of larger firms, but quite unique in their own right.

Perhaps the most detailed definition of a small business was provided by Reynolds et al. (1994). They suggested that the following characteristics make up the organizational environment in which a small business operates. These include:

- small management team,
- strong owner influence,
- centralized power and control,
- lack of specialist staff,
- multi-functional management,
- a close and loyal work team,
- informal and inadequate planning and control systems,
- lack of promotable staff,
- lack of control over business environment,
- limited ability to obtain finance,

- labor intensive work,
- limited process and product technology,
- narrow product/service range,
- limited market share,
- heavy reliance on few customers,
- decisions - intuitive instead of rational,
- leadership - personal but not task oriented,
- education experience and skill - practical but narrow,
- low employee turnover,
- product dedication rather than customer orientation,
- reluctance to take risks,
- management swayed by personal idiosyncrasies,
- strong desire to be independent, and
- intrusion of family interests.

When the introduction of IT into small business is considered, there are marked differences between small firms and their larger counterparts (Barnett and Mackness (1983). Khan and Khan (1992) suggest that most small firms avoid sophisticated software or applications. This view is supported by studies carried out in the United Kingdom by Chen (1993). Cragg and King (1993) suggest that small firms often lack the necessary expertise to fully utilize IT. This view is supported by the findings of Holzinger and Hotch (1993) and Delvecchio (1994). Indeed, Yap et al. (1992) have shown that many small firms use consultant or vendor expertise in the identification of hardware and software as their first critical step towards computerization. They conclude that ongoing success with IT is positively associated with vendor support, vendor training, vendor after sales service and vendor expertise. This is supported in recent studies (MacGregor and Cocks, 1994; Wood and Nosek, 1994; MacGregor and Bunker, 1998).

Added to the views and findings concerning small business, are the variety of definitions of what actually constitutes an SME. Some definitions tend to be based purely on a quantitative perspective, such as number of staff, or amount of turnover, while others attempt to utilize qualitative definitions, similar to those provided by Reynolds et al. (1994). Meredith (1994) suggests that any definition of a SME must include a qualitative as well as a quantitative component. The quantitative component should examine tangible financial measures, while the qualitative component should reflect less tangible factors such as mode of operation as well as organizational procedures.

Not only is there a myriad of views concerning the nature of small business, but also from a governmental standpoint, there is a variety of definitions of SMEs. In the United Kingdom, a small business is defined as:

having fewer than 50 employees and was not a subsidiary to any other company

In the United States:

a small business concern shall be deemed to be one which is independently owned and operated and which is not dominant in its field of operation' (United

States Small Business Administration - based on section 3 of the Small Business Act 1953)

While in Australia, a small business is defined as:

> one in which one or two persons are required to make all the critical decisions (such as finance, accounting personnel, inventory, production, servicing, marketing and selling decisions) without the aid of internal (employed) specialists and with the owners having knowledge in one or two functional areas of management (Meredith, 1994, p 31)

We can see from this selection of definitions that researchers are far from agreement on this matter. For the purposes of this study, however, the UK definition was selected as an appropriate reflection of the SME situation within Australia.

This study has been carried out primarily to examine the nature of the adoption of information technology by SMEs. As background to this study, findings that impact upon the level of adoption of EDI in Australian SMEs, were also examined.

11.3. IT and EDI in Small/Medium Enterprises

A number of studies examining the acquisition and use of computer technology in the SME environment (Doukidis et al., 1992; Neergaard, 1992; Yap et al., 1992), have found that small business managers use vendor expertise in the identification of hardware and software as their first critical step towards computerization. The vendor becomes the surrogate IT department for the SME. Swanson (1988) suggested that failure of the vendor to understand the nature of small business operations or the level of skill of the personnel who will be using the technology often leads to dissatisfaction or abandonment of IT.

Where larger businesses will call upon the technical expertise of their IT department to supplement vendor support, there is a heavy reliance by an SME on the vendor, prior and subsequent to purchase. Not only does vendor support and ability affect the overall level of small business management's satisfaction with computer technology, but a recent study (MacGregor and Bunker, 1998) suggests that the level of vendor expertise and support can significantly affect a small businesses ongoing ability to implement new systems and to manage staff responsible for IT. Thus, despite recent findings (DelVecchio, 1994) which suggest that there is a genuine desire by small business managers to require requisite knowledge of IT, most small businesses have tended to rely on vendors for the necessary background knowledge to purchase and use computers.

This may have implications for the implementation and subsequent use of EDI technology, if, as suggested by Harvey (1992) and Mackay (1992), EDI should only be considered a special case of the implementation of IT in SMEs.

An examination of the literature would suggest that there are many advocates supporting the use and expansion of EDI in the small business environment. Pletsch (1994) suggests that an SME's acceptance of EDI systems implementation and use is becoming a business necessity. This view is supported by Huttig (1994) who suggests the use of pooled microcomputers in an EDI environment increases the purchasing power of those organizations within the pool. Britt (1995) suggests that there is a 'push' being mounted by the US banking fraternity for the adoption of EDI by SMEs and Tuunainen and Saarinen (1997) suggest that economies of scale are gained from EDI used for integration of the value chain and efficiency gains from functional integration.

Many researchers point to specific tangible benefits with EDI. Hinge (1989) and Tuunainen and Saarinen (1997) suggest that EDI allows both intra- and inter-organizational functions to be carried out more effectively and efficiently. Rockart and Short (1989) suggest that the use of EDI allows the organization to respond more quickly to global competition, risk, service and costs, while Kavan and Van Over (1990) suggest that EDI allows better cash management throughout the organization.

In most instances, these authors tend to point to specific organizations that have adopted EDI and have shown specific improvement. Fallon (1988), for example, utilized General Motors as the example where design and manufacturing time were significantly reduced, while Sehr (1989) has identified the Levi Strauss company as one which has benefited through the analysis of market trends using EDI techniques.

More recently Pletsch (1994) has used examples from K-Mart, Wal-Mart and Sears as companies using EDI in their claims processing, while The EDI World Institute (1995) has used Preister Supply (US) and SJ Dixon (UK) as evidence of profit increase, improvement in transaction processing, reduction of document cycle time and increased employee satisfaction with the introduction of EDI.

It is interesting to note that while most of these authors advocate the adoption of EDI in the small business environment, most provide examples from large businesses. Not only are the examples questionable to the SME marketplace, but few authors point out the problems which arise when small business adopts EDI technology.

Huttig (1994) suggests that in order for a small business to successfully adopt EDI there is a need to develop computerized outsourcing and to establish a system of control and management. Evans-Correia (1994) considers the major hurdle for small businesses is the lack of technical, financial and administrative resources to comply with both EDI and the subsequent organizational partners. This view is supported by Udo and Pickett (1994). Higgins (1995) suggests that one of the problems is security while Buchanan (1995) points to the high setup cost as a disincentive to EDI use. Tuunainen and Saarinen (1997) touch upon most of the above issues in their study of SME suppliers to the Finnish automotive industry.

Of particular interest are figures supplied by Anson (1995) who demonstrates that despite all that EDI appears to offer, in that year, only 35,000 companies had adopted it in the US, 15,000 in the UK and 5,500 in Australia. Anson (1995) and Chatfield and Alston (1997) further add that EDI only takes up a small part of the information flow within the chain of many companies.

Mindful of the problem of IT implementation in SMEs, and with the awareness of EDI technologies forming a subset of that problem, a study was conducted of SME's IT implementation and use in Australia.

11.4. Survey Method

A number of authors (Harvey 1992, Mackay 1992) suggest that when attitudes to EDI are being considered, these must be taken in the context of attitudes to IT in general. Based on this view, a questionnaire was developed which sought SME managers' attitudes to the implementation of IT within their organizations. In particular, the questionnaire sought information concerning the number of employees, suitability of the computer technology being used, the rationale for computerization, the practices adopted by the business with the acquisition of IT as well as the education level and requirements of the organization.

A mailing list was developed by the Illawarra Chamber of Commerce. The geographic area covered included the southern suburbs of Sydney, the cities of Wollongong and Nowra (population approx. 500,000). The sampling frame included companies with a work force of less than 50, where the company was not a subsidiary of a larger company.

Respondents were asked the amount of time (in hours per week) devoted by the organization to developing new systems for the computer. Respondents were also asked to rate the importance (not important/of some importance/very important) and their own business' ability (poor/passable/good) with regard to using technology to meet business requirements; implementing new hardware and software; knowing what information was needed to run the business; designing new systems; evaluating; the benefits of computer technology and implementing new systems for specific applications. This list is based on work by Jackson (1986), Neergaard (1992), Yap et al. (1992) Doukidis et al. (1991) and Igbaria (1992).

Finally, respondents were asked to rank the following as the major reason for the acquisition of computer technology: actual performance against specified measures, cost, benefits, ease of use, and future enhancement possibilities.

11.5. Results

A total of 600 questionnaires were distributed. Responses were obtained from 131 businesses, over a range of market activities, representing a response rate of 21.8%. All respondents indicated that they were using IT in their day-to-day work. Table 1 indicates the number of hours spent on developing new projects using IT.

Table 2 indicates small business rating of the importance of: using technology to meet business requirements, implementing new hardware and software, knowing what information was needed to run the business, designing new systems, evaluating the benefits of computer technology and implementing new systems for specific applications.

Table 3 indicates the respondent's perception of their own organization's abilities in these areas. Respondents were asked to rank the criteria (actual performance against specified measures, cost, benefits, ease of use, future enhancement possibilities) in their order of importance when computer technology was being acquired. Table 4 indicates the ratings. A chi-squared analysis was applied to the data in Table 4 to determine whether the changes in ranking were associated with changes of criteria used in the acquisition of computer technology.

Table 1. Number of new project hours spent using IT.

No. of Hours	No of Respondents	Percentage
0 - 1	67	51.1
1 - 2	19	14.5
2 - 5	27	20.6
> 5	18	13.7

Table 2. Importance of activities connected with IT.

Activity	Not Very Important	Some Importance	Very Important
Using technology to meet business requirements	12	63	36
Implementing new hardware and software	15	75	20
Knowing what information was needed to run the business	9	65	41
Designing new systems	20	62	27
Evaluating the benefits of computer technology	13	71	27
Implementing new systems for specific applications	18	68	21

Table 3. Ability in activities connected with IT.

Activity	Not Very Good	Passable Good	Very Good
Using technology to meet business requirements	14	86	17
Implementing new hardware and software	24	82	11
Knowing what information was needed to run the business	14	71	32
Designing new systems	20	60	27
Evaluating the benefits of computer technology	19	80	18
Implementing new systems for specific applications	27	71	11

Table 4. Acquisition criteria used for IT

Criteria	Ranking				
	Highest			Lowest	
	1	2	3	4	5
Actual performance against specified measures	41	11	11	13	18
Cost	24	26	20	16	17
Benefits	35	25	22	14	10
Ease of use	15	18	27	31	10
Future enhancement possibilities	12	17	16	23	32

11.6. Analysis

Advocacy for the adoption of EDI in SMEs is often premised upon the desire and the ability of the organization to implement such technologies. Reynolds et al. (1994) have suggested that, among other qualities, SMEs are characterized by: lack of specialist staff; informal and inadequate planning and control systems; lack of promotable staff; narrow product/service range; limited market share; product dedication rather than customer orientation; reluctance to take risks; and strong desire to be independent.

A number of authors (Khan and Khan 1992, Cragg and King 1993, Delvecchio 1994) suggest that when confronted with computer technology, these factors manifest themselves firstly, in a reluctance to use sophisticated hardware and software or applications, and secondly in a utilization of applications provided with little thought or need to develop enhancements to them. An examination of Table 1 would tend to support this. More than half the organizations surveyed spent less than one hour per week on the development of new applications. The SMEs surveyed would seem to regard new applications (and enhancements) as of little consequence. Likewise, if we examine Table 4, it can be seen that less than 10% of respondents considered future enhancements utilising computer technology to be important when IT was acquired. This finding would seem to indicate a lack of long- and short-term planning expertise and implementation in the use of IT within these SMEs, which supports the Reynolds et al. (1994) view that SMEs have 'informal and inadequate planning and control systems'.

An examination of Table 2 suggests that there is some expression of importance for the factors: using technology to meet business requirements, implementing new hardware and software, knowing what information was needed to run the business, designing new systems, evaluating the benefits of computer technology and implementing new systems for specific applications. With the exception of the factors 'using technology to meet business requirements' and 'knowing what information was needed to run the business', most small business respondents are, at best, equivocal concerning future enhancement of their current computer usage. Indeed, if the factors 'implementing new hardware and software' and 'implementing new systems for specific applications' are considered, less than 16% of respondents considered them of great importance to the on-going success of the small business. This finding again, reinforces the lack of IT long- and short-term planning within these SMEs.

An examination of the figures in Table 3, suggests that most SME's knowledge of, and skills in, IT are at best passable. This finding highlights the tendency that most small businesses have to rely on third party hardware and software suppliers to provide expertise in IT use and management. This suggests a preoccupation by SMEs on important operational business matters rather than the acquisition of a sophisticated knowledge and use of IT, due to lack of in-house resources and reliance on third-party suppliers as a de facto IT department. This reliance may, in turn, influence or be influenced by the lack of SME emphasis on long- and short-term IT planning.

11.7. Conclusion

Most advocates of EDI in small business tend to suggest that the benefits of EDI to the small business manager include:

- improving the bottom line,
- working faster and better within the organization,
- gaining strategic advantage,
- strengthening customer relations, and
- preparing for the future in business.

However, studies carried out by Rotch (1987), Reynolds et al. (1994), Delvecchio (1994), and supported by the current study would suggest that these factors are not necessarily those upon which small business managers base their decisions. It would seem that the more tangible measures of performance, cost, benefits and ease of use dominate SME IT evaluation criteria. Long and short-term planning activities (which rely heavily on less tangible information and inputs) are of little importance to these SMEs.

This in turn would seem to suggest that many of the assumptions on which the benefits of EDI are based (gaining strategic advantage; preparing for the future in business) are far more relevant to a large business that to an SME.

If EDI is to be applicable to SMEs, designers and advocates alike may need to examine the nature of SMEs far more closely, especially with regard to their planning environments. They need to realise that many are product rather than customer based, that most small businesses are interested in maintaining stability of operations rather than attempting to increase market share and that most need to maintain a position of independence from larger organizations they may interact with.

The current thrust of theory about EDI use in SMEs tends to push the idea of the use of IT planning processes which result in the SME gaining a strategic edge over competitors and improving the bottom line through changes to the business structure and function. The current study suggests that these factors have little importance for most small business managers.

11.8. References

Alter, S.: 1996, *Information Systems: A Management Perspective*, Benjamin/Cummings, Menlo Park.

Anson, R.: 1995, The shape of future EDI, *Lan Magazine*, May, 77-80

Barker, P.: 1995, Fear, resistance holding back electronic commerce, *Computing Canada*, 21(13), 36.

Barnett, R. R. and Mackness, J. R.: 1983, An action research study of small firm, *Management Journal of Applied System*, 10, 63-83.

Britt, P.: 1995, EDI/EFT moves forward, *America's Community Banker*, 4(8), 7-8.

Buchanan, L.: 1995, The business outlook, *CIO Webmaster Supplement*, 52-57.

Brigham, E. F. and Smith, K. V.: 1967, The cost of capital to the small firm, *The Engineering Economist*, 13(1), 1-26

Chatfield, A. T. and Alston, M.: 1997, Small and medium enterprises in electronic commerce: A case study of barriers to financial EDI adoption, *Proceedings 5th European Conference on Information Systems*, Cork, Ireland, June, pp. 1219-1233.

Chen, J. C.: 1993, The impact of microcomputers on small businesses: England 10 years later, *Journal of Small Business Management*, 31(3), 96-102.

Cochran, A. B.: 1981, Small business mortality rates: A review of the literature, *Journal of Small Business Management*, 19(4), 50-59.

Cragg, P. B. and King, M.: 1993, Small firm computing: Motivators and inhibitors, *MIS Quarterly*, 17(1), 47-60.

Delone, W. H.: 1988, Determinants for success for computer usage in small business, *MIS Quarterly*, 51-61.

DelVecchio, M.: 1994, Retooling the staff along with the system, *Bests Review*, 94(11), 82-83.

Doukidis, G. I., Smithson, S. and Naoum, G.: 1992, Information systems management in Greece: Issues and perceptions, *Journal of Strategic Information Systems*, 1, 139-148.

EDI World Institute: 1995, *The WHY EDI Guide for Small and Medium-Sized Enterprises*, EDI World Institute, Canada.

Evans-Correia, K.: 1994, New company lets small suppliers in on EDI, *Purchasing*, 116(4), 76.

Fallon, J.: 1988, GM Europe blaze EDI trail: Will link 200 suppliers in seven countries, *MIS Week*, 19 December.

Harvey, D.: 1992, A discussion of the organizational impacts of EDI, *Proceedings 3rd Australian Conference on Information Systems*, Wollongong, Australia, pp. 609-620.

Higgins, K. J.: 1995, The Internet beckons, *EDI Information Week*, 2 October, 66-70.

Hinge, K. C.: 1989, *Electronic Data Interchange: From Understanding to Implementation*, American Management Association, New York.

Holzinger, A. G. and Hotch, R.: 1993, Small firms usage patterns, *Nations Business*, 81(8), 39-42.

Huttig, J. W.: 1994, Big lessons for small business, *Secured Lender*, 50(5), 44-49.

Kavan, B. C. and Van Over, D.: 1990, Electronic Data Interchange: A research agenda, *Proceedings 23rd Annual Hawaii International Conference on Systems Science*, pp. 192-197.

Khan, E. H. and Khan, G. M.: 1992, Microcomputers and small businesses, *Bahrain Industrial Management and Data Systems*, 92(6), 24-28.

MacGregor, R. C. and Cocks, R. S.: 1994, Computer usage and satisfaction in the Australian veterinary industry, *Australian Veterinary Practitioner*, 25(1), 43-48.

MacGregor, R. C. and Bunker, D. J.: 1998, The effect of criteria used in the acquisition of computer technology on the ongoing success with information technology, *Small Business*, forthcoming

Mackay, D.: 1992, The contribution of EDI to the structural change of the Australian automotive industry, *Proceedings 3rd Australian Conference on Information Systems*, Wollongong, Australia, pp. 633-652.

Meredith, G. G.: 1994, *Small Business Management in Australia*, 4th edn, McGraw Hill.

Neergaard, P.: 1992, Microcomputers in small and medium sized companies: Benefits achieved and problems encountered, *Proceedings 3rd Australian Conference on Information Systems*, Wollongong, Australia, pp. 575-604.

Pletsch, A.: 1994, Study showing EDI acceptance level on the rise, *Computing Canada*, 20(19), 13.

Reynolds, W., Savage, W. and Williams, A.: 1994, *Your Own Business: A Practical Guide to Success*, ITP.

Rockart, J. F. and Short, J. E.: 1989, IT in the 1990's: Managing organizational interdependence, *Sloan Management Review*, 30(2), 7-17.

Rotch, W.: 1967, *Management of Small Enterprises: Cases and Readings*, University of Virginia Press.

Roy Morgan Research: 1995, *Link Telecommunications Survey Carried Among 500 Small Business Across Australia*, Roy Morgan Research,

Sehr, B.: 1989, Levi Strauss strengthens customer ties with electronic data interchange: Levilink network carries order and shipment information, *Computerworld*, 30, January.

Swanson, E. B.: 1988, *Information Systems Implementation*, Homewood, IL.

Tsai, T. C., Richards, T. C. and Kappelman, L. A.: 1995, Electronic data interchange: Guidelines for development, implementation and use, *Association for Information Systems 1st Conference*, Pittsburgh, August, pp. 463-465.

Tuunainen, V. K. and Saarinen, T.: 1997, EDI and Internet-EDI: Opportunities of effective integration for small business, *Proceedings of 5th European Conference on Information Systems*, Cork, Ireland, June, pp. 164-177.

Udo, G. J. and Pickett, G. C.: 1994, EDI conversion mandate: The big problem for small businesses, *Industrial Management*, 36(2), 6-9.

Walker E.W.: 1975, Investment and Capital Structure Decision Making in Small Business in Walker E.W. (ed.) The Dynamic Small Firm: Selected Readings Austin Press, Texas

Wood, J. G. and Nosek, J. T.: 1994, Discrimination of structure and technology in a group support system: The role of process complexity, *International Conference on Information Systems*, Vancouver, pp. 187-199.

Yap, C. S., Soh, C. P. P. and Raman, K. S.: 1992, Information systems success factors in small business, *International Journal of Management Science*, 20, 597-609.

Zack, M. H.: 1994, The state of EDI in the US housewares manufacturing industry, *Journal of Systems Management*, 45(12), 6-10.

CHAPTER 12

Paying for Goods and Services in the Information Age

Implications for Electronic Commerce

BOON-CHYE LEE
University of Wollongong

12.1. Introduction

In the last decade, the Internet has grown exponentially in terms of the numbers of both users and applications. Until just a few years ago, however, there prevailed among users a widespread informal understanding that frowned upon any commercial material on the "Net". Violators of this code of conduct were routinely cowed into submission by a chorus of indignant email messages. Companies and individuals have since begun to realise the seemingly endless commercial possibilities of the Internet and to exploit them. Commercial transactions initiated, and often completed, on the Internet are now a commonplace.

.   Initially, although the agreements to buy and sell were entered into via the Internet, payment tended to be arranged off the Internet by more conventional means; for example, by cheque or credit card details provided by mail, fax or telephone. The main reason for using conventional means of payment was the lack of security of the Internet as a channel for communicating such sensitive information. This was clearly unsatisfactory because, among other things, it necessitated an additional step to be taken via a different medium of communication before transactions could be completed.

Partly in response to this deficiency, much effort and resources have been put into the development of secure protocols for such communications, as well as alternative means of payment that could be made on the Internet. At the same time, other developments that have taken place more or less independently - in particular, in stored-value cards and smart card technology - also offer solutions to the problem of secure payment on the Internet. These developments have the potential to spur the growth of electronic commerce and, in doing so, transform the way in which business is transacted. This chapter is an overview of the major non-currency methods of payment and the likely impact they will have on electronic commerce. As the emphasis is on broad trends, we will not be taking a detailed look at the features of the different payment methods; rather we will focus on the key characteristics that make them more or less likely to be used in Internet transactions.

The chapter is structured as follows. In the following section we review alternative payment methods in existence, focusing in particular on those with actual and potential applications to Internet commerce. Section 3 is a survey of some recent trends in the use of non-currency payment methods in the developed countries, and what they imply for electronic commerce. Section 4 then looks at the implications of the foregoing for electronic commerce. We summarize in Section 5.

12.2. Payment Methods

The basic model of a payment method envisages the transfer of value from the payer to the payee without the involvement of intermediaries. This may be called the "direct transfer" method of making payments (Ledingham 1996). In the case of currency (notes and coin), the transfer takes the form of currency being handed from the payer directly to the payee.

When money is represented by physical objects, the storage and transfer of monetary value involves a logistical as well as a security problem. The costs of holding and transferring money with an adequate level of security would constitute a significant proportion of the costs of conducting any transaction paid for with money, and it is not difficult to see why physical forms of money have evolved down the ages towards progressively less cumbersome forms.

Variations on the method of direct transfer involve some other form of value which substitutes for currency and which is accepted as payment for a range of goods and/or services. This range may in fact be quite limited, as in the case of telephone cards and travel passes; or it may be virtually as wide as that for currency, as with some "stored value cards" (SVCs) whose acceptability is limited only by the availability of merchants with the appropriate card-reading devices. The substitute value is purchased from an issuer who assumes the responsibility for redeeming it.

A less direct means of effecting payment involves at least one financial intermediary who manages an account on behalf of the customer (the payer or payee in a transaction). This may be termed the "account transfer" system of making payments (Ledingham 1996). When people's holdings of money are stored in bank deposit accounts, the holding costs are correspondingly reduced - money having taken the form of an entry in the bank's records. The cost of transferring that value has also fallen; all that is required is a debit of the payer's account balance and a corresponding credit of the payee's account balance. The instructions to effect the transfer may vary - e.g., the writing of a cheque, which is an instruction to the payer's bank authorising the transfer to the payee's account; a telex or fax instruction; or some other form of communication. Transfer of value therefore relies on a transfer of information from the payer to the financial intermediary. When a payer wishes to make a payment to another party, the payer sends an instruction to his or her financial intermediary authorising the release of a specified amount of value from the payer's account in favor of the payee's account. The payer's financial intermediary, of course, is not necessarily the same as the payee's, in which case another set of instructions (between financial intermediaries) is required.

From the payer's point of view, one important difference between direct transfer and account transfer payment systems is the possibility of anonymity in the former. Direct transfer payment methods are good for immediate value, and there is no further requirement to link the payment with an individual or company. This is not the case with account transfer systems, where the availability of funds in the account has to be verified before payment can be authorized, and indeed the necessity for an online link between the merchant and financial institution adds to the cost of such transactions, and is a significant impediment to using such payment methods to settle low-value transactions. In a variety of situations, anonymity may be desired by the payer. On the other hand, account transfer systems provide proof of payment and a record of transactions, features that may appeal to people in other situations.

The availability of a range of payment methods therefore serves a variety of needs. There is no suggestion that different payment methods cannot coexist.[1] However, what we are likely to see is the continuing evolution of payment methods towards less costly, more efficient ways of effecting payments some of which are more suited to particular situations than others. As a result of this process, consumers today are faced with a wider range of choices than has been the case before. Apart from currency and cheques, the choices include credit cards, debit cards, and stored-value cards. In addition, most of these methods are accessible by telephone banking and Internet banking. We focus our attention on the applicability of these methods to Internet commerce.

12.2.1. CHEQUES

In essence, a cheque is an instruction from an account holder to his or her financial institution authorising payment to a third party. While cheques are overwhelmingly of the physical variety, some schemes involve electronic cheques comprising an email instruction with an electronic signature attached. Cheques, however, do not play a significant part in Internet commerce, and are unlikely to do so. In the range of physical-world transactions for which they have traditionally been used, alternative payment methods (mainly card-based methods) are proving more efficient and are increasingly being preferred over cheques (see Section 3). It is likely that this preference will extend to Internet transactions.

12.2.2. CREDIT CARDS

The main impediment to the more widespread use of credit cards as a means of payment for Internet transactions has been the fear in many people's minds that such communications lack security. However, the major credit cards companies have been working cooperatively to develop a system, Secure Electronic Transactions (SET), which allows credit card details to be passed from buyer to merchant on the Internet. While it is still in the pilot stage, and is only one of many electronic payments protocols that have been proposed, the SET protocol has the great advantage of being able to ride on the reputations of the major credit card and software

---

[1] Note, however, that a prerequisite for the wide acceptance of any payment method is that it should be secure, and perceived as being secure.

companies, which are well known, and hence can act as a sort of stamp of approval for SET.[2] Credit cards seem likely to remain the principal means of making payments over the Internet for medium- to high-value transactions for some time yet, and card readers may well become a standard feature of personal computers in the future.

On the other hand, the relatively high cost of making credit card transactions means that this is not a suitable means of payment for low-value transactions. Table 1 in the Appendix gives an indication of the cost of alternative card-based payment methods. In addition, there is a lack of anonymity for people choosing this method.

12.2.3. DEBIT CARDS

Debit cards such as those used at electronic funds transfer at point of sale (EFTPOS) terminals offer another potential means of making payment on the Internet, using, for example, personal computers equipped with card readers. Like credit cards, however, debit cards are a relatively high-cost means of payment because of the need to authenticate the payment instruction. As with credit cards, debit cards also do not offer users anonymity.

12.2.4. ELECTRONIC MONEY

The term "electronic money" denotes digitally-encoded currency balances which represent floating claims on a bank or other issuer. Consumers purchase the claims with conventional money and exchange them for goods and services with merchants who are willing to accept them as payment.

In the search for more efficient means of effecting transactions, the evolution of electronic forms of money is in the forefront of current developments. Electronic money, indeed, is just the latest stage in an evolutionary process towards more efficient media of exchange that began thousands of years ago when people first began using money as an improvement on barter arrangements in trade. It also represents a significant shift from concrete, more tangible forms of money, to a much more abstract medium consisting in its essence of an instruction. In what has come to be known as the Information Age, money has itself become an aspect of information.

Electronic money takes two forms. In the first, it is typically stored on a "stored-value card" (SVC) (also known as a prepaid card or electronic purse); in the second, known as "network money", it is software-based and is stored in the hard disk of a computer.

Stored-value cards are already well established in many countries, particularly in Europe, and they are expected to become even more widely used. There were an estimated 440 million in circulation worldwide in 1994[3], 600 million in 1995[4]; the majority of these were telephone cards. It has been predicted that there will be 3.8

---

[2] The SET protocol is supported by Visa and MasterCard, two leading credit card companies, as well as by a number of leading companies in Internet commerce, including Microsoft, IBM, and Netscape.
[3] FSI (1996).
[4] *Asiaweek* (1995).

billion SVCs in use around the world by the turn of the century[5], a growth rate of more than 40 per cent per annum over the period. Network money is less established, but a number of systems are offered by different companies.

In both forms of electronic money, transfer of value can take place with or without intermediaries, depending on the system. That is, electronic money is not necessarily linked to any particular account, and hence anonymity is possible. This is an important feature of electronic money systems. Furthermore, some systems allow user-to-user transfers of value, in much the same way that cash can be passed from one individual to another without having to go through a third party, and without the need for one of the individuals to be a merchant, as is the case with credit card payments. Very small payment amounts are economically feasible and security is extremely good.[6] To the extent that electronic money offers anonymity, ease of use, and convenience, it is a substitute for currency — indeed, it may be argued, it is an improvement over currency because of the negligible storage and transportation costs associated with its use.

The extent and the speed with which electronic money is adopted for Internet payments will depend partly on how quickly people adopt SVCs in their everyday habits, since there will be flow-on aspects of that behavior on to the Internet. The growing popularity of card-based payment means (see next section) may be a precursor to wider acceptance of SVCs; note that SVCs may be regarded as a substitute for debit cards, although the latter are more advantageous and convenient to consumers. From Table 1, the cost-effectiveness of SVCs over alternative payment cards in relative terms is clear. Harper and Leslie (1995), from whom the figures are taken, note that although the estimated processing cost for SVCs is conservative, the marginal cost of using a stored-value card is at least 70 per cent less than the cheapest card-based alternative.

Table 1. Costs of alternative payment cards.

	Transaction Range	*Processing Cost*
Credit Cards	$50 - $1000	$0.80 - $2.50
Debit Cards	$20 - $100	$0.50 - $1.00
Stored-Value Cards	$1 - $20	$0.05 - $0.15

Source: Harper and Leslie (1995)

While SVCs are not currently linked to the Internet, the technology for that certainly exists. It is a simple matter for card-readers used for credit and debit cards to be modified to take SVCs as well. A PC equipped with such a card-reader could be used to connect to the Internet and payments made using an SVC.

In functional terms, the two forms of electronic money are identical. Each represents a means of effecting value transfers without the use of bank accounts. As well, it is not far-fetched to imagine the establishment of links between SVCs and

---

[5] *The Economist* (1996).

[6] At least one network money system "allows payment of amounts as low as one cent, and all payments are made with the security technology currently used by large financial institutions for international money transfers" (DigiCash, 1996).

network money so that value can be transferred from one medium to the other. For this reason network money and SVCs can be discussed under the common term electronic money. A summary of the characteristics of the main non-currency payment methods is given in Table 2.

Table 2. Characteristics of main payment methods.

Payment Method	Typical/Best Payment Size	Physical World or Internet Use?	Anonymity	Certainty of Transfer
Currency	Small to Medium	Physical	Yes	High
Cheques	Small to Large	Both	No	Medium
Credit Cards	Medium to Large	Both	No	High
Debit Cards	Medium	Both	No	High
SVCs	Very Small to Small	Both?	Yes	High
Network Money	Very Small to Large	Internet	Yes	Medium?

12.3. Recent Trends in the Use of Payment Methods

While our focus in this chapter is on payment methods that are applicable to Internet transactions, it is relevant to look at patterns in the use of payment methods in the physical world for what they tell us about people's preferences for different methods, and their readiness to adopt new methods. For example, although credit cards have been available since the early 1970s, they did not really become widespread as a means of payment until more than a decade later.

It remains the case that for low-value, everyday consumer purchases the predominant means of payment is currency. Humphrey (1995) reports, for example, that cash transactions as a proportion of the total volume of all transactions in the U.S. has been estimated at 83 per cent; the corresponding estimates for Germany, the Netherlands, and the UK were 86 per cent, 78 per cent, and 90 per cent respectively. Historically, the value of currency on issue in most countries has increased at a rate roughly equal to that of nominal income (see Table 3 for figures for some countries for the period 1991-95).

In the case of non-cash payments, there is an evident trend towards electronic means of effecting payments. While in general the industrialized countries have advanced furthest down this path, they differ markedly from each other in their relative use of the various payment methods (see Tables 4 and 5). However, two trends are broadly discernible. The first is the decline in the use of cheques, measured in terms of both volume and value of transactions. This reflects the relative inefficiency of cheques as a means of transmitting payment instructions.

Second, in terms of volume of transactions, card payments have increased in importance, in some cases (e.g., in Canada, the Netherlands, Switzerland, and the United Kingdom) quite dramatically. However, in terms of value of transactions, the trend is not as pronounced, reflecting the fact that card payments are a predominantly retail payment method.

Table 3. Notes and coin in circulation as % of GDP, selected countries.

	1991	1992	1993	1994	1995
Australia	3.6	3.8	3.9	4.0	4.0
Belgium	6.2	5.9	6.0	5.2	5.3
Canada	3.1	3.3	3.4	3.4	3.4
France	3.7	3.6	3.5	3.4	3.7
Germany	6.0	6.5	6.7	6.8	6.9
Italy	5.4	5.7	5.8	5.9	5.5
Japan	9.4	9.0	9.5	9.7	10.4
Netherlands	6.8	6.5	6.5	6.3	6.0
Sweden	5.3	5.1	5.3	5.0	4.7
Switzerland	8.0	8.0	7.9	7.9	7.7
UK	2.7	2.9	2.8	2.8	2.8
USA	4.6	4.8	5.0	5.2	5.2

Sources: BIS (1996), APSC (1995)

Table 4. Relative importance of cashless payment methods, selected industrialized countries (% of total volume of cashless transactions).

Country	Method	1991	1992	1993	1994	1995
Belgium	Cheques	21.6	18.8	16.0	11.7	10.6
	Cards	13.3	15.6	16.5	18.0	19.7
	Credit transfers	57.0	56.9	58.5	60.9	60.2
	Direct debits	8.2	8.8	9.0	9.4	9.5
Canada	Cheques	64.8	62.4	58.7	52.8	46.9
	Cards	27.8	28.9	31.1	35.3	40.0
	Credit transfers	3.9	4.4	5.2	6.4	7.3
	Direct debits	3.5	4.3	5.0	5.5	5.8
France	Cheques	52.2	50.6	49.1	46.9	44.8
	Cards	14.5	15.0	15.7	16.3	17.3
	Credit transfers	15.2	15.4	15.4	15.7	16.0
	Direct debits	9.3	10.2	10.6	11.7	12.2
Germany	Cheques	9.6	8.8	8.1	7.9	7.0
	Cards	1.8	2.1	2.6	3.1	3.6
	Credit transfers	51.3	49.8	45.6	48.7	49.5
	Direct debits	37.3	39.3	43.7	40.3	39.9
Italy	Cheques	41.6	40.0	37.2	34.0	32.8
	Cards	3.1	3.7	4.1	5.2	6.6
	Credit transfers	40.9	42.1	44.6	46.8	45.9
	Direct debits	3.8	4.1	4.4	4.7	5.4
Netherlands	Cheques	14.3	12.3	8.1	6.0	4.0
	Cards	1.8	2.6	4.1	7.9	13.6
	Credit transfers	61.3	61.3	66.4	64.2	60.6
	Direct debits	22.6	23.9	21.5	21.9	21.8
Switzerland	Cheques	5.4	4.4	3.3	2.6	2.0
	Cards	9.7	11.8	13.8	16.2	18.4
	Credit transfers	82.7	81.3	80.1	78.1	76.3
	Direct debits	2.3	2.5	2.8	3.1	3.3
UK	Cheques	48.5	45.4	43.0	40.2	36.7
	Cards	16.4	18.8	21.0	23.3	25.9
	Credit transfers	20.9	20.6	20.4	20.1	19.7
	Direct debits	14.2	15.1	15.6	16.5	17.7

USA	Cheques	81.6	81.1	80.1	78.9	77.4
	Cards	16.0	16.2	16.9	18.0	19.1
	Credit transfers	1.6	1.8	1.9	2.1	2.3
	Direct debits	0.8	0.9	1.0	1.1	1.2

Source: BIS (1996)

Notes: (1) Card payments include payments by credit card and debit card; (2) credit transfers are those initiated by the payer in which paper-based and paperless funds are sent directly to the payee's account through the banking system without the payee's involvement; (3) direct debits are pre-authorized payments by which the payer gives the bank authority to debit an account; (4) the total for some countries may not sum to 100% because of other payment methods that are not included in the categories above.

Table 5. Relative importance of cashless payment methods, selected industrialized countries (% of total value of cashless transactions).

Country	Method	1991	1992	1993	1994	1995
Belgium	Cheques	5.4	6.2	5.4	4.6	4.3
	Cards	0.1	0.2	0.1	0.1	0.2
	Credit transfers	94.3	93.4	94.2	94.7	95.2
	Direct debits	0.2	0.2	0.3	0.5	0.3
Canada	Cheques	99.0	98.8	98.8	98.7	98.1
	Cards	0.3	0.3	0.3	0.3	0.5
	Credit transfers	0.6	0.7	0.7	0.7	1.1
	Direct debits	0.1	0.2	0.2	0.2	0.3
France	Cheques	7.3	6.4	4.6	4.4	4.7
	Cards	0.2	0.2	0.2	0.2	0.2
	Credit transfers	89.9	91.2	93.5	94.0	93.3
	Direct debits	0.7	0.6	0.7	0.8	0.6
Germany	Cheques	2.8	2.4	2.3	2.3	2.1
	Cards	0.02	0.02	0.02	0.02	0.03
	Credit transfers	95.4	95.5	95.7	95.7	95.8
	Direct debits	1.8	2.1	2.0	2.0	2.1
Italy	Cheques	9.1	7.1	5.4	4.5	4.5
	Cards	0.04	0.04	0.03	0.04	0.05
	Credit transfers	88.6	91.1	93.2	94.2	94.1
	Direct debits	0.3	0.2	0.2	0.2	0.2
Netherlands	Cheques	0.2	0.2	0.1	0.1	0.1
	Cards	0.0	0.0	0.0	0.1	0.2
	Credit transfers	98.4	98.6	98.8	98.7	98.6
	Direct debits	1.4	1.2	1.1	1.1	1.2
Switzerland	Cheques	0.2	0.1	0.1	0.1	0.1
	Cards	-	-	-	-	-
	Credit transfers	99.8	99.9	99.9	99.8	99.8
	Direct debits	-	-	-	0.1	0.1
UK	Cheques	16.1	11.6	9.4	7.6	5.3
	Cards	0.2	0.2	0.2	0.2	0.2
	Credit transfers	82.5	87.1	89.5	91.2	93.4
	Direct debits	1.2	1.1	1.0	1.0	1.0
USA	Cheques	13.7	13.1	12.6	12.2	11.9
	Cards	0.1	0.1	0.1	0.1	0.1
	Credit transfers	85.4	85.8	86.4	86.8	87.0
	Direct debits	0.8	1.0	0.9	0.9	0.9

Source: BIS (1996)

Interestingly, these developments have taken place against a background of more or less stable currency holdings as a percentage of GDP. While a number of industrialized countries (including Australia, Canada, Germany, Japan, and the United States) have seen an increase in the ratio of currency in circulation as a percentage of GDP between 1991 and 1995, some (including Belgium, the Netherlands, Sweden, and Switzerland) have exhibited declines, while for still others (France, Italy, and the United Kingdom) the ratio has been more stable. The rise in currency holdings in some countries during this period, it may be noted, may be due partly to the general fall in inflation rates and nominal interest rates, and a corresponding decline in the opportunity cost of holding currency. Overall, these developments indicate that, at least during the period surveyed, and somewhat contrary to predictions of a move to a "cashless economy", the transition to card-based means of payment has taken place at the expense of cheque payments rather than currency. As SVCs become more widely used, however, it is expected that this will take place at the expense of currency use.

12.4. Implications for Electronic Commerce

Of the payment methods available and currently in various stages of development, the ones most likely to impact on electronic commerce are credit cards and the various forms of electronic money. A major obstacle to more rapid development of Internet commerce has been consumer concerns about the security of information transmitted over open network lines. However, the development of common secure transfer protocols for credit card and other sensitive information is currently proceeding apace. Once common standards have been developed, tested, agreed to and implemented, consumers are likely to have fewer objections to using their credit cards for payments over the Internet. This, together with their familiarity with this medium of payment, provide strong indications that credit cards will continue to be the most common payment method for medium- and large-value transactions.

However, credit card payments are inefficient and uneconomical for small transaction amounts. The development of electronic money forms that are capable of carrying out extremely small payment amounts economically and efficiently is therefore an important innovation. Its importance lies in the fact that it has the potential not just to cater to the requirements of this end of the market but, more significantly, to bring about fundamental changes in the way goods and information are marketed and transacted, and in the laws governing these activities, particularly in the area of copyrights.

What appears to be an emerging trend is the unbundling of products such as music and information. This may be indicative of a growing demand on the part of consumers to pick and choose only those parts of previously bundled products like newspapers, magazines, research journals, and compact disks that they want. The fact that the delivery of products of this nature can be effected over the Internet, thereby obviating the need for costly physical packaging (paper, ink, binding, plastic), means that the marginal cost of delivering each article or song will be driven down towards zero. The development of electronic money and its ability to process micropayments at low cost would be well placed to cater to the requirements of the emerging market in microtransactions. Perhaps more to the point, the ability to make micropayments means that microtransactions are now economically feasible.

These developments could spur changes in the existing distribution system and fee structure for such products (Tanaka, 1996). For example, Cox (1994) describes a new paradigm in marketing and distribution, known as "superdistribution", which is based on the fact that although monitoring the copying of electronic goods is impossible, it is "trivially" easy to monitor their usage. The revenue stream of a vendor using superdistribution is based not on the number of copies that are made of its product but on the number of times its product is used. There is then every incentive for vendors to make their products freely available and then to charge on a pay-per-use basis.

In fact, as Choi et al. (1997, chap. 11) argue, there is an economic impulse driving the demand for microtransactions and micropayments which is based on the inability of consumers on the Internet to assess the quality of vendors' products. This is particularly so in the case of the vast majority of Internet vendors who do not have a reputation to trade on. To illustrate this argument, consider the case of a subscription for a bundled product, e.g., a magazine subscription. If the vendor has an established reputation for quality, this in itself may be a sufficient guarantee of quality. If not, however, a subscription would mean that the consumer is required to commit to a bundle of products of uncertain quality. There would not be many customers who are prepared to make such a commitment.

One mechanism to resolve this problem is to unbundle the magazine and allow consumers to purchase individual articles. Because the commitment required of the consumer is extremely short-term in nature and minimal in terms of price, there would be much less reluctance on the part of consumers to try out the vendor's products. If the quality does not meet the consumers' expectations, they will be reluctant to make further purchases. The mechanism therefore also provides an incentive for the vendor to strive for quality. What makes this mechanism possible, however, is the availability of a payment method that is able to make very small payment amounts economically.

12.5. Summary

The development of widely acceptable secure payment methods on the Internet is proceeding apace. A common standard has been formulated for the major credit cards, and this will drive the growth in Internet commerce especially in medium- to high-value transactions.

Important though these developments are, however, it is the development of payment methods that can handle low-value transfers economically that potentially will have the greatest impact. This is because these methods, which have been available for some time, make possible a whole range of microtransactions that were not feasible before. This aspect of Internet commerce has the potential to completely change the way in which transactions are marketed and carried out.

The drive towards micropayments and microtransactions has an economic rationale: the resolution of the problem of uncertain quality that is endemic on the

Internet. In allowing consumers to "try out" unbundled parts of what would previously have been bundled products, microtransactions actually enhance both consumer and producer welfare by making possible transactions which would not otherwise be completed.

12.6. References

Asiaweek: 1995, The card that could rule our lives, *Asiaweek*, 3 November, pp. 52-59.

Australian Payments System Council (APSC), *Annual Report*, various years.

Bank for International Settlements (BIS): 1996, *Statistics on Payment Systems in the Group of Ten Countries*, December.

Choi, S-Y., Stahl. D. O. and Whinston, A. B.: 1997, *The Economics of Electronic Commerce*, Macmillan.

Cox, B.: 1994, Superdistribution, *Wired*, September.

DigiCash: 1996, Press release, 24 October.

Economist: 1996, Going for Olympic gold cards, *The Economist*, 30 March.

Financial System Inquiry (FSI): 1996, Inquiry into the Australian financial system, *Discussion Paper*, December.

Harper, I. R. and Leslie, P.: 1995, Electronic payments systems and their economic implications, *Policy*, Autumn, 23-28.

Humphrey, D. B.: 1995, Payment systems: Principles, practice, and improvements, *World Bank Technical Paper No. 260*, The World Bank, Washington, DC.

Ledingham, P.: 1996, The policy implications of electronic payments, Paper presentation, *Consumer Payment Systems Conference*, May, Auckland.

Tanaka, T.: 1996, Possible economic consequences of digital cash, *First Monday*, 1(2), 5 August.

CHAPTER 13

Channel Integration

A New Focus in Electronic Banking

KRISTEEN GLEASON AND DAN HEIMANN
Applied Communications, Inc.[1]

13.1. Electronic Banking

Electronic banking, remote banking, home banking—whatever term you prefer, each means different things to different people. A withdrawal at an automated teller machine (ATM) may be considered electronic banking by some, others may consider a telephone call to a financial institution's call center as electronic banking. Still others view electronic banking on a much more complex scale and see it as the ability to access and initiate a wide selection of financial services using a variety of technologies such as ATMs, the telephone, self-service kiosks, and personal computers. Depending on where you bank and in what part of the world you live, electronic banking may assume a different form, combining a variety of services and access devices.

Customers of financial institutions in the United States may choose to browse the bank's service offerings and pay their bills over the Internet, while customers in Japan may call a bank's call center to pay their bills. Customers of Brazilian banks expect their ATMs to dispense personal checks that are then used as negotiable items. In the United Kingdom, bank customers are being introduced to self-service kiosks that can be used to cash checks. In the Netherlands, where ATM "smart" cards are equipped with microchips that store customer and bank information, checking accounts are almost unheard of. Dutch customers use their smartcards to withdraw funds, transfer between accounts and pay bills, all at the ATM. Today, customers all over the world expect to access their banking services in a wide variety of manners using a broad choice of delivery technologies.

---

[1] Applied Communications, Inc. (ACI) is a subsidiary of Transaction System Architects, Inc. (TSA), and has developed a transaction processing engine called BASE24 which is deployed in more than 600 financial institutions and retail companies in more than 69 countries worldwide. BASE24 incorporates message-oriented middleware with a variety of fully integrated transaction processing applications including teller, ATM, POS, smartcard, and remote banking.

To the financial institution, remote banking has evolved to encompass many forms of direct customer access to an increasing array of financial products and services. These can be as simple as requesting an account balance or paying a bill, or as complex as applying for credit or initiating a stock trade. To meet the needs of particular market segments and to differentiate themselves from their competitors, financial institutions have access to a variety of technologies that can be used to offer electronic banking services to their customers. Access devices include everything from ATMs and self-service kiosks to telephones and personal computers. Delivery channels may include ATM networks, web servers, and call center systems, as well as interfaces to third-party service providers who may provide credit card authorization, Internet access, brokerage services, or bill presentment and remittance services.

The challenge financial institutions face today is to structure their electronic banking product to provide high levels of service and information integrity while accommodating a multitude of access devices and delivery channels (Figure 1). This can be difficult, given the vast selection of service "solutions" available in today's market. Part of the challenge is that the information and services customers want to access reside on a wide variety of applications and systems, some maintained internally and others outsourced to third parties. Compounding the challenge, financial institutions must almost consult a crystal ball to look beyond the needs of today's customers, and anticipate the customers' future requirements. Electronic banking solutions must be designed today with a high degree of flexibility in order to be able to meet the ever changing and diverse needs of tomorrow's customers.

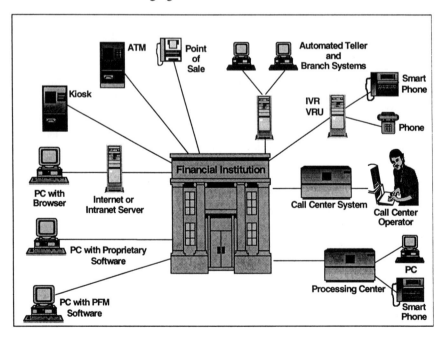

Figure 1. Financial services delivery channels.

13.2. Electronic Banking: Creating the Ideal Solution

Depending on local market competition and available resources, financial institutions have initiated a variety of approaches when implementing electronic banking services. Some have adopted a wait-and-see attitude, allowing other institutions to make the initial investment and expend the resources required to test the market. In this case, the financial institution may plan to enter the market once successful, proven remote banking solutions emerge.

Other financial institutions have decided on a phased-in approach. The first step is usually to bring a product to market as quickly as possible in order to meet the immediate demand and to protect its customer base against aggressive competitors. Here, the financial institution may initially offer a basic remote banking service package providing bill payment services and access to checking and savings information via telephone and/or PC. At a later date, they may decide to upgrade and expand electronic banking functionality and access methods as market demand dictates.

Some financial institutions have taken the shotgun approach to remote banking. With the broad range of home banking solutions available, these institutions have decided to implement a variety of applications. Here, the strategy is to make sure customers have enough choices at "their" financial institution, so they have no reason to move to the competition.

Still others have implemented a comprehensive, high-capability remote banking strategy. In this approach, the institution provides both retail and commercial customers remote access to information and services on checking, savings, lending, credit, and investment products. The customer is provided entry via a wide range of access devices and a variety of channels, including the Internet. The electronic banking market has evolved rapidly with new technologies, services and service providers entering the market on a regular basis. As financial institutions implement these new technologies and services, the job of integrating them into a comprehensive, long-term electronic banking solution becomes more challenging.

13.3. Comprehensive Solutions

No matter what initial approach is taken, most institutions would agree that long term, electronic banking service offerings must be comprehensive, providing the customer access to a broad range of information and services using a variety of access devices. At the same time, the service must encompass those elements of the electronic banking offering to which loyal customers have become accustomed. The ultimate vision of remote banking should include most, if not all, of the following attributes:

- *Support for a wide variety of access devices and delivery channels, including the Internet.* The advent of electronic banking has blurred the lines between access devices and services they support. Transactions once supported only by a teller or ATM are now available at self-service kiosks. Transactions that have traditionally been available through telephone banking systems are now supported in PC. The look and feel of accessing banking information by PC is now being duplicated by Web-enabled ATMs that include browser technology. As a result, financial institutions must be prepared to support a wide range of services over multiple access devices and delivery channels.

- *Support for proprietary and/or commercial Personal Financial Management (PFM) software such as Intuit's Quicken, MECA's Managing Your Money or Microsoft Money.* Although these packages support the export and import of financial data from electronic banking services, avid users of PFM software are religious about keeping financial records in sync. New releases of software and the latest electronic banking services support an automatic download of data from the bank site to the records retained in PFM software. This is an important feature for PFM users who represent a relatively small percentage of electronic banking customers overall, however, they tend to be the more highly educated, higher income customers the financial institution most wants to retain.

- *24-hour/7-day-a-week service availability.* By nature of the service, Internet users expect to access information anytime of the night or day. Financial institutions which offer electronic banking services via the Internet should expect their customers to attempt to access bank information and services at any time. This can prove difficult for financial institutions that still depend on a few hours of downtime each night to refresh account and balance information. 24-hour availability is a must for electronic banking.

- *Real-time access to current and accurate customer account and financial information.* Providing the customer with access to current balance and account information is important. Given the diverse options customers have for accessing account information, they expect that a transfer from a savings account to a demand or current account which was initiated through PC banking should be available at the ATM without the delay of overnight posting.

- *Ability to scale the offering as subscribers and transaction volumes increase.* Financial institutions worldwide are placing greater emphasis on alternate methods of service delivery in an attempt to lessen customer dependence on more expensive branch-based operations. As new delivery channels are added, the average number of times customers access their account information each month increases. When developing a long-term strategy for electronic banking, financial institutions must structure the system architecture in a way that allows it to be scaled to support higher and higher transaction volumes.

- *Incorporation of existing delivery channels such as ATM, point of sale (POS), and teller, so that the customer view of account information is consistent across all channels.* Over the years, as financial institutions have grown their account base, added major new services, and acquired other financial institutions, the number of processing platforms required to support these customers and services has grown. Typically, there is a one-to-one ratio between an access point and the system that supports it. For instance, teller stations are supported by the teller transaction processing platform, ATMs are supported by an ATM system, etc. If a customer initiates a transaction through the teller, that transaction is usually not immediately reflected in the account balance. If the customer went on to make a withdrawal at the ATM, it is likely that the balance at the ATM would differ from the balance received from the teller. A comprehensive electronic banking solution will support the integration of these systems so that customers are able to access the same information regardless of the device used to access the information.

- *Flexibility to add new services and delivery technologies as customers demand.* Main frame legacy systems are complex systems designed to maintain large databases of information. Adding new services or access points via new delivery technologies to legacy systems can be a lengthy and expensive process. With new NT server technology, financial institutions are able to incorporate a higher degree of flexibility to their processing systems. Servers interact with larger main frame processing systems using application programming interfaces (APIs) which send messages to the mainframe in a programming language it can understand. To ensure a high level of flexibility to add new services, a financial institution's processing systems must support a variety of APIs.

- *High degree of transaction and data integrity.* Because electronic banking transactions can be initiated from a variety of devices and processed on any of many processing systems, it is important that transaction requests and the data supplied in response be treated with a high degree of integrity. Every transaction must be tracked as it is routed through the system to ensure that each request is handled through resolution. Because of the variety of technologies required to process transactions over the Internet, it is possible for one link or another to go down, before a total transaction can be processed. For instance, if a customer requests a transfer from one account to another and only the debit from one account is processed when the modem link goes down, the debit must be reversed so that the customer can re-enter the request when the system is again available.

- *Infrastructure that leverages existing investment in legacy systems.* Financial institutions have invested millions of dollars in their existing legacy systems. It would be impossible and impractical to replace these systems with newer, more flexible operating systems. To leverage the use of these existing systems, new electronic banking applications must incorporate the traditional operating systems and technology currently in place.

- *Flexibility to add new services and delivery technologies as customers demand.* Flexibility in today's market is achieved through open systems which support a variety of interface standards. Without this level of flexibility, adding new access devices and access to new services and information would be cost-prohibitive.

- *Flexibility to integrate service provider technologies with the technologies currently owned by the financial institution in order to offer a complete remote banking service package.* Most financial institutions maintain relationships with outside service providers who fulfill the need for services the financial institution is unable or unwilling to provide in-house. Electronic banking solutions must be designed to also support the incorporation of these systems.

- *A solution that allows the financial institution to differentiate itself and build customer loyalty.* Flexibility to add new services as the market demands, transaction processing integrity that translates into customer confidence, 24-hour availability and more contribute to the financial institution's ability to differentiate its product in the marketplace.

13.4. Deployment Considerations

Meeting the objectives outlined above is becoming an increasingly complicated and costly task that can hamper a financial institution's quick entry to market. In addition to acquiring new delivery technologies, integrating them into existing financial systems can require significant modification to existing systems. The following is a list of considerations that must be taken into account when planning to integrate new delivery technologies into existing operating systems:

- Existing systems must be enhanced to provide network connectivity necessary to support PCs, IVRs, the Internet, PFM software and other technologies that may be deployed.
- New application software may have to be developed to process requests and transactions from new access devices and delivery channels.
- Existing applications and systems may need to be modified to integrate solutions so that financial institution customers receive consistent information across existing and new access devices and delivery channels.
- Interfaces to external service providers must be developed to support the various customer products and services a financial institution chooses to outsource to third party providers.
- New application software may need to be purchased or built to provide complicated remote banking and bill payment services like warehousing future-dated bill payment transactions, maintaining and managing "payee" lists, authorizing funds availability, etc.
- Specific interface software must be built and/or maintained to support messaging formats required by particular service providers and delivery technologies.
- Existing systems and procedures may need to be modified to provide 24-hour availability, support high transaction volumes, and ensure integrity and security of the services.

Industry experts all agree that innovative remote banking efforts will require integration of new technologies into existing infrastructures and systems. These efforts will cost institutions a great deal in time, money, and resources. In fact, the resources required for the integration of a new technology may exceed the initial cost of the technology itself.

> **"A bank's ability to integrate its content with its navigation will be dependent on the current legacy systems. Upgrading these systems will require an investment that is several orders of magnitude greater than that required to create the front end."**
> -Boston Consulting Group, The Information Superhighway and Retail Banking

While the initial technology investment in electronic banking alone can be large, long-term operations and maintenance costs of interface and application software residing on multiple systems can also skyrocket. Without an integrated strategy that crosses all delivery channels, many institutions will suffer the brutal costs of maintaining an environment where multiple delivery devices must connect to multiple back-end systems using multiple interfaces. If all delivery channels do not utilize identical customer account information, customers will see a different view of their "current" account relationships depending upon the device or delivery channel used. This potentially serious product weakness would undermine customer confidence and acceptance of the service.

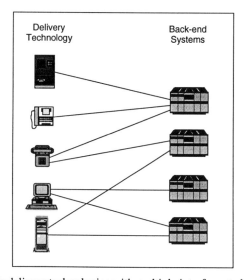

Figure 2. Multiple delivery technologies with multiple interfaces to back-end systems.

As technologies change and customers demand remote access to more products and services, it becomes increasingly hard for the financial institution to respond in a cost-effective manner. With each new delivery technology added, a new interface to the processing system must be established, making it even more difficult to ensure that consistent account information can be accessed across all delivery channels (Figure 2). Before long, this type of environment becomes unmanageable and cost prohibitive for the financial institution to maintain.

13.5. The Challenge of Integration

When financial institutions begin to analyze and develop plans to implement a long term system architecture to support electronic banking, they will be challenged to address the most complex and costly aspect of implementation - integrating new delivery devices and channels in a way that minimizes modifications to existing systems and does not require the development of new back-end systems.

Financial institutions faced a similar challenge in the past when integrating divergent ATM and POS devices manufactured by a variety of vendors. By adding a "transaction processing engine" between the access devices and the host systems, financial institutions have been able to integrate the new technology with existing systems.

A transaction processing engine combines the power of message-oriented middleware with a transaction processing system that is capable of authenticating, authorizing, and routing transactions to back-end legacy systems for processing and storage (Figure 3). Designed to support a standard messaging interface and a variety of host system interfaces, the addition of a transaction processing engine can simplify the integration of multiple access devices and channels with divergent legacy systems. System integration using this type of transaction processing technology has been successfully deployed in electronic funds transfer systems by financial institutions all over the world. This same type of configuration can be utilized just as successfully in electronic banking system implementations.

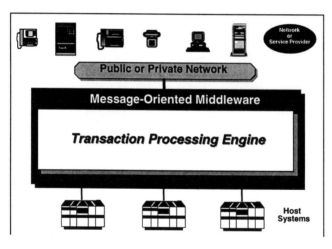

Figure 3. Integrating delivery technologies with a transaction processing engine.

One example of a transaction processing engine that has been utilized in electronic banking, ATM, teller, and POS deployments worldwide is BASE24, a suite of electronic transaction processing applications designed by ACI, based in Omaha, Nebraska. BASE24 applications have been implemented by more than 600 financial institutions in 69 countries, providing a bridge between diverse access technologies and multiple legacy systems.

13.6. A Proven Solution

Employing a transaction processing engine enables financial institutions to quickly and cost-effectively integrate and support new delivery technologies, such as PC software, Web servers, IVRs and others. As depicted in Figure 4, end-to-end electronic banking implementations consist of several components of disparate hardware and operating systems. Each component in the configuration plays a complementary role best suited to the strengths of that particular component.

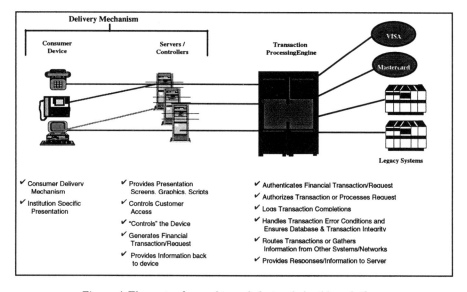

Figure 4. Elements of an end to end electronic banking platform.

Delivery technology consists of a combination of customer access devices and server/controllers. Today, financial institutions provide electronic banking services that support access via personal computers, telephones, ATMs, screenphones, and self-service kiosks. Devices planned for future inclusion in electronic banking programs include WebTV, or interactive television, and personal digital assistant or PDAs.

The second element of delivery technology is the server/controller such as an IVR or Web server which provides the presentation of screens or voice scripts to the customer as well as the corresponding data in response to information or service requests.

Information databases which contain customer bank records and transaction information reside on large mainframe computer systems, usually referred to as legacy systems. Some of these systems may be maintained within the bank and others may be maintained by an outside service provider that delivers processing services for the financial institution, such as a credit card processor or ATM network.

The transaction processing engine is positioned between the server/controllers and the legacy systems and drives customer authentication processes, provides real-time customer account, statement, and vendor information, and routes and authorizes financial and bill payment transactions generated by electronic banking devices. In effect, it acts as a high-performance, highly reliable, fault-tolerant server that processes financial transactions for delivery technologies of all types. Through standard interfaces to back-end systems, switch networks or third-party processors, the "engine" can also access other systems and networks for information and services that may not reside on the transaction processing system itself. It creates the cooperative computing environment that leverages existing systems to deliver a full set of electronic banking products and services through new delivery channels.

When the delivery channels need customer-specific information such as an account balance or statement information; or need to authorize a financial transaction such as a funds transfer or bill payment, they communicate the request to the processing engine. The engine can be designed to act as a stand-in processor for the host if the host is unavailable, or it may be designed to act in place of the host, maintaining a subset of customer data and information. The engine fulfills the request and/or authorizes and routes the financial transaction to the appropriate legacy system for processing. It then provides the requested information back to the delivery channels which communicate an appropriate response for the customer via the access device.

If delivery channels need to access data or services that do not reside on the processing platform, the engine can intelligently route requests to other systems, gather information from those systems and then forward responses to the delivery channel for presentation to the customer. In this way, host systems are modified to communicate only with the processing engine, and do not have to be programmed to interface with each individual server, controller, or access device. The processing engine simplifies the typically time-consuming and difficult task of developing and managing multiple interfaces and minimizes programming on the host systems protecting the financial institution's investment in these expensive and complex systems.

13.6.1. CONNECTIVITY

Enabling delivery technology to communicate to existing systems within the financial institution is an absolute requirement for the real-time processing of electronic banking transactions and inquiries. The types of devices and networks customers will use to access financial information and services will vary widely. The wider the variety of entry points, the greater the pressure on existing systems to support the telecommunications protocols necessary to connect with a wide range of networks. Modifying applications on existing systems to support the technical requirements of public networks (like the Internet), proprietary networks, card networks, in-house local area networks, and existing system networks can be costly and time-consuming.

The transaction processing engine is built on message-oriented middleware which supports all the protocols necessary to communicate with any delivery technology the financial institution chooses (see Figure 5). This important layer of middleware also supports communications with existing systems including demand deposit (current) systems, credit systems, loan systems, and others, to provide customers with the products and services they desire.

Whether the financial institution needs to create a cooperative computing environment with existing SNA, bisync or X.25 networks, or a network like the Internet that uses TCP/IP protocols, middleware solutions allow the institution to save time and development costs associated with building mission-critical, scaleable, and flexible networking capability.

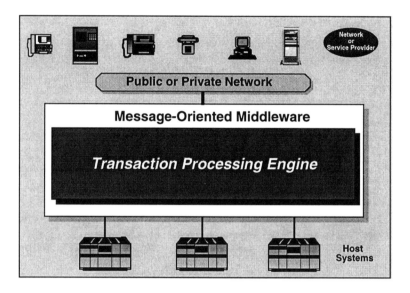

Figure 5. Transaction processing engine built on message-oriented middleware.

13.6.2. COMPREHENSIVE OPERATIONS AND MONITORING

This approach can provide a single point of monitoring and control across the entire network including connections to all forms of delivery mechanisms, back-end systems, third-party service providers, switch networks, and distributed processing systems. This single view of the overall service operation enables the financial institution to ensure that all delivery channels, network connections, and processing systems are operable.

Having a single point from which computer and network monitoring can be performed is crucial to providing the highest level of service required in today's competitive environment. Without this capability, it is possible that a PC banking customer may attempt to logon to a financial institution's remote banking service, and even though the server is operable, the customer cannot connect because the institution is unaware that its modem bank is down.

13.6.3. SUPPORT FOR OPEN SYSTEMS

A transaction processing engine designed to facilitate electronic banking applications will support a variety of messaging standards, enabling it to accept and process transactions from virtually any technology provided by any vendor or developed by the financial institution. To ensure the greater degree of compatibility in the financial services industry, the transaction processing engine should support the following:

- Delivery products based on common industry platforms such as UNIX, Windows NT, OS/2, DOS, Tandem NSK, and others,
- PC products like Microsoft's Money, Intuit's Quicken, or software authored by the financial institution or a third party,
- Service systems operated by third party information service providers,
- Industry standard Internet browsers and Web server technologies from a variety of vendors.

13.6.4. MISSION-CRITICAL FUNDAMENTALS

The financial services industry has long believed that mission-critical fundamentals are prerequisites in the deployment of electronic funds transfer systems. The same is true for electronic banking. Customers will expect reliable service where they want it and when they want it. A transaction processing engine should be developed to run on a fault-tolerant operating system, such as Tandem NSK (Non-stop Kernel).

This type of system is designed to deliver the following benefits demanded in a competitive financial services environment:

- 24-hour availability,
- Linear scalability of the platform to grow as the customer base and usage of services grow,
- Highest levels of transaction and data integrity, ensuring that transactions are not lost or processed incompletely,
- Fault-tolerance to isolate the impacts of system outages from the customer,
- High-performance transaction processing to ensure very quick response times,
- Ability to handle extremely large transaction volumes and high peak loads that will occur given the nature of the services being offered.

13.7. Benefits of the Transaction Processing Engine

Once the initial flurry of interest and implementations of new electronic banking technologies and services settles down, financial institutions will begin the process of incorporating the many diverse elements of their electronic banking services into a long-term system architecture. Developing a platform that supports electronic banking with reliability, flexibility and a high level of processing performance will be the primary objectives. The inclusion of a transaction processing engine that can authorize, route, and process financial transactions and requests generated by any electronic banking delivery technology will provide the following advantages:

- Reduce time to market and deployment costs by greatly reducing in-house software development - there is no longer a need to write multiple interfaces between access devices or delivery channels and each back-end system.
- Allow the integration of all forms of electronic banking (ATM, POS, teller, phone banking, PC banking, PFM software, Internet banking, and others), so that customers can access consistent information and services across all technologies.
- Support standard message interface that enables other vendor technologies (i.e., Voice Response Units, Web servers, etc.) to easily communicate with the transaction processing engine.
- Provide secure, reliable, high-performance financial transaction processing, 7 days a week, 24 hours a day, 365 days a year, as proven around the world in EFT networks.
- Provide the scalability required to respond to growing customer demand for remote banking and the flexibility to easily support new delivery technologies, financial products, and services as they become available.

13.7.1. INCORPORATION OF NEW TECHNOLOGIES

As new technologies and services become available, the transaction processing engine can enable a financial institution to easily incorporate new capabilities into an electronic banking service offering. It is expected that the next generation of personal computers expected on the market in late 1998 will include chipcard or smartcard readers in the keyboards. These readers will support stored-value schemes and customer authentication using chipcard technology. Also anticipated in the very near future are server-based ATMs with chip reader capabilities, providing the electronic banking customers with greater levels of service flexibility and processing security. It will be  important for the financial institution to be able to incorporate these new technologies quickly, easing the effort required to integrate new technologies into an electronic banking service offering.

Whether a financial institution has jumped into electronic banking with both feet or has taken a more conservative and methodical approach, it will be important to keep an eye to the future. At some point in the evolution of a financial institution's electronic banking offering, it will be necessary to execute a plan to integrate the diverse access devices and delivery channels demanded by the market with the current infrastructure of the financial institution's operating systems. The implementation of a transaction processing engine will enable the financial institution to keep pace with the demands of the future, while leveraging their investment in existing legacy systems.

CHAPTER 14

Information Systems for Electronic Banking

The Case of the Central Bank of Indonesia

CELIA ROMM
University of Wollongong

FARIDA PERANGINANGIN
Bank Indonesia

14.1. What is Electronic Banking?

The literature reveals that the term 'electronic banking' is still not well defined. This term is often used interchangeably with 'electronic payment system' to refer to a subset of electronic commerce. It covers the electronic ways of transmitting payment data, and the settlement of payment from the payer to the payee.

Banking services traditionally include deposit-taking, distribution of loans and provision of payment services. In addition banks are also commonly involved in funds management, insurance, financial advisory services, and trading activities. The players in the banking industry are not only the banks, but also non-bank financial institutions such as building societies, mortgage originators and brokers, and insurance companies.

The proliferation of electronic banking has introduced further "non-banks players", such as software houses and telecommunication companies. In the US, reports suggest that AT&T's is enabling consumers to make purchases with AT&T credit cards over AT&T telephone lines, using AT&T telephone services (Waterhouse, 1996). In Australia, Telstra announced its $100 million investment in smart cards and infrastructure, declaring that the company views smart cards as the core technology of the next payment system (Allard, 1997).
In this study, the definition of electronic banking includes:

- Automated teller machines (ATMs),
- Electronic funds transfer at point-of-sale (EFTPOS),
- Electronic home banking (banking by personal computer, telephone banking, interactive television),
- Smart cards,
- Credit/debit cards,
- Electronic purse or electronic wallet,

- Digital cash,
- Electronic clearing.

The following case study describes the electronic banking planning process of Bank Indonesia, the central bank of the Republic of Indonesia.

14.2. Electronic Banking in Indonesia

The ever-increasing level of competition among financial service organizations in Indonesia, especially banks, has led commercial banks there to invest heavily in information technology to enable them to improve their services to customers. Non-cash payments, including electronic banking, are among the services offered by banks that have gained wide acceptance from the customers. The Indonesian payment system has a number of payment instruments that fall into the category of electronic banking. These include: debit cards, credit cards, automated teller machines, smart cards, EFTPOS, prepaid cards, and direct/phone banking (Bank Indonesia, 1997).

14.3. The Development of Electronic Banking in Indonesia

The central bank of Indonesia commenced its Electronic Payment System Development project in 1995. It was a long-term project that included the formulation of the Payment System Blue Print, a master plan for the development of the payment system in Indonesia and its subsequent activities. Note that by 1995 several electronic banking technologies had been widely offered by commercial banks, such as ATMs, credit cards, and debit cards. The electronic banking plan was intended to build on and extend that infrastructure.

As part of the 22 projects suggested in the Payment System Blue Print, the electronic banking projects were considered a high priority because of their importance and urgency (Bank Indonesia, December 1995). There were three information technology plans or projects closely related to electronic banking, namely:

1. Jakarta's electronic clearing project
2. online accounting system network
3. electronic transfer system that links the central bank's accounting system with the commercial banks.

Among the three projects, the Jakarta Electronic Clearing Project is still in the planning stage, whilst the online accounting system network among Bank Indonesia offices' accounting system is already in place and the electronic transfer system is going to be implemented in the very near future.

The following sections describe in detail the planning processes of all three projects. The data is presented in terms of seven major issues that are mentioned in the literature as crucial to all planning processes: (i) the internal environment; (ii) the external environment; (iii) planning resources; (iv) planning issues; (v) the plan; (vi) the plan's implementation; and (vii) the plan's alignment.

14.3.1. THE INTERNAL ENVIRONMENT

In this study, the internal environment refers to both informational inputs from within the organization and organizational factors that contribute to or affect the planning process. Issues included in this part were the factors identified by interviewees and the reason(s) behind the interviewees' considerations.

Members of the central bank of Indonesia who were interviewed for this study reported that the major internal issues that influenced the planning process were top management guidance, especially guidance from the Board or the Head of the End-User Department, their perceptions of the central bank role in the payment system, and the central bank's strategic plan. The following excerpt from an interview with one of the top managers reflects the way the strategic plan was seen as contributing to the planning process:

> The strategic plan is the main direction to be followed in developing our IT systems. In the case of electronic banking, it was clear that the Payment System Blue Print has been aligned with the strategic plan. This guaranteed that the electronic banking projects, as a part of the payment system development projects, were going to be aligned with the whole strategic plan.

It is interesting to note that even though most interviewees commented on the importance of the central bank's strategic planning in the electronic banking planning process, none of the interviewees mentioned the influence of the organization's culture, size, or structure.

14.3.2. THE EXTERNAL ENVIRONMENT

The external environment was defined as factors outside the organization that have been taken into account in the planning process.

There were several factors outside the organization that the interviewees considered as relevant to the planning process. They included: (i) pressures from the commercial banks' and the banks' customers for a reliable electronic banking system; (ii) the rapid development of IT which made electronic banking services technically feasible; and (iii) changes in the Indonesian economy and its links with the global economy that made electronic banking desirable. The following excerpt from an interview with one of the low-level managers reflects the identification of one of these external factors:

> There are various banking technologies that have been adopted by the commercial banks. We realise it. As the central bank, we should be able to accommodate this development and also be ready for the future development of electronic banking in Indonesia. We conducted meetings with the commercial banks and talked about it, and we used these discussions as an input for our planning.

14.3.3. PLANNING RESOURCES

Planning resources were defined here as resources from within the organization as well as from outside the organization that have been utilized during the planning process.

Two issues were mentioned by the interviewees as important resources: (i) management involvement in the planning process, and (ii) the contribution of the central bank of Indonesia's strategic plan. Most of the interviewees found that financial resources were not a constraint in the planning process. In contrast, consideration of time and human resources were inherent in the planning. The following excerpt from an interview with one of the middle managers reflects the common perception of the management of resources in the planning process:

> Funds are not a big issue here. It is not a constraint that management has to consider in the first place. We do have yearly financial planning, but it is not such a rigid figure. We have to be concerned more with the availability and skills of our human resources. It is important to consider whether or not our human resources are sufficient and capable in implementing the plan. We also have to refer to the schedule, the deadline at which the plan should have been completed and implemented.

14.3.4. PLANNING ISSUES

Planning issues were defined here as a series of activities conducted by the organization in order to formulate its plan. The findings indicated that the planning process in this case consisted of the following issues: (i) the conduct of the electronic banking planning process; (ii) the level of formalization of the planning process; and (iii) the similarity between the electronic banking planning process and other information systems planning processes within the organization.

Interviewees had various versions regarding how the electronic banking planning process was conducted. Nevertheless, most of them referred to a bottom-up planning process. In this context, the user department initiated the plan in the form of a proposal addressed to top management, from whom approval was required. The following excerpt from the interview with a middle manager reflects the bottom-up approach of the electronic banking planning process:

> It started from the user department. In the Jakarta Electronic Clearing Project, for example, the clearing division firstly submitted a proposal to the Head of the Accounting and Clearing Department, to get their approval. Even though the electronic clearing project has already been written as a part of the payment systems development project, it still needed a formal approval to realise it as a project. With the approval of the Head of Department, the proposal was then brought up to the Payment Systems Working Group, to be followed up. From there, it continued like any other project.

Most of the low and middle level managers reported that the electronic banking planning processes had been undertaken through several meetings that involved multi-related departments, with a steering committee in charge of every project. Nevertheless, there was no project manager in charge, no formal working group had been formed, and no formal documentation was produced. The following excerpt extracted from an interview with a low-level manager reflects the degree of formalization of the electronic banking planning process:

> Well, just like any other IT planning process. It was the urgency felt by the user department that had become the starting point for the planning process. But there was no formal planning process to be followed. It was conducted through a series of meetings that were held on the basis of urgency. It was not regular. At the beginning, the meetings were very intense and frequent. Then, they became less frequent. We are basically on recess now, awaiting the procurement. (Was there any project manager?) No, there was no project manager. There was a steering committee, but no formal working group. There was also no formal documentation of the progress of the project.

All managers involved in electronic banking had been involved with other IS planning before. In comparing the electronic banking planning project with other IS planning projects, most of the managers claimed that the prior was similar to the latter. In saying this, they referred to the common steps that the planning has gone through. Few of the interviewees saw dissimilarity in terms of resources used to support the planning process.

The following two excerpts reflect the similarity and then the difference between the electronic banking project and other IT projects within the bank. The first interview was with a middle manager, and the second was with a low-level manager:

> I think (this project) was similar to other information systems projects. There was user requirements analysis conducted at the early stage, meetings among related departments, and consultant involvement. There was a steering committee which consisted of the heads of the departments involved. There was no formal documentation, but we did have minutes of meetings, and we did report the progress to the Board.

> It was slightly different from other IT projects I have been involved in. Compared with the Jakarta Automatic Clearing Project (the changing from manual clearing to automatic), for instance, it was less hectic. The Jakarta Automatic Clearing Project was more intense. Our current project is not that intense in terms of resource employment. Perhaps because we already have had experience with this kind of project. But, compared with the accounting IT project that I was involved with before (the accounting electronic transfer system), the Jakarta Electronic Clearing planning process used more consultancy services.

14.3.5. THE PLAN

The plan refers here to all written documents generated from the planning process that describe the specification of the project, and/or some other aspects, such as its time schedule and budget. The interview findings regarding this topic included the followings issues: (i) the physical form of output of the planning, (ii) the time horizon, and (iii) the degree of detail of the plan.

Referring to the online accounting system project, the interviewees reported that there was a clear output from the planning process. The following excerpt from an interview with one of the middle managers discusses the physical form of the plan:

> There were some written reports that can be seen as the physical output of the planning process. It consisted of technical design, functional specification, time schedule, and budget planning. It also touched on the legal aspects.

Due to their urgency, the three electronic banking plans were all short term. They had to be completed within a five-year period. In this context, all the interviewees had the same understanding regarding the time horizon of the projects.

All the interviewees agreed that the final output of the electronic banking plans should have been written in considerably greater detail. The interviewees argued that documentation had not been thorough as it should have been because the details that were important were clear enough to be implemented.

14.3.6. PLAN IMPLEMENTATION

Plan implementation is defined here as the actions carried out by the organization to realise the information system plan. Issues covered in this topic included: (i) the planning-implementation gap, and (ii) the project management post the planning process.

Most of the interviewees reported that there was a time gap between the planning process and its implementation. This time lag has been attributed to the procurement of both hardware and software. The following excerpt from an interview with one of the middle managers reflects the interviewees' opinions regarding this gap:

> Just like any other IT project, procurement has been the bottleneck in the electronic banking project which has led to the delay of the implementation. The Jakarta Electronic Clearing Project was targeted to be implemented in August 1997, but as you can see, we are still waiting for the decision of the procurement right now. It has been a four-months-delay until now. Hopefully, we can implement it in December 1997.

Overall, the interviewees reported that the management of the project, post the planning process, was part of the user department's responsibility. However, the IT Department was still seen as having some responsibility after the implementation stage was completed, especially for the hardware and software maintenance. The following excerpts quoted from interviews with two middle managers discuss issues related to how the project was conducted within the central bank:

> After the planning process, the control and evaluation of the project was undertaken by the user department. Nevertheless, it did not mean that it was only the user department working on it, but all of the team. The IT Department was involved after the implementation with issues relating to maintaining and development of the system.

> Management kept monitoring the plan and its implementation. Any discrepancies between the two were discussed within the internal Bank Indonesia team as well as with the consultant. The IT Department was

involved in the implementation stage, but their role was more focussed on maintenance rather than on research and development.

14.3.7. PLAN ALIGNMENT

Alignment is defined here as the degree to which the information system plan is in line with the overall organization's strategic plan and is in support of the organization's vision or mission. Issues that were included in this topic are: (i) the success level of the electronic banking plans, (ii) the alignment of the electronic banking plans with the overall Bank Indonesia's strategic plan, and iii3) the level of sufficiency of current electronic banking systems within the central bank in meeting the commercial banks' needs.

Most of the interviewees expressed satisfaction with the success level of the plans. However, in this context they mentioned different indicators of success. The following excerpts from two interviews, with middle and top managers respectively, reflect such opinions:

> Oh yes, we can say that the previous electronic banking project has successfully met its objective. We overcame the problems that existed before the project. Automation of the Jakarta clearing, for instance, has eliminated the hassles of the jobs that were done manually before. It also speeded the process, and enhanced its accuracy.

> We received a letter of congratulation from the Bank of International Settlement (BIS) regarding our Payment System Development project. They congratulated us for our success in completing the Payment Systems Blue Print. It was a success story....

The interviewees unanimously argued that the electronic banking plans have aligned with the central bank's strategic plan. Few of the interviewees stated that the current electronic banking systems of the central bank were sufficient in meeting the commercial banks needs. Most of the interviewees stated that the central bank still was a little bit behind the commercial banks. The following excerpt from an interview with one of the top managers reflects the opinion of the group that perceived the insufficiency of the current system:

> Part of our systems have already answered the banking system's needs. But we are just starting to catch up with everything. We are now in a better position, but, still, there are many things we have in our agenda, as you can see in the Payments Systems Blue Print....

14.4. Conclusions

This case reflects the fact that the internal environment has played a more important role in the planning process than the external environment. Nevertheless, there was a shift in the central bank to being more concerned with the external environment. This was reflected in management concern for the commercial banks' needs and bank customers' needs.

Perhaps the fact that Bank Indonesia has a history of being more inward looking in its planning process, can be attributed to its nature as a non profit organization which had no culture of trying to provide the best service for its customers. This is not surprising. Similar phenomena have been reported in numerous studies of information systems planning in other government institutions. For instance, studies in the U.K. Metropolitan Council Planning Process over a period of 11 years revealed that the external business environment has not been formally studied in the planning process (Flynn and Hepburn, 1994).

In regard to the internal environment, the findings from this study reveal that while the organizational size, structure, and culture were not seen as influencing the planning process, careful consideration was given to the organization's role in developing the Indonesian payment system.

As regards the external environment, interviewees did not indicate the effect of government legislation in the planning process. Much emphasis was put, however, on the importance of the customers, namely the commercial banks in Indonesia, as sources of input and the major justification for the initiation of the project.

In conducting its electronic banking planning process, the central bank did not refer to any organization business plan. Understandably, this is due to the nature of the organization. i.e. a non profit organization, which has no business plan.

There was no indication of a clear approach having been adopted by the central bank of Indonesia in its planning processes. However, the data suggests that in the past the central bank of Indonesia has undertaken its planning process in a non-integrated way (ad-hoc approach) or with a bottom-up approach. The adoption of the ad-hoc approach can be attributed to the fact that at the time there was no clear direction for information systems, and thus every IT development was made merely as a response to emerging needs (Ahituv, et al., 1994).

Referring to McFarlan's (1984) strategic grid, Coote and Gough (1992) argued that government organizations are likely to be in either a strategic or turn around IT environment. This is due to the considerable strategic importance of information for government agencies. The data from this case study suggests the opposite, i.e., that in the past, the central bank of Indonesia has overlooked the importance of its IS strategic planning. It was only with electronic banking that plans were deliberately aligned with the organization's IT vision and strategy.

Thus, it can be argued that the electronic banking plan represented a new era for the central bank of Indonesia, with integrated planning which involved a number of departments (end-users department(s), from whom the plan was initiated, the IT Department, the Internal Planning and Development Department, and the Logistics Department) and a continuous process of consultation with internal and external advisers. As noted earlier, Bank Indonesia consistently referred to its strategic plan as the basis for its planning of the electronic banking information systems.

This case study demonstrated that there was a shift toward multiple approaches in Bank Indonesia's planning process. While the high level plan, i.e. the Payment System Blue Print, was generated through a top down approach, the more operational level planning was done through a bottom up approach. The three electronic banking projects, as have been noted in the earlier sections, were all based on an evaluation of the current systems and yet consistently referred to the Payment

System Blue Print and Bank Indonesia's Strategic Plan. This phenomenon is in line with Earls' (1989), Galliers and Bakers' (1996), and Mentzas' (1997) arguments that there is a tendency for organizations to move from the adoption of one single approach to planning towards multiple methods.

In this sense the planning process at Bank Indonesia should not be seen as unique. Historically, most planning approaches have been bottom-up, piecemeal and driven by IS issues rather than the business demand for information systems (Ward, et al., 1993).

The data from this case study reveals that the planning of the Bank Indonesia's electronic banking system was, to some extent, formal. The existence of a steering committee, which is typical of organizations with a fairly formal planning process, supports this argument (Doll and Torkazdeh, 1987). This claim is also supported by the fact that the process produced a written plan, involved an agreement on development priorities, and had funding available for the planning process, i.e., the four characteristics of a formal planning process. The only characteristic that was not found in the Bank Indonesia's electronic banking planning projects was the separation of the activities of maintenance and development.

In conclusion, this case study suggests that the electronic banking planning projects at Bank Indonesia have aligned with the overall strategic plan of the central bank. This alignment can be attributed to the fact that the process was systematically incorporated into the bank's overall strategic plan, thus ensuring the immediate implementation of the project and, hopefully, its longer term success.

14.5. References

Ahituv, N., Neumann, S., and Riley, H. N.: 1994, *Principles of Information Systems for Management*, 4th edn, Business and Educational Technologies.

Allard, T.: 1997, Telstra may take on banks in the payment system, *The Sydney Morning Herald*, 12 May, p. 37.

Bank Indonesia: 1995, Overview of Payment System Technology, Jakarta (Unpublished Material), December.

Bank Indonesia: 1997, *Annual Report*, Jakarta.

Coote, G. and Gough, C. A.: 1992, Information planning in a large government agency, *in* R. Clarke and J. Cameron (eds), *Managing Information Technology's Organizational Impact, II*, North Holland, The Netherlands.

Doll, W. J. and Torkazdeh, G.: 1987, The relationship of MIS Steering Comittees to size of firm and formalization of MIS planning, *Communications of the ACM*, November, 972-978.

Earl, M. J.: 1989, *Management Strategies for Information Technology*, Prentice Hall, NJ.

Flynn, D. J. and Hepburn, P. A. 1994, Strategic planning for information systems: A case study of a UK metropolitan council, *European Journal of Information Systems*, 3(3), 207-217.

Galliers, R. D.: 1996, Strategic information systems planning; myths, reality and guidelines for successful implementation, *in* R. D. Galliers and B. S. H. Baker, *Strategic Information Management: Challenges and Strategies in Managing Information Systems*, Butterworth-Heinemann.

McFarlan, F. W.: 1984, Information technology changes the way you compete, *Harvard Business Review,* 62, 98-103.

Mentzas, G.: 1997, Implementing an IS strategy - A team approach, *Long Range Planning,* 30, February, 84 - 95.

Ward, J. P., Griffiths and Whitmore, P.: 1990, *Strategic Planning for Information Systems,* John Wiley, New York.

Waterhouse, M.: 1996, How does regulation affect the future role and competitiveness of banks?, *The Australian Banker,* April, pp.50-55.

CHAPTER 15

The Use of EDI at BHP Steel

An Industry Perspective

KARL ROMMEL
BHP Steel

BHP Steel is the world's 14th largest steelmaker and a leader in coated steel technologies, with a range of metallic coated and painted steels being manufactured worldwide. BHP Steel operates four integrated steelworks. Three steelworks are in Australia - Port Kembla and Newcastle, New South Wales, and Whyalla, South Australia - and one in New Zealand - Glenbrook, near Auckland. BHP Steel has iron ore mines in Australia and ironsands mines in New Zealand that supply its raw materials. A series of rolling, coating and painting facilities throughout Australia and the Pacific Rim process the steel into finished product.

BHP Steel produces a wide range of flat and sheet steel products, rail and structural steels, building products, coated, painted and rollformed steel and reinforcing mesh products. Finished products include wire, engineering pipe and tube, rails, roof and wall claddings. In percentage terms, BHP is one of the world's largest exporters of steel, with approximately 40 per cent of products exported globally, in particular to Asia and North America.

Since the 1980s BHP Steel has invested more than A\$7 billion to maintain itself as a world-class steel business and establish a significant presence around the Pacific Rim as a leading producer and supplier of metallic and coated flat products.

In total BHP Steel operations employ 29,500 people worldwide.

15.1. The Early Days - Supply at the Port Kembla Steelworks

In 1987 the supply function was very fragmented, with the various tasks being performed by the Finance, Engineering, Operations and Technical Departments. Following a review, a single Supply Department was created, with targets being set that were commensurate with the company's overall objectives.

15.1.1. THE STRATEGY

To provide improved service to the plant customers while holding less inventory on site required a radical re-think of the way the purchasing function was conducted.

The General Store held approximately 8,000 line items that were all purchased under yearly contracts. Almost all the other items procured were purchased individually, often from different vendors each time. It was resolved to work towards eliminating the inventory in the Store, reducing the spares inventory and the supplier base; whilst at the same time improving relationships and communications with vendors.

15.1.2. THE TACTICS

To eliminate the stores, a re-think and re-engineering of the supply processes was required. This was achieved by:

- commissioning an in-house integrated supply system, which enabled customers to generate orders for contract lines without any manual interference by supply personnel,
- initiating a system of stockless purchasing, that is, outsourcing the inventory,
- providing customers with a guaranteed 24 hour delivery of contracted items from our vendors' premises,
- providing a rapid communications mechanism to transport purchase orders and other business documents.

Thus emerged the implementation of value managed partnerships and the establishment of an EDI (electronic data interchange) network of BHP Port Kembla Steelworks.

15.1.3. EDI PILOT

The EDI pilot commenced in September 1988 with twelve trading partners on a PC based system. At that time, EDI in Australia was very much in its infancy. The published pilot objective was therefore an ambitious target to achieve:

> In Partnership with our Suppliers to prove both Technically and Commercially that a new Technology Based Supply System can replace the Manual Systems with:
> - no significant data errors,
> - reduced administration costs,
> - improved management control,
> - reduced order lead times.

The pilot concluded in January 1989 and was declared a success.

15.1.4. 1989-1993

The plan then allowed for the addition of vendors in a controlled manner, with a view to:

1. having 80 per cent of all orders placed through the EDI network by December 1989,
2. reducing and rationalising the supplier base.

Unfortunately our 80 per cent target was not achieved until December 1990. The objective was ambitious to say the least and the effort required to achieve the target was underestimated.

The period May 1991 to February 1992 saw the rationalization of the internal systems together with the integration of EDI to the newly developed mainframe Supply System.

15.1.5. THE BENEFITS

The Port Kembla Steelworks is currently transacting EDI documents with more than 60 trading partners, accounting for some 70 per cent of all purchasing transactions. In addition some 29 per cent of transactions are transmitted electronically by fax. The supplier rationalization program has resulted in twelve (12) major partnerships accounting for 60 per cent of invoices by volume.

General Store's inventories have been eliminated with some 7,500 line items now sourced direct from the vendor. The General Store ceased operations in March 1993 resulting in major cost savings in warehousing. Shorter lead times in the day-to-day purchase and supply process from more than 10 days to 26 hours for contract lines (partnerships) and 42 to 10 days approximately for items purchased direct from vendors.

15.2. Electronic Trading Gateway Initiative

In April 1990 BHP Steel initiated the Electronic Trading Project with the objective of establishing a "gateway" to facilitate EDI between its trading partners and the various steel divisions.

The gateway approach enabled the different divisions of BHP Steel to present a straightforward, single access point for EDI to all trading partners at minimal cost and with minimal duplication of effort. It also provided other advantages including:

- high level of security, making use of X25 and X400,
- ability to translate between UN Edifact and ANSI X12 document formats and the various versions and implementations of these,
- ability to meet the needs of trading partners with the added benefit of insulating the BHP applications from the need to cater for different standards and paths for each trading partner. BHP applications only have one link and one standard to support,
- ability to allow trading partners to use a VAN of their choice or directly connect to BHP (subject to volumes transmitted),
- auditing, monitoring and tracking facilities to control and account for all documents,
- archiving of all documents in transmission format to meet legal requirements.

Adoption of the electronic gateway strategy followed an 18 month study by a Steel Group Steering Committee which assessed the EDI approach of other companies worldwide. The group found that many suppliers to large organizations were being forced to adopt EDI in order to remain competitive. EDI was still very much in its infancy worldwide, particularly in Australia, and this provided BHP and its customers with a significant strategic opportunity by taking a pro-active approach. BHP had learned from the experiences of other companies, and did not approach EDI simply as a technical issue, but as a long-term business strategy. The project involved a phased implementation of EDI over three years and three stages:

15.2.1. STAGE 1: CUSTOMER FOCUS

The objectives of Stage 1 included the development and commissioning of the gateway and implementing EDI both internally and with major customers. A feature of this stage was the considerable amount of development and integration involved and the significant role played by BHP Information Technology as a major consultant and facilities manager.

BHP's desire to support International Standards (X400, UN Edifact, ANSI X12) was incorporated into the design, with the recognition and knowledge that ANSI would migrate to Edifact in due course.

Internal Pilots

An important element in Stage 1 was the establishment of electronic trading within BHP. During September 1991 the first internal pilot commenced, with the second in October. The documents exchanged were the Purchase Order and Purchase Order Acknowledgement, both in the ANSI X12 standard.

External Customers

By the end of December 1991 two major steel distributors were using EDI to purchase steel products.

Steel Industry Working Party (SIWP)

A Steel Industry Working Party under the auspices of the EDI Council of Australia (now Tradegate ECA) was established with the responsibility for creating EDI implementation guidelines for the Australian Steel Industry. This Working Party comprized members of EDICA and other standard associations, strategic trading partners, value added network providers (VANS) and BHP Steel representatives.

SIWP subsequently restructured to become the Metals Industry Working Party which later amalgamated with the Electronic Procurement and Supply (EPAS) Working Group. Stage 1 of the project had a strong marketing focus with initial business documents aimed at improving ordering efficiency and materials management.

15.2.2. STAGE 2: ROLL-OUT

This stage aimed to "roll-out" ETG access to those trading partners that had reached the "EDI ready" stage. Other functional areas would also be supported, e.g. supply, finance.

In addition this stage set out to define document standards and provide Gateway services for the following documents:

- invoices,
- debtor statements,
- debit/credit advices,
- test certificates.

Electronic Test Certificates

Through the SIWP, and in conjunction with the Institute of Steel Service Centres of Australia (ISSCA, now the Steel Institute of Australia Inc), a successful approach was made to the National Association of Testing Authorities (NATA) in early 1991 to gain acceptance for transmission of the BHP Test Certificate to trading partners using EDI.

Previously BHP Test Certificates were mailed to customers after despatch of products. This was slow and expensive. The EDI system provided for a more timely despatch of the data, more efficiently and cost-effectively.

Supply

Following considerable effort in introducing suppliers to EDI, at the Port Kembla Steelworks, a strategy was developed to introduce suppliers to other BHP Steel Divisions via the Gateway.

With the assistance of the third party network provider, National Electronic Interchange Services, the first supplier was connected to the Gateway on 9 December 1992. More suppliers were connected soon after and the Port Kembla Steelworks system migrated to the ETG in June 1993.

International Trade - APEC Project

BHP Steel, in conjunction with the EDI Council of Australia, Australian and New Zealand Governments and shipping agents, became involved in an Asia Pacific Economic Co-operation (APEC) EDI project (Figure 1). On 10 December 1992 Steel and Tube Pty Ltd, a large New Zealand steel distributor, became the first international trading partner to connect to the BHP Gateway. In addition EDI is being used to provide pre-arrival clearance of BHP products via NZ Customs as a service to customers, where previously they were responsible for this task.

Substantial savings to customers, including an improved service, were achieved at the completion of the APEC project in April 1993.

15.2.3. STAGE 3: CULTURAL CHANGE

The third stage involved the progressive introduction of an education and awareness program that would encourage the re-engineering of business processes that electronic trading requires.

A part of the awareness program was the production of a 10-minute video and accompanying Awareness Booklet and regular newsletters throughout the Project. In addition, this stage set out to define document standards and provide Gateway service for electronic funds transfer, electronic mail, and technical and product data.

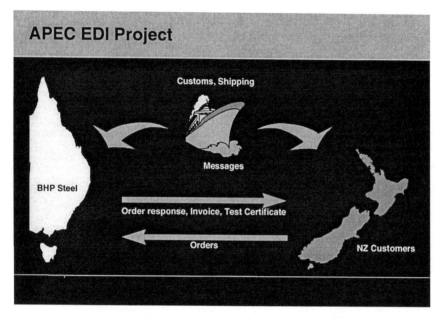

Figure 1. Asia Pacific Economic Co-operation (APEC) EDI Project.

Electronic Funds Transfer

A pilot between Port Kembla Steelworks, six suppliers and the ANZ Bank aimed to lead to the elimination of cheque payments to BHP suppliers in favor of an EDI payment order/remittance advice and subsequent funds transfer between banks.

The Steelworks already had 90 EDI-capable suppliers (for purchase orders, request for quotes, quotations); a complementary project to introduce electronic invoicing was also implemented. Invoices are now received electronically either on diskette upload or EDI. Some 65 per cent of all invoices to this Division are now received electronically.

This has completed the electronic trading cycle from ordering to payment and has provided the opportunity to re-engineer the receipting/payment process to an extent that the invoice can actually be eliminated in favor of an electronic despatch advice.

The learnings and process changes from this initial pilot have now been migrated to the other major BHP Steel sites.

Stage 3 of the Project was completed in June 1993. Most BHP Steel Divisions were using the Gateway for day-to-day business with some 40,000 EDI documents per month being transmitted to more than 130 trading partners, including major customers and suppliers, shipping agents, the ANZ Bank and the National Rail Corporation. Purchase orders, material release schedules, test certificates, invoices, shipping manifests, and payment orders being some of the EDI messages involved. Messages were also being traded in both UN Edifact and ANSI X12 standard.

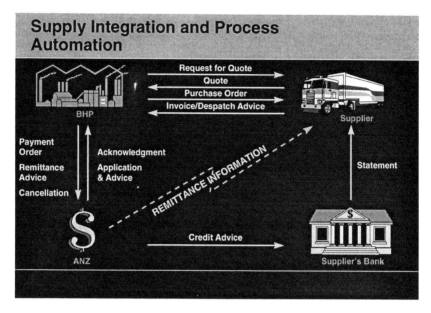

Figure 2. Supply integration and process automation.

15.3. Barcoding and Product Numbering Project

The importance of barcoding as a complementary technology was recognized during 1994. Substantial savings in the cost of materials and products handling through the introduction of barcoding across Steel Group were identified in a Materials Movement Study. In order to capitalize on this potential, Management approved the formation of a Barcoding Project Team dedicated to achieving the savings.

The project aimed to achieve its objective through the development and co-ordinated implementation of a "best practice" international standards based approach to barcoding across the Steel Group.

It was recognized that the real gains are achieved when barcoding is linked to fully integrated computer systems both within BHP and with the computer systems of its trading partners.

The project examined barcoding applications across the entire supply chain, from procurement of parts and materials, through the manufacturing operations to warehousing and delivery to the customer's store. It was expected that the project would dovetail with and accelerate the level of EDI message implementation within BHP in the areas of Supply, Sales, Finance and Transport.

The project was progressed in three phases:

15.3.1. STAGE 1

Firstly and most importantly a scoping study was undertaken to produce a "best practice" guideline and standards for barcoding within BHP Steel. This was achieved through an intensive schedule of interviews, internally and with customers, suppliers, peak industry and regulatory bodies, and barcode equipment suppliers. This study was completed in mid 1995 and found that:

- There was strong acceptance of the need for a co-ordinated approach to barcoding, making use of internationally recognized standards and methods.
- BHP's adoption of the European Article Numbering Association (EAN) system needed to be managed in concert with customers to ensure that their needs are also met.
- The Hardware and Retail industries had mandated the use of EAN barcodes by suppliers.
- A number of BHP business units had already implemented or were planning to introduce and support barcoding.
- Areas of potential barcode usage were identified as was the quantifying potential cost savings. One of the major areas of cost savings that was universally identified was the reduction of error rates in product tracking and despatch.

Resulting from the study was the recognition (and subsequent policy decision) that it would be mandatory for BHP to utilize the internationally recognized EAN-128 Item Identification numbering standard in order to comply with the published EAN Metals Industry Guidelines.

15.3.2. STAGE 2

Stage 2 of the project involved the implementation of a number of pilot projects using the principles defined in the "BHP Best Practice Barcoding Standards and Guidelines" (April 1995) document to prove that the recommended approach worked and delivered the expected savings/benefits.

Six pilots, representing a range of activity across BHP's supply chain were selected to demonstrate the benefits of barcoding. The pilots included diverse applications such as using barcoding in conjunction with radio frequency (RF) data capture, receipting and inventory management, despatch and transportation, improved scheduling, materials tracking, spares management.

15.3.3. STAGE 3

With the best practice approach now confirmed, Stage 3 involved rolling out the concept to all identified applications, with the aim of transferring the barcoding skills and technology to all parts of the organization. This has been successfully achieved in the distribution centres where barcoding technologies have now been implemented across Australia. Stage 3 was deemed a success and formally completed in June 1997.

The use of barcoding and product numbering has improved the processes of product and information handling and can give rise to significant benefits, but benefits can be maximized when EDI messages are used as well.

An example is provided (Figure 3) showing how the scanning of a barcode on despatch of a product can automatically trigger the transmission of an EDI Despatch Advice to the customer's computer.

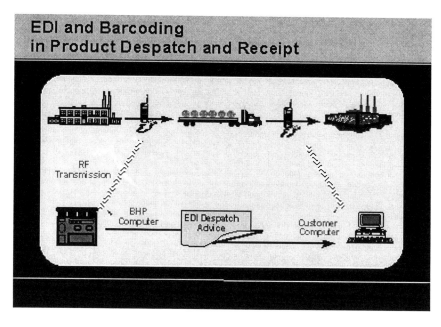

Figure 3. EDI and barcoding in product despatch and receipt.

Thus, when the customer scans the barcode on receipt of the product, all of the necessary information is already available. Other EDI messages such as Purchase Orders, Order Responses, Invoices and Payments can assist in providing a timely and error-free supply chain.

Since the commencement of the Barcoding Project in 1994, BHP Steel has received the support of EAN Australia. The EAN guideline for the Australian Metals Industry that was developed and published by EAN, has underpinned BHP's approach. BHP Steel would like to acknowledge the contribution and support provided by EAN Australia during this project.

Many of the barcoding projects underway or in the planning process are in the areas of product despatch, materials receipt and inventory management. However, the accuracy of data capture and the opportunities for automation that barcoding offers, open up possibilities for many applications. Some examples are:

1. *Document Distribution*

    BHP Steel's Infolink project was established to improve customer service by developing a central Customer Support Centre where all product information enquiries can be handled. The accurate collation and timely distribution to customers of the various items of product and marketing material was determined to be a key success factor, and a barcoding solution was seen to facilitate the necessary control.

During a customer's phone call, the operator can nominate brochures, information packs and other material from a list on a computer. In the storehouse, an operator uses a hand-held terminal to view the picking-lists and a barcode scanner to select, verify and transfer the barcoded items from the shelves to locations in a trolley. The trolley, containing material for many inquiries, is then periodically transferred to an assembly workstation where barcode scanning is used to select and assemble the correct material with each barcoded covering letter for distribution to the customer.

The result is improved service in that the customers always receive the items as discussed in their inquiry, as well as in-house benefits of reduced manual effort and improved management of material usage and replenishment.

2. *Asset Tracking*

BHP-IT are moving to the use of barcoding to assist in the management and stocktaking of their assets, across all sites. Each asset and each location will be identified using a barcoded label. The stocktaking will simply be a matter of scanning a location (e.g., room) and then scanning each of the assets in that room.

The use of barcode scanning during stocktaking will dramatically reduce the time involved in both the actual stocktaking process, and in the subsequent reconciliation process. Other benefits include the simplification of asset labelling, the ease of updating asset information when assets move from one site to another, and the potential to establish a single source and a single collection process for asset information for all parts of the business.

15.4. Internet Developments

Although BHP has been involved with Web sites on the Internet, principally for the display of Corporate information, for some time, interest in the use of the "Net" for transmitting transactional documents escalated during the second half of 1996.

This interest resulted from a realization that EDI was not readily accepted by the small to medium sized enterprises (SME's). It had been suggested (EDI World Institute 1995) that the benefits of EDI to small business include:

- improving the bottom line,
- working faster and better within the organization,
- gaining strategic advantage,
- strengthening customer relations,
- preparing for the future in business.

Despite the availability of EDI and its perceived benefits SMEs have not embraced the technology.

BHP's experience with SMEs suggests the reluctance to implement an EDI solution is that:

- it is difficult to implement,
- it is expensive to implement and maintain,
- SMEs generally do not have the IT resources or expertise,
- volumes generally to not justify the costs or provide the benefits,
- tasks often need to be duplicated after the installation of EDI.

These views were supported in a Pilot Study undertaken by the University of Wollongong in 1997.

In order to receive maximum benefits from electronic trading, it is essential for the majority of trading partners to trade electronically. The Internet provides one solution to this problem.

15.4.1. PILOT

In January 1997 a pilot involving a strategic supplier, J Blackwood & Son Limited; a software/network provider, Sterling Commerce; and the BHP ETG engaged in a pilot to transmit EDI Purchase Orders and Invoices over the Internet using e-forms.

The desire to trial and then implement an Internet solution was driven by the following factors:

1. *Cost*
   EDI using value added network providers (VANS) was increasingly seen to be a costly way of trading. The Internet, on the other hand, was perceived to be a low cost way of transporting messages between trading partners.

2. *Small Trading Partners*
   BHP Steel was desirous of providing a solution to SMEs as well as reaching new trading partners.

The purpose of the pilot was to test, understand and obtain data on a number of criteria, i.e.:

- Timeliness,
- document integrity,
- security,
- proof of arrival,

as well as collecting data on the performance of the Internet as a transport medium as the basis of an appraisal of its suitability for use for Electronic Commerce at BHP.

In summary the pilot found that:

- there was no data loss in any of the tests,
- typically delivery performance was acceptable,
- the e-form product was easy to use,
- the software and hardware used in the pilot would be suitable for low and medium volume trading partners.

15.4.2. TEST CERTIFICATES

Following on from the pilot experience a project was initiated to migrate the transmission of EDI Test Certificates to a managed Web site using the Internet.

Historically these Certificates were transmitted automatically to customers using traditional EDI and the value added networks. Customers logged on to the VAN, downloaded the messages to their PCs and printed the Certificate as required. A facility for requesting individual Certificates from BHP by EDI was also in existence and utilized by customers.

The Internet was seen as a viable, lower cost alternative. An externally managed Web server was commissioned and all Test Certificates transmitted through the BHP Gateway to the NEIS VAN by EDI. At the NEIS VAN all Test Certificates are uploaded into the Web based database. The Web application determines whether the Test Certificates need to be sent on automatically or retained on the database. The customer using a browser and Internet connection can download the Certificates to their PC and print or can electronically request Certificates from an archive.

Significant benefits to the customer have been identified, namely:

- lower operating costs,
- better quality documents.

The Test Certificate Internet service became operational on 15th December 1997 and is the first transactional Internet based system in BHP.

15.5. Conclusion

From BHP Steel's early involvement in Electronic Commerce in 1988 with the initial twelve pilot suppliers using a PC based system through to Electronic Trading Gateway Project, BHP has seen some fundamental changes in the way it conducts its business.

Currently the ETG processes some 1.8 million documents per annum and is a central face for trading partners conducting business electronically. The Company provides a range of commercial documents in a variety of standards.

15.6. References

BHP: 1997, *Factsheets 97*, Corporate Communications.
BHP Steel: 1990, *Gateway: Electronic Trading Project Newsletter*, 1 October.
BHP Steel: 1991, *Gateway: Electronic Trading Project Newsletter*, 2 May.
BHP Steel: 1991, *Gateway: Electronic Trading Project Newsletter*, 3 December.
BHP Steel: 1993, *Gateway: Electronic Trading Project Newsletter*, 4 March.
BHP Steel: 1994, *Steel Group Barcoding Project Newsletter*, 1 October.
BHP Steel: 1994, *Steel Group Barcoding Project Newsletter*, 2 December.
BHP Steel: 1995, *Steel Group Barcoding Project Newsletter*, 3 June.
BHP Steel: 1995, *Steel Group Barcoding Project Newsletter*, 4 November.

BHP Steel: 1996, *Steel Group Barcoding Project Newsletter*, 5 April.

BHP Steel: 1996, *Steel Group Electronic Commerce Newsletter*, 1 September.

BHP Steel: 1997, *Steel Group Electronic Commerce Newsletter*, 2 April.

MacGregor, R. C., Waugh, P. and Bunker, D.: 1997, Attitudes of small business to the implementation and use of IT: Are we basing EDI design initiatives for small business on myths, University of Wollongong, Australia.

MacGregor, R. C., Waugh, P. and Bunker, D.: 1997, Adoption of EDI by small business: Are the advocates in tune with the views of small business: A pilot study, University of Wollongong, Australia.

INDEX

ABOUT THE CONTRIBUTORS

Alice P. Chan (apc18@cornell.edu) is an Assistant Professor in the Department of Communication and a Faculty Research Associate of the Interactive Multimedia Group (IMG) at Cornell University. Her research centers on the uses and impacts of new information technologies in such contexts as organizational communication, inter-firm relationships and electronic commerce. Alice has contributed to articles and given presentations in several countries on electronic network use and coordination of buyer-seller transactions. (Most of these writings are under Alice's former last name, Plummer.)

Kristeen M. Gleason (gleasonk@tsainc.com), is the Strategic Marketing Manager for Applied Communications, Inc. (ACI), in Omaha, NE. She is responsible for marketing and establishing the strategic product direction for ACI's remote banking services worldwide. Before joining ACI, she was an account executive for CheckFree Corporation, a home banking and bill pay service bureau in Atlanta, GA. She has more than twenty year's experience in the banking industry and has extensive experience in developing and marketing financial services and products.

Dan Heimann (heimann@tsainc.com) is the Director of Applied Communications, Inc (ACI) Strategic Marketing. He is responsible for promoting ACI's products and strategic direction worldwide. Before his appointment to director in 1996, he was responsible for marketing ACI's retail banking products and held positions with ACI in product management department. A ten year ACI veteran, he received his associate degree in data processing from Southeast Community College.

Stefan Klein (klein@wi.uni-muenster.de) is Professor for Information Systems at the Institute for Information Systems, University of Muenster, Germany. Prior to assuming his current position he was Professor at the University of Koblenz-Landau, Assistant Professor for information management and project manager of the Competence Center Electronic Markets at the University St. Gallen, Switzerland, a Fellow at the Center for European Studies, Harvard University, and a research associate at the GMD (National Research Center for Computer Science), Cologne, Germany. He received his Dipl.-Kfm. and Dr. rer. pol. (PhD in business administration) from the University of Cologne.

Robert E. Kraut (kraut+@andrew.cmu.edu) is Professor of Social Psychology and Human-Computer Interaction at Carnegie Mellon University. He previously directed the Interpersonal Communications Research Program at Bellcore, was a Member of Technical Staff at AT&T Bell Laboratories, and was a member of the faculty at Cornell University and the University of Pennsylvania. He has broad interests in the design and social impact of computing. He has conducted empirical research on office automation and employment quality, technology and home-based employment, the communication needs of collaborating scientists, the design of information technology for small-group intellectual work, and the impact of national information networks on organizations and families. He was instrumental in the design and testing of several new information technologies including video telephony systems and software for collaborative writing.

Albert L. Lederer (lederer@ukcc.uky.edu) is Professor of Management Information Systems in the Gatton College of Business and Economics of the University of Kentucky. He holds a PhD in Industrial and Systems Engineering from the Ohio State University, MS in Computer and Information Sciences from Ohio State, and BA in Psychology from the University of Cincinnati. His articles on his major research area, information systems planning, have appeared in many academic and practitioner journals.

Boon Chye Lee (boon@uow.edu.au) is a senior lecturer in economics at the University of Wollongong. He holds degrees in Business Administration and a PhD from the University of New South Wales. His research interests include international debt and electronic money/commerce. He has published articles in these areas in international journals as well as a book, *The Economics of International Debt Renegotiation* (Westview, 1993).

Robert MacGregor (robert_macgregor@uow.edu.au) is a Senior Lecturer in the Department of Business Systems at the University of Wollongong and is also a member of the University's research program entitled *Analysing, Developing and Integrating Internet Commerce Technologies in Organisations.* He is Editor of the Australian Journal of Information Systems and is currently researching Small Business Computerisation Success Factors. Rob has had extensive experience within industry in various IS professional roles.

Dinesh Mirchandani (dinesh0@sac.uky.edu) is a PhD candidate at the Gatton College of Business and Economics, University of Kentucky. In 1999, he joins the Seidman College of Business, Grand Valley State University, as Assistant Professor. He holds an MS in Electrical Engineering from Purdue University and BS in Electronics Engineering from the University of Bombay. His research has been published in the *Journal of Organizational Computing and Electronic Commerce* as well as in several international conference proceedings. His research interests include global information systems planning and electronic commerce.

Rex Eugene Pereira (pereira@mail.utexas.edu) obtained his BS and MS degrees in Computer Science, and MBA and PhD degrees in Management Information Systems from the University of Texas at Austin. He is currently a Lecturer at the University of Texas at Austin in the Department of Management Science and Information Systems. His research interests are in electronic commerce, decision making, and cognitive science. His research has been published in journals such as *International Journal of Electronic Commerce, International Journal of Research in Marketing, Journal of the Institute of Engineers,* and *Journal of Consumer Research.*

Celia Romm (celia_romm@uow.edu.au) is an Associate Professor in the Department of Business Systems, University of Wollongong, Australia. She received her PhD in Applied Psychology from the University of Toronto, Canada. She has been a lecturer, consultant, and visiting scholar in Israel, Japan, Germany, Canada, USA and Australia. Her research interests lie in the area of the impact of information systems on organisations, with particular emphasis on human resources, culture, power, and electronic commerce issues. She has recently completed a book entitled *Virtual Politicking* (Hampton Press, 1998). She is currently working on a second volume on electronic commerce, *Doing Business on the Internet: Opportunities and Pitfalls* (Springer, London). In addition to these, she has published over sixty papers in refereed journals and chapters in collective volumes. She has presented her work in over forty local and international conferences..

Karl Rommel (Rommel.Karl.K@bhp.com.au) is the Manager of Electronic Commerce at BHP Steel, Australia. He joined BHP Port Kembla Steelworks in 1968 as a commercial degree trainee and worked in a number of commercial areas both on Plant and in Finance before joining the Purchasing Department in 1971. He has a Bachelor of Commerce from the University of NSW. Following various appointments within Purchasing he was appointed Purchasing Superintendent in 1979. As a result of further rationalization within the Company was appointed to the position of Superintendent Materials Supply in 1987 and Materials Supply Manager in August 1992; being responsible for all purchases other than raw materials. He was responsible for the implementation of electronic data interchange (EDI) in 1988; member of the BHP Steel Electronic Trading Gateway Project Steering Committee, and BHP Steel Group Barcoding Steering Committee. He lectured at Wollongong TAFE for three years, teaching Supply Management, Economics and Commercial Law and has been a keynote speaker at a number of Supply and EDI conferences .

Neal G. Shaw (n.shaw@ttacs.ttu.edu) is currently a doctoral student in Management Information Systems in the College of Business Administration at Texas Tech University. He has published several papers on various aspects of electronic commerce and has presented his work at major national and international conferences. In addition, he is a NASA research fellow, where he investigates the proliferation of emerging network technologies in organizations.

Kenneth Sims (kenpc@ukcc.uky.edu) is Assistant Professor of Computer Information Systems at Cumberland College in Williamsburg, Kentucky. He is a PhD candidate at the Gatton College of Business and Economics of the University of Kentucky. He holds master's in Business Administration and Information Management from Washington University, St. Louis, and a BS in Accounting and Data Processing from Cumberland. His research has been published in the *Journal of Organizational Computing and Electronic Commerce* as well as in several international conference proceedings. His research interests include electronic commerce and decision support systems.

Andrew Slade (Andrew.Slade@sunderland.ac.uk) is currently Director of the Graduate Research School of Sunderland University in the UK. where he has responsibility for the development of the research strategy for the University across all disciplines. He has worked at several Universities in the UK including 14 years as a lecturer in Computer Science at Durham University. He has held many grants and contracts and has published papers in many fields of computer science including software development methodologies for distributed systems and artificial intelligence in fault diagnosis. Andrew is also Director of the Centre for Electronic Commerce at Sunderland which is pursuing research and development in all areas of electronic commerce.

Charles Steinfield (steinfie@pilot.msu.edu) is a Professor in the Department of Telecommunication at Michigan State University. In addition to numerous articles, he has published several award-winning books on such topics as organizations and information technology, international telecommunications policy, and telecommunications and media convergence. He was a member of technical staff at Bellcore as well as a visiting researcher at CNET, the national telecommunications research center in France. He has also been a visiting faculty member at the Institut National des Telecommunications in France, and at the Helsinki School of Economics and Business Administration.

Fay Sudweeks (fays@arch.usyd.edu.au) is a Research Associate at the University of Sydney, a doctoral candidate in Business Systems at the University of Wollongong, and has degrees in Psychology and Cognitive Science. She has given lectures in Israel, Sweden, Germany, Bulgaria, Russia. Her research interests are social, cultural and economic aspects of computer mediated communication. She has published 13 edited books and edited proceedings, and 30 papers in books, journals and proceedings. Her most recent book is *Network and Netplay: Virtual Groups on the Internet* (MIT Press, 1998), co-edited with Margaret McLaughlin and Sheizaf Rafaeli, and is currently working on a second volume on electronic commerce, *Doing Business on the Internet: Opportunities and Pitfalls* (Springer London). She has recently co-edited a special issue of *the Journal of Computer Mediated Communication*, and is co-editor of a special issue of *the Journal of Global Information Technology Management.*

Philip Waugh (philip_waugh@uow.edu.au) is a Professional Officer with the Department of Business Systems at the University of Wollongong. He has worked extensively in the area of Electronic Commerce over the last 5 years as a consultant and researcher.

David Whiteley (D.Whiteley@doc.mmu.ac.uk) is a Senior Lecturer at Manchester Metropolitan University. He teaches on Information Systems in the Department of Computing and researches into Electronic Trading in the Telematics Research and Application Centre (TRAC).

Contents

Preface

My experience over many years lecturing in land surveying and organizing the training of graduates in setting out procedures, has led me to believe that there is a real need for a book which covers the academic theory and the practical procedures used to complete the setting out work accurately.

The normal object of land surveying is to produce a scaled plan of an area. The process of setting out involves locating precisely the position of a building using the information provided by the architect's or engineer's drawing. Every building or engineering structure that is constructed must undergo a setting out procedure to ensure that it is the correct size, in the correct plan position and at the correct level.

The basic equipment used in traditional surveying and setting out are: the tape for measuring lengths, the level for measuring height differences and the theodolite for measuring angles. Over the years many developments have been introduced in setting out equipment to improve the speed of operation and to achieve a higher standard of accuracy.

This book follows the many developments in instrumentation which have taken place over the years and the corresponding changes adopted to site setting out procedures in order to meet the specified accuracies as efficiently as possible. The later chapters examine in detail the practical methods of setting out many types of engineering work such as roads, tunnels, buildings, sewers, etc.

In recent years the scarcity of building land and the use of modular prefabricated building have created a demand for higher accuracy specification enabling buildings to be placed in the correct positions with the units of the building fitting together precisely. In order to meet those requirements the text examines suitable measuring techniques, suggests checking procedures and indicates the errors which may be permitted in a range of situations.

Since the early 1980s there has been a rapidly accelerating introduction of electronic instruments in land surveying and the book examines their usage in levelling, angle and distance measurement, data collection and interpretation.

The book would be particularly suitable for civil engineering and building site engineers who have recently graduated and will shortly be putting into site practice the academic knowledge gained from their undergraduate or B/TEC courses. Students should find this a valuable textbook and extremely useful when they start their practical site work. Practising engineers will no doubt wish to refer to sections on new instruments and up-to-date procedures involving data collection and interpretation by electronic means.

Acknowledgements

I wish to thank all who have contributed to the preparation of this book and in particular the following people:

Professor F. C. Harris of Wolverhampton Polytechnic for his initial and continued encouragement.
Jill Pearce, publisher, who has kindly assisted me at all stages.
Carmela Billingham for patiently typing the original manuscript.
J. Billingham for help in correction of some of the errors.
W. H. Hatfield for his assistance in the field.
R. Spooner who has allowed me to use his drawings in the final chapter.
All of my colleagues at Wolverhampton Polytechnic.

I also wish to thank the following companies which have given me photographs and permission to reproduce them:

Husky Computers Ltd
Sokkisha (UK) Ltd
Spectra Physics Ltd
Wild Heerbrugg (UK)
Zeiss West Germany

My thanks are due to the Controller of Her Majesty's Stationery Office for permission to use extracts from Road Curve Data in DTp 'Highway Link Design' Standard TA/43/84 and to quote from the Building Research Establishment Digest No. 234 *Accuracy in Setting Out*. Thanks are due also to the County Surveyors' Society for permission to make use of the highway transition curve tables.

My special thanks go to my wife for her patient support throughout this venture.

One

General responsibilities of a land surveyor

1.1 Overall responsibility

On arrival at a site, a land surveyor is expected to be responsible for:

1. The efficiency of the surveying task.
2. The accuracy of the work.
3. The safety of the surveying personnel.
4. The care and security of the surveying instruments.

In order to achieve efficiency, the surveyor must be aware of all the up-to-date information regarding the site and the nature of the task to be completed. To achieve accuracy the work must be done with care and incorporate a comprehensive checking system.

The surveyor must be familiar with the implication of the Health and Safety at Work Act 1974 and appreciate the need for security and care of the instruments.

1.2 Site knowledge

Before starting surveying or setting out work, useful information can be obtained from:

1. A site reconnaissance (site walk).
2. The most recent ordnance sheet of the area.
3. The latest issues of site drawings.

In the site walk, checks must be made to see that all bench marks and reference points are well defined, and that boundaries and all visible permanent features are correctly positioned and indicated on the drawing. The site walk should be used to check out the terrain and to assess possible solutions to the difficulties created by site obstacles.

The surveyor should prepare the proposed plan of campaign before taking out the instruments.

1.3 Care of personnel

The Health and Safety at Work Act 1974 requires an employer to provide a written safety policy and insists that all employees take reasonable care of themselves and others. In land surveying work:

Do not
- Allow nails to project from discarded timber.
- Enter unsupported trenches.
- Look into a laser beam.
- Run – but walk and work steadily.
- Signal a chainman to move into danger.

Do
- Wear an approved protective safety helmet without a brim.
- Wear high visibility waistcoats.
- Wear approved safety footwear.
- Correct immediately any dangerous practices or emissions.

1.4 Care and security of equipment

A surveyor is responsible for the care and security of his equipment used on site. In land surveying work:

Do not
- Leave instruments unattended on site.
- Leave instruments set up in the site offices.
- Put an instrument away until it has dried out after rain.

Do
- Store equipment carefully in a dry place.
- Inspect all instruments before work commences.
- Make a list of equipment taken from security.
- Return a complete set of equipment on completion.
- Make sure that the equipment is used in a manner which does not endanger it or people.

■ Adopt procedures which ensure the instrument achieves the accuracy for which it is designed.

■ Clean and oil tapes and chains at regular intervals.

1.5 Checks

All surveying should be planned to have checks at as many stages as is practical to ensure that errors are detected as early as possible.

A good surveyor will estimate the value to be measured before using the instrument. Predictions will be made of distance, value of an angle or difference in level between two positions. A gross difference between predicted and measured values will suggest the need for a repeat reading to confirm the result.

Items checked

■ **Distances** are checked by repetition.

■ **Triangles** are confirmed by the use of check lines as shown in Figure 1.1.

■ **Rectangular buildings** should be checked by measuring the diagonals as shown in Figure 1.2.

■ **Angles** are checked by repetition of face left and right readings.

■ **Traverse angles** have a misclosure given by:

$(2n - 4)\ 90° -$ Sum of measured internal angles

where n is the number of sides of the traverse.

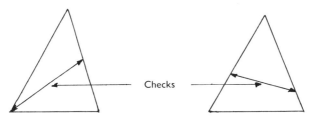

Figure 1.1 Check that measurement in field equals value on scaled drawing.

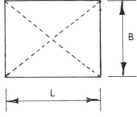

Figure 1.2 Each diagonal $= \sqrt{(L^2 + B^2)}$.

■ **Levelling.** Here it is essential that a levelling operation starts at a point whose value is known and finishes either at the same point or at a second position with a precisely known value. The difference between the levelled value and the known value is the *misclosure*.

1.6 Accuracy

Every surveying operation is subject to errors, and the British Standard document 'Accuracy in Building PD 6440 Part 2' lays down guidelines to the deviations permissible in setting out. For general site work the following values are normally acceptable.

Typical acceptable misclosures for levelling

Accurate roadwork ± 3 mm$\sqrt{\text{Number of CPs}}$

Contour work ± 12 mm$\sqrt{\text{Number of CPs}}$

where CPs are change points or set ups.

Typical acceptable misclosures for traverse angles

Normal theodolite work $\pm 3e\sqrt{N}$

where N = number of stations and e = least count or error expected from centring, etc.

Typical acceptable misclosures for distance measurement

Normal site electromagnetic distance measurement

Error expected is ± 10 mm $\pm$ 5 parts per million
Accuracy over 1 km is approximately 1/100 000
Accuracy over 50 m is approximately 1/10 000

Steel tape measurement
The Building Research method advocates that a tension of approximately 70 N should be applied to a steel tape either fully supported or in catenary. If corrections for temperature of 1 mm per 10 m for each 10 °C difference between standard and air temperature, and the sag correction are applied in the catenary case then:

Accuracy up to 1 km is approximately 1/10 000

Two

Levelling

2.1 Levelling definitions_____

See Figure 2.1.

- **Levelling** is the determination of the differences in elevation between two or more points.
- A **level line** is a line lying throughout on one level surface and normal to the direction of gravity at all points.
- A **horizontal or tangent line** is a straight line passing through a point in a direction normal to the direction of the gravity at the point.
- A **refracted sight line** is the normal sight line which bends towards the earth due to refraction.
- A **bench mark (BM)** is a fixed point or datum of predetermined height.

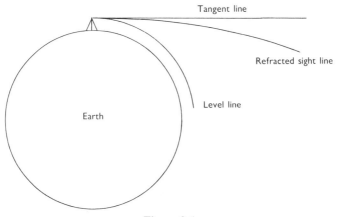

Figure 2.1

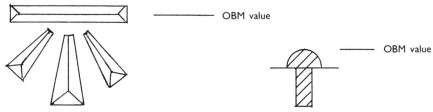

Figure 2.2

- A **temporary bench mark (TBM)** is a datum fixed by a surveyor for his own convenience for a particular job.
- An **ordnance bench mark (OBM)** is a datum based on zero at the mean level at Newlyn, Cornwall, 1915–21.
- A **reduced level** is the height of a point with reference to the particular datum in use.

Note that the difference in reading between sight line and level line is approximately $K^2/15$ m where K is sight length in kilometres.

The locations of Ordnance Survey datums are published in Ordnance Survey bench marks lists and Ordnance Survey plans. In the field they are indicated as shown in Figure 2.2.

2.2 The level staff

See Figure 2.3.

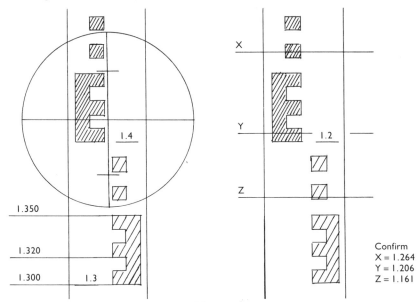

Figure 2.3

2.3 Techniques to increase the accuracy of level readings____

By instrument operative

1. Ensure that the bubble is central.
2. Focus staff clearly.
3. Focus cross hairs.
4. If there is no change in staff reading when the eye is moved up and down then focusing is complete. However, if there is change as the eye moves then **parallax** is present and must be eliminated by the following procedure:
   (a) Place a piece of white paper in front of the telescope and adjust eyepiece to sharpen the cross hairs.
   (b) Focus on the staff. This will eliminate the parallax for the operator and refocusing on the staff at differing distances should now be all that is necessary. An occasional check on parallax is a good precaution.
5. Ensure that the staff is vertical relative to the vertical part of the cross hair and indicate to the staff operative if the staff appears to be non-vertical.
6. Take the mid cross hair reading on the staff.

By the staff holder

1. The base of the staff must be kept clean.
2. The staff must be held on solid ground or on a change plate.
3. The staff should be held vertically using a staff bubble if available. Alternatively rock the staff slowly backwards and forwards so that the instrument operative may observe the smallest level reading which occurs in the vertical position.

2.4 Levelling principles_____

A level in adjustment will sweep out a level plane.

- A **backsight (BS)** is the first reading taken at a new level station.
- A **foresight (FS)** is the last reading before moving from a level station.
- **Intermediate sights (IS)** are all sights which are neither backsight nor foresight.

Figure 2.4 shows a bench mark (BM) of level 100.00 AOD (above Ordnance datum) and positions A, B, C, D and E are levels are required.

First the level is placed at X where staffs can be seen at BM, A, B and C. Second the level is placed at Y where staffs can be seen at C, D and E.

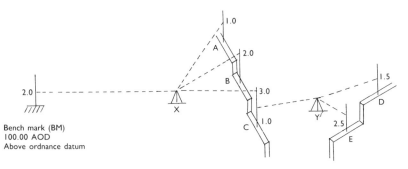

Figure 2.4

Level at X   BS to BM   2.00
             IS to A and B 1.00 and 2.00
             FS to C   3.00

Level at Y   BS to C   1.00
             IS to D   1.50
             FS to E   2.50

Rise and fall method of determining levels with respect to ordnance datum

This method considers relative ground levels between adjacent positions. If the latter is higher it is a rise, if lower a fall.

Here the level at A is a rise from BM, B is a fall from A, C is a fall from B, etc. In the example, the level at BM is 100.00.

Level at A = 100.00 + 1.00 = 101.00
Level at B = 101.00 − 1.00 = 100.00
Level at C = 100.00 − 1.00 = 99.00
Level at D = 99.00 − 0.50 = 98.50
Level at E = 98.50 − 1.00 = 97.50

Height of collimation method

The level of the dotted line at X is the height of collimation or height of instrument and is 100.00 AOD + 2.00 = 102.00.

Level at A = 102.00 − 1.00 = 101.00
Level at B = 102.00 − 2.00 = 100.00
Level at C = 102.00 − 3.00 = 99.00

Level of dotted line at Y is height of collimation or height of instrument and is 99.00 AOD + 1.00 = 100.00.

Level at $D = 100.00 - 1.50 = 98.50$
Level at $E = 100.00 - 2.50 = 97.50$

2.5 Level booking using the rise and fall method_____

Consider the levelling situation shown in Figure 2.5.

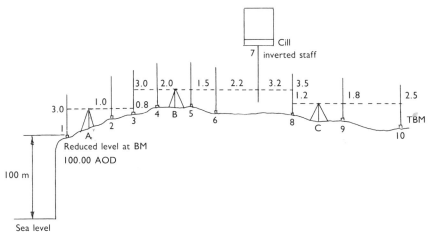

Figure 2.5

BS	IS	FS	Rise +	Fall −	Reduced level	Remarks
3.00					100.00	1 BM (bench mark)
	1.00		2.00			2
3.00		0.80	0.20			3
						4
						5
						6
						7 Cill
						8
						9
						10 TBM

Readings taken from instrument at A (shaded)

■ First reading onto 1, i.e. *back* onto a known reading, is a **backsight**.
■ Second reading onto 2 is not a first or last reading, it is an **intermediate sight**.
■ Third reading onto 3 is the *last* reading before moving forwards and is a **foresight**.

  1 to 2 = 3.00 − 1.00 = + 2.00 (rise)
  2 to 3 = 1.00 − 0.80 = + 0.20 (rise)
  Reduced level at 2 = 100.00 + 2.00 = 102.00
  Reduced level at 3 = 102.00 + 0.20 = 102.20

Readings taken from instrument at B

■ First reading onto 3, where the reduced level is known, is a **backsight**.
■ Readings onto 4 to 7 are all **intermediate sights**.
■ Reading onto 8 is the *last* reading and is a **foresight**.

  3 to 4 = 3.00 − 2.00 = + 1.00 (rise)
  4 to 5 = + 0.50 (rise)
  5 to 6 = − 0.70 (fall)
  6 to 7 = + 5.40 (rise)
  7 to 8 = − 6.70 (fall)
  Reduced level at 4 = 102.20 + 1.00 = 103.20
  Reduced level at 5 = 103.20 + 0.50 = 102.70

Complete the rest of the table. (Solution is shown in section 2.7.)

*2.6 Height of instrument or height of collimation method*____

Consider the levelling situation shown in Figure 2.6.

Instruments at A

■ Level at 1 is 100.00 AOD. Level of collimation, i.e. height of instrument or the dotted line at A, is 100.00 + 3.00 = 103.00.
■ Level at 2 is 103.00 less 1.00 = 102.
■ Level at 3 is 103.00 less 0.80 = 102.20

Instrument at B

■ Reduced level at 3 is 102.20 AOD. Level of collimation, i.e. height of instrument or the dotted line at B, is 102.20 + BS = 102.20 + 2.00 = 105.20.

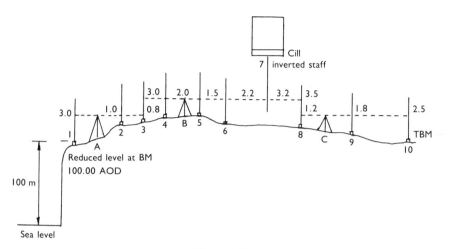

Figure 2.6

BS	IS	FS	Height of collimation	Reduced level	Remarks
3.00			103.00	100.00	1 BM (bench mark)
	1.00			102.00	2
3.00		0.80		102.20	3
	2.00				4
	1.50				5
	2.20				6
	− 3.20				7 Cill
1.20		3.50			8
	1.80				9
		2.50			10 TBM

- Levels at 4, 5, 6, 7 and 8 are found by subtracting their staff values from 105.20. Care must be taken with 7 where the value is $105.20 - (-3.20) = 108.40$.

Complete the rest of the table. (Solution is shown in section 2.7.)

2.7 Method of checking arithmetic and the accuracy of the levelling

Arithmetical checks

$$\text{Sum of backsights} - \text{Sum of foresights} = K$$
$$\text{Sum of rises} - \text{Sum of falls} = K$$
$$\text{Last reduced level} - \text{First reduced level} = K$$

If all the values of K are the same then the arithmetic is correct.
[Note that the height of collimation method does not consider the second check.]

Rise and fall method and height of collimation method considered together

BS	IS	FS	Rise	Fall	Height of collimation	Reduced level	Remarks
3.00					103.00	100.00	1 BM (bench mark)
	1.00		2.00			102.00	2
3.00		0.80	0.20		105.20	102.20	3
	2.00		1.00			103.20	4
	1.50		0.50			103.70	5
	2.20			0.70		103.00	6
	−3.20		5.40			108.40	7 Cill
1.20		3.50		6.70	102.90	101.70	8
	1.80			0.60		101.10	9
		2.50		0.70		100.40	10 TBM 100.396
Σ7.20		Σ6.80	Σ9.10	Σ8.70			

$\Sigma \mathrm{BS} \quad - \Sigma \mathrm{FS} \quad = 7.2 - 6.8 = 0.4$
$\Sigma \mathrm{Rises} - \Sigma \mathrm{Falls} = 9.1 - 8.7 = 0.4$
Last reduced level − First reduced level $= 100.40 - 100.00 = 0.40$

Accuracy of the levelling

True level at the temporary bench mark (TBM) is	100.396
Level at TBM found by site work is	100.400
Misclosure in site levelling is	0.004

Precise work would be expected to be within:

± 3 mm $\sqrt{\text{Number of set ups}}$
± 5.2 mm

Contour work would be expected to be within:

± 12 mm $\sqrt{\text{Number of set ups}}$
± 20.8 mm

The work on site falls statistically within the limits of precise work.

Exercise 2.1 *General levelling problem*_____

Procedure

A tilting level was used to conduct a circuit of levels A, B, C, D, E, F, G, A, as shown in the figure.

1. The bubble was level before every reading.
2. The telescope was focused correctly.
3. The staff was held vertically at each station.
4. The backsights and foresights were made approximately equal in length.

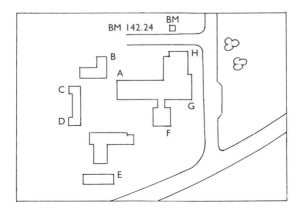

BS	IS	FS	Rise	Fall	Reduced level	Remarks
2.358						BM 142.240 AOD
	1.866					A
3.216		1.326				B
2.861		0.236				CP 1
1.562		0.833				C
0.234		1.687				D
0.486		3.468				CP 2
0.346		2.326				E
	0.878					F
1.845		2.364				G
2.137		1.487				H
		1.324				BM 142.240 AOD

(a) Complete the levelling table with full checks.
(b) Check that levelling accuracy falls within a permissible error of ±3 mm $\sqrt{\text{Number of set ups}}$.

Exercise 2.2 Levelling using older instruments

Procedure

A dumpy level was used to take ground levels at A to K and gutter levels at 1 and 2 as shown in the figure. Precautions were taken to ensure:

1. Fine adjustment of the level bubble at each station.
2. The telescope was focused correctly.
3. The vertical staff was used at every reading.
4. The backsights and foresights were made to be of similar length.

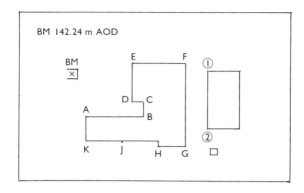

BM 142.24 m AOD

BS	IS	FS	Height of collimation	Reduced level	Remarks
1.384					BM 142.240 AOD
	1.872				A
	1.785				B
	1.783				C
	1.779				D
1.875		1.776			E
2.472		1.876			F
	− 2.972				1
	− 2.976				2
1.873		2.478			G
	1.870				H
	1.872				J
1.562		1.876			K
		1.164			BM 142.240 AOD

(a) Complete the levelling table with full checks.

(b) Check that levelling accuracy falls within a permissible error of ± 3 mm $\sqrt{\text{Number of set ups}}$.

2.8 The modern surveying telescope

The objectives of a telescope are:

1. To provide a general overview.
2. To focus clearly on distant objects.
3. To magnify distant objects.
4. To introduce cross hairs which provide a reference from which measurements may be taken.
5. To facilitate the insertion of differing diaphragm patterns suitable for specific purposes.
6. To allow for the adjustment of the line of collimation.

In Figure 2.7 the focusing screw adjusts the position of the central concave lens which facilitates the focusing of distant objects. The image of the object, when focused sharply, indicates clearly the markings of the cross hairs superimposed on the object focused.

At this point it is important to check that cross hairs and object are truly in the same plane by moving the eye about the eye piece. If there is no differential movement between object and cross hairs then true readings can be taken. If there is differential movement then parallax is present, and until it is removed readings should not be taken.

Removing parallax

To remove parallax, place a piece of white paper in front of the telescope and adjust the eyepiece to sharpen the cross hairs. Then focus the object. Repeat until there is no differential movement.

All patterns shown in Figure 2.8 give horizontal and vertical reference and all indicate stadia lines used in distance measurement. One is suitable for sighting ranging rods and the other a fixed point.

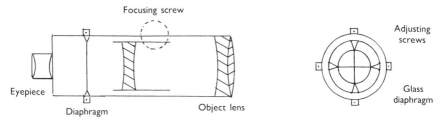

Figure 2.7 The modern, internally focusing telescope showing, on the right, a section at the diaphragm.

Figure 2.8 Diaphragm pattern.

Adjustment of the line of collimation

Adjusting screws on the diaphragm can be adjusted to correct collimation errors.

2.9 Lines of sight of optical levels

The central diaphragm position shown in Figure 2.9 indicates the line of sight through a telescope. In the case of a level the line of sight should be truly horizontal.

Figure 2.9

Means of obtaining a horizontal line of sight

1. The level bubble.
2. The automatic level with free suspension compensators.
3. The automatic level with mechanical compensators.

   The level is adjusted until the bubble shown in Figure 2.10 is in the centre of its run. A more sensitive method of ensuring the bubble is central is to use the levels with split image bubbles (shown in Figure 2.11) which, by a system of prisms, enable both ends of the bubble to be viewed and aligned simultaneously.

Automatic levels

All automatic levels need coarse adjustment by three footscrews or by a 'ball and socket' device built into the level (or between instrument and

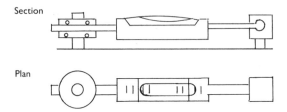

Figure 2.10 The spirit level.

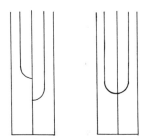

Figure 2.11 Split bubble.

the tripod). Most automatic levels vibrate under windy or heavy traffic conditions.

Free suspension compensators

The type of automatic level shown in Figure 2.12 relies on a system of prisms which are suspended within the telescope tube in such a way that the final line of sight is horizontal. The prisms may be suspended either by wire or in a liquid.

Mechanical compensators

This type of automatic level relies on prisms, but here the prisms may be attached by spring to the telescope itself.

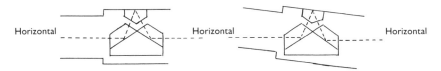

Figure 2.12

2.10 Surveying levels

There are basically three types of level used in practical surveying:

1. Dumpy level.
2. Tilting level.
3. Automatic level.

The dumpy level

Shown in Figure 2.13(a). This is an old instrument which has lost favour because it is slow to use compared with modern instruments. Here the telescope and the levelling plate are cast in one piece, the level bubble is large and very sensitive and the tribrach screws have fine threads and are also very sensitive. As a result of the sensitivity, setting up takes a long time but, once set up, all sights are horizontal.

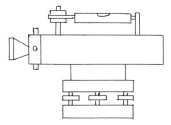

Figure 2.13(a) Dumpy level.

The tilting level

Shown in Figure 2.13(b). This instrument can be set up quickly using coarse tribrach screws and a pond level, and then sensitively levelled using the tilting screw. Although setting up is rapid every reading needs a tilting screw adjustment. This type of level is suitable for refinements. The tribrach may be replaced by a ball and socket to produce a quickset level. The incorporation of the split bubble or coincidence bubble will give greater accuracy in centring the bubble.

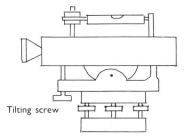

Figure 2.13(b) Tilting level.

The automatic level

Shown in Figure 2.13(c). This level is extremely quick because it needs only to be levelled approximately and then the compensator moves automatically to give a truly horizontal line of sight. High winds and vibrations cause variations in readings and in these conditions several readings may have to be taken.

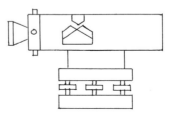

Figure 2.13(c) Automatic level.

2.11 The two peg test used to measure the collimation error of a level

A level is in perfect adjustment if the line of sight is truly horizontal when the bubble is in the centre of its run. The two peg test is used at regular intervals to check whether the adjustment needs attention.

A two peg test example

1. The instrument is placed at C, midway between pegs placed firmly at B and D, which are 30 m apart as shown in Figure 2.14.

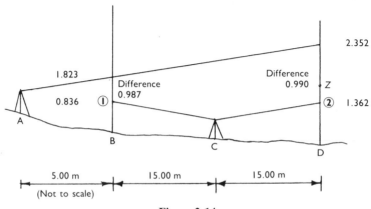

Figure 2.14

2. Vertical staff readings are taken onto the pegs at B and D.
3. The instrument is then placed at A which is, say, 5 m from B in the line D, C, B, A.
4. Vertical staff readings are taken at pegs B and D.

Results

CB = CD. The reduced levels 1 and 2 are equal. If the difference between the two staff readings at B equals the difference between the two staff readings at D then the collimation error is zero.

Here the staff differences at D exceed the staff differences at B by 3 mm, so over 30 m there is a collimation error of + 3 mm. Over 100 m there is a collimation error of + 10 mm.

To establish a true horizontal line of sight from level to staff at Z

1. The reading of the staff at D from instrument at A is 2.352 m.
2. The line of sight rises 10 mm in 100 m.
3. Between A and D, which is 35 m, the line of sight rises $\frac{35}{100} \times 10$ m = 3.5 mm.
4. True reading on D from A, i.e. Z, is 2.352 − 0.0035 = 2.3485 m

2.12 Correction of collimation errors_____

Field levelling procedures

To reduce significantly the effects of collimation errors, ensure that the backsight and foresight distances are equalized and that all sight distances in the levelling operation are restricted to below 30 m.

Permanent adjustment of the collimation error

If the results of a two peg test indicate a collimation error exceeding ± 1 mm in a length of 20 m or ± 5 mm in 100 m then permanent adjustments are required.

The two peg test example above showed that there was an error of

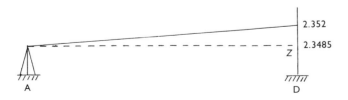

Figure 2.15

+ 10 mm over a length of 100 m. Now the actual reading on D was 2.352, and the true horizontal reading on D, i.e. Z, was calculated as 2.3485 (as indicated in Figure 2.15). The adjustment for various levels are indicated below.

The tilting level

In Figure 2.16, Z is sighted using the tilting screw. The bubble is no longer central. Adjust the capstan screws to centralise bubble maintaining sight to Z.

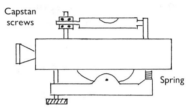

Figure 2.16

The dumpy level

In Figure 2.17 the 'fine levelling' procedure must be completed (described in section 3.5) before the two peg test. In this case, Z is sighted by adjusting diaphragm screws.

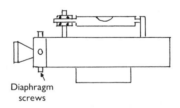

Figure 2.17

The automatic level

For most automatic levels (indicated in Figure 2.18) Z can be sighted by adjusting diaphragm screws. Others require adjustment to the compensator which is best left to the manufacturer.

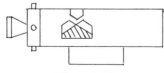

Figure 2.18

Plate 1 Wild automatic level.

Plate 2 Wild precise automatic level.

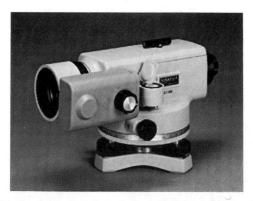

Plate 3 Sokkisha level: an illumination device LA4 for levelling in tunnels or at night. The device is able to illuminate wedge reticle lines for levelling in dark places. It is equipped with a light emitting diode as its light source, and can be used continuously for about ten hours with two UM3 batteries.

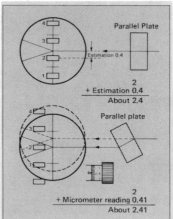

Plate 4 Sokkisha precise level. This has built-in sharp wedge reticle lines, essential for high precision levelling in combination with the optical parallel micrometer (optional). Graduations on the staff can be bisected to obtain the height difference up to 0.1 mm. There are also reticle stadia lines, important for determining the mid point between fore- and backsights.

2.13 Contouring

A **contour line** is a continuous line drawn on a map or plan representing the points which are at the same level.

The **vertical** or **contour interval** is the difference in level between adjacent contours.

The **gradient** between two points is given by considering the horizontal distance between the points and the difference in level between the points. Generally, gradient is the difference in level divided by horizontal distance. In contouring, gradient is the contour interval divided by the horizontal distance between contours.

2.14 Methods of contouring

Direct method

This method involves locating positions of similar level in order to produce a series of contours.

A level is set up and a backsight taken to a position of known level. To establish the height of collimation the backsight and the known level are added. The staff is placed on a series of points with the same intermediate sight and these points are located accurately thus establishing a continuous contour line. Other contour lines are positioned by changing the intermediate sight to suitable staff readings.

This is a very accurate method, but as every point has to be carefully located it is slow and hence costly.

Grid method

Here a grid network is set up and levels taken at each grid intersection. The contours are established by interpolation.

Methods of setting out grid of levels

There are numerous methods of setting out grids but most methods have the following features in common:

1. The grids are square and vary in size according to the accuracy required: 30 m squares are used for the least accurate work while 5 m squares are called for in very precise work.
2. Two base lines are set out at right angles to each other and all points can be defined as coordinates from the base lines.
3. All distances should be measured horizontally using step chaining to establish a truly horizontal grid.
4. Levelling should start at a known bench mark and return to the same bench mark or a second one with a known value.

2.15 Grid levels and contours_____

If the levels at each grid intersection are known, the levels of intermediate points may be established by interpolation. Interpolation methods include:

1. Judgement.
2. Radial graph.
3. Mathematical calculations indicated in Figures 2.19–2.21.

Consider two grid points with levels 14.0 m AOD and 23.0 m AOD spaced 10 m apart. Using each method determine the position of the 20 m AOD level assuming a uniform gradient.

Judgement

- 20 is 6 units from 14 and 3 units from 23.
- 20 lies in the position which divides the line in the proportion 6 : 3.

Practice enables a good eye judgement of this position.

Figure 2.19 Contours by judgement.

Graph method
A large graph on tracing paper enables points to be plotted accurately: here 20 m.

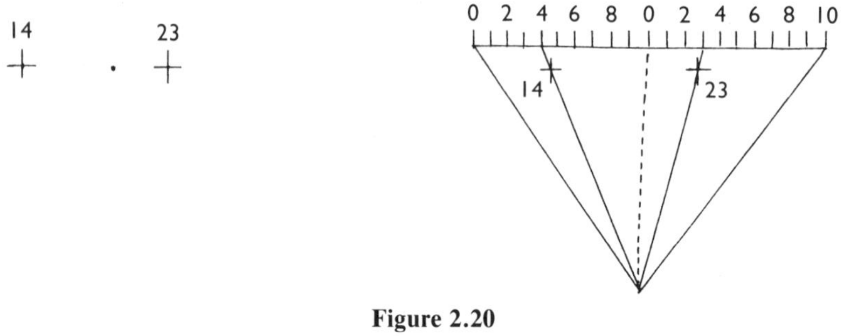

Figure 2.20

Mathematical

$$\frac{a}{6} = \frac{10 - a}{3} \qquad 3a = 60 - 6a \qquad 9a = 60$$

$$a = \frac{60}{9} = 6.66$$

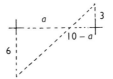

Figure 2.21

Using grid levels to obtain the average level of a site

Average level of site

$$= \frac{\Sigma \text{ Level at grid point} \times \text{Number of associated squares}}{4 \times \text{Number of squares}}$$

In Figure 2.22, A has 1 associated square; B has 3 and C has 2. The number of squares is 3.

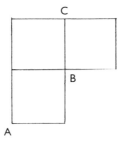

Figure 2.22

Example 2.1 *Grid levels and contours*_____

For the grid shown below:

(a) Find the average level of the site.
(b) Draw the contours at 5 m intervals using judgement.

8	9	14	
+	+	+	
10	15	19	24
+	+	+	+
12	17	22	28
+	+	+	+

Solution

Average level

$$= \frac{\Sigma \text{ Level at grid point} \times \text{Number of associated squares}}{4 \times \text{Number of squares}}$$

Number of associated squares			
1	2	3	4
Level at grid point			
8 14 24 28 12	9 22 17 10	19	15
86	58	19	15
×1	×2	×3	×4
86	116	57	60

Average level $= \dfrac{86 + 116 + 57 + 60}{4 \times 5} = 15.95$ m AOD

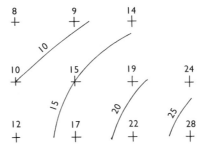

Exercise 2.3

For the grid shown:

(a) Show that average level is 75.265 m AOD.
(b) Complete the contours at 10 m intervals.

```
  48.6      59.2      67.7      56.4
   +         +         +         +

  64.1      76.6      82.2      68.3
   +         +         +         +

  71.4      82.6      93.1      83.5
   +         +         +         +

  69.8      75.6      79.8      80.1
   +         +         +         +

  64.2      68.5      74.2      70.3
   +         +         +         +
```

2.16 Levelling used to determine heights of sight rails to control the gradient of a drain or sewer

Basic definitions used in sewer control

See Figure 2.23.

- **Gradient**. This refers to the slope at which the sewer or drain must be laid in order to achieve self cleaning.

  Drains and sewers with no access to storm water are normally laid at 1 : 40, 1 : 60, and 1 : 90 for 100 mm, 150 mm and 225 mm diameter pipe respectively. Where drains and sewers have access to storm water, shallower gradients are used depending on the quantity of water flow.
- **Invert level**. The lower level of the inside of a pipe at a section is known as the invert level.
- **Outfall**. The lowest invert level in a drainage section is the outfall.
- **Cover**. The cover at a section is the depth of earth between the existing

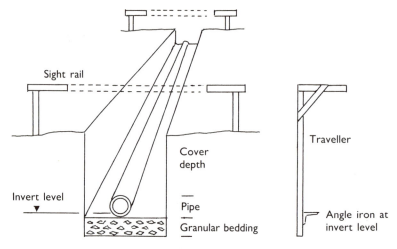

Figure 2.23

ground level and the top of the pipe. Ideally cover is above 1 m. Below 1 m and above 6 m special protection is needed in the form of at least 150 mm thick concrete surround to avoid cracking of the pipe due to surface or earth pressures.

- **Sight rail**. This horizontal rail is placed at a precise distance above the invert level of the sewer. Machine operations require the dotted section to be excluded.

  Always use at least three sets of sight rails so that a disturbance of one sight rail due to the normal building operations is detected by the others.

- **Traveller**. The traveller is constructed to have length equal to the precise distance between top of sight rail and lower level of granular bedding. An angle iron is placed at the position of the invert level.

Example 2.2 *Sewer and drainage calculations*_____

A sewer AB is 48 m in length and is to be laid at a gradient of 1 in 60 from its outfall at A which has a reduced level of 146.362 m AOD. The pipe is 150 mm diameter and 10 mm thick. The granular bedding is to be 150 m.

Design the heights of suitable sight rails at each end and centre of its run, and dimension a traveller to use in the operation. The levels were taken on pegs placed at A, B and C, the mid point of the sewer length.

BS	IS	FS	Rise	Fall	Reduced	Remarks
2.864					147.214	BM(x)
	2.276		0.588		147.802	A
	1.596		0.680		148.482	C
	1.678			0.082	148.400	B
		2.864		1.186	147.214	BM(x)

Σ2.864   Σ2.864 Σ1.268 Σ1.268

Diff. = 0   Diff. = 0

Solution

Assume a traveller measuring 2 m from top to angle iron at invert.

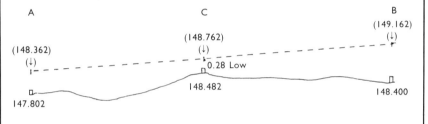

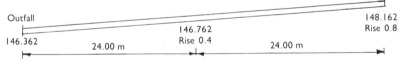

Sewer rises 1 m in 60 m: Sewer rises in 24 m $\frac{24}{60} \times 1 = 0.4$ m

Sewer rises in 48 m $\frac{48}{60} \times 1 = 0.8$ m

	A	C	B
Level at ground	147.802	148.482	148.400
Level at invert	146.362	146.762	147.162
Level at sight rail	148.362	148.762	149.162
Height of sight rail above ground for a 2.0 m traveller	0.560	0.280	0.762
	(too low)	(too low)	(ok)
If traveller is 3.0 m to angle	**1.560**(ok)	**1.280**(ok)	**1.762**(ok)

Suitable traveller total length = 3.0 m + 150 mm + 10 mm
= 3.16 m

Exercise 2.4 *Sewer and drainage calculations*_____

The levelling operation was carried out to establish the ground levels at A, B, C and D, four points on the line of a sewer where AB = BC = CD = 16 m.

The level of the outfall of the sewer at A was 124.36 m AOD, and the gradient between A and D was 1 in 40.

The sewer had a thickness of 10 mm and a granular bedding of 150 mm.

From these details show that suitable sight rail heights at A, B, C and D would be 1.5, 1.4, 1.3 and 1.6 m respectively assuming a traveller measuring 3.16 m was used.

BS	IS	FS	Rise	Fall	Reduced level	Remarks
2.264					125.742	BM(Y)
	2.146					A
	1.646					B
	1.146					C
	1.046					D
		2.264				BM(Y)

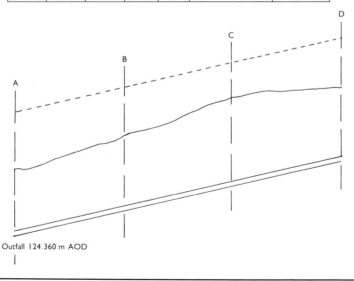

Outfall 124.360 m AOD

2.17 Curvature and refraction errors_____

Short sights

For short sights the level line, the horizontal line and the tangential line can be considered to coincide.

Long sights

Longer sights must consider the effects of the curvature of the earth's surface as shown in Figure 2.24.

Curvature effect

C_C is the difference in reading on a staff between a tangent line and a level line over a distance of K (km). By Pythagoras' theorem:

$(C_C + R)^2 = R^2 + K^2$
$C_C{}^2 + 2C_C R + R^2 = R^2 + K^2$
$C_C{}^2$ is negligible $\therefore C_C = K^2/2R$
Diameter of earth $= 2R = 12\,730$ km
C_C in m $= 0.0786K^2$ (K in km)

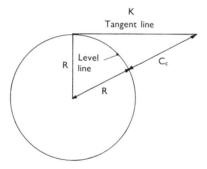

Figure 2.24

Refraction effects

Lines of sight are affected by air movement and changes in air density. Sights which pass close to the earth's surface are subjected to errors due to the turbulence of the air caused by the ground and air being at different temperatures.

In steady conditions, usually in the middle of the day, the effect of refraction is taken as one-seventh that of curvature but acting in the opposite direction.

Consequently, the effects of both curvature and refraction errors are often taken as $0.0786K^2 \times \frac{6}{7}$, i.e.

$$C_C - C_R = 0.0674K^2 \; (K \text{ in km})$$

Methods of reducing refraction effects

1. Sights should be taken in the middle of the day when refraction is small and steady.
2. Sights should not be allowed to pass within 1 m of the earth's surface.
3. Take reciprocal levels.

2.18 Precise levelling

If levelling is required to meet a very high specification for accuracy, special equipment is required and careful procedures must be followed.

Equipment

- The **precise level**. This instrument is a very precise tilting level with a high-powered telescope. The level must be fitted with a very sensitive split bubble and a parallel plate micrometer.

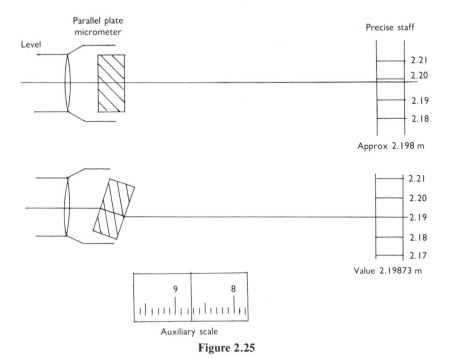

Figure 2.25

Note that automatic levels are not usually used in this type of work as they cannot meet the accuracy specification.

■ The **precise staff**. This staff is normally faced with invar steel to restrict temperature displacement. The staff is provided with a level bubble to ensure that the staff is vertical.

■ The **parallel plate micrometer**. Figure 2.25 shows a glass with parallel sides pivoting in front of the telescope. When the glass is vertical the cross hairs take up an intermediate position. When the glass (i.e. parallel plate) is tilted, the line of sight can be made to pass through the centre of a graduation. The tilt and displacement are related and the displacement recorded accurately on an auxiliary scale.

Procedures

1. Use short sights.
2. Equalize backsights and foresights carefully using tapes or strides.
3. Focus accurately and ensure that the bubble is central.

Three

Angle measurement

3.1 The basic theodolite_____

Purpose and general description

The theodolite is designed to measure accurately both vertical and horizontal angles. The instrument chosen for a description is an old pattern of theodolite illustrated in Figure 3.1: selected because it shows clearly the main working parts common to all theodolites.

The figure shows how the telescope is mounted on the trunnion axis fitted in the index frame. The vertical circle moves with the telescope about the trunnion axis. Vertical angles are measured by the horizontal index arm.

The upper and lower horizontal plates are supported by a level head consisting of a tribrach with three levelling screws fitted to a horizontal foot plate.

Horizontal angles are measured by clamping the lower circle and using the upper plate as an indicator.

3.2 Types of theodolite_____

Older instruments

The vernier theodolite is rarely used commercially but is used as a training instrument because it is very basic in structure and its working components can be clearly seen.

The circles of this instrument are normally brass and they are read by vernier measurement. The vertical angles are assessed using vernier scales

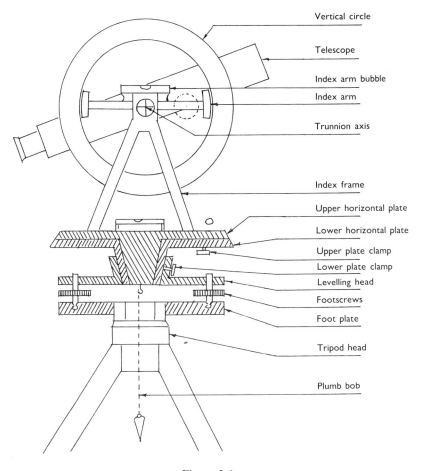

Vertical circle

Telescope

Index arm bubble

Index arm

Trunnion axis

Index frame

Upper horizontal plate

Lower horizontal plate

Upper plate clamp

Lower plate clamp

Levelling head

Footscrews

Foot plate

Tripod head

Plumb bob

Figure 3.1

on the index arm against the vertical circle, while the horizontal angles are obtained by using vernier scales on the upper horizontal plate.

Modern instruments

Modern instruments normally incorporate many of the developments which have taken place over the years including:

1. Alternatives to vernier measurement of angles.
2. Smaller circles in glass with fine etched graduations for precise work.
3. Axes are no longer tapered but are in steel cylinders with self-centring ball races.
4. Introduction of optical plummets for centring accuracy.

5. Improvement in lens giving greater magnification and better vision.
6. Introduction of internal lighting for night work.
7. Automatic vertical collimation.

3.3 Classification of modern theodolites by angle reading system

- **Optical scale theodolite** employs a transparent scale graduated over a whole glass circle division normally one degree.
- **Single reading micrometer theodolite** relies on a parallel plate micrometer to deflect light to read index mark. The amount of deflection is read on the micrometer scale.
- **Double reading micrometer theodolite** has a light system which reads the opposite sides of the main circle and reflects them together. Rotation of the micrometer brings the readings into coincidence. This gives a reading free of eccentricity error.
- **Electronic theodolites** have the graduated circles replaced by coded ones and readings appear on a crystal display.

3.4 Classification of modern theodolites by precision

- **Low order instruments** are theodolites reading directly to 20″ or more and are used for general engineering and construction work and setting out where high accuracy is not required.
- **One-second theodolites** read directly to 1″ and are used by land surveyors for large-scale surveys and third-order triangulation work.
- **Geodetic theodolites** read directly to 0.2″ and are used for primary and secondary triangulation and first-order traverse work.

3.5 Temporary adjustments of a theodolite

Set up tripod

Ensure the following:

1. Tripod is in a stable position.
2. Points are firmly in the ground.
3. Tripod screws are tight.
4. Tripod head is horizontal.
5. Tripod is centrally placed over station peg.

Plate bubble levelled

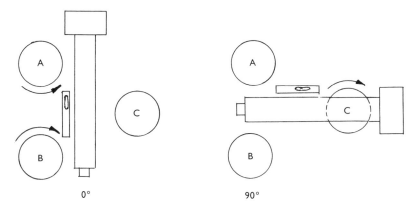

Figure 3.2

Levelling procedures

1. Place the telescope parallel to the footscrews at A and B as shown in Figure 3.2.
2. The footscrews at A and B should be turned as shown in the diagram or in the opposite direction. The bubble will follow the direction of the *left thumb*.
3. Centralize the bubble.
4. Rotate the telescope through 90°.
5. Centralize the bubble by turning footscrew C, appreciating that the bubble will follow the direction of the left thumb.
6. Repeat the operation until the bubble remains central in both positions.
7. Check to see if bubble remains in the centre of its run at 180°.
8. If the bubble remains central there is zero bubble error.
9. If the bubble is out at 180° there is bubble error.

Fine levelling

Fine levelling is a method of neutralizing bubble error. If a test shows that the bubble is consistently central at 0° and 90° and slightly out at 180° there is bubble error. If the error at 180° is reduced by half, by turning the footscrews, the plane will be perfectly horizontal even though the bubble will appear off-centre for the whole 360°.

Permanent adjustment is required to ensure the bubble is central throughout a complete rotation.

3.6 Setting up above stations

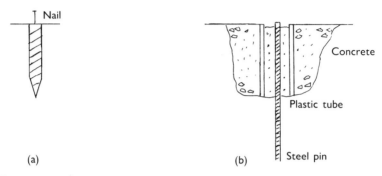

Figure 3.3 (a) Stations wooden peg. (b) Permanent ground marker (PGM).

Setting up above a mark on a peg

Using a plumb bob

1. Place legs equidistant from peg with tripod head levelled by eye.
2. Hang plumb bob and note error and direction between it and the mark.
3. Move each leg in turn, this amount in the noted direction.
4. Place instrument on tripod and level up.
5. If optical plummet shows a small error, release centring clamp and centre.
6. Fine level and centre again.

If the error is too large for centring then repeat the process.

Using optical plummet only

1. Place legs equidistant from peg with tripod head levelled by eye.
2. Place instrument on tripod and locate peg using optical plummet.
3. Using footscrews centre above mark.
4. Level using sliding legs.
5. Fine level using footscrews.
6. Release centring clamp and centre above mark.

Using a 'kern' tripod

1. Place legs equidistant from peg.
2. Loosen the collar under the tripod head.
3. Lower centring rod on mark, ensuring that it is screwed tightly into the tripod head.
4. Level the circular bubble by adjusting the tripod legs.

5. Push in small button on tripod head and move the head to centre bubble precisely.
6. Tighten the collar.
7. Rotate the centring rod through 180°. If there is bubble movement then loosen the collar and adjust the bubble to the mean position.
8. Check that the centring rod is directly above the mark on the peg. If so, the rod will be vertical and the instrument directly above the mark.

3.7 The face of a theodolite

If an observer looks through the eyepiece of a theodolite, as shown in Figure 3.4, and the vertical circle is on his left then the readings taken from this position will be **face left** readings.

If the vertical circle is on his right, the readings taken from this position will be **face right** readings.

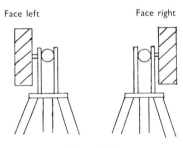

Figure 3.4

3.8 Measurement of horizontal angles using a theodolite

For the situation shown in Figure 3.5:

1. Level up instrument at A through 360°.
2. Clamp lower plate.
3. With upper plate free sight B approximately.
4. Clamp upper plate, and, using fine adjustment, sight B very accurately.
5. Read angle using scale to give angle OAB using the methods described in section 3.11.
6. Repeat with point C and read angle OAC.
7. Subtract to obtain angle BAC.
8. Repeat the procedure on the opposite face and take the mean value.

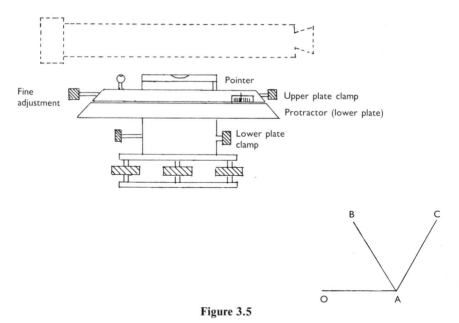

Figure 3.5

3.9 Vertical angles

The measurement of vertical angles is more complex than measuring horizontal because:

1. Vertical angles are measured with respect to a horizontal datum.
2. The pattern of vertical circle figuring varies with different theodolites.

Establishing horizontal datums

The method of determining horizontal datum varies with the type of theodolite. Some instruments are fitted with an altitude bubble on the vertical circle which may be levelled by a clip screw. Before taking readings with this type of instrument the altitude bubble must be centralized.

Most modern theodolites have an automatic vertical indexing facility provided by a damped pendulum device. Electronic theodolites are normally automatic and will enable the operator to set zero either at the horizontal horizon or the zenith at the touch of an internal switch.

Vertical circle figuring patterns

Whichever pattern in Figure 3.6 is used, the angle should be reduced to an elevation or depression with respect to the horizontal.

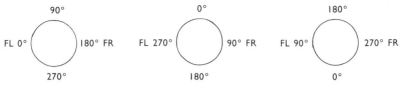

Figure 3.6

Measurement of vertical angles using a theodolite

With the instrument placed in position indicated in Figure 3.7:

1. Level up through $360°$.
2. Level the index-arm spirit level in older instruments or accept automatic horizons with the new.
3. Sight approximately onto D and clamp circle.
4. Using fine adjustment sight D accurately.
5. Read angle using the scale as indicated in section 3.11.
6. Repeat the process using the opposite face.
7. Reduce the angles and determine the mean.

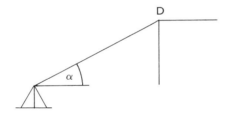

Figure 3.7

3.10 Booking procedures

It is usual to adopt a procedure in booking which will give optimum precision. Such a procedure should indicate:

1. The use of a reference object which is preferably a distinct, distant point which gives a reliable base reading to which all other horizontal readings are referred.
2. The use of face left and face right readings on each station helps to cancel out many instrument errors.
3. Swinging to the right on face left and swinging to the left on face right helps to eliminate creep and slip in the older instruments.

4. To have a value for the reference object (RO) slightly above zero. This cuts out the need for zeroing and protects the instrument from over-clamping on zero.
5. Repeat readings over a different part of the circle. This is mainly a check reading but averaging will reduce any scale distortion.

A typical angle booking is shown in the table below.

Theodolite		Personnel			Contract details	
Number Station A Height (stn) 1.42		Observer Booker Date			Title Job. no.	
Point			Horizontal angles			
	Face left	Face right	L & R mean	Angle w.r.t. RO		
RO B C D	00–08–30 64–16–50 123–24–30 184–36–40	180–09–10 244–17–10 303–24–20 4–37–30	00–08–50 64–17–00 123–24–25 184–37–05	00–00–00 64–08–10 123–15–35 184–28–15		
RO B C D	90–04–50 154–13–40 213–20–30 184–33–30	270–05–40 234–14–00 33–20–50 4–33–50	90–05–15 154–13–50 213–20–40 184–33–40	00–00–00 64–08–35 123–15–25 184–28–25		
Pt Target height			Vertical angles			
	Face left	Face right	FL corr.	FR corr.	Average	
B 1.42 C 1.42 D 1.42	93–04–10 87–42–20 86–18–40	266–53–40 272–20–50 273–43–20	– 03–04–10 02–17–40 03–41–20	– 03–06–20 02–20–50 03–43–20	– 03–05–15 + 02–19–15 + 03–46–20	

- Horizontal angles 1st line (RO)(FL) is slightly above 0°. (RO)(FR) is approximately 180° and is used to correct minutes and seconds. L and R mean is average of 00–08–30 and 00–09–10, i.e. 00–08–50. All angles are referred to (RO) by subtracting 00–08–50 from means.
- Horizontal angles 5th line (RO)(FL) is slightly above 90°. L and R mean is average of 90–04–50 and 90–05–40, i.e. 90–05–15. All angles are referred to (RO) by subtracting 90–05–15 from means.
- Vertical angles 1st line, horizontal (FL) is 90–00–00. Because of figuring pattern here, 93–04–10 is depression of 03–04–10 and 266–53–40 is a depression of 03–06–20. Mean depression is – 03–05–15.

Note that true vertical angles need instrument and target heights to be the same value.

Exercise 3.1 Booking procedure_____

Complete the horizontal angle booking shown in the table and deduce the following:

1. The corrected horizontal angles measured with respect to reference object (RO).
2. The horizontal angles between adjacent stations.
3. The elevations and depressions to the targets assuming the figuring pattern is as shown in the figure.

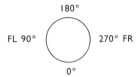

Theodolite	Personnel	Contract details
No. Station 0 Height 1.48	Observer FB Booker WHH Date: 2.9.90	Title: Compton Broadway Job. no. 136

Point	Horizontal angles			
	Face left	Face right	L & R mean	Angle w.r.t. RO
RO	00–10–20	180–11–40		
A	41–42–50	221–44–20		
B	93–10–10	273–11–50		
C	186–52–30	6–53–10		
D	247–27–40	67–28–30		
E	302–15–10	122–16–50		
RO	00–10–20	180–11–40		
RO	90–08–40	270–10–20		
A	131–40–30	311–41–50		
B	183–08–50	03–09–40		
C	276–50–40	96–51–20		
D	337–26–20	157–27–50		
E	32–13–40	212–15–10		
RO	90–08–40	270–10–20		

Pt Target height	Vertical angles			
A 1.48	88–18–20	271–41–30		
B 1.48	86–43–50	273–16–50		
C 1.48	91–51–10	268–09–20		
D 1.48	94–10–30	265–50–10		
E 1.48	96–36–40	263–15–10		

3.11 Types of angle reading device_____

Optical methods

Optical direct reading scales

In the example illustrated by Figure 3.8 transparent scales etched between
0' and 60' are placed in the optical paths between the circle eyepiece and
the highly magnified horizontal and vertical circles. The transparent scale
is constructed to be exactly equal to the length on each circle corresponding
to 1°. The position at zero on the transparent graduated scale defines the
angle. Here the pointer zero is between 54° and 55°. The value is given by
intersection of scales, i.e. 54°49'.

Figure 3.8

Single reading optical micrometer

When light is passed through a glass wedge the path of the light is diverted,
as shown in Figure 3.9. Lateral movement of the wedge will mean greater
or less diversion. This can be used to establish accurate angle readings if
lateral movement is graduated.

With auxiliary scale on zero, the reading lies between 63°30' and 63°40'.
Lateral movement of the wedge gives a reading of exactly 63°20' on the
main scale and an auxiliary scale reading of 11' 40". Therefore the true
reading is 63°31'40".

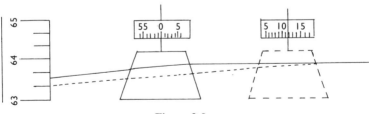

Figure 3.9

Double reading optical micrometer

This optical micrometer comprises two parallel plates or wedges which can
be made to rotate in opposite directions allowing images of both sides of

the circle to be brought together. A micrometer screw can be used to achieve coincidence.

Here coincidence is achieved between the upper and lower scales. In Figure 3.10 the reading is 93°20′ plus 3′51″. Thus the true reading is 93°23′51″.

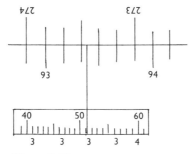

Figure 3.10

Simple micrometer methods

The drum micrometer
One complete turn of the drum of the micrometer is designed to move a hair line laterally on a scale through one circle graduation. The drum perimeter is suitably divided to give accurate intermediate values.

In Figure 3.11, with A set up at zero the two cross hairs straddle the groove. Turn A until the nearest lower division is straddled. This measures

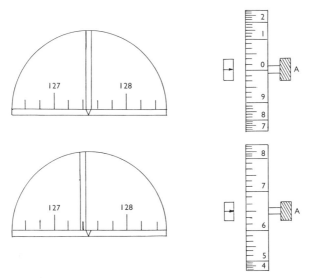

Figure 3.11

the movement from groove to lower division very accurately. Here the reading is 127°20′00″ plus 6′31″, which gives 127°26′31″ as the true reading.

The three window digital micrometer

This instrument has a soft display with sharp graduations to give a rapid read out.

In Figure 3.12 the horizontal angle is 137° plus 33′26″. The true horizontal reading is 137°33′26″. In order to find the vertical angle the micrometer must be adjusted to place a reading between the marks and then a new reading should be taken on the micrometer scale.

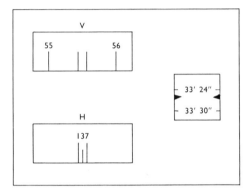

Figure 3.12

Example 3.1

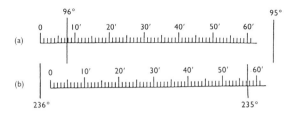

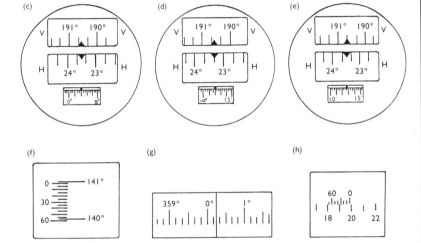

(a) Zero lies between 96° and 97°. How far from 96° 7 mins + say 40 sec reading is 96°7′40″?

(b) Zero lies between 235° and 236°. How far from 235° 57 mins + 20 sec reading is 235°57′20″?

(c) ▲ does not lie on any line therefore no reading is to be taken.

(d) The ▲ lies on line between 23 and 24, therefore the reading is 23°20′ plus the reading of 12′ shown on the lower scale. The reading is 23°32′.

(e) The ▲ lies on a line between 190° and 191°, i.e. 190°40′, and the reading shown on the lower scale is 12′40″. Therefore the reading is 190°52′40″.

(f) Zero lies between 140° and 141°; the reading = 140°58′.

(g) Reading between 0 and 1° and between 10′ and 20°, i.e. 16′, therefore the reading is 0°16′.

(h) Zero lies between 19° and 20° and the reading shown on the upper scale is 36′, therefore the reading is 19°36′.

50   *Surveying and setting out procedures*

Exercise 3.2

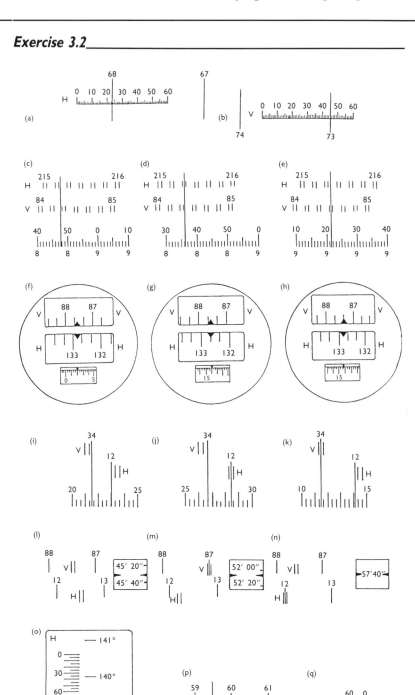

(a) H = 68°23′20″	(g) H = 132°56′00″	(m) V = 87°52′07″
(b) V = 73°45′00″	(h) V = 87°35′40″	(n) H = 12°57′40″
(c) No result	(i) No result	(o) H = 140°36′
(d) H = 215°28′36″	(j) H = 12°28′30″	(p) V = 59°29′
(e) V = 84°39′21″	(k) V = 34°11′28″	(q) H = 19°30′
(f) No result	(l) No result	

3.12 Theodolite adjustments

The theodolite adjustments should be completed in the following order:

1. Plate level adjustment.
2. Horizontal collimation or vertical hair adjustment.
3. Trunnion axis.
4. Vertical circle index.
5. Optical plummet.

Plate bubble errors

1. Place a spirit level parallel to footscrews at A and B as shown in Figure 3.13, i.e. at 0°.
2. The footscrews should be turned in the direction shown or in the opposite direction. The bubble will follow the direction of the *left thumb*.
3. Centralize the bubble.
4. Rotate the spirit level through 90°.
5. Centralize the bubble by turning footscrew at C.
6. Repeat the operation until the bubble remains central at both 0° and 90°.

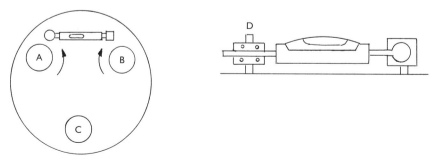

Figure 3.13 Spirit level.

7. Turn the spirit level through $180°$. If the bubble remains in the centre of its run the plate will be truly horizontal.
8. If the bubble moves off centre at $180°$ the plate is not horizontal but can be made to be so by adjusting A and B to take the bubble half-way back.
9. If the bubble is taken half way it will remain in the same position throughout a revolution of $360°$.
10. To correct the bubble the capstan screws at D should be carefully adjusted to centralise the bubble so that it remains central throughout a complete revolution.

Horizontal collimation (vertical hair error)

If the vertical hair is displaced horizontally as the telescope revolves around the trunnion axis, as shown in Figure 3.14, the angle swept out by the cross hair sight will not be a $90°$ plane but a very shallow cone. The plan Figure 3.15 shows the diversion on one face only.

The vertical hair collimation line on one face diverts from true by angle $2c$.

Figure 3.14

Figure 3.15

Horizontal collimation adjustment

1. Place an arrow at approximately 200 m from a wall in an area where the ground is relatively flat, as shown in Figure 3.16.
2. Set up and level the theodolite at T mid-way between the arrow and the wall.
3. Using face left, carefully sight the arrow at E and with the instrument clamped transit and make a mark on the wall at F. At F the diversion to the left is $2c$.
4. Using face right, carefully resight the arrow at E and with the instrument clamped transit and make a mark on the wall at G. At G the diversion to the right is $2c$.

5. Measure TH where H is mid-way between F and G.

The results are shown as:

TH = _____ m   FG = _____ m   FH = $\frac{1}{2}$FG = _____ m

tan $2c$ = FH/TH $2c$ = _____ ° c = _____ seconds

Correction of error

In the test procedure in Figure 3.16, the last face right reading was on to G. Place a point X mid-way between H and G. Using the diaphragm screws L and R as shown in Figure 3.17 alter the sight to pass through X. Recheck the whole procedure to ensure that the horizontal collimation error is no longer present.

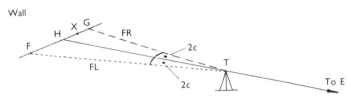

Figure 3.16

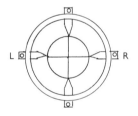

Figure 3.17

The trunnion axis error of the theodolite

Ideally, the trunnion axis is perpendicular to the vertical axis and will be horizontal when the instrument is levelled. If the trunnion axis is not horizontal, the telescope will not define a vertical plane and will give rise to incorrect vertical and horizontal angles. Angle i is the inclination of the trunnion axis as shown in Figure 3.18.

The spire test

It is normal when checking the trunnion axis to make use of a church spire or lightning conductor to provide a well defined elevated point as shown in Figure 3.19.

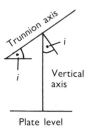

Figure 3.18

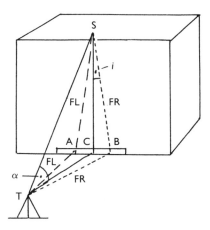

Figure 3.19

1. Place the theodolite so that a spire is seen elevated between 30 and 50°.
2. Place a horizontal staff at approximately the same level as the theodolite.
3. Using face left, note the vertical angle at S and staff reading at A.
4. Using face right, note the vertical angle at S and staff reading at B.
5. C is the mid-point between A and B.
6. Measure CT and CB.

The results are shown as:

$$\tan \alpha = \frac{SC}{CT} \quad \therefore \ SC = CT \tan \alpha$$

$$CB = \tfrac{1}{2}AB = \underline{\hspace{1.5cm}}$$

$$\tan i = \frac{CB}{SC} = \underline{\hspace{1.5cm}}$$

$$i = \underline{\hspace{1.5cm}}° \quad i = \underline{\hspace{1.5cm}} \text{ seconds}$$

Station	Sight to	Face	Vertical angle α	Value at A	Value at B
T	S	FL			
T	S	FR			
Average angle(α) =				AB =	CT =

Correction of error

1. The last reading taken in the above test was a face right to B.
2. Use the upper tangent screw to sight C mid-way between A and B.
3. Elevate the telescope to spire and locate S by adjusting the trunnion axis screws.
4. Check the accuracy of the adjustment by depressing telescope and note whether the sight passes through C.

Vertical circle index

Ideally, for all types of theodolite a perfectly horizontal line of sight should give a vertical angle reading which is a multiple of 90°.

Some theodolites establish the horizontal line of sight by use of the altitude bubble while others use automatic levelling.

Vertical circle tests

1. Set up and level the theodolite.
2. Establish a horizontal datum by:

   (a) centralizing the altitude bubble by means of the clip screw, or
   (b) by automatic means.

3. Direct the telescope face left in a horizontal position at vertical staff placed at, say, 60 m.
4. Set vertical circle to read the nearest angle exactly a multiple of 90° by using tangent screw.
5. Take a reading on the vertical staff.
6. Repeat the whole operation using face right.
7. If the staff readings differ there is vertical circle index error.
8. The methods of correction depend on the type of theodolite.

Vertical circle adjustment for theodolites with altitude bubble

1. Complete the test and find the mean staff reading.
2. Direct the telescope to the mean staff reading using the telescope tangent screw.

3. The angle reading will not now be a multiple of 90°. Reset using the altitude resetting screw.
4. Altering the altitude resetting screw will decentralize the altitude bubble. Centralize using the bubble capstan screws.

Vertical circle adjustment for automatic theodolites

1. Complete the test and find the mean staff reading.
2. Adjust the cross hairs to obtain coincidence with the mean reading.

Vertical circle adjustment for electronic theodolites with telescope bubble

1. Complete the test and find the mean staff reading.
2. Sight multiple of 90° on mean reading.
3. The bubble will be out. Correct using capstan screws.
4. Press the indexing button.

Optical plummet located in the plate

This is a popular method of providing a vertical line of sight coinciding with the vertical axis of the levelled theodolite. Here the plate can be rotated about the vertical axis.

Test

1. Set up and level the theodolite.
2. Mark the position on the ground intersected by the optical plummet.
3. Turn the instrument horizontally through 180°.
4. Locate a second mark.
5. If the marks coincide no adjustment is required.
6. If the marks do not coincide establish the position of the mid-point.
7. Adjust the capstan screws until the mid-point is located.
8. Repeat the test until all error is removed.

Optical plummet located in the tribrach

This method provides a vertical line of sight coinciding with the vertical axis of the instrument but its accuracy is difficult to assess in the field. The tribrach cannot be rotated without disturbing the levelling.

Test

1. Set the theodolite on its side on a bench with its base facing the wall.
2. Mark the position on the wall intersected by the optical plummet.
3. Rotate the tribrach through 180° and locate the second mark.

4. If the marks coincide no adjustment is required.
5. If the marks are apart, establish the mid-point by adjustment of the capstan screws until the mid-point is located.
6. Repeat the test until all error is removed.

The kern plumbing pole

This method of providing a vertical line relies on the bull's eye bubble on the plumbing pole being in good adjustment.

Test

1. Set up the theodolite and centre it above a mark with a central bubble.
2. Rotate the plumbing pole through 180°.
3. If the bubble remains central, no adjustment is required.
4. If the bubble moves off centre, bring it half-way back with the capstan adjusting screws.
5. Repeat the test and adjustment until all error has been removed.

3.13 Field methods used to reduce the effects of theodolite permanent errors

Most common errors

Plate bubble errors

The bubble is levelled at 0 and 90°. A check is made at 180°. If the bubble is out, it is brought back to the half-way point by the foot screws. This is known as fine levelling.

When the instrument has been fine levelled, a complete revolution of the horizontal circle should see the bubble in the same position. In this situation the plate is truly horizontal and the vertical axis vertical even though the bubble is out. The results given in this situation are very reliable.

The mean of face left and face right readings will reduce considerably the errors due to plate level error.

Horizontal collimation (on vertical hair error)

Collimation error is largely cancelled by taking the means of the readings on two faces.

Optical plummets and kern plumbing pole

Inaccuracy in any of these devices causes centring error which can have a considerable effect on the accuracy of the angle measurement and should be eliminated as soon as possible.

Fortunately the errors which most commonly occur are those which are most easily checked and corrected. Bubble error can be checked at each station; the plumbing and the horizontal collimation errors can be checked and corrected monthly.

Less common errors

Trunnion axis error
In most modern theodolites the trunnion axis errors are kept extremely small and often there is no means of adjusting the error. An occasional check is desirable to see that the error remains small. The mean of the readings on both faces gives a very reliable reading.

Vertical circle index error
In well designed theodolites this error is small and the index error is cancelled by taking the mean of face left and face right angles. Monthly checks are advisable.

3.14 Care of theodolites and accessories

Security

- When not in use the equipment is normally kept in a store under lock and key.
- List the items taken from security when they are required.
- Never leave the instrument unattended.
- Check all the items when they are returned to security.

Safety

- The surveyor is responsible for the safety of his personnel and his equipment.
- Potential dangers and hazards should be anticipated. Approaching plant and passing vehicles are a danger to both personnel and equipment.
- The instrument should be set up in a stable condition. Under normal site conditions the tripod legs can be secured in the ground.
- It is ill-advised to set up the instrument in the site office or on a smooth hard surface where a small push may cause a great deal of damage to the instrument.

Care

- The instrument should be carefully taken from the box noting how it lies so that replacement will be an easier process.
- Set up the instrument over its peg in a stable condition and ensure that it is protected against severe weather conditions.
- Use the instrument with care and do not over-tighten the clamps.
- Make sure the instrument is in a clean condition and give special attention to the lens which should be cleaned with a special tissue or dusting brush.
- On returning the instrument to its box make sure it fits snugly and that the clamps are locked before closing the lid.

Method of use

- The correct theodolite should be chosen for the appropriate accuracy.
- A checking system must be employed at as many stages as possible.
- Physical checks should be made on angles close to the horizon or close to $180°$ to ensure the directions are correct.

Tests

- There should be a daily check on the plate bubble and approximately monthly checks made on the trunnion axis error, the collimation axis error, the index error, the optical plummet or the plumbing rod.
- The errors should be either corrected on-site or sent away to a specialist or the manufacturer.

Four

Distance measurement

4.1 Distance measurement by tape_____

Types of tape

Basically there are three types of tape used in surveying work:

1. Synthetic tapes.
2. Carbon steel tapes.
3. Invar steel tapes.

Synthetic tapes are linen, glass fibre or plastic and are useful in low order accuracy work such as chain surveying. This type of tape is robust and does not suffer cracking but it shrinks and stretches with temperature and moisture content. The graduations are normally shown at 5 mm intervals.

Carbon steel tapes are less affected by weather conditions and are used largely in setting out work. Although this tape is strong in tension it is brittle when a person inadvertently treads on its edge. Here the accuracy is higher and the graduations are marked at 1 mm intervals.

Invar steel tapes are very resistant to temperature and moisture content and consequently suffer little change in length due to weather conditions. This type of tape is used for very accurate setting out work and base line measurement.

Measurement of short distances by tape

For very short distances a 2 or 3 m long, a spring-loaded pocket tape is useful. This type of tape is usually fitted with a hook end which will secure itself to a peg nail or the corner of a building, etc. to enable one person to take a quick measurement.

Measurement of intermediate distances by tape

For intermediate distances the most popular tape is the 30 m steel tape with a protective coating which is in an open frame winder. This size is comfortable to carry and will measure most offset distances. The protective coating retards rusting and the open winder does not collect dirt to the same extent as the more compact encased winder.

Care of steel tapes

- Tapes should be cleaned and lightly oiled at regular intervals.
- The winder mechanism should be well maintained to give a smooth action.
- Care should be exercised to see that the tape is not pulled from the winder and that the tape is not stretched, kinked or broken.

4.2 Building Research Establishment findings

The Building Research Establishment in their *Digest 234* (1980) indicate that even experienced site personnel are liable to have errors in the order of 25 mm in the measurement of a length of 30 m using a steel tape. Further work by the Building Research Establishment suggested that reading errors and calibration errors are unlikely to exceed 2 mm and 3 mm respectively, and are not normally significant when compared with other sources of error.

4.3 Reasons for inaccuracies in tape measurements

1. Roughness of ground surface.
2. Humidity.
3. Sag.
4. Slope.
5. Tension.
6. Temperature.

How to compensate

1. Roughness is reduced by measurement between intermediate pegs or catenary measurement.
2. Humidity is avoided using steel.

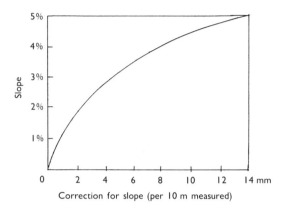

Figure 4.1 Corrections for slope.

3. Sag is reduced by using 70 N pull for 10 mm tape or 105 N pull for 13 mm tape.
4. Slopes are corrected by the graph shown in Figure 4.1.
5. Tension problems are avoided by using standardized tensions.
6. Temperature change is approximately 1 mm every 10 m for every 10°C from 20°C.

If the corrections are made the errors should fall within the accuracies shown below for carbon steel tapes.

Distance	Sag	Slope	Tension	Temperature	Accuracy (mm)
5 m	✓	✓	✕	✕	±5
25 m	✓	✓	✕	✕	±10
25 m +	✓	✓	✕	✕	±15
10 m	✓	✓	✓	✓	±3
30 m	✓	✓	✓	✓	±6
100 m	✓	✓	✓	✓	±15
500 m	✓	✓	✓	✓	±25
500 m +	✓	✓	✓	✓	1/20 000

✕ means no special precautions taken
✓ means special precautions taken

4.4 Base line measurement

When precise measurement is required from a tape it is usual to use catenary measurement as shown in Figure 4.2 and to apply a series of corrections.

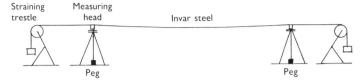

Figure 4.2

Practical base line measurement

1. Pegs are placed at intervals of approximately 30 m in a straight line ranged by a theodolite.
2. Measuring heads are set up above the pegs and the levels of the successive heads are established.
3. The tape is set up in catenary and checked for twists.
4. Take readings at beginning and end of the tape at the same time.
5. Note temperatures and tensions.
6. Repeat this procedure entirely using different values on the measuring scales at each end (say 6 times).
7. Apply corrections for sag, tension, temperature, slope and height above sea level.

Precautions

■ Protect the tape from wind.
■ Avoid varying temperatures.
■ Use standardized tape with low coefficient of expansion.

Corrections to apply to a catenary

$$\text{Sag} = -\frac{W^2 L}{24 N^2}$$

$$\text{Tension} = +\frac{(N - N_s)L}{AE}$$

$$\text{Temperature} = +\alpha L(\theta - \theta_s)$$

$$\text{Slope} = -\frac{h^2}{2L}$$

$$\text{Sea level} = -\frac{HL}{R}$$

where W = weight of tape in catenary (Newtons); N = pull (Newtons);

N_s = pull at which tape was standardized; A = area of tape (mm²); θ = temperature of the tape; θ_s = temperature at which tape was standardized; H = height above sea level; h = difference in level between heads; E = Young's modulus (kN/mm²); and α = coefficient of expansion.

The true length between A and B is:

$$L - \frac{W^2 L}{24 N^2} + \frac{(N - N_s)L}{AE} + \alpha L (\theta - \theta_s) - \frac{h^2}{2L} + \frac{HL}{R}$$

In normal calculations the value of L is the difference in tape readings. In even more precise work, where a computer program is used, each value of L is the value corrected by the previous terms. The order is as indicated above.

Example 4.1 *Base line measurement*_____

A base line was measured by a steel tape in catenary with the following level differences 0.1, 0.1, 1.3, 0.2 m in four separate bays as 30.010, 29.655, 30.025, 17.672 m under respective pulls of 60, 60, 60 and 55 N at respective temperatures of 18, 18, 18, and 25°C, the length used being 30.0 m at 20°C under a pull of 45 N on a plane surface.

Given that 30 m of the tape weighs exactly 8 N with steel at 0.00008 N/mm³, the coefficient of expansion α as 0.0000112 and E is 210 kN/mm², determine the length of the base to three decimal places.

Height above sea level is 40 m. Radius of the earth is 6371 km.

Weight of tape = Volume × Density.

∴ $8\,N = 30\,000 \times A \times 0.00008\,N/mm^2$

∴ $A = 3.333\,mm^2$

Constants

$$AE = 3.333 \times 210 = 700\,000\,N$$

$$\frac{H}{R} = \frac{40}{6371 \times 1000} = 0.00000627$$

Bay	L	W	W^2	$(N - N_s)$	$(\theta - \theta_s)$	h	h^2
1	30.010	8	64	15	−2	0.1	0.01
2	29.655	8	64	15	−2	0.1	0.01
3	30.025	8	64	15	−2	1.3	1.69
4	17.672	4.71	22.2	10	+5	0.2	0.04
	107.362						

	Legs 1, 2, 3	**Leg 4**

$$\text{Sag} = \frac{W^2 L}{24 N^2} \qquad \frac{-64 \times 89.69}{24 \times 60^2} \qquad \frac{-22.2 \times 17.672}{24 \times 55^2}$$

1, 2, 3	-0.006644
4	$+0.00540$

$$\text{Tension} = \frac{+(N - N_s)L}{AE} \qquad \frac{+15 \times 89.69}{700\,000} \qquad \frac{+10 \times 17.672}{700\,000}$$

1, 2, 3	$+0.00192$
4	$+0.00025$

$$\text{Temperature} = +\alpha L(\theta - \theta_s) =$$

Legs 1, 2, 3

$$0.0000112 \times 89.69 \times -2 \qquad 1, 2, 3 - 0.00201$$

Leg 4

$$0.00000112 \times 17.672 \times 5 \qquad 4 + 0.000099$$

Legs 1, 2

$$\text{Slope} = -\frac{h^2}{2L} \qquad \frac{0.01}{2 \times 30.01} \qquad \frac{0.01}{2 \times 29.655}$$

1	-0.00017
2	-0.00017

Legs 3, 4

$$\frac{-1.69}{2 \times 30.025} \qquad \frac{-0.04}{2 \times 17.672}$$

3	-0.02815
4	-0.00113

Legs 1 to 4

$$\text{Sea level} = \frac{-HL}{R} \qquad -0.00000627 \times 107.362$$

$$1 \text{ to } 4 - 0.00067$$

$$-0.10098$$

$$\text{Total length} = +107.362 - 0.10098 = \mathbf{107.261} \text{ m}$$

Distance measurement using tapes

In recent years little use has been made of the full base line measurement equipment on site, but a less expensive version shown in Figure 4.3 incorporating a spring balance and ranging rods has been used to establish accurate distances between points.

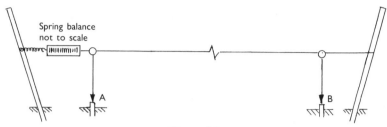

Figure 4.3

The true length between A and B is:

$$\text{Sag} \qquad \text{Tension} \qquad \text{Temperature} \quad \text{Slope} \quad \text{Sea level}$$

$$L - \frac{W^2 L}{24 N^2} + \frac{(N - N_s)L}{AE} + \alpha L(\theta - \theta_s) - \frac{h^2}{2L} - \frac{HL}{R}$$

The approximate length between A and B is:

$$L + \begin{pmatrix} \text{Zero if sag} \\ \text{and tension} \\ \text{are equalized} \end{pmatrix} + \begin{pmatrix} 1 \text{ mm for every} \\ 10 \text{ m for every} \\ 10°C \text{ from } 20°C \end{pmatrix} - \begin{pmatrix} \text{Graph} \\ \text{slope} \\ \text{value} \end{pmatrix} - \frac{HL}{R}$$

Exercise 4.1

A tape was used in catenary for the situation shown above to measure distance AB. The details were as follows: AB = 29.985 m on the tape. $N_s = 50$ N. $N = 80$ N. $\theta_s = 25°C$. $\theta = 30°C$. $W = 8$ N. $A = 2$ mm^2. $E = 200$ kN/mm^2. $\alpha = 0.00001$. $H = 300$ m. $h = 1.36$ m. $R = 6397$ km.
Show that values of the corrections were:

(a) Sag = −0.0125 m
(b) Tension = +0.0022 m
(c) Temperature = +0.0015 m
(d) Slope = −0.0308 m
(e) Sea level = −0.0014 m
(f) The true distance AB = 29.944 m.

Exercise 4.2

The distance AB was measured and the details were as follows: AB = 29.976 m on tape. $N_s = 40$ N. $N = 100$ N. $\theta_s = 25°C$. $\theta = 30°C$. $W = 6$ N. $A = 2$ mm^2. $E = 200$ kN/mm^2. $\alpha = 0.00001$. Slope = 4.5%. $H = 300$ m. Show that:

(a) Tension and sag corrections cancel each other out.

(b) Temperature correction is $+0.0015$ m.
(c) Slope correction is -0.03 m.
(d) Sea level correction is -0.0014 m.
(e) The true distance AB $= 29.946$ m.

4.5 Optical distance measurement

Tacheometry

Tacheometry is an inexpensive distance measurement method which involves no specialist equipment. The method employs the normal level or theodolite and a levelling staff.

Marked on the diaphragm of most levels and theodolites are stadia lines as indicated in Figures 4.4(a) and (b).

Basic theory

Consider Figure 4.5: $U =$ distance from lens to object, $V =$ distance from lens to image, $f =$ focal length of lens, $c =$ distance from lens to instrument,

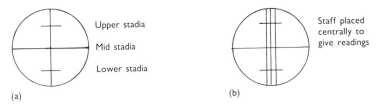

(a) (b)

Figure 4.4

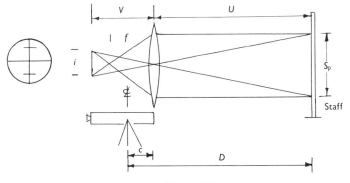

Figure 4.5

S_p is staff intercept perpendicular to line of sight, i = image of staff between stadia lines, C_1 and C_2 are tacheometric constants of the instrument.

The law of optics states that $f^{-1} = U^{-1} + V^{-1}$. Multiply by fU:

$$u = f + \frac{fU}{V}$$

But $U/V = S_p/i$ by similar triangles, therefore:

$$L = U + C = f + f\frac{S_p}{i} + C$$

$$L = C_1 S_p + C_2$$

where $C_1 = f/i$ and $C_2 = f + C$.

In most levels and theodolites C_1 is designed to be 100. In modern instruments C_2 is made to be zero by the introduction of an anallactic lens. A telescope with $C_1 = 100$ and $C_2 = 0$ is known as an anallactic telescope.

Finding horizontal distance and difference in level using a vertical staff

The distance between the trunnion axis of the telescope and the mid stadia reading on the staff is given by L where $L = C_1 S_p + C_2$. Consider the situations shown in Figures 4.6–4.9.

C_1 and C_2 are multiplying and additive constants respectively. S_p is the staff intercept perpendicular to the line of sight.

$S = (u - l)$ when V is zero.
$S_p = (u - l)\cos V$ when V is below 30°
$L = C_1 S_p + C_2$
$D = L \cos V$
$H = L \sin V$

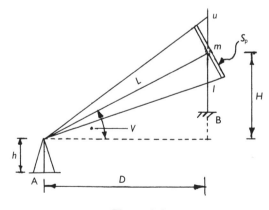

Figure 4.6

In Figure 4.6:

Horizontal distance AB $= D$
Level of B above A $= h + H - m$

In Figure 4.7:

Horizontal distance AB $= D$
Level of B above A $= h - H - m$

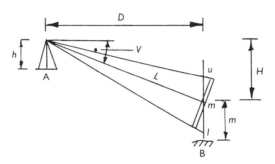

Figure 4.7

Finding horizontal distance and difference in level using an inclined staff

$$S = (u - l)$$
$$S_p = (u - l) \times 1$$
$$L = C_1 S_p + C_2$$
$$D = L \cos V$$
$$H = L \sin V$$

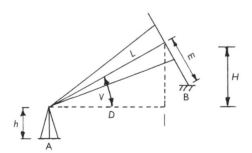

Figure 4.8

In Figure 4.8:

Horizontal distance AB $= D + m \sin V$
Level of B above A $= h + H - m \cos V$

In Figure 4.9:

Horizontal distance $AB = D - m \sin V$
Level of B above $A = h - H - m \cos V$

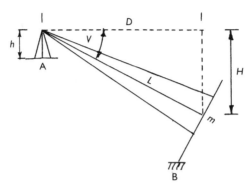

Figure 4.9

4.6 Use of tacheometric tables_____

Tacheometry enables the surveyor to establish the coordinates of points in an area around a theodolite station. The effectiveness of the operation depends on the accuracy required, the speed at which the readings are taken, and how quickly the results can be worked out.

The accuracy is not of a high order but it competes well with chain surveying and taping over rough terrain. The speed at which results are taken depends largely on the operation and the way in which the readings are taken. The rate at which results can be produced are also dependent on the methods used.

Redmond, in his work on tacheometric tables, has produced a method which is simple to operate, produces accuracy which is more than sufficient for the purpose, and will give rapid results on site.

Redmond's method

Redmond recommends that the operator should use the following procedure:

1. Sight the vertical staff in a suitable preparatory position.
2. Use the tangent screw to bring the vertical reading to nearest 20 minute mark.

3. Record this vertical angle *V* and the central hair reading *m*.
4. Use the tangent screw to bring the apparent lower stadia reading to the nearest 0.1 m reading.
5. By subtraction of this reading from the apparent upper stadia reading record *S*.
6. Establish *G* where $G = C_1S$. Note that C_1 is normally 100.
7. Use the values of *G* and *V* in Redmond's tacheometric tables to establish *D* and *H*.

Example 4.2

Use extracts from Redmond's tacheometric table to find:

(a) The horizontal distance AB.
(b) The level of B above A.

The instrument was at A and vertical staff at B. Height of instrument at A = 1.42 m. Vertical angle = $V = +5°20'$ when $m = 1.38$. When $l = 1.0$, $u = 1.72$, $C_1 = 100$.

$V = 5°20'$		
G	D	H
70	69.46	6.48
71	70.29	6.57
72	71.38	6.66
73	72.37	6.76
74	73.36	6.85
75	74.35	6.94

Extract from Redmond's tacheometric tables.

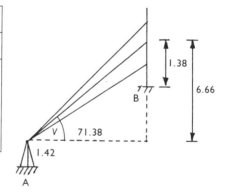

Solution

$V = 5°20'$.
$S = (u - l) = 1.72 - 1.0 = 0.72$.
$G = 100S = 72$.

From Redmond's table, $D = 71.38$, $H = 6.66$.

Horizontal distance AB = 71.38.
Level of B above A = $1.42 + 6.66 - 1.38 = 6.70$ m

*Tacheometric calculations*_____

Exercise 4.3_____

If A, B and C lie in the same plane, and $C_1 = 100$ and $C_2 = 0.1$, show that:

(a) Horizontal distances BA and BC are 62.841 and 79.813 m respectively.
(b) The levels at A and B are 89.318 and 107.394 m respectively.
(c) The gradient between A and C is 1 in 7.836.

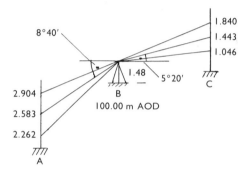

Staff at A		Staff at C	
$S = (u - l)$	$=$	$S = (u - l)$	$=$
$S_p = (u - l)\cos\ V =$		$S_p = (u - l)\cos\ V =$	
$L = C_1 S_p + C_2$	$=$	$L = C_1 S_p + C_2$	$=$
$D = L \cos\ V$	$=$	$D = L \cos\ V$	$=$
$H = L \sin\ V$	$=$	$H = L \sin\ V$	$=$
Level at A	$=$	Level at C	$=$

Exercise 4.4_____

In the situation shown in the diagram the coordinates at O are:

$X = 1\,000$ m, $Y = 1\,000$ m.
Level $= 100$ m AOD.
Height of instrument above O is 1.46 m.
$C_1 = 100$, $C_2 = 0.0$.

Readings taken from station O:

To A, $m = 1.43$, $S = 0.740$, $V = +5°20'$
To B, $m = 1.37$, $S = 0.715$, $V = -5°20'$
To C, $m = 1.56$, $S = 0.320$, $V = +8°40'$
A is east of O

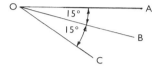

Show that:

(a) Plan lengths OA, OB, OC are 73.36 m, 70.835 m, 31.27 m respectively.
(b) The levels at A, B and C are 106.88 m, 93.475 m and 104.667 m respectively.
(c) The X coordinates at A, B and C are 1073.36 m, 1068.421 m and 1027.081 m.
(d) The Y coordinates at A, B and C are 1000.00 m, 981.667 m and 984.365 m.

$V = 5°20'$			$V = 8°40'$		
G	D	H	G	D	H
70	69.46	6.48	30	29.32	4.469
71	70.29	6.57	31	30.30	4.618
72	71.38	6.66	32	31.27	4.767
73	72.37	6.76	33	32.25	4.916
74	73.36	6.85	34	33.23	5.065
75	74.35	6.94	35	34.21	5.714

Extract from Redmond's tacheometric tables.

4.7 Subtense bar

Under the best conditions the subtense bar shown in Figure 4.10 provides the most accurate optical method of distance measurement. The basic principle of the method is simple, but to achieve the best results care and good quality equipment are required.

Basic principles

$$D = \frac{S}{2} \cot \frac{\theta}{2}$$

where D is the horizontal distance between instrument and the centre of the bar.

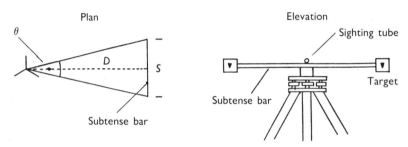

Figure 4.10

Measures used to obtain best results

1. The distance between the targets should be maintained as near to 2 m as possible. The use of invar steel will ensure that the difference between 2 m will not exceed 0.05 mm over a temperature range of 30°C.
2. A one second theodolite should be used to centre above the ground mark and to give the angles of θ to the nearest second after taking a series of readings.
3. The subtense bar should be supported by a tripod and tribrach which is used for levelling up the bar and centring above the ground mark.
4. A sighting tube attached at 90° to the bar should be used to ensure that the bar is perpendicular to the line of sight from the one second theodolite.
5. The distance to be measured is restricted to between 30 and 50 m in order to give the highest accuracy. Distances above 50 m involve small angles of θ and a 1 second error assumes more significance. Distances below 30 m are more difficult to centre on target.

Typical accuracies

Distance	20 m	30 m	40 m	60 m	100 m	200 m
Approximate accuracy	$\frac{1}{1000}$	$\frac{1}{8000}$	$\frac{1}{10\,000}$	$\frac{1}{6800}$	$\frac{1}{4200}$	$\frac{1}{2000}$

Accuracy of the subtense angle

To achieve an accuracy of one second the mean of several readings is required. For this purpose, ten readings would be appropriate. When taking the readings it is good practice to vary the positions on the horizontal circle. As the targets are the same level there is little need to change face.

4.8 Subtense bar calculations

The theodolite is designed to measure angles either in the horizontal or vertical plane. Where the theodolite is used to take angles between the targets on the subtense bar, the horizontal angle or plan angle is measured even though there is a considerable difference in level between instrument and the subtense bar. This means that D is always the horizontal distance in the expression:

$$D = \frac{S}{2} \cot \frac{\theta}{2}$$

where S is distance between targets on subtense bar and θ is horizontal angle measured by theodolite.

The difference in level between instrument and subtense bar, as shown in Figure 4.11, is given by:

$$H = D \tan \alpha$$

where H is the level difference between instrument and subtense bar, and α is vertical angle.

Measurement of longer distances using the subtense bar

It can be shown that the accuracy in measuring a distance D by a 2 m subtense bar with a theodolite measuring to 1 second is given by:

$$\frac{\Delta D}{D} = \frac{D\sqrt{n}}{206\,265 \times 2 \times n^2}$$

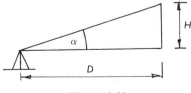

Figure 4.11

where D is total distance, n is number of bays and 2 is length in metres of subtense bar.

Consider a length of 160 m measured as:

(a) One length as shown in Figure 4.12.

Figure 4.12

(b) Four lengths of 40 m, as shown in Figure 4.13.

Figure 4.13

$$\text{Accuracy (a)} = \frac{160\sqrt{1}}{206\,265 \times 2 \times 1^2} = \frac{1}{2578}$$

$$\text{Accuracy (b)} = \frac{160\sqrt{4}}{206\,265} = \frac{1}{20\,626}$$

It can be shown that the accuracy in measuring a distance D using a base with the main length perpendicular as shown in Figure 4.14 is given by:

$$\frac{\Delta D}{D} = \sqrt{\left(\frac{2D}{2}\right)} \Big/ 206\,265$$

D is total distance and 2 is length in metres of subtense bar.

$$\text{Accuracy} = \frac{\sqrt{160}}{206\,265} = \frac{1}{16\,306}$$

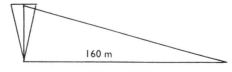

160 m

Figure 4.14

Subtense bar calculations_____

Exercise 4.5_____

If the horizontal and vertical angles taken from a one second theodolite on to a horizontal 2 m subtense bar were $1°30'30''$ and $5°40'$ respectively, show that:

(a) The horizontal distance between instrument and subtense bar is 75.968 m.
(b) The level of the bar above the theodolite is 7.538 m.

Exercise 4.6_____

The trunnion axis of a theodolite is 1.48 m above a peg A which has a reduced level of 107.36 m AOD.

The theodolite takes horizontal and vertical angles onto a horizontal 2 m subtense bar 1.56 m above a peg B.

If the horizontal angle is $2°10'20''$ and the vertical angle is a depression angle of $6°36'$ show that:

(a) The horizontal distance AB is 52.747 m.
(b) The difference in level between the instrument and the subtense bar is 6.103 m.
(c) The level at B is 101.177 m AOD.

Exercise 4.7_____

Assume that the accuracy in a length D measured in equal bays is given by:

$$\frac{\Delta D}{D} = \frac{D\sqrt{n} \times 1}{206\,265 \times 2 \times n^2}$$

where D is total distance, n is number of bays, 2 is the length of subtense bar in metres, and 1 is the accuracy of the instrument in seconds.

If the distance to be measured is 200 m, the subtense bar 2 m, and the accuracy of the theodolite is 1 second, show that the accuracy:

(a) Using one bay of 200 m is 1/2062.
(b) Using two bays of 100 m is 1/5834.
(c) Using four bays of 50 m is 1/16 501.

Exercise 4.8_____

Assume that the accuracy in measuring a distance D using a base with the main length perpendicular is given by:

$$\frac{\Delta D}{D} = \frac{\sqrt{\left(\frac{2D}{2}\right)}}{206\,265}$$

where D is total distance, 2 is the length of the subtense bar in metres, and 1 is accuracy in seconds.

If the distance measured in 150 m, the subtense bar is 2 m and the accuracy is to the nearest second, show that the accuracy:

(a) Due to direct measurement of 1 bay is 1/2750.
(b) Due to use of base and perpendicular is 1/16 841.

Special optical distance measurement methods

Until the advent of electromagnetic distance measurement there was a considerable market for expensive, accurate, quick reading optical measurement equipment. This market has virtually gone but the existing equipment is still used.

4.9 Diagram tacheometers_____

Diagram tacheometers are instruments with the same characteristics as the normal theodolite but the stadia lines are designed to vary with the inclination of the telescope.

There are three stadia lines: the lower is the datum line, a second a horizontal distance line, and lastly a vertical distance line to which a factor is added.

A special vertical staff is sighted and the datum line set onto the zero of the staff. Horizontal distance from instrument to the vertical staff is given by:

   $100 \times$ Upper stadia reading on staff

Difference in level is given by:

   $100 \times$ (Factor) $\times$ Middle sloping reading on staff

4.10 Optical wedge system

This instrument is a theodolite with a special optical wedge attachment, as shown in Figure 4.15, which allows some light to pass directly through while the rest is diverted at an angle with a gradient of 1 in 100. Both readings are observed on the horizontal staff.

Slope distance from instrument to the horizontal staff is given by:

$100 \times$ Difference in horizontal staff readings

Horizontal and vertical distances are calculated from the slope distance and vertical angle.

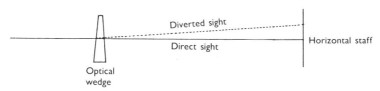

Figure 4.15

4.11 The teletop

This instrument, shown in Figure 4.16, works on similar principles to the range finder but here the parallactic angle is fixed, the base length is altered and the length accurately established at coincidence.

At R_2 the ranging rod is seen in the same position directly and through prisms. Horizontal distance OR_2 is $100 \times x$.

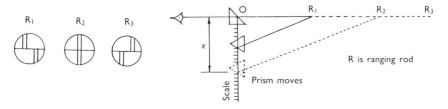

Figure 4.16 (a) View through eyepiece of teletop. (b) Plan.

4.12 Wave theory and electromagnetic distance measurement

Basic terms used in wave theory

An electrical disturbance creates a wave which spreads outwards, as shown in Figure 4.17. The type of disturbance affects the frequency, wavelength and period. The velocity of an electromagnetic wave depends on the medium through which it travels.

- **Wavelength** is the length of one wave, i.e. λ, in metres.
- **Frequency** is the number of waves per second, i.e. f, in hertz (Hz).
- **Period**, the time taken for one wave to travel through one wavelength, is t seconds.
- **Velocity of flow** is the velocity at which the wave travels through the medium. If the medium is a vacuum, the velocity C will be the velocity of light which is 299 792.5 km/s.
- **Distance** is the progress of a wave in a certain time. Generally:

$$D = Ct$$

where D is distance (metres), C is velocity of light (m/s) and t is time (seconds).

Figure 4.17

4.13 Basic electronic limitations

These are physical limits that the electronics engineer cannot breach without incurring undue costs. At present, the measurement of time is limited to $\pm 1 \times 10^{-9}$ s. Frequencies are limited to 7.5 to 500 MHz.

In order for the wave to be suitable for transmission at these frequencies, the wave must be modulated to reduce effects such as interference, reflection, fading and scatter.

4.14 Methods of modulation

Amplitude modulation

In Figure 4.18 the carrier wave has a constant frequency and the modulated wave is conveyed by the amplitude of the carrier wave.

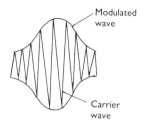

Figure 4.18

Frequency modulation
In Figure 4.19 the carrier wave has a constant amplitude but its frequency varies with the amplitude of the modulating wave.

Figure 4.19

4.15 The basic principles of electromagnetic distance measurement

Electromagnetic distance measurement (EDM) instruments send out modulated pulses which may be made up of micro, infra-red, radio or light waves. The pulses reach the prism or remote station and are returned to the instrument.

Measurement of the distance between instrument and prism or remote station may be achieved by two different methods:

1. Timing the wave.
2. By measuring phase difference using various pulse lengths.

Timing the wave

$$D = Ct$$

where D is distance measured, C is 299 792.5 km/s and t is time measured $\pm \times 10^{-9}$ s. The accuracy over shorter distances is not high.

By measuring phase difference using various pulse lengths
When a pulse is sent out to the prism or remote station it will normally
return out of phase. This phase comparison can be measured accurately
using phase detectors.

If the process is repeated using a different pulse a new phase comparison
will be detected as shown in Figure 4.20. Using this information and
solving simultaneous equations, D can be established. In most modern
instruments electromechanical devices solve the problem automatically and
display the result.

Consider the simplified situation shown in Figure 4.20.

$$D = N\phi_1 + \phi_{1R}$$

$$D = N\phi_2 + \phi_{2R}$$

$$N = \frac{\phi_{2R} - \phi_{1R}}{\phi_1 - \phi_2}$$

To nearest lower integer:

$$D = N\phi_1 + \phi_{1R}$$

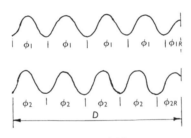

Figure 4.20

Example 4.3_____

If pulse lengths are $\phi_1 = 10.00$ m, $\phi_2 = 9.900990099$ m and the phase
comparisons are $\phi_{1R} = 1.34$ m, $\phi_{2R} = 7.79$ m, determine D.

Solution

$$N = \frac{\phi_{2R} - \phi_{1R}}{\phi_1 - \phi_2} = \frac{7.79 - 1.341}{10 - 9.900990099} = 65.135, \text{ say } N = 65$$

$$D = 65 \times 10 + 1.34 = 651.34 \text{ m}$$

Exercise 4.9

If pulse lengths are $\phi_1 = 10.00$ m, $\phi_2 = 9.900990099$ m and the phase comparisons are $\phi_{1R} = 2.68$ m, $\phi_{2R} = 6.83$ m, show that $D = 412.68$ m.

Exercise 4.10

If pulse lengths are $\phi_1 = 10.00$ m, $\phi_2 = 9.99000999$ m and the phase comparisons are $\phi_{1R} = 1.21$ m, $\phi_{2R} = 8.46$ m, show that $D = 7251.21$ m.

4.16 Classification of electromagnetic distance measurement equipment

The first electromagnetic distance device was the tellurometer which was a development from radar techniques. The instrument was designed in 1954 for geodetic work in South Africa.

Since then there have been considerable developments in electronics and solid state design which have introduced electromagnetic distance devices for a range of purposes making use of different frequency ranges.

4.17 Microwave instruments

Microwaves have frequencies between 10^8 and 10^{12} Hz. These instruments are built primarily for long range work. The master station transmits a signal which is received by the remote station. As the signal is weak on arrival at the remote station, it amplifies the signal and returns the signal in exactly the same phase.

This system employs an operator at each end and requires a communication system between the two. In order to dispel ambiguity in results, a range of four or five frequencies is employed. The method is appropriate for a range of 30–80 km and gives accuracies of ± 15 mm ± 5 mm/km.

The microwave instrument is used for large trilaterations, i.e. triangulation, where the sides are measured and for the control of very large civil engineering projects.

4.18 Visible light instruments

Visible light has frequencies between 10^{14} and 10^{16} Hz. Visible light instruments are for intermediate range. Here the remote station is replaced by a corner cube prism which reflects back the signal close to and parallel to the outcoming signal.

Light wave instruments normally measure the distance with three different wavelengths to ensure accuracy. The method is used up to 25 km and gives an accuracy of ± 10 mm ± 2 mm/km.

4.19 Infra-red instruments

Infra-red waves have frequencies between 10^{12} and 10^{14} Hz. These are short wave instruments. The infra-red instrument is very popular due to its low costs. The carrier wave source is gallium arsenide which is an infra-red emitting diode. These diodes are easily amplitude modulated at high frequency and consequently provide a cheap and simple method of obtaining a modulated carrier wave. The simple design of this instrument makes it compact and light allowing theodolite mounting.

Because the infra-red wavelength is close to visible light it can be controlled by lenses in the same way as light. The main disadvantage of the diode is that power is low and the range limited to 2 or 3 km. The accuracy is normally ± 10 mm within its range.

The method is now used for setting out where the distances are beyond the reach of a 30 m tape.

4.20 Problems, errors and corrections

It is unwise to assume that the results of electromagnetic distance measurement are always of high accuracy. Care must be taken to set up the instrument level and to ensure that the instrument and target are directly above the ground marks.

In addition to the normal problems of the basic instrument, there are problems within the electromagnetic distance measuring systems which must be considered.

Weak signals

These are caused by:

1. The non-alignment of the prism. The operator at the prism should ensure that it points directly at the EDM equipment.

2. Poor cable connections. Here a spare set of cables is advisable.
3. Low batteries. A couple of spare batteries should always be available.

System zero error

This error is due to:

1. The centre of the theodolite and the centre of the EDM unit not coinciding.
2. The centre of the prism not coinciding with the prism station.

To find the system zero error
Set out three points A, B and C in a straight line with the distances between the points exceeding 30 m. Place instrument at A and measure AC. Place instrument at B and measure BA and BC.

$$\text{System zero error} = (BA + BC - AC)$$

Atmospheric corrections

Atmosphere retards the velocity of the waves in the EDM unit and corrections can be made if the pressure and the wet and dry bulb temperatures are known. If highest accuracy is required the values should be measured at both ends of the line. If accuracy is required to 1 in 100 000 the conditions need only be measured once a day.

Corrections are usually made from graph sheets. It is becoming more usual to incorporate an atmospheric correction switch which can be set to prevailing weather conditions and all measurements will be corrected automatically.

Problems with mounted instruments

Assume the following general procedure:

1. The prism is placed perpendicular to the line of sight.
2. The optical and signal axes are parallel and displaced by distance d.
3. The prism optical centre and the target on prism are displaced by distance d.

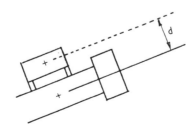

Figure 4.21 Telescope mounting. Optical distance = Signal distance.

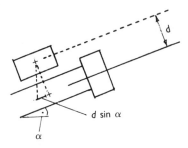

Figure 4.22 Standard mounting. Optical distance = Signal distance + *d* sin α.

Collimation error

Sight target on the prism optical centre, adjust the capstan screws until strongest return signal is recorded. For most work the distance measured is little affected by slight collimation error.

4.21 Use of electromagnetic distance measurement in practical situations

Assuming that the problems, errors and corrections in 4.20 have been dealt with, the procedures outlined are best employed in the following situations:

Short distance setting out work

- Carefully centre above the instrument station.
- Place a target prism in the line of the point to be set out at approximately the correct distance.
- Measure accurately the distance between instrument and prism and then using a steel tape add or deduct the amount required to complete the true measurement.
- If 'tracking mode' is available the readings can be taken more quickly allowing for a trial and error procedure. Unfortunately the 'tracking mode' is less accurate.

Short distance accurate work

- Use the three tripod method outlined in 7.6 where the instrument and prism heads are interchangeable.
- The mean of several forward and back sights gives good accuracy.

Larger distance accurate work

- Use a cluster of prisms at the target to produce a strong return signal.
- Take a series of readings from each end.
- Apply carefully the corrections for slope and sea level outlined in 4.4.
- Make the necessary atmospheric correction as shown in 4.20.
- Reduce the horizontal distance to a grid distance by multiplying by a scale factor obtained from Table 6.1.

4.22 Typical ranges and accuracies in distance measurement__

Short distance measurement

	Range	Approximate accuracy
Most short distance setting out work is done using the 30 m steel tape which is corrected for slope errors	0–30 m	1 : 2000
Synthetic tapes are less accurate	0–30 m	1 : 500
Steel tapes with corrections for slope, tension and temperature	0–30 m	1 : 10 000
Steel tapes with corrections for sag, sea level, slope, tension and temperature	0–30 m	1 : 30 000

Note that the accuracies are quoted for a 30 m tape. The accuracies would improve with a longer tape.

Base line measurement

	Range	Approximate accuracy
Where a base line is required for a large scale control triangulation for geodetic work, all corrections are applied to an invar band in catenary	30 m per bay	1 : 100 000
If wind protection is used and many readings taken		1 : 1 000 000

Optical distance measurement

Optical distance measurement is often used where taping would be difficult but where the accuracy of the work is not so important – contouring, earthworks, volumes, etc.

	Range	Approximate accuracy
Stadia tacheometry	20–100 m	1 : 300
Teletop	20–60 m	1 : 500
Moving stadia methods	20–100 m	1 : 5 000
Optical wedge	20–100 m	1 : 5 000
Subtense bar (best)	40 m	1 : 10 000
	30 m	1 : 8 000
	60 m	1 : 7 000

Electromagnetic distance measurement

The initial use of this equipment was for long range, accurate, geodetic work but now these instruments are used for all but the short distances.

	Range	Approximate accuracy
Microwave instruments	30 m–80 km	± 15 mm ± 5 mm/km
Lightwave instruments	15 m–5 km	± 10 mm ± 2 ppm
Lightwave with laser	15 m–10 km	± 6 mm ± 1 ppm
Infra-red (best)	0–2 km	± 3 mm ± 1 ppm

(ppm = parts per million)

Electromagnetic instruments have a zero error and an error which varies as the distance. The accuracy improves with distance.

Five

Systems involving lasers and electromagnetic beams

The word _laser_ is an abbreviation for Light Amplification by Stimulated Emission of Radiation. British Standard BS 4803 'Safety and the Use of Lasers' indicates that although surveying site instruments fall into a lower category of danger, care must be taken in their use.

As far safety is concerned, the sun and lasers follow a similar pattern of risk. In each case the operative should not look directly into the beam nor direct a telescope into the beam.

5.1 Laser beams used in surveying

In surveying there are basically two types of laser beam: visible and invisible.

Visible beams

Visible beams are normally produced by a 12 volt DC energy source acting on a helium neon plasma to emit a small coherent beam to produce a visible red light. The laser beam is of single frequency and is virtually parallel, meaning that the thin beam loses little energy and a bright beam of light can be projected over considerable distances. In most conditions the red spot can be seen up to 200 m away.

Surveyors use the pencil of light as a reference for horizontal, vertical and sloping control. A weightless ray provides a far more accurate reference than a string line, or tape.

For short distances lining in of the laser beam can be carried out using templates or boning rods, but to allow level and position measurement to be made in high ambient lighting conditions, standard photodetector units are usually employed.

In principle the great advantage of the visible beam is that it can be seen by the surveyor and this gives him more confidence that everything is functioning correctly. The visible beam has many practical surveying applications.

Invisible beams

Invisible beams are normally produced by a rechargeable 6 volt nickel cadmium battery source acting on gallium arsenide to emit and produce a beam which is not visible. This beam can be picked up by a detector which indicates the height of the beam relative to the detector on the LCD display. Arrows indicate the direction of the detector and a horizontal illuminated strip appears when the detector is central.

In addition, an audible signal generator can also be switched on so that the position of the detector can be recognized even in extremely difficult measuring conditions.

The invisible beam is cheap to produce and uses nickel cadmium batteries which are light in weight. A second battery pack in reserve increases the scope.

This method is used primarily with the rotating beam for levelling.

5.2 Levelling using lasers

The rotating prism laser

The basic unit consists of a laser, a telescope and a rotating prism. When the instrument is levelled up and the laser turned on, the rotating prism enables a narrow pencil of red light to project over a considerable distance sweeping out a horizontal plane. If the rotations are rapid, a red line will be seen at all points having the same level as the instrument.

A staff man at points surrounding the instrument can readily establish the ground levels if the height of collimation of the rotary prism is known.

With the non-visible light laser or with the light laser in high ambient lighting conditions a photodetector assembly unit is required to establish the correct level point.

Detectors

In the beam seeking device shown in Figure 5.1, the photo cell moves up and down the staff until the laser beam halts it, to give the level.

In the invisible laser detector shown in Figure 5.2, the height of the detector relative to the beam is indicated on the LCD displacement panel. The arrow indicates the direction, and audio sounds give an indication of beam position.

The accusensor is similar to the invisible laser detector of Figure 5.2 but has, in addition, a three-light system to locate the beam. The sensor has a remote readout option.

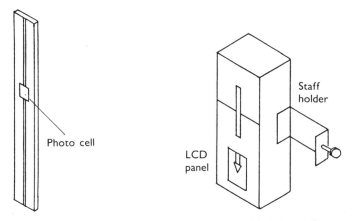

Figure 5.1 Beam seeking device. **Figure 5.2** Invisible laser detector.

Site observations

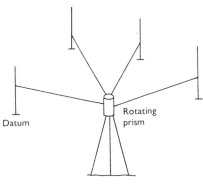

Figure 5.3

5.3 Laser control of pipe laying_____

The laser can be placed in one of three positions shown in Figure 5.4 to set out a pipe run:

1. On a theodolite above the ground.
2. On top of the first pipe.
3. In the first pipe.

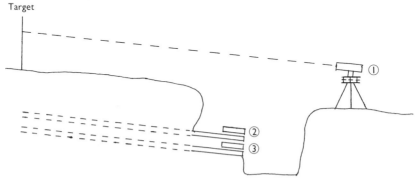

Figure 5.4

Considering these three positions in turn:

1. If the instrument is above the ground it must be clamped onto a tripod. The whole outfit should be lined up in the direction of the sewer. The grade setting crank should be adjusted to produce a line of sight parallel to the proposed line of the sewer. A distant target should be used to indicate any disturbance during the workings. A vertical pole and detector are placed at the invert of the first pipe and adjusted to receive the laser signal. Subsequent pipes are laid in positions indicated by the vertical pole and detector, acting as a traveller throughout the whole job.
2. If the instrument is placed on the top of the pipe, it must be placed in the clamp and the base stabilized using the screws. Set the gradient and operate as before but with a shorter traveller.
3. With the development of smaller laser instruments, it is now more usual to set up the instrument within the pipe itself. The instrument is secured within the pipe, levelled and the grade set out. Targets are employed to ensure that subsequent pipes are set at the same gradient.

Plates 5 and 6 Wild LNA2 automatic rotating laser used for setting out foundations.

Plate 7 The use of the Dialgrade in drop manholes and large pipes.

Plate 8 The Dialgrade laser used for pipelaying.

5.4 Lasers used in construction

Earth moving operations

In Figure 5.5 a vibration, shock, and moisture proof accusensor are placed on the blade. The rotating laser is set at the desired level. Audible sounds and a panel of lights indicate to the operator how near the level is to the correct level.

The survey mode

This is a control box with digital sensor elevation display. When switched to 'survey mode' the sensor tracks the plane of the laser light, continually reading out site elevations as the machine is driven over the site in a grid pattern. This allows a quick engineering site evaluation to guide in preparing a cut sheet for the finished work.

Vertical alignment

Most of the rotating lasers with the visible beams can be turned through 90° to sweep through a vertical plane enabling the unit to be used as an accurate plumb for vertical alignments which are useful for setting out curtain walling, partitions, etc.

Plumbing

A laser mounted to point up or down can be used to set up a plumb line. The advantage of the laser is that it is a one-man operation, but few lasers would have similar accuracy to the auto plumb.

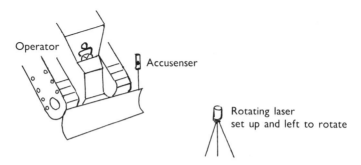

Figure 5.5

Tunnel work

The laser is useful for the control of line and level in tunnel work. The instrument should be placed so that it projects a beam parallel to the centre line a short distance below the crown. Once the direction is set, work can continue without an operator at the laser station.

Screed levelling

The levelling can be done by one person as illustrated in Figure 5.6.

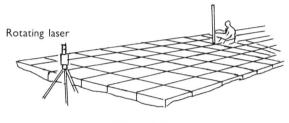

Rotating laser

Figure 5.6

5.5 Electronic tacheometers

Surveying electronic communication network

Surveying has seen a great number of advances in recent years in the area of instrumentation, data collection and computer processing. The introduction of electromagnetic distance measurement and the electronic theodolite has speeded up field measurements. The interfacing of the electronic theodolite and electronic fieldbooks has led to automatic recording of the field data which may be utilized in a selection of surveying software programs to produce processed results.

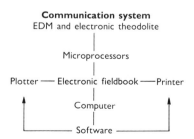

Communication system
EDM and electronic theodolite

Microprocessors

Plotter —— Electronic fieldbook ——Printer

Computer

Software

5.6 Basic systems

Electronic tacheometers

An electronic tacheometer is an electronic theodolite with an integral EDM (electromagnetic distance measurement) system. It is fitted with an electric socket ready to connect up with an electronic field book.

A total station

A total station is an expensive instrument. Basically, it is the same as the electronic tacheometer and is capable of reading vertical angle, horizontal angle and slope distance to a point and displays the results electronically on panels.

Keyboard-initiated programs can establish a range of factors such as horizontal distances, differences in level, and coordinates. The basic information automatically fed into an electronic fieldbook is capable of generating sophisticated programs which may be expressed on printers, plotters or transferred to a second computer.

A semi-total station

The semi-total station is a less expensive piece of equipment than the total station, requiring the operator to read out the vertical and horizontal angles. If the operator manually transfers the basic readings to the keyboard panel and to the electronic fieldbook, this instrument is capable of duplicating all the qualities of the total station.

Alternative systems

An electromagnetic distance measurement (EDM) system mounted on a theodolite will serve as a semi-total station. Entering the basic information manually into the fieldbook can initiate the same programs as the total station.

5.7 The total station

The total station is a surveying instrument which will give distance and angle measurements in the field and be capable of passing on this information to a computer via an electronic fieldbook.

Total station design has benefited greatly from the development of EDM and electronic theodolites in recent years and now there is a good range of total station equipment available. Basically, the manufacturers have recognized two markets: one offering high accuracy and sophistication, and the other a lower price with slightly less accuracy.

5.8 Distance measurement features

Present technology allows the inclusion of the following desirable features in the distance measurement area of the total station.

- **Automatic self-diagnosis.** Each time the power is turned on, the instrument self-checks for problems in operation. If there are problems the facts are displayed on LCD.
- **Upright digital display.** The liquid crystal readout is always upright whatever the telescope reading.
- **Atmospheric corrections.** Before measuring the values, barometric pressure and temperature are keyed in. The instrument automatically compensates for these environmental factors before displaying the distance.
- **Automatic curvature and refraction correction.** When the appropriate internal switches are set the instrument automatically compensates for the earth's curvature and differences in air density.
- **Prism constant.** The instrument retains the pre-set prism constant until a new value is set via the keyboard.
- **Audible and digital target acquisition.** If the signal is interrupted by traffic or other obstacles the instrument ceases operation until the path is clear. Measurement resumes when the path is cleared.
- **Moving prism tracking function.** In tracking mode the distance meter can measure to a target held for less than a second. Generally the accuracy is less, but this facility is invaluable in construction staking.
- **Stake-out function.** If a pre-set distance is entered. The display indicates the difference between prism distance and pre-set distance. This is a useful feature when setting out stakes.
- **Change of parameter.** This enables the operator to select units such as metres or feet.

5.9 Angle measurement features

Having already considered the factors making the total station an effective distance measuring instrument, consideration will be made on the desirable features that should be included in the angle reading process.

- **Coaxial tangent locking and fine adjustment screws.** These are convenient and quick to use.

- **Optical plummet**. An optical plummet built into the instrument's alidade will ensure erect unreversed images which permits quick and precise orientation over the station.
- **Telescope diameter**. A large diameter telescope with an extra wide view provides a clear erect image which makes sighting more accurate.
- **Coaxial telescope**. If the EDM signal and the optical telescope are on the same optical axis then the angle and distance measurements can be performed simultaneously. Also collimation errors are minimized.
- **Retical illumination**. To maintain instrument's operating ease at night or in dark conditions an LED is built in to illuminate the telescope reticle.
- **Optical sight (finder)**. For quick sighting, a collimator target finder is provided on the top of the telescopic housing.
- **Built-in automatic zenith index**. The built-in automatic compensator allows a quick instrument set up and ensures accurate measurement of vertical angles.
- **Easy-to-read angle display**. The angles are shown on the scales softly illuminated and in digital form.

5.10 Microprocessors

It is usual for total stations to carry in their keyboard in-built simple programs which allow instant compilation at the touch of a key. Such **keyboard initiated application programs** are based on the measured angles and distance data; they include:

1. Slope distances, horizontal distances, height differences.
2. Horizontal distances and height distances between two prism points.
3. Values of coordinates.
4. Remote elevations.
5. Setting out by distance or coordinates.

5.11 Information collection

Traditionally, many land surveying processes have consisted of information gathering, storage and use of the information to solve problems and produce drawings with details. In modern times the process has been speeded up using electronics. The information is electronically gathered, stored and the computer is now used to solve problems and produces plots and printouts.

5.12 Field data loggers

Data loggers rely on recording media to provide memory units. The most commonly used are:

1. Magnetic tape cassettes.
2. Solid state.
3. 'Bubble' memory units.

Magnetic tapes have a reasonable capacity but the tapes are vulnerable to moisture, dust and breakage. The solid state memories are widely used but restricted in capacity. The bubble memories are expensive but have large capacities.

5.13 Basic types of data logger

Dedicated loggers are produced by surveying equipment manufacturers to collect and store observations from survey instruments such as electronic theodolites and EDM equipment. A complete range of user friendly field data collection programs and calculation programs is provided so that observations can be checked and verified in the field. Observations are taken automatically from electronic surveying instruments and can be entered via the keyboard for optical instruments.

The stored data can be transmitted to a variety of different data processors in a variety of ways.

General purpose loggers require the introduction of special programs to give them the capability of accepting manual and automatic recording and the ability to pass on the information to an office microcomputer.

5.14 The influence of data loggers in surveying

Data loggers speed up the process of taking details, thus giving surveyors more time to select their points carefully in order to achieve more accurate results.

Checking the work at each stage is very important. If a mistake is made in the numbering of stations, the office computer may have corrected the whole system before the error is spotted.

Dedicated loggers, being user friendly, are easy to use but surveyors should be aware that if they are not to become the servants of technology they should play an active part in developing their own programs.

5.15 General recommendations for the practical application of lasers and electromagnetic beams __

Lasers

Ensure safety when using laser equipment. It is dangerous to look along the beam or to search for it with a level or theodolite. British Standard BS 4803 'Safety and the use of lasers' outlines these dangers and illustrates safety procedures.

In site situations the laser is easily disturbed. The engineer must continually check that the beam is on line.

The laser method of setting out drains and sewers is especially useful for deep trenches where the alternative method involves long travellers which are difficult to hold vertical.

Tunnels are appropriately set out by lasers but the line and level should be continually checked by theodolite and level.

Electromagnetic beams

Electromagnetic beams are found in distance-measuring devices and total stations which have the advantages of saving time and are more accurate than other methods in certain situations.

Setting out distances greater than 30 m are readily accomplished by these measuring devices and give high accuracy.

Normally difficult measurement exercises such as river crossings and busy traffic areas are readily established using electromagnetic beams.

Traverses employing the total station and the three-tripod method outlined in 7.6 are very quick and accurate.

Total stations may be used to collect basic surveying information, store it, solve problems and be able to reproduce the basic information and the solutions to the problems in detailed printouts or plots.

Plate 9 Wild TM 3000V motorized precision theodolite with built-in CCD video camera for automatic target-point recording.

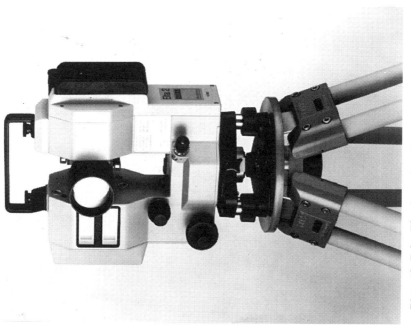

Plate 10 Zeiss Elta 2 total station computer recording instrument.

Plate 12 Sokkisha data logger.

Plate 11 Sokkisha total station.

Six

National control

6.1 The national projection and national grid

When consideration of a project is made it is essential to show how it fits into the whole scheme of things. It is normal to control accurately the whole then to work down in stages to the detail. This is often referred to as 'working from the whole to the part'. In Britain, the whole is the national grid which is based on the national projection.

6.2 The national projection

It is impossible to represent any considerable area of the earth's surface on a flat plane without distortions being introduced. Various projections have been derived, some to maintain correct areas, some to give consistency of scale in certain directions and others to give minimum distortions and fair generalizations.

Cassini produced a projection which gave correct east–west scales and a correct scale at the meridian, i.e. the main north–south line, but which changed as the distance away from the meridian increased. The transverse meridian projection was developed from the Cassini projection by introducing a scale error in the east–west direction to balance the error in the north–south direction. This projection has the virtue of having the local scale equal in all directions. This is basically the national projection.

6.3 True north, magnetic north and grid north_____

True north is the direction on the earth taken towards the North Pole. The North and South Poles are points on the axis of the earth's daily rotation.

Magnetic north is the direction on the earth taken towards the magnetic pole which is on the axis of the earth's magnetic field.

Grid north. In order to provide a reference system it is common practice on maps to have a system of squares or rectangles. The vertical grid line at the centre of the system is normally true north. The other grid lines will not be true north but will converge.

6.4 Convergence of the meridians_____

Grid norths are parallel and only one will be true north, all the others will converge as shown in Figure 6.1 by a value given by:

$$\text{Convergence} = \Delta\lambda \, \sin \phi \text{ or } \frac{L}{R} \tan \phi \times 3437.8 \text{ minutes}$$

where $\Delta\lambda$ is difference in longitude in minutes, ϕ is latitude, L is distance from meridian (km) and R is the radius of the earth (6384 km).

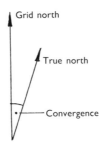

Figure 6.1

6.5 The national grid and local scale factors_____

The meridian of the national grid, where true north and grid north coincide is chosen to be 2°W longitude, as shown in Figure 6.2.

The meridian passes through the centre of the country and minimizes the effects of convergence. The origin of the grid is 400 km west of the meridian and approximately 100 km south of Land's End. The scale factor is

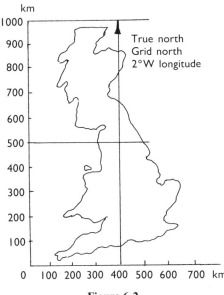

Figure 6.2

true 180 km each side of the meridian. This minimizes the effects of scale factor as shown in Table 6.1.

Points on the national grid are specified by quoting:

Distance measured eastwards from 0.0 (**Eastings**)

Distance measured northwards from 0.0 (**Northing**)

$$\text{Ground distance} = \frac{\text{Projected distance}}{\text{Local scale factor}}$$

Local scale factor is introduced to compensate for transverse meridian projection errors.

To calculate a traverse A–B as shown in the diagram in Example 6.1 it is necessary to apply local scale factor (LSF) to all measured distances before traverse is completed.

National grid projections do not necessitate any correction to measured angles or bearings.

Table 6.1

Nat. grid	Easting (km)	Scale factor (F)
400	400	0.99960
390	410	60
380	420	61
370	430	61
360	440	62
350	450	63
340	460	65
330	470	66
320	480	68
310	490	70
300	500	72
290	510	75
280	520	78
270	530	81
260	540	84
250	550	88
240	560	92
230	570	0.99996
220	580	1.00000
210	590	04
200	600	09
190	610	14
180	620	20
170	630	25
160	640	31
150	650	37
140	660	43
130	670	1.00050

Example 6.1 Local scale factors_____

OS stn E422841.570 m   N283542.210 m

OS stn E418835.970 m   N281889.570 m

Difference = 4005.600 m   1652.640 m

Projected distance $= \sqrt{(4005.600^2 + 1\,652.640^2)}$

$\qquad\qquad\qquad\ = 4433.134$ m

Ground distance $= \dfrac{4333.134}{0.99961}$

$\qquad\qquad\quad = 4334.826$

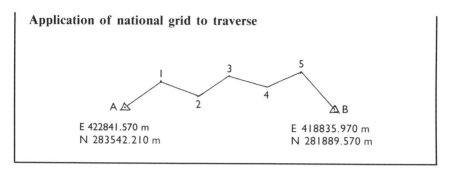

Application of national grid to traverse

6.6 Use of national grid for distant stations

Consider the projected distance shown dotted between A and a distant point B in Figure 6.3. The projected distance AB will not equal the measured distance AB. The projected path AB will not be the line sighted between A and B.

In Figure 6.3:

$$\text{Projected distance AB} = \sqrt{(N_B - N_A)^2 + (E_B - E_A)^2}$$

$$\text{True ground distance (AB)} = \frac{\text{Projected distance}}{\text{Local scale factor}}$$

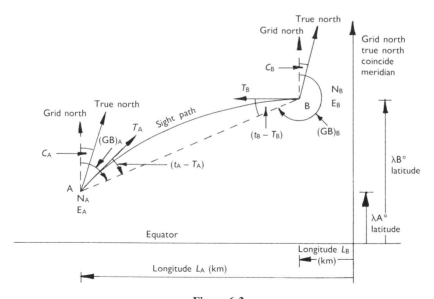

Figure 6.3

$$\text{Grid bearing at A} = (GB)_A = \tan^{-1} \frac{(E_B - E_A)}{(N_B - N_A)}$$

$$\text{Grid bearing at B} = (GB)_A + 180°$$

$$C_A \text{ convergence at A} = \frac{L_A \tan \lambda_A}{R} \ 3437.8 \text{ minutes}$$

$$C_B \text{ convergence at B} = \frac{L_B \tan \lambda_B}{R} \ 3437.8 \text{ minutes}$$

$$R = \text{radius of earth} = 6384 \text{ km} \qquad K = 845 \times 10^{-6}$$

$(t_A - T_A)$ is the angular difference between projected path AB and sighted path AB

$(t_B - T_B)$ is the angular difference between projected path BA and sighted path BA

$(t_A - T_A) = (2E_A + E_B)(N_A - N_B)K$ where units of N and E are km and value is in seconds;

$(t_B - T_B) = (2E_B + E_A)(N_B - N_A)K$

Example 6.2

If true north and grid coincide at 600 000 m east and the mean latitude of the area is 55° using the details below:

	Easting (m)	Northing (m)
Ordnance survey station A	499 000	282 500
Ordnance survey station B	501 000	285 000

Determine:

(a) Projected distance AB.
(b) True distance AB.
(c) The grid bearing of A to B.
(d) The convergence of meridians at A.
(e) The angular differences between projected path AB and sighted path AB.
(f) The direction of T_A with respect to true north.

Assume R = 6384 km   K = 845 × 10⁻⁶

(a) Projection distance AB $= \sqrt{(285\ 000 - 282\ 500)^2 + (501\ 000 - 499\ 000)^2}$
$= 3201.5 \text{ m}$

Average easting $\qquad$ $= (499 + 501)/2 = 500$ km
Scale factor $\qquad$ $= 0.999\ 72$ from Table 6.1
True distance AB $\qquad$ $\dfrac{3201.5}{0.999\ 72} = 3202.4$ m

The grid bearing of A to B
$$= (GB)_A = \tan^{-1} \frac{(501\ 000 - 499\ 000)}{(285\ 000 - 282\ 000)}$$
$$= 38°\ 39'\ 35''$$

$$C_A = \frac{L_A \tan \lambda_A}{R}\ 3437.8 \text{ minutes}$$

$$= \frac{600\ 000 - 499\ 000}{6384} \times \tan 55° \times 206\ 265 = 4660 \text{ seconds}$$

$(t_A - T_A) = (2E_A + E_B)(N_A - N_B)k$
$\qquad = (2 \times 499 + 501)(282.5 - 285) \times 845 \times 10^{-6} = {}^-3$ seconds

Direction T_A with respect to true north
$\qquad = (GB)_A - C_A + (t_A - T_A)$
$\qquad = 38°\ 39'\ 35'' - 4660'' - 3''$
$\qquad = \underline{37°\ 21'\ 52''}$

Calculations using the national grid

Complete the exercises using the extract from the local scale factor table and other information given below.

National grid	Easting (km)	Scale factor
250	550	0.99988
240	560	0.99992
230	570	0.99996
220	580	1.00000
210	590	1.00004

$(t_A - T_A) = (2E_A + E_B)(N_A - N_B)K$

$$C_A = \frac{L_A \tan \lambda_A}{R} \times 3437.8 \text{ mins}$$

$$\text{True area} = \frac{\text{Projected area}}{(\text{Scale factor})^2}$$

$K = 845 \times 10^{-6}$
$R = 6384$ km

Exercise 6.1 _____

If true north and grid north coincide at 400 000 m east and the mean latitude of the area is 49° using the details below:

	Easting (m)	*Northing* (m)
Ordnance survey station A	222 030.025	297 582.629
Ordnance survey station B	228 004.727	302 671.207

Show that:

(a) Projected distance AB is 7847.974 m.
(b) True distance AB is 7848.131 m.
(c) The grid bearing of A to B is N49°34′46″E.
(d) The convergence at A is 1°50′14.9″.
(e) The angular difference between projected path AB and sighted path AB is 2.9″.
(f) The bearing of the sighting from A to B is 47°44′28.2″.

Exercise 6.2_____

If true north and grid north coincide at 340 000 m east, the mean latitude of the site is 55°, and a traverse A, B, C, D, A has the coordinates indicated.

Ordnance station	A	B	C	D
Northing (km)	282	285	281	276
Easting (km)	236	242	246	244

Show that:

(a) Projected distance AB is 6708.204 m.
(b) Local scale factor mid AB is 0.99992.
(c) True distance AB is 6708.741.
(d) The grid bearing of A to B is N63°26′06″E.
(e) The convergence at A is 79.98 minutes.
(f) The angular value between projected line AB and sighted line AB is 1.8 seconds.
(g) The uncorrected area A, B, C, D, A is 44 km^2.
(h) The corrected area A, B, C, D, A is 44.007 km^2.

6.7 Using the national grid for map numbering

The Ordnance Survey has devised a unique reference system as shown in Figure 6.4. A position of 400 km west of 2°W and 100 km north of latitude 49°N was chosen as origin. The grid system was first divided into major squares 500 × 500 km and each given a fore letter. The major square is divided into twenty-five 100 km squares each lettered alphabetically starting at top left and omitting I. Each square of 100 × 100 km is identified by two letters.

Scale

- SJ refers to 100 km square — 1 : 250 000
- SJ 82 refers to 10 km square 80 km E and 20 km N — 1 : 25 000
- SJ 8123 refers to 1 km square 81 km E and 23 km N — 1 : 2500
- SJ 814231 refers to 100 m square 81.4 km E and 23.6 km N — 1 : 250
- SJ 8123NW   SJ 8123NE⎫
  SJ 8123SW   SJ 8123SE⎭ — 1 : 1250

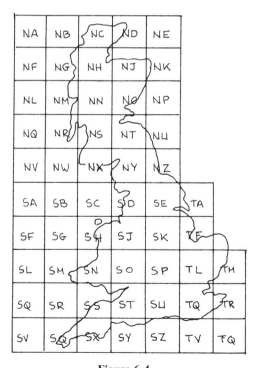

Figure 6.4

6.8 Using the national grid for grid or map reference_____

The location of a grid or map reference is similar to the system used for map numbering. Two letters identify the 100 km square. The rest of the figures give the position relative to the south-west corner of the square. There is always an even number of figures. The first half of the number gives the easting and the rest the northing.

- SJ 873 237 refers to a point in square SJ. Its position is 87.3 km east and 23.7 km north of the south-west corner. The reference is to the nearest 100 m.
- SJ 87321 23786 refers to a point in square SJ. Its position is 87.321 km east and 23.786 km north of the south-west corner. The reference is to the nearest 1 m.
- SJ 87321456 23786868 defines the point to the nearest 1 mm.

6.9 National surveying control systems_____

For a century Britain has possessed an extremely reliable network of controlling triangulation stations.

Primary triangulation

Applying the principle of working from the whole to the part, the whole of Britain was covered by a network of well conditioned large triangles with side lengths in the order of 50–80 km.

Permanent stations – normally concrete pillars – were set up and geodetic theodolites giving accuracies to 0.1 second with allowances of closure error in triangles of 2 seconds. Base lines giving accuracies of one part in a million were used and the whole system of primary triangulation coordinated.

Within the primary triangulation secondary and tertiary triangulation have been developed to increase the density of available triangulation stations.

Secondary triangulation

This is a second stage development of triangulation which relies on the existing primary triangulation. Here the side lengths are normally 8–40 km and the closing error in triangles is allowed to be 5 seconds.

Tertiary triangulation

This is the final stage of the development of the national triangulation and depends on both primary and secondary triangulation schemes. Here the distances are more varied and the targets are less reliable; the resulting accuracies are considerably reduced.

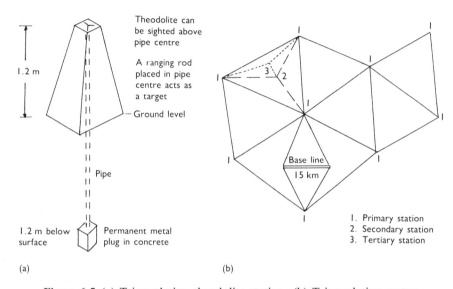

Figure 6.5 (a) Triangulation theodolite station. (b) Triangulation system.

6.10 Triangulation, trilateration and triangulateration

So that surveyors may relate their own work to the national grid, the co-ordinates of many permanent positions throughout the country have been accurately established and are obtainable from the Ordinance Survey, Southampton.

These coordinates are the results of computation of a network of well conditioned triangles measured by several means.

Triangulation

Triangulation relies on the accurate measurement of all the angles of a triangle and the knowledge of the length of one of the sides which is obtained by base line methods. This has been the traditional way of achieving extremely good values for the coordinates of permanent survey stations.

By modern standards, triangulation is considered slow, and it can be demonstrated that the results tend to be less reliable the further from the base line.

Trilateration

Trilateration depends on the ability to measure accurately all the sides of a triangle. Since the event of very accurate electromagnetic distance measuring equipment this method has come to the fore: it is accurate and produces results very quickly. On a national basis, triangulation has been replaced by trilateration.

Triangulateration

Triangulateration depends on the measurement both of angles of the triangle and of the lengths of the sides. Here there are redundant terms, but by using the theory of least squares and a computer it is possible to achieve the most probable results. This method should give good results and provide good checks.

Control on construction sites

The construction surveyor finds Ordnance Survey coordinates extremely useful for checking against but is normally reluctant to use triangulation methods on site. The main reason for this is that triangulation, trilateration or triangulateration methods rarely allow marker positions to be placed in convenient locations relative to the construction in hand. The site surveyor tends to prefer to use the traverse which is more adaptable and less complex to calculate.

Seven

The traverse

7.1 Traverse control

The framework preferred for the control of large-scale land surveys and construction projects is the traverse. In this method a number of stations are chosen which are convenient for the construction workings. The plan lengths or legs between stations are measured and the angles between pairs of lines established.

There are two types of transverse:

1. A closed traverse which starts at a station and returns to the same station completing a closed polygon as shown in Figure 7.1.
2. An open traverse as shown in Figure 7.2.

The closed traverse should be used whenever possible because it provides a means of checking angles, lengths and coordinates. The open transverse is not really suitable for engineering surveys unless the coordinates of the starting and finishing position are known with precision.

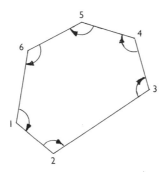

Figure 7.1 Closed traverse.

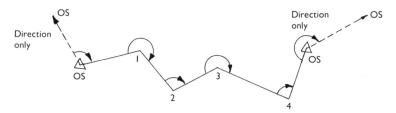

Figure 7.2 Open traverse.

Road, rail and pipe line surveys use traverse with Ordnance Survey triangulation points at each end to give the necessary checks.

Setting out pegs

Care must be taken in the positioning of the pegs for the traverse and the following precautions taken:

1. A reconnaissance of the area should be made.
2. Intervisibility between adjacent stations should be ensured.
3. Pegs to be placed where measurement is practicable.
4. Control surveys should follow direct routes using long lengths.
5. Detail surveys to pass close to the detail.
6. Pegs should be clearly marked and referred to local detail.

7.2 Traverse bearings basic theory

Bearing definitions

WCB   A whole circle bearing is the angle measured between north and the leg considered in a clockwise direction.

FB   A forward bearing is the WCB measured in the direction the pegs are set out.

BB   A backward bearing is the WCB measured in the direction opposite to which the pegs are set out.

RB   Is the reduced bearing and is the smallest angle between the leg and the N–S line. Prefix the angle by N or S and suffix the angle by E or W according to the direction of the leg.

(Note that the difference between forward bearing and backward bearing should be 180°.)

If the stations are marked in an anti-clockwise direction then:

New FB = Last BB + Clockwise angle of the traverse where 360° may be deducted.

Example 7.1

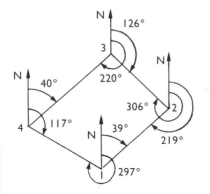

Leg	1–2	2–3	3–4	4–1
FB°	39	306	220	117
BB°	219	126	40	297
Diff.	180	180	180	180

Example 7.2

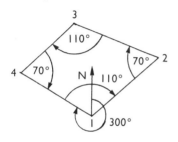

FB(1–2) = 300 + 110 = 410
$$= 50°$$
BB(1–2) = 230
(to give 180° diff.)
FB(2–3) = 230 + 70 = 300°
BB(2–3) = 120
(to give 180° diff.)
FB(3–4) = 120 + 100 = 230°
BB(3–4) = 50
(to give 180° diff.)
FB(4–1) = 50 + 70 = 120°
BB(4–1) = 300°
(to give 180° diff.)

Example 7.3

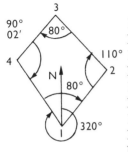

Final values

FB(1–2) = 320 + 80 = 40°   39°59′30″
BB(1–2) = 220
FB(2–3) = 220 + 110 = 330°   329°59′
BB(2–3) = 150
FB(3–4) = 150 + 80 = 230°   229°58′30″
BB(3–4) = 50
FB(4–1) = 50 + 90°2′ = 140°2′   140°0′
BB(4–1) = 320°2′
Error 2 min = 120 sec
Reduce FB by 30″ on 1st, 60″ on 2nd,
90″ on 3rd, 120″ on 4th

7.3 Calculation of coordinates

A traverse may be checked if the coordinates of the first and last station are known. Coordinates of each of the stations are obtained by calculating the east and north components ΔE and ΔN for each line in turn as indicated in Figure 7.3. East and north are treated as positive and west and south as negative.

In a perfect traverse where the end coordinates are known:

$\Sigma\Delta E$ = Difference between eastern coordinates at each end
$\Sigma\Delta N$ = Difference between northern coordinates at each end

In perfect closed traverses:

$\Sigma\Delta E = 0$
$\Sigma\Delta N = 0$

Normally there is a small error in eastings and a small error in northings.

$$\text{Linear error} = \sqrt{(\text{Error in eastings})^2 + (\text{Error in northings})^2}$$

$$\text{Accuracy} = \frac{\text{Linear error}}{\text{Perimeter}}$$

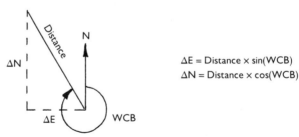

$\Delta E = \text{Distance} \times \sin(\text{WCB})$
$\Delta N = \text{Distance} \times \cos(\text{WCB})$

Figure 7.3

7.4 Traverse adjustment

Bowditch method
This method adjusts the eastings and northings components proportionally to the length of the individual traverse lines expressed by:

Correction to easting component

$$= -\,\text{Total easting error} \times \frac{\text{Length of line}}{\text{Perimeter}}$$

Correction to northing component

$$= -\,\text{Total northing error} \times \frac{\text{Length of line}}{\text{Perimeter}}$$

Transit method

This method adjusts the eastings and northings components proportionally to the size of the individual easting and northing components.

$$\text{Correction to easting component} = -\text{Total easting error} \times \frac{\Delta E}{\Sigma \Delta E}$$

$$\text{Correction to northing component} = -\text{Total northing error} \times \frac{\Delta N}{\Sigma \Delta N}$$

$\Sigma \Delta E$ and $\Sigma \Delta N$ are the addition of all easting components and northing components irrespective of signs.

Exercise 7.1 *Angle measurement*_____

A traverse was set out to meet the following requirements:

(a) The traverse was to close.
(b) The pegs were set out with forward direction anti-clockwise.
(c) Angles were measured clockwise.
(d) The first face left is chosen at approximately 10′.
(e) The first face left in second round is chosen at approximately 90°10′.

The angles at 1 and 2 of the diagram have been completely worked out to confirm the clockwise angles at 1 and 2 are correct.

Work out the values of the angles at 3 and 4 and confirm that they are also correct.

Clockwise angles:

1	91	36	20
2	79	23	40
3	121	15	30
4	67	43	50

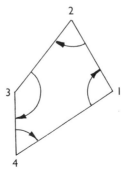

Stn	To	Order	Face left	Order	Face right	Mean	Value
1	4	1	00 09 40	4	180 10 00	00 09 50	
	2	2	91 46 00	3	271 45 40	91 45 50	91 36 00
1	4	5	90 10 00	8	270 09 40	90 09 50	
	2	6	181 47 00	7	1 46 00	181 46 30	91 36 40
						Mean	91 36 20
2	1	1	10 00	4	180 08 00	00 09 00	
	3	2	79 33 20	3	259 32 20	79 32 50	79 23 50
2	1	5	90 04 30	8	270 06 30	90 05 30	
	3	6	169 18 50	7	349 29 10	169 29 00	79 23 30
						Mean	79 23 40
3	2	1	00 11 00	4	180 10 30		
	4	2	121 26 40	3	301 25 30		
3	2	5	90 09 30	8	270 11 20		
	4	6	211 25 50	7	31 26 20		
						Mean	
4	3	1	00 09 40	4	180 10 20		
	1	2	67 53 10	3	247 54 50		
4	3	5	90 11 00	8	270 10 30		
	1	6	147 54 30	7	327 54 20		
						Mean	

Exercise 7.2 *Traverse bearings*

A traverse was set up to meet the following requirements:

(a) The traverse was to close.
(b) The pegs were set out with forward direction anti-clockwise.
(c) All angles were measured clockwise which will mean:

    (i) New forward bearing = Backward bearing + Clockwise angle where 360° may be deducted;
    (ii) Backward bearing and forward bearing differ by 180°.

The uncorrected forward bearings have been established at (1–2) and (2–3). Complete the forward bearings at (3–4) and (4–1) and note the error in backward bearing (4–1). Distribute the errors and confirm that the corrected forward bearings are: 347 07 10, 187 46 40 and 75 30 40 respectively.

    Angles of figure:

        Backward bearing (4–1) = 255 30 40

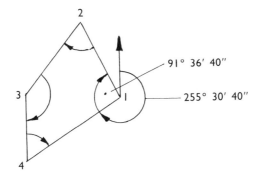

Clockwise angles:

1	91	36	20
2	79	23	40
3	121	15	30
4	67	43	50

New FB(1–2) = BB(4–1) + Clockwise angle 1
                = 225 30 40 + 91 36 20 = 347 07 00

Corrected FBs

Angle 1
FB(1–2)   = 347 07 00   _____

BB(2–1)   = 167 07 00 (180° diff.)
                 79 23 40 (clockwise 2)

Angle 2
FB(2–3)   = 246 30 40   _____

BB(2–3)   66 30 40 (180° diff.)
                121 15 30 (clockwise 3)

Angle 3
FB(3–4)   = _____   _____

BB(3–4)

Angle 4
FB(4–1)   = _____   _____

BB(4–1)

Exercise 7.3 Eastings and northings

A closed traverse 1, 2, 3, 4, 1 was set out and the lengths and corrected forward bearings were:

Line	1–2	2–3	3–4	4–1
Line length (m)	490.5	500.0	445.5	649.0
Forward bearing	347 07 10	246 31 00	187 46 40	75 30 40

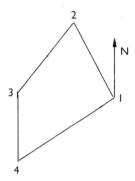

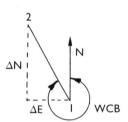

ΔE = Line length × sin WCB
ΔN = Line length × cos WCB
In this case WCB will be forward bearing

The values of the eastings and northings, i.e. ΔE and ΔN have been established for lines (1–2) and (2–3).

Complete the table and show that the errors in eastings = +0.139 m and in northings = 0.111 m. Show that linear error is 0.178 and that accuracy is 1 in 11 713.

Line	Length	WCB	sin WCB	cos WCB	ΔE	ΔN
1–2	490.5	347 07 10	−0.222919	+0.974837	−109.342	+478.157
2–3	500.0	246 31 00	−0.917176	+0.398482	−458.588	−199.241
3–4	445.5	187 46 40				
4–5	649.0	75 30 40				

Linear error = $\sqrt{(\text{Error in eastings})^2 + (\text{Error in northings})^2}$ = _____

Traverse accuracy = $\dfrac{\text{Linear error}}{\text{Perimeter}}$ = _____

Exercise 7.4 *Traverse adjustment using the Bowditch method*_____

A closed traverse 1, 2, 3, 4, 1 was seen to have small errors in eastings and northings as shown:

Line	1–2	2–3	3–4	4–1	Sum
Line length (m)	490.5	500.0	445.5	649.00	2085
ΔE	− 109.342	− 458.588	− 60.290	+ 628.359	+ 0.139
ΔN	+ 478.157	− 199.241	− 441.401	+ 162.374	− 0.111

$$\text{Correction to } \Delta E = \frac{-\text{Error in eastings} \times \text{Line length}}{\text{Perimeter}}$$

$$\text{Correction to } \Delta N = \frac{-\text{Error in northings} \times \text{Line length}}{\text{Perimeter}}$$

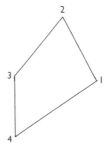

The values of corrections to ΔE and ΔN have been established for lines (1–2), (2–3). Complete the table and show that the sum of the corrections to ΔE and ΔN are − 0.139 and + 0.111.

Determine the true values of ΔE and ΔN in lines (3–4), and (4–1). Show that the sum of the true values of ΔE and ΔN are both zero.

$$\text{Let } E_E = \frac{\text{Error in eastings}}{\text{Perimeter}} = \frac{0.139}{2085} = 6.67 \times 10^{-5}$$

$$\text{Let } E_N = \frac{\text{Error in northings}}{\text{Perimeter}} = \frac{-0.111}{2085} = -5.32 \times 10^{-5}$$

Line	Length	Correction to ΔE, i.e. C_E	Correction to ΔN, i.e. C_N
1–2	490.5	$-E_E \times 490.5 = -0.033$	$-E_N \times 490.5 = +0.026$
2–3	500.0	$-E_E \times 500.0 = -0.033$	$-E_N \times 500.0 = +0.027$
3–4	445.5		
4–1	649.0		
Totals	2085.0		

Line	ΔE	C_E	True ΔE	ΔN	C_N	True ΔN
1–2	− 109.342	− 0.033	− 109.375	+ 478.157	+ 0.026	+ 478.183
2–3	− 458.588	− 0.033	− 458.621	− 199.241	+ 0.027	− 199.214
3–4	− 60.290			− 441.401		
4–1	+ 628.359			+ 162.374		
Totals	0.139	− 0.139		− 0.111	+ 0.111	

Exercise 7.5 *Traverse adjustment using the transit method*_____

A closed traverse 1, 2, 3, 4, 1 was seen to have small errors in easting and northings as shown:

Line	1–2	2–3	3–4	4–1	Sum
Line length	490.5	500.0	445.5	649.0	2085
ΔE	− 109.342	− 458.588	− 60.290	+ 628.359	+ 0.139
ΔN	+ 478.157	− 199.241	− 441.401	+ 162.374	− 0.111

$$\text{Correction to } \Delta E = \frac{-\text{Error in eastings} \times \Delta E}{\text{Total } \Delta E}$$

$$\text{Correction to } \Delta N = \frac{-\text{Error in northings} \times \Delta N}{\text{Total } \Delta N}$$

Total ΔE and total ΔN are the addition of all easting and northing components irrespective of signs. Assume in above formula that ΔE and ΔN have positive values.

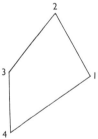

The values of corrections to ΔE and ΔN have been established for lines (1–2), (2–3). Complete the table and show that the sum of the corrections to ΔE and ΔN are − 0.139 and + 0.111.

Determine the true values of ΔE and ΔN in lines (3–4) and (4–1). Show that the sum of the true values of ΔE and ΔN are both zero.

$$\text{Let } E_{ET} = \frac{\text{Error in eastings}}{\text{Total } \Delta E} = \frac{0.139}{1256.574} = + 11.1 \times 10^{-5}$$

$$\text{Let } E_{NT} = \frac{\text{Error in northings}}{\text{Total } \Delta N} = \frac{-0.111}{1281.175} = 8.66 \times 10^{-5}$$

Line	ΔE	ΔN	Correction to ΔE, i.e. $(C_{ET}) = -E_{ET} \times$ Signless ΔE	Correction to ΔN, i.e. $(C_{NT}) = -E_{ET} \times$ Signless ΔN
1–2	− 109.342	+ 478.157	− 0.012	+ 0.041
2–3	− 458.588	− 199.241	− 0.051	+ 0.017
3–4	− 60.290	− 441.401		
4–1	+ 628.359	+ 162.374		
Totals	0.139	− 0.111		

Line	ΔE	C_{ET}	True ΔE	ΔN	C_{NT}	True ΔN
1–2	− 109.342	− 0.012	− 109.354	+ 478.157	+ 0.041	+ 478.198
2–3	− 458.588	− 0.051	− 458.639	− 199.241	+ 0.017	− 199.224
3–4	− 60.290			− 441.401		
4–1	+ 628.359			+ 162.374		
Totals	0.139			− 0.111	+ 0.111	

Exercise 7.6 Compilation of coordinates

The eastings and northings of a closed traverse 1, 2, 3, 4, 1 were corrected using both the Bowditch and transit methods with the results shown in the tables:

Bowditch method

Line	1–2	2–3	3–4	4–1
Corrected ΔE	− 109.375	− 458.621	− 60.320	+ 628.316
Corrected ΔN	+ 478.183	− 199.214	− 441.377	+ 162.408

Transit method

Line	1–2	2–3	3–4	4–1
Corrected ΔE	− 109.354	− 458.639	− 60.296	+ 628.289
Corrected ΔN	+ 478.199	− 199.224	− 441.363	+ 162.388

East coordinate at point on the traverse
= East coordinate at 1 + ΔE between 1 and the point

North coordinate at a point on the traverse
= North coordinate at 1 + ΔN between 1 and the point

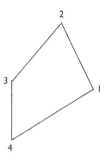

The values of the coordinates at 2, 3 and 4 have been established for the Bowditch method assuming the coordinates at 1 are 1000E, 1000N.

Show that the coordinates at 2, 3 and 4 are as shown for the transit method:

  2. 890.648E   1478.199N
  3. 432.009E   1278.975N
  4. 371.712E   837.612N

Bowditch method

Easting at 1 =   = 1000
Easting at 2 = 1000 + − 109.375   = 890.625
Easting at 3 = 1000 − 109.375 − 458.621   = 432.004
Easting at 4 = 1000 − 109.375 − 458.621 − 60.320 = 371.684
Easting at 1 = 371.684 + 628.316   = 1000.000

Northing at 1 =   = 1000
Northing at 2 = 1000 + 478.183   = 1478.183
Northing at 3 = 1478.183 − 199.214   = 1278.969
Northing at 4 = 1278.969 − 441.377   = 837.592
Northing at 1 = 837.592 + 162.408   = 1000.000

Exercise 7.7 Determination of area of closed traverse

The eastings and northings of a closed traverse 1, 2, 3, 4, 1 were corrected using both the Bowditch and transit methods with the results shown:

Bowditch method

Line	1–2	2–3	3–4	4–1
Corrected ΔE	− 109.375	− 458.621	− 60.320	+ 628.316
Corrected ΔN	− 478.183	− 199.214	− 441.377	+ 162.408

Transit method

Line	1–2	2–3	3–4	4–1
Corrected ΔE	– 109.354	– 458.639	– 60.296	+ 628.289
Corrected ΔN	+ 478.199	– 199.224	– 441.363	+ 162.388

Area of traverse 1, 2, 3, 4, 1 = Area of enclosing rectangles less the areas of triangles and rectangles numbered

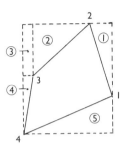

The area of the traverse derived by using the Bowditch method values has been established. Show that the area using the transit method values gives an area of 254 309.4 m².

Bowditch method

Area of enclosing rectangle

$= 628.316 \times (478.183 + 162.408)$ $\qquad = 402\,493.57 \text{ m}^2$

1.	$109.375 \times 478.183/2 =$	$26\,150.63$
2.	$458.621 \times 199.214/2 =$	$45\,681.86$
3.	$60.32 \times 199.214 \quad =$	$12\,016.59$
4.	$60.32 \times 441.377/2 =$	$13\,311.93$
5.	$628.316 \times 162.408/2 =$	$\underline{51\,021.77}$
		$148\,182.78$

Area of traverse $= 402\,493.57 - 148\,182.78$ $\qquad = \mathbf{254\,310.79 \text{ m}^2}$

Exercise 7.8 *Determination of area of closed traverses*

The eastings and northings of a closed traverse 1, 2, 3, 4, 1 were corrected using both the Bowditch and transit methods with the results shown below:

Bowditch method

Line	1–2	2–3	3–4	4–1
Corrected ΔE	– 109.375	– 458.621	– 60.320	+ 628.316
Corrected ΔN	+ 478.183	– 199.214	– 441.377	+ 162.408

Transit method

Line	1–2	2–3	3–4	4–1
Corrected ΔE	– 109.354	– 458.639	– 60.296	+ 628.289
Corrected ΔN	+ 478.199	– 199.224	– 441.363	+ 162.388

Quick method of finding areas using columns

- Columns a, b and c are given.
- Column d shows the progressive values of ΔN.
- Column e is obtained by adding adjacent ΔE values from column c.
- Column f is the product of values in columns d and e.

The area of the traverse corrected by the Bowditch method was found by using the method of columns as shown below.

Show that the area of the traverse corrected by the transit method gives an area of 254 309.4 m^2 using the method of columns.

Bowditch results

a	b	c	d	e	f
Leg	ΔN	ΔE	$\Sigma\Delta$N	Adj ΔE	Product (d $\times$ e)
1–2	+ 478.183	– 109.375	+ 478.183	– 567.996	– 271 606.03
2–3	– 199.214	– 458.621	+ 278.969	– 518.941	– 144 768.45
3–4	– 441.377	– 60.320	– 162.408	+ 567.996	– 92 247.09
4–1	+ 162.408	+ 628.316			

$$2 \mid -508\,621.57$$
$$-254\,310.79$$

Area of traverse = **254 310.79 m^2**

(Note that if the pegs are placed in a clockwise direction the area will be given as a positive value. Here the pegs were placed in an anti-clockwise direction giving a negative value.)

Exercise 7.9 *Bearings of a linked traverse*_____

A link traverse was set out between ordnance survey triangulation points while direction was established using a further two triangulation stations. All angles were measured clockwise in an anti-clockwise traverse giving new forward bearing = backward bearing + clockwise angle where 360° may be deducted.

The uncorrected forward bearings have been established for the

lines (OS2–1) and (1–2). Complete the unmarked bearings for lines
(2–3), (3–OS3), (OS3–OS4).

Distribute the errors and confirm the forward bearings are respectively: 71 35 55, 122 56 30, 63 12 25, 123 19 10 and 32 00 05.

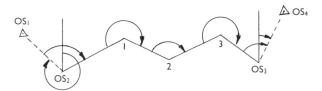

Clockwise angles:

OS2	131 15 30
1	231 20 20
2	120 15 40
3	240 06 30
OS3	88 40 40

Backward bearing (OS2–OS1) = 300 20 10
Forward bearing (OS3–OS4) = 32 00 05

New FB(OS2–1) = BB(OS2–OS1) + Clockwise angle
                = 300 20 10 + 131 15 30
                = 431 35 40
                = 71 35 40

                                        Corrected FBs

FB(OS2–1) = 71 35 40   _____
BB(OS2–1) = 251 35 40 (180° diff.)
            231 20 20 clockwise 1
  FB(1–2) = 122 56 00   _____
  BB(1–2) = 302 56 00 (180° diff.)
            120 15 40 clockwise 2
  FB(2–3) = _____   _____
  BB(2–3) =
FB(3–OS3) = _____   _____
BB(3–OS3) =
FB(OS3–OS4) = _____   _____
FB(OS3–OS4)
     (given)
     Error =

Exercise 7.10 Eastings and northings of a link traverse_____

A linked traverse was conducted between two ordnance survey triangulation points whose coordinates had been precisely determined.

The corrected horizontal line lengths and forward bearings are shown below:

Line	OS2–1	1–2	2–3	3–OS3
Line length	426.5	312.5	337	327.5
FB	71 35 55	122 56 30	63 12 25	123 19 10

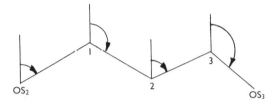

	Easting	*Northing*
OS2	6512.346	8632.868
OS3	7753.848	8569.392

Note: ΔE = Line length $\times$ sin WCB
ΔN = Line length $\times$ cos WCB
In this case WCB will be forward bearing

Using the above information, show that the errors in eastings between OS2 and OS3 is -0.067 and that the error in northings between OS2 and OS3 is $+0.128$.

Line	OS1–1	1–2	2–3	3–OS3
Length	426.5	312.5	337	327.5
WCB	71 35 55	122 56 30	63 12 25	123 19 10
sin WCB	$+0.948868$	$+0.839225$		
cos WCB	$+0.315672$	-0.543785		
ΔE	$+404.692$	$+262.257$		
ΔN	$+134.634$	-169.993		

Errors in eastings = $\Sigma\Delta E$ – Diff. in eastings (OS2 – OS3) = _____
Errors in northings = $\Sigma\Delta N$ – Diff. in northings (OS2 – OS3) = ____

Exercise 7.11 *Traverse adjustment using the Bowditch method on a linked traverse*

A linked traverse OS2, 1, 2, 3, OS3 was seen to have errors in eastings and northings. The derived values are shown below:

Line	OS2–1	1–2	2–3	3–OS3	Sum
Line length	426.5	312.5	337	327.5	1403.5
ΔE	404.692	+262.257	+300.820	+273.666	1241.435
ΔN	134.634	−169.993	+151.909	−179.898	−63.348

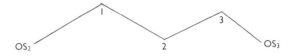

$$\text{Correction to } \Delta E = \frac{-\text{Error in eastings} \times \text{Line length}}{\text{Total line length}}$$

$$\text{Correction to } \Delta N = \frac{-\text{Error in northings} \times \text{Line length}}{\text{Total line length}}$$

The error in the eastings is -0.067 and the error in the northings is 0.128 m. The corrected values for ΔE and ΔN in the first two legs are shown in the table below.

Complete the table and show that the sum of the corrected values of ΔE and ΔN equal the difference in coordinate values at OS2 and OS3.

$$\text{Let } E_E = \frac{\text{Error in eastings}}{\text{Total line length}} = \frac{-0.067}{1403.5} = 4.77 \times 10^{-5}$$

$$\text{Let } E_N = \frac{\text{Error in northings}}{\text{Total line length}} = \frac{+0.128}{1403.5} = 9.12 \times 10^{-5}$$

Line	Length	Correction to ΔE, i.e. C_E	Correction to ΔN, i.e. C_N
OS2–1	426.5	$-E_E \times 426.5 = +0.020$	$-E_N \times 426.5 = -0.039$
1–2	312.5	$-E_E \times 312.5 = +0.015$	$-E_N \times 312.5 = -0.028$
2–3	337.0		
3–OS3	327.5		
Totals	1403.5		

Line	ΔE	C_E	True ΔE	ΔN	C_N	True ΔN
OS2–1	+ 404.692	+ 0.020	+ 404.712	134.634	− 0.039	+ 134.595
1–2	+ 262.257	+ 0.015	+ 262.272	− 169.993	− 0.028	− 170.021
2–3	+ 300.820			+ 151.909		
3–OS3	+ 273.666			− 179.898		
Totals	1241.435		+ 1241.502	− 63.348		− 63.476

Exercise 7.12 *Traverse adjustment using the transit method on a linked traverse*_____

A linked traverse OS2, 1, 2, 3, OS3 was seen to have errors in eastings and northings. The derived values are shown below:

Line	OS2–1	1–2	2–3	3–OS3	Sum
Line length	426.5	312.5	337	327.5	1403.5
ΔE	+ 404.692	+ 262.257	+ 300.820	+ 273.666	1241.435
ΔN	+ 134.634	− 169.993	+ 151.909	− 179.898	− 63.348⎫
					or 636.434⎭

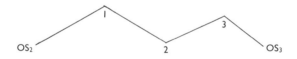

$$\Delta E \text{ correction} = \frac{-\text{Error in eastings} \times \Delta E}{\text{Total } \Delta E}$$

$$\Delta E \text{ correction} = \frac{-\text{Error in northings} \times \Delta N}{\text{Total } \Delta E}$$

Total ΔE and Total ΔN are the addition of all easting and northing components irrespective of signs. Assume in above formula ΔE and ΔN have positive values.

The error in the eastings is − 0.067 and the error in the northings is 0.128 m. The corrected values for ΔE and ΔN in the first two legs are shown in the table below.

Complete the table and show that the sum of the corrected values of ΔE and ΔN equals the difference in coordinate values at OS2 and OS1.

$$\text{Let } E_{ET} = \frac{\text{Error in eastings}}{\text{Total } \Delta E} = \frac{-0.067}{1241.435} = -5.40 \times 10^{-5}$$

$$\text{Let } E_{NT} = \frac{\text{Error in northings}}{\text{Total } \Delta N} = \frac{+0.128}{636.434} = 20.1 \times 10^{-5}$$

Line	ΔE	ΔN	Correction to ΔE, i.e. $C_{ET} = -E_{ET}$ × Signless ΔE	Correction to ΔN, i.e. $C_{NT} = -E_{NT}$ × Signless ΔN
OS2–1	+404.692	+134.634	+0.022	−0.027
1–2	+262.257	−169.993	+0.014	−0.034
2–3	+300.820	+151.909		
3–OS3	+273.666	−179.898		
Totals	1241.435	−63.348		

Line	ΔE	C_{ET}	True ΔE	ΔN	C_{NT}	True ΔN
OS2–1	+404.692	+0.022	404.714	+134.634	−0.027	+134.607
1–2	+262.257	+0.014	262.271	−169.993	−0.034	−170.027
2–3	+300.820			+151.909		
3–OS3	+273.666			−179.898		
Totals	1241.435	+0.067	1241.502	−63.348	−0.128	−63.476

Exercise 7.13 *Compilation of coordinates for a linked traverse*_____

The eastings and northings of a closed traverse OS2, 1, 2, 3, OS3 were corrected using both the Bowditch and transit methods with the results shown in the tables:

Bowditch method

Line	OS2–1	1–2	2–3	3–OS3
Corrected ΔE	+404.712	+262.272	+300.836	+273.682
Corrected ΔN	+134.595	−170.021	+151.878	−179.928

Transit method

Line	OS2–1	1–2	2–3	3–OS3
Corrected ΔE	+404.714	+262.271	+300.836	+273.681
Corrected ΔN	+134.607	−170.027	+151.878	−179.934

East coordinates at a point
   = East coordinates at OS2 + ΔE between OS2 and point
North coordinates at a point
   = North coordinates at OS2 + ΔN between OS2 and point

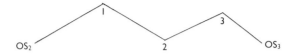

The values of the coordinates of 1, 2, 3 and OS3 have been established for the Bowditch corrected results assuming the coordinates at OS2 are 1620.5E 1435.5N.

Show that the coordinates at 1, 2, 3 and OS3 using the transit results are:

1	2025.214E	1570.107N
2	2287.485E	1400.080N
3	2588.321E	1551.958N
OS3	2862.002E	1372.024N

Bowditch method

Easting at 1   = 1620.5   + 404.712 = 2025.212E
Easting at 2   = 2025.212 + 262.272 = 2287.484E
Easting at 3   = 2287.484 + 300.836 = 2588.320E
Easting at OS3 = 2588.320 + 273.682 = 2862.002E

Northing at 1   = 1435.5   + 134.595 = 1570.095N
Northing at 2   = 1570.095 − 170.021 = 1400.074N
Northing at 3   = 1400.074 + 151.878 = 1551.952N
Northing at OS3 = 1551.952 − 179.928 = 1372.024N

7.5 Precision in traverse work

Traverses are used for basically three types of survey:

1. **Geodetic surveys** used to supply precise control points in flat areas unsuited for triangulation or to provide accurately positioned reference points to be used by engineering surveys.
2. **Engineering surveys** used for secondary control and setting out work.
3. **Topographical surveys** used for less accurate work such as reconnaisance surveys or large scale detail map work.

Equipment used and permissible errors recommended

Survey type	Geodetic	Engineering	Topographic
Theodolite	0.1 sec	1–20 sec	20 sec–1 min
Permissible error in angle (sec)	$2n^{1/2}$ n = no. of angles	$20n^{1/2}$ n = no. of angles	$60n^{1/2}$ n = no. of angles
Distance measurement method	Precise EDM	EDM, steel tape or subtense bar	Synthetic tape or tacheometry
Permissible accuracy in length	$\dfrac{1}{20\,000} - \dfrac{1}{100\,000}$	$\dfrac{1}{5000} - \dfrac{1}{20\,000}$	$\dfrac{1}{100} - \dfrac{1}{5000}$

Closure errors

Angular
For a closed traverse closure error is the difference between the total internal angles and $(2n-4)\,90°$ where n is the number of sides of the traverse.

Linear
For a closed traverse, accuracy = linear error/perimeter.

Causes of inaccuracies

1. Poor centring of theodolite or target.
2. Displacement of pegs during site operations.
3. Inaccurate sighting of target.
4. Parallax.
5. Theodolite errors.
6. Setting up errors.
7. Booking and reading errors.
8. Wrongly numbering stations.
9. Not reducing slope distance to horizontal.
10. Not correcting for scale factor.

7.6 Methods used to increase accuracy in traverse work____

Three tripod traversing equipment

Many modern theodolites have the additional feature of being able to detach the upper part of the theodolite from the tribrach. Special targets and prisms are made to fit into the tribrachs occupying exactly the same positions as the removed theodolites. If three or more tripods are set up with tribrachs carefully levelled and centred above ground stations very accurate traverse work can be achieved.

The theodolite is set up at one station and targets set in tribrachs at adjacent stations. The elevated target is clearly visible, ground refraction effects are minimized and the target is directly above the ground station. This situation means that accurate horizontal and vertical angles can be achieved relatively quickly.

If the targets are replaced by prisms and the theodolite is provided with electromagnetic distance measuring equipment the slope distances can be found automatically. Horizontal distances can be calculated using the vertical angle and the slope distance.

The pace of the operation is governed by the availability of quick reading instruments such as total and semi-total stations and the number of tripods and tribrachs which are available.

The placement of station markers

Station markers should not be easily disturbed and should be clearly visible. The markers should be placed near to the required detail in lines which are long and of similar spacing.

A 50 mm square peg driven almost flush into the ground with a central nail, or a coloured pipe nail driven flush into a road surface is very suitable. This will give stability and the points will be easy to locate especially if a reference or witnessing sketch is used to indicate the point's position relative to nearby site features. If the distance between adjacent stations is long, the centring error will be minimized.

National grid coordinates

When using national grid coordinates at the ends of a link traverse care must be taken to convert the traverse lengths measured in the field into grid lengths using:

Grid length = Measured ground length × Scale factor

The scale factor depends on the value of the eastings on site. (Note that national grid projections do not necessitate any correction to measured angles.)

*7.7 Recent developments in traverse work*_____

Electromagnetic distance measurement

The introduction of electromagnetic distance measurement to traverse operations has brought about considerable improvements especially in the accuracy achieved and the speed at which the work is carried out.

The measurement of 600 m using EDM would be ±6 mm which is a vast improvement over the use of steel tape over the same distance and the operation would be far quicker. However, for distances less than 60 m the steel tape would still be competitive in accuracy, possibly quicker but much cheaper in price.

The use of EDM has made it possible to replace secondary short length traverses which tend to be lacking in accuracy and to replace polar methods.

In Figure 7.4 the points 1, 2, 3 and 4 are positions where site detail is required. The coordinates at 1, 2, 3 and 4 are more accurately established by measuring distances and bearings from A. In the figure, A, B, C, etc. is the main traverse and 1, 2, 3, 4 is the secondary traverse.

The total station

The introduction of the total station has meant that in three tripod traversing the optical sight and the signal axis will coincide making it possible for the instrument directly to display vertical angles, horizontal angles and slope distances. Horizontal distances or vertical distances may be obtained at the press of a button. Refraction and centring errors will be considerably reduced. The fieldbook or data logger will automatically record the readings taken. The results may then be entered into computers either in the field or office and used to determine the corrected coordinates, areas, etc., and then to plot or print out the final required values.

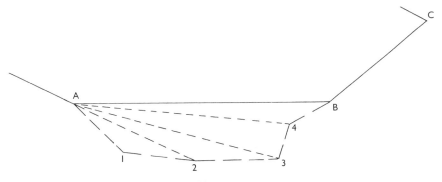

Figure 7.4

Eight

Local control

The levels at numerous stable points are known throughout Great Britain.
These are known as bench marks.

Types of bench mark

- The **Ordnance Survey bench mark** (OSBM) is the level with respect
  to mean sea level (MSL) taken over the years 1915–21 at Newlyn,
  Cornwall.

  Ordnance Survey plans show the positions of the bench marks and
  the values when the plans were published. Due to subsidence and earth
  movement the values may change. Ordnance Survey print-sheets can be
  purchased indicating bench mark values which are of recent date. It is
  customary to design projects based on the Newlyn datum.
- The **master bench mark** (MBM) is normally an OSBM chosen near to
  where the project is to be positioned. The MBM is agreed in writing
  between engineer and contractor and if necessary other OSBMs in the
  area are corrected according to the MBM.
- **Transferred or temporary bench marks** (TBM) are bench marks established near the work in progress but away from possible disturbance.
  They can be established in several ways: metal pins, bolts, tubes or an
  angle iron can be set in concrete. Existing features such as manholes or
  kerbs can be used if the point is specifically indicated. Coloured pipe
  nails driven into the road surface can also provide a temporary bench
  mark.

(a)

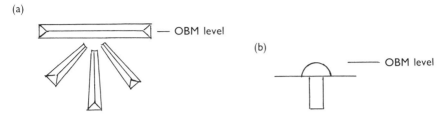

Figure 8.1 Ordnance Survey bench mark.

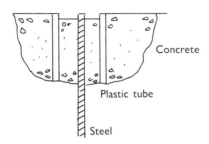

Figure 8.2 Temporary bench mark.

8.2 Level checks and adjustments

Arithmetic checks

Sum of backsights − Sum of foresights = K
Sum of rises − Sum of falls = K
Last reduced level − First reduced level = K

Survey checks

Last BM level − First BM level = K_1

- If all the K values are equal the arithmetic is correct.
- If $K - K_1$ exceeds acceptable error the operation must be repeated.
- If $K - K_1$ is within acceptable error then the error may be redistributed.

Distribution of error

- If distances are known the distribution can be made according to distance.
- If distances are not known divide the error according to the number of set ups.
- The distribution will be to nearest millimetre.

Example 8.1

Consider the level operation shown if acceptable error is:

$$\pm 10 \text{ mm}\sqrt{\text{No. of sets ups}}$$

BS	IS	FS	Rise	Fall	Reduced level	Distance	Remarks
3.575					206.065	0	206.065BM
	3.682			0.107		100	
	3.767			0.085		200	
	3.880			0.113		300	
2.735		2.880	1.000			400	
	2.005		0.730			500	
		2.390		0.385		600	207.113BM

Show that:

(a) Sum of backsights − Sum of foresights = 1.040.
(b) Sum of rises − Sum of falls = 1.040.
(c) Last reduced level − First reduced level = 1.040.
(d) The error is − 8 mm.

Distance distribution

Add 8 mm at 600, 4 mm at 300, 1.33 mm at 100, 2.66 mm at 200, 5.33 mm at 500, giving values:

0	100	200	300	400	500	600
206.065	205.959	205.876	205.764	206.765	206.497	207.113

Set up distribution

Two set ups: 4 mm at each set up, 1 mm for first four readings, 2 mm for the rest.

0	100	200	300	400	500	600
206.065	205.959	205.875	205.763	206.764	206.496	207.113

Exercise 8.1 Level checks and adjustments_____

The levels at A, B, C, D, E, F, G, H, J, K, L and M were found by using the level at five positions between A and M with the results as indicated below:

> Position 1 Sight to BM at A, 2.680; to B, −(0.875); to C, 0.980; to D, −(0.430).
> Position 2 Sight to D, 1.665; to E, −(1.440); to F 0.625.
> Position 3 Sight to F, 0.580; to G, 1.690; to H, 1.225.
> Position 4 Sight to H, 2.455; to J, 3.880; to K, 2.880.
> Position 5 Sight to K, 2.735; to L, 2.005; to BM at M, 2.390.

If this level operation has an acceptable error of:

$\pm 5 \text{ mm} \sqrt{\text{No. of set ups}}$

(a) Plot the backsights, intermediate sights and foresights and reduce the levels.

(b) Show that:

The sum of the backsights − Sum of the foresights = 3.425
The sum of the rises − Sum of the falls = 3.425
Last reduced level − First reduced level = 3.425
Last BM level − First BM level = 3.436
Error = 0.011

(c) Distribute the errors between BM'A' 204.110 and BM'M' 207.546.

Distributed values

A	B	C	D	E	F
210.110	207.666	205.812	207.223	210.329	208.265

G	H	J	K	L	M
207.156	207.622	206.198	207.199	207.930	207.546

BS	IS	FS	Rise	Fall	Reduced level	Distance	Remarks
					204.110	0	BM'A'
						50	B
						100	C
						150	D
						200	E
						250	F
						300	G
						350	H
						400	J
						450	K
						500	L
						550	BM'M' 207.546

8.3 Probable values for a level network

There are several ways of determining the most probable values of a series of results. The method of least squares gives the most satisfactory solutions as long as the data has been carefully produced.

Assumed factors in the solution of a level network

1. Large errors do not occur.
2. Negative and positive errors are equally frequent.
3. Smaller errors are more frequent than larger ones.
4. The sum of the squares of the individual errors in turn should be minimal.
5. The number of equations is given by:

Number of links − Number of stations other than datum

6. The error in the links are directional.
7. The reliability of the results depend on the number of times it has been checked and the length of the link. This reliability is expressed as w, where

$$w \propto \frac{\text{No. of times}}{\text{Length}} \quad w \text{ is known as weight}$$

8. The error in a route from datum back to datum is given by K.

Example 8.2

Levels (m):

A to B = + 10   B to C = + 10
C to D = − 9.8   D to A = − 10.21
C to A = + 20.01

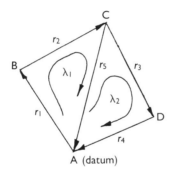

A (datum)

Direction of errors as indicated.

    No. of equations
       = No. of links − No. of stns other than datum
       =   5   −   3   = 2

Consider two routes λ_1 and λ_2, A back to A.

λ_1: $r_1 + r_2 + r_5 = K_1$
λ_2: $-r_5 + r_3 + r_4 = K_2$

Then:

$K_1 = + 10 + 10 - 20.01 \quad\quad = - 0.01$
$K_2 = + 20.01 - 9.8 - 10.21 = + 0.02$

Note the change of sign for direction opposite to error.

Exercise 8.2_____

Levels (m):

> A to B = +8.22   B to C = +18.37
> C to D = +4.32   D to E = −10.85
> E to A = −20.00 C to A = +26.61
> D to A = −30.90

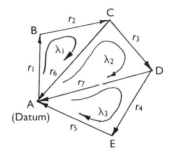

Show that:

> Number of equations or routes = 3
> λ_1: $r_1 + r_2 + r_6 = -0.02$
> λ_2: $-r_6 + r_3 + r_7 = +0.03$
> λ_3: $-r_7 + r_4 + r_5 = +0.05$

These are basic equations with too many unknowns to solve without a least squares approach (see next section).

Example 8.3 *Use of a tabular method to obtain basic equations in a level network*_____

Leg	Direction	Level diff.	Weight
1	A to B	+10.1	1
2	B to C	+9.9	1
3	C to D	+10.2	1
4	D to E	−15.4	1
5	E to A	−14.7	1
6	D to A	−30.1	2
7	D to F	+9.9	1
8	F to A	−40.1	2
9	F to G	−19.3	2
10	G to A	−20.6	2

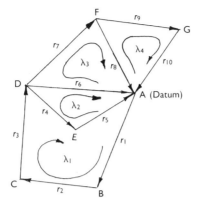

Number of equations

= Number of links − Number of stations other than datum

=   10   −   6   = 4

Route λ_1 has r_1, r_2, r_3, r_4 and r_5 in it and is indicated in column 4. K_1 is the sum of the errors in route λ_1, i.e. r_1, r_2, r_3, r_4 and r_5 as column 8.

Leg	$1/w$	r	λ_1	λ_2	λ_3	λ_4	K_1	K_2	K_3	K_4
AB	1	r_1	1				+ 10.1			
BC	1	r_2	1				+ 9.9			
CD	1	r_3	1				+ 10.2			
DE	1	r_4	1	− 1			− 15.4	+ 15.4		
EA	1	r_5	1	− 1			− 14.7	+ 14.7		
DA	$\frac{1}{2}$	r_6		1	− 1			− 30.1	+ 30.1	
DF	1	r_7			1				+ 9.9	
FA	$\frac{1}{2}$	r_8			1	− 1			− 40.1	+ 40.1
FG	$\frac{1}{2}$	r_9				1				− 19.3
GA	$\frac{1}{2}$	r_{10}				1				− 20.6
							$\Sigma 0.1$	$\Sigma 0.0$	$\Sigma - 0.1$	$\Sigma 0.2$

Note that negative is used when the error direction is opposite to the route direction.

Basic equations

$$\lambda_1: \quad r_1 + r_2 + r_3 + r_4 + r_5 = \quad 0.1$$
$$\lambda_2: \quad -r_4 - r_5 + r_6 \qquad\quad = \quad 0.0$$
$$\lambda_3: \quad -r_6 + r_7 + r_8 \qquad\quad = -0.1$$
$$\lambda_4: \quad -r_8 + r_9 + r_{10} \qquad\quad = \quad 0.2$$

These are basic equations with too many unknowns to solve without using a least squares solution.

8.4 Use of least squares method to find the most probable values

Consider the basic equations:

$$\lambda_1: \quad r_1 + r_2 + r_5 = -0.01$$
$$\lambda_2: \quad -r_5 + r_3 + r_4 = +0.02$$

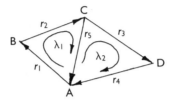

Figure 8.3

These equations have too many unknowns to be solved by normal means. If the data are reliable, the least squares assumption can be made which adds the extra equation:

$$w_1 r_1^2 + w_2 r_2^2 + w_3 r_3^2 + \cdots \qquad\qquad = \text{Min}$$

r_1	r_2	0	0	r_5	$= -0.01$ (1)
0	0	r_3	r_4	$-r_5$	$= +0.02$ (2)
$w_1 r_1^2$	$w_2 r_2^2$	$w_3 r_3^2$	$w_4 r_4^2$	$w_5 r_5^2$	$= \text{Min}$ (3)

Let each of these equations be partially differentiated and multiplied by a chosen factor:

Diff (3) $\times \frac{1}{2}$	$w_1 r_1 \partial r_1$	$w_2 r_2 \partial r_2$	$w_3 r_3 \partial r_3$	$w_4 r_4 \partial r_4$	$w_5 r_5 \partial r_5 = 0$
Diff (2) $\times -\lambda_2$	0	0	$-\lambda_2 \partial r_3$	$-\lambda_2 \partial r_4$	$+\lambda_2 \partial r_5 = 0$
Diff (1) $\times -\lambda_1$	$-\lambda_1 \partial r_1$	$-\lambda_1 \partial r_2$	0	0	$-\lambda_1 \partial r_5 = 0$
	0	0	0	0	0

Each independent variable equals zero. Here:

$$w_1 r_1 \partial r_1 + 0 - \lambda_1 \partial r_1 \quad = 0 \quad \therefore r_1 = (\lambda_1/w_1) + 0$$
$$w_2 r_2 \partial r_2 + 0 - \lambda_1 \partial r_2 \quad = 0 \quad \therefore r_2 = (\lambda_1/w_2) + 0$$
$$w_3 r_3 \partial r_3 - \lambda_2 \partial r_3 + 0 \quad = 0 \quad \therefore r_3 = 0 + (\lambda_2/w_3)$$
$$w_4 r_4 \partial r_4 - \lambda_2 \partial r_4 + 0 \quad = 0 \quad \therefore r_4 = 0 + (\lambda_2/w_4)$$
$$w_5 r_5 \partial r_5 + \lambda_2 \partial r_5 - \lambda_1 \partial r_5 = 0 \quad \therefore r_5 = +(\lambda_1/w_5) - (\lambda_2/w_5)$$

$$\lambda_1: \quad r_1 + r_2 + r_5 = \frac{\lambda_1}{w_1} + \frac{\lambda_1}{w_2} + \frac{\lambda_1}{w_5} - \frac{\lambda_2}{w_5} = -0.01$$

$$\lambda_2: \quad -r_5 + r_3 + r_4 = -\frac{\lambda_1}{w_5} + \frac{\lambda_2}{w_5} + \frac{\lambda_2}{w_3} + \frac{\lambda_2}{w_4} = +0.02$$

If all weights are equal to 1 then the normal equations are:

$3\lambda_1 - \lambda_2 = -0.01$	(1)	$\lambda_1 = -0.00125$
$-1\lambda_1 + 3\lambda_2 = +0.02$	(2)	$\lambda_2 = 3\lambda_1 + 0.01 = 0.00625$
$9\lambda_1 - 3\lambda_2 = -0.03$	(eqn 1) × 3	$r_1 = -0.00125$
Add $8\lambda_1 \quad 0 = -0.01$		$r_2 = -0.00125$
		$r_3 = 0.00625$
		$r_4 = 0.00625$
		$r_5 = -0.00750$

Check $r_1 + r_2 + r_5 = -0.01$
Check $-r_5 + r_3 + r_4 = +0.02$

Example 8.4 *Determination of basic and normal equations in a level network using a tabular method*_____

Leg	Direction	Level diff.	Weight
1	A to B	+ 10.00	1
2	B to C	+ 9.90	1
3	C to D	+ 10.10	1
4	D to F	− 15.10	2
5	F to A	− 15.00	2
6	D to E	− 19.82	1
7	E to A	− 10.20	1

Number of equations
= Number of links − Number of stations other than datum
=   7   −   5   = 2

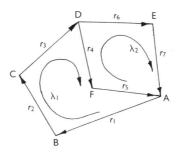

When the first seven columns have been established, obtain the normal equations by dividing into sections equalling the number of routes.

1. In the first section multiply λ_1/w by λ_1, λ_2, λ_3 ... in turn in the correct order.

2. In the second section multiply λ_2/w by λ_1, λ_2, $\lambda_3 \ldots$ in turn in the correct order.
3. In the third section multiply λ_3/w by λ_1, λ_2, $\lambda_3 \ldots$ in turn in the correct order, etc.

In this case there will be two sections.

							1st section	2nd section		
							$K_1 = -0.10$	$K_2 = +0.08$		
Leg	$1/w$	r	λ_1	λ_2	K_1	K_2	$\dfrac{\lambda_1\lambda_1}{w}$	$\dfrac{\lambda_1\lambda_2}{w}$	$\dfrac{\lambda_2\lambda_1}{w}$	$\dfrac{\lambda_2\lambda_2}{w}$
AB	1	r_1	$+1$		10.00		1	0	0	0
BC	1	r_2	$+1$		9.90		1	0	0	0
CD	1	r_3	$+1$		10.10		1	0	0	0
DF	$\frac{1}{2}$	r_4	$+1$	-1	-15.10	$+15.10$	$\frac{1}{2}$	$-\frac{1}{2}$	$-\frac{1}{2}$	$\frac{1}{2}$
FA	$\frac{1}{2}$	r_5	$+1$	-1	-15.00	$+15.00$	$\frac{1}{2}$	$-\frac{1}{2}$	$-\frac{1}{2}$	$\frac{1}{2}$
DE	1	r_6		$+1$		-19.82	0	0	0	1
EA	1	r_7		$+1$		-10.20	0	0	0	1
					-0.10	$+0.08$	4	-1	-1	3

In each section, first column gives λ_1 value, second column gives λ_2 value, etc. All equal K values.

Here, the normal equations are:

$$4\lambda_1 - \lambda_2 = -0.1 \tag{1}$$
$$-1\lambda_1 + 3\lambda_2 = +0.08 \tag{2}$$

Solving gives $\lambda_2 = 0.02$ and $\lambda_1 = -0.02$.

Exercise 8.3 *Finding the most probable values in a level network using a tabular method*

Leg	Direction	Level diff.	Weight
1	A to B	10.00	1
2	B to C	20.00	2
3	C to D	-15.00	2
4	D to E	-7.56	1
5	E to A	-7.36	1
6	D to A	-15.10	1

Level at A = 100.00 mm AOD

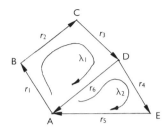

Leg	$1/w$	r	λ_1	λ_2	$K_1 =$		$K_2 =$	
					$\dfrac{\lambda_1\lambda_1}{w}$	$\dfrac{\lambda_1\lambda_2}{w}$	$\dfrac{\lambda_2\lambda_1}{w}$	$\dfrac{\lambda_2\lambda_2}{w}$
AB	1	r_1	1	0	1	0		
BC	$\frac{1}{2}$	r_2	1	0	$\frac{1}{2}$	0		
CD	$\frac{1}{2}$	r_3	1	0				
DE	1	r_4	0	1				
EA	1	r_5	0	1				
DA	1	r_6	1	-1				
					Σ	Σ	Σ	Σ

Complete the table and show that the normal equations are as follows:

$$3\lambda_1 - 1\lambda_2 = -0.10 \qquad\qquad (1)$$
$$-1\lambda_1 + 3\lambda_2 = +0.18 \qquad\qquad (2)$$

Solution of λ_1 and λ_2

$$
\begin{aligned}
3\lambda_1 - 1\lambda_2 &= -0.10 \quad &(\text{eqn } 1)\\
-3\lambda_1 + 9\lambda_2 &= +0.54 \quad &(\text{eqn } 2) \times 3\\
\text{Add:} \quad 8\lambda_2 &= +0.44 \quad &\therefore \lambda_2 = 0.055\\
3\lambda_1 - 0.055 &= -0.10 \quad &\therefore \lambda_1 = -0.015
\end{aligned}
$$

Complete the calculated errors (r) and corrections (C):

$$
\begin{aligned}
r_1 &= (\lambda_1/1) + 0 &= -0.015 &\qquad C_1 = +0.015\\
r_2 &= (\lambda_1/2) + 0 &= -0.0075 &\qquad C_2 = +0.0075\\
r_3 &= &= &\qquad C_3 = +0.0075\\
r_4 &= &= +0.055 &\qquad C_4 =\\
r_5 &= &= &\qquad C_5 = -0.055\\
r_6 &= &= &\qquad C_6 = +0.070
\end{aligned}
$$

Find the levels at B, C, D, E and A (complete):

Level at B $= 100 + 10.00 + 0.015$ $=$
Level at C $= 110.015 + 20.00 + 0.0075 =$
Level at D $= 130.0225 - \quad + \quad = 115.030$
Level at E $= \quad -7.56 - \quad = 107.415$
Level at A $= 107.415 \quad - \quad - \quad = 100.000$

Exercise 8.4 *Finding the most probable values in a level network*_____

Leg	Direction	Level diff.
1	AB	− 6.299
2	BC	+ 1.165
3	CD	+ 8.664
4	DE	+ 3.815
5	EF	+ 0.544
6	FG	+ 1.870
7	GH	+ 1.437
8	HJ	− 3.182
9	JK	− 4.364
10	KA	− 3.663
11	EA	− 7.360
12	KF	+ 4.236

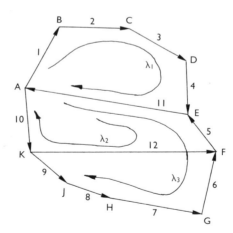

In the above situation show that:

(a) Three circuits are needed.
(b) Circuit λ_1 has an error of -0.015.
    Circuit λ_2 has an error of $+0.005$.
    Circuit λ_3 has an error of $+0.002$.

(c) If the weights are all equal show that the normal equations are:

$$5\lambda_1 - \lambda_2 - \lambda_3 = -0.015$$
$$-1\lambda_1 + 4\lambda_2 + 3\lambda_3 = +0.005$$
$$-1\lambda_1 + 3\lambda_2 + 7\lambda_3 = +0.002$$

(d) Show that $\lambda_1 = -0.002922$; $\lambda_2 = +0.000911$; $\lambda_3 = 0.000522$ and corrected values are:

Circuit λ_1	Circuit λ_2	Circuit
−6.296	+7.357	+7.357
+1.168	+0.544	+0.544
+8.667	−4.237	+1.870
+3.818	−3.663	+1.437
−7.357	0.001	−3.181
0.000		−4.363
		−3.663
		0.001

(e) If the weights of 1, 2, 3 and 4 are double the rest, show that the normal equations are:

$$3\lambda_1 - \lambda_2 - \lambda_3 = -0.015$$
$$-1\lambda_1 + 4\lambda_2 + 3\lambda_3 = +0.005$$
$$-1\lambda_1 + 3\lambda_2 + 7\lambda_3 = +0.002$$

(f) Show that $\lambda_1 = -0.005058$; $\lambda_2 = +0.000461$; $\lambda_3 = -0.000635$, and corrected values are:

Circuit λ_1	Circuit λ_2	Circuit λ_3
−6.296	+7.355	+7.355
+1.167	+0.544	+0.544
+8.666	−4.236	+1.871
+3.818	−3.663	+1.437
−7.355	0.000	−3.181
0.000		−4.363
		−3.663
		0.000

The remaining sections of this chapter are concerned with **vertical control**.

8.5 Methods of ensuring vertical alignment_____

- **Spirit level**. This is effective for plumbing columns and formwork up to a height of one storey.
- **Plumb bobs**. These give a visual indication of the vertical when used in a suitable situation. The best conditions are a wind-free environment with a heavy bob immersed in a liquid to dampen the pendulum effects.
- **Two theodolites**. These are placed away from the building in positions where they can check verticality in two directions at right angles to each other.
- **One theodolite employing a diagonal eyepiece**. The optical plummet is used to set above a mark. The diagonal eyepiece makes it possible to view through the telescope when the telescope tube points vertically upwards.
- **Optical plumbing device (auto plumb)**. This is a tripod-mounted instrument which produces a vertical sight upwards and one downwards, and automatically levels itself when the instrument is approximately level.
- **Laser light**. Many laser instruments can be adjusted to project the red laser light vertically up or down. In most conditions the practical range is limited to around 60 m.
- **Plumbing devices**. (See Figure 8.4.)

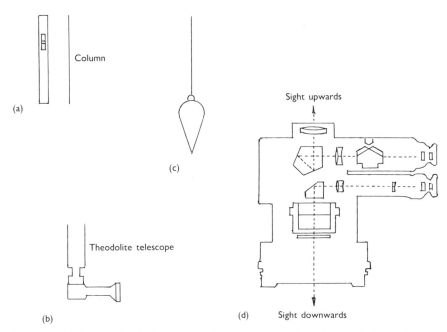

Figure 8.4 (a) Spirit level. (b) Diagonal eyepiece. (c) Plumb bob. (d) Auto plumb.

8.6 Vertical alignment of tall buildings_____

General method

As each floor is added a new datum should be established directly above the datums on the floors beneath. Measurements to column centres should be referred to the new datum to ensure verticality as the building progresses.

Ensuring vertical alignment using two theodolites

Consider the situation illustrated in Figure 8.5. A, B, C, D should be established before the job starts in positions where disturbance is unlikely. A and D should be placed far enough away to give vertical angles less than 30°. B, E, C should be a right angle.

At each floor level establish a new datum in the vertical planes AB and DC. Use average values of face left and face right marks on the structure.

Ensuring vertical alignment using the auto plumb

The auto plumb is set up above E, approximately level. The instrument will sensitively level and give a vertical sight when viewed through the upper eyepiece.

The position of the line of sight may be located on a target on the floor above. If this is repeated with the instrument at 90°, 180° and 270° a total of four marks will be located. if they all coincide the instrument is in perfect adjustment. It is normal to adjust the cross hairs to the mean position to ensure adjustment.

Some instruments are capable of moving the pentagonal prism. In these cases a position on the target is located by adjusting the micrometer drum giving a reading of R_1. Repeating the operation at 180° the micrometer drum gives a value of R_2.

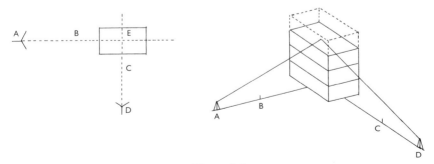

Figure 8.5

If the value of $(R_1 + R_2)/2 = 10$ the instrument is in perfect adjustment. If $(R_1 + R_2)/2 = x$ then the instrument will give perfect vertical readings when the drum reading is x.

8.7 Practical alignment of tall buildings

Internal use of the auto plumb

The best practical method to establish a good grid system for each floor level is to use the auto plumb internally at three or preferably four points as shown in Figure 8.6(c). This requires that holes be placed in each floor directly above the ground reference marks.

A transparent plastic sheet in a frame shown in Figure 8.6(a) is placed above each hole in turn and intersecting lines of a chinagraph pencil mark on the plastic can provide a target. When the target is accurately located the frame is partially screwed down until a final check is made. Final adjustment, if necessary, is made by a slight tap with a hammer and then the frame is screwed down.

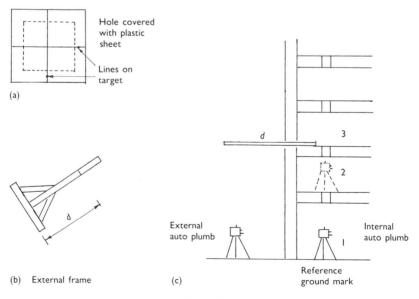

Figure 8.6

External use of the auto plumb

To check the verticality of walls or columns the auto plumb may be set up externally at a distance *d* from the edge and checked at each floor level using the external frame shown in Figure 8.6(b).

The laser

A laser can be used as an alternative to the autoplumb. It does have the advantage of providing a visible sight line which means the whole line can be set out by one man, thereby reducing the communication problems usually experienced at the higher levels with the auto plumb. However, the length of laser sight line is less than 60 m in most conditions and the accuracy of the vertical line is not as good as the auto plumb.

8.8 Verticality of old buildings

A surveyor is often called upon to check the verticality of an existing building indicated in Figure 8.7 thought to be suffering differential settlement. If a check is made every six months over a period of years, the severity of the problem will be disclosed. If the rate of change of inclination increases then steps must be taken to alleviate the problem.

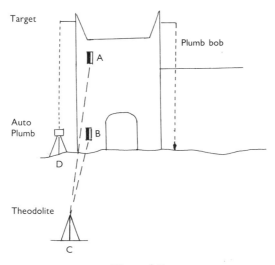

Figure 8.7

Methods of checking verticality

Fixed plates and a theodolite

The plates indicated in Figure 8.8 are fixed at A and B, where A is high on the face of the building and B is directly below near to ground level. Each time a check is made a theodolite is placed at C, a very stable position. A is sighted face left and the telescope depressed to measure the displacement at B. This is repeated on face right and the average displacement between A and B noted in mm.

Plate

Figure 8.8

Upper target and auto plumb

An auto plumb is set up above a very stable point D. An upper target is adjusted vertically above.

Each time a check is made the auto plumb is placed at D and the pentagonal prism is moved to sight target to give a value of R_1 at $0°$ and a value of R_2 at $180°$.

$R_1 - R_2$ is the angular displacement of the mark from vertical. Displacement over H metres between auto plumb and target is:

$$(R_1 - R_2)/1000 \times H \text{ mm}$$

Plumb bob

In low wind conditions a suitably damped plumb bob will indicate any large errors in verticality.

Nine

Setting out

9.1 Preparation for site work

Office work

Shortly before the surveyor starts site work the following information must be checked:

1. The latest drawings showing all the project detail.
2. Lists of temporary bench marks with location and level.
3. Lists of permanent and temporary reference points with their positions and levels.
4. Dated revisions which have been made to the drawing.
5. Other revisions expressed in writing.
6. Confirmations in writing of orally expressed instructions.

From the above information investigation should be made into the following:

1. The anticipated setting out problems and their recommended solutions.
2. The completeness of the information supplied and whether it is sufficient to enable the work to be set out without resorting to scaling from the drawings.
3. The compatability of the information given. Do the overall dimensions equal the sum of the individual dimensions?
4. The planning of a sequence of setting out operations and the incorporation of a checking system which will control the dimensions.
5. The checking over of the availability of personnel and equipment on the proposed setting out dates.

Site reconnaissance

Before starting to set out any new work the surveyor should check out the following in the field:

1. Do the existing features closely match those shown on the drawing?
2. Is it feasible to fit the proposed project into the space available?
3. Are the level values of the temporary bench marks still correct?
4. Have the marker positions been disturbed?
5. Are the clearances still available?
6. If there are any discrepancies found, report them in writing as soon as they are discovered.
7. Investigate the nature of the activities which will be taking place on the site over the duration of setting out and building work and plan accordingly.
8. Amend the method and sequence of the setting out operations according to the latest information gathered from site.

9.2 Use of lines in setting out

In general terms, setting out consists of transferring detail from a drawing to a piece of ground. On the drawing details are given of nearby existing buildings and features and the proposed work to be set out.

It is possible to extract from the existing detail lines of reference to which new work can be referred such as building lines, base lines and grid lines.

Building lines

The local authorities normally define the building line and insist that all building frontages must lie on or behind this line.

The building line is usually a continuation of the building line of the existing adjacent premises. Often the majority of measurements are taken at right angles or parallel to the building line as shown in Figure 9.1.

Figure 9.1

Base lines

A base line is an accurately measured distance between two stations. Buildings are set out by taping well conditioned triangles from the stations as indicated in Figure 9.2.

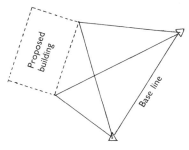

Figure 9.2

Grid lines

Generally, two main perpendicular base lines are set out and lines parallel to these are grid lines. The intersection of grid lines often indicates a setting out position. In Figure 9.3 a series of piles are indicated at the intersection points.

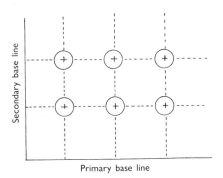

Figure 9.3

9.3 Setting out using coordinate mathematics of a simple grid

On-site people tend to be confused by the amount of information supplied. It must be remembered that when performing coordinate calculations the relationship between two points only is considered at any one time. The problem is reduced to a simple mathematical process, as shown in the following worked example.

Example 9.1 *The calculation of the whole circle bearings and distances given the relative coordinates*_____

Consider an instrument at station A, as shown in the diagram.

Sign convention

4th quad.	− E + N	+ E + N	1st quad.
3rd quad.	− E − N	+ E − N	2nd quad.

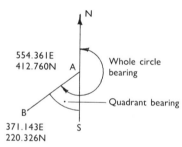

554.361E
412.760N

Whole circle bearing

Quadrant bearing

B
371.143E
220.326N

$$\text{Quadrant bearing } AB = \tan^{-1}\frac{(E_B - E_A)}{(N_B - N_A)}$$

$$\text{Distance } AB = \sqrt{(E_B - E_A)^2 + (N_B - N_A)^2}$$

$$\text{Quadrant bearing } AB = \tan^{-1}\left(\frac{371.143 - 554.361}{220.326 - 412.760}\right)$$

$$= \tan^{-1}\left(\frac{-183.218}{-192.434}\right)$$

The signs indicate 3rd quadrant.

$$\text{Quadrant bearing } AB = 43°35'41''$$

$$\text{Whole circle bearing} = 43°35'41'' + 180° = 223°35'41''$$

$$\text{Distance } AB = \sqrt{(183.218)^2 + (192.434)^2} = 265.706 \text{ m}$$

Exercise 9.1_____

Show that:

Quadrant bearing AC = $32°18'06''$
Whole circle bearing AC = $327°41'54''$
Distance AC = 134.358 m
Quadrant bearing AD = $11°58'54''$
Whole circle bearing AD = $168°01'06''$
Distance AD = 92.924 m

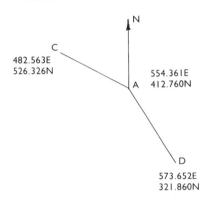

Example 9.2 *The calculation of coordinates from whole circle bearings and distances*_____

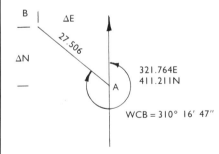

Sign convention			
4th	$-E$	$+E$	1st
quad.	$+N$	$+N$	quad.
3rd	$-E$	$+E$	2nd
quad.	$-N$	$-N$	quad.

Quadrant bearing

$360° - WCB$	WCB
$WCB - 180°$	$180° - WCB$

In the diagram, quadrant bearing = $360° - WCB = 49°43'13''$

$$\sin QB = \frac{\Delta E}{AB} \qquad \Delta E = AB \sin QB \text{ (note: negative in the fourth quadrant)}$$

$$\cos QB = \frac{\Delta N}{AB} \qquad \Delta N = AB \sin QB \text{ (note: positive in the fourth quadrant)}$$

$\Delta E = -27.506 \sin 49°43'13'' = -20.984$
Easting at B $= 321.764 - 20.984 = \textbf{300.78E}$

$\Delta N = +27.506 \cos 49°43'13'' = +17.783$
Northing at B $= 411.211 + 17.783 = \textbf{428.994N}$

Exercise 9.2_____

Show that:

(a) Easting at C = 348.497N.
(b) Northing at C = 435.845N.
(c) Easting at D = 292.834E.
(d) Northing at D = 380.946N.

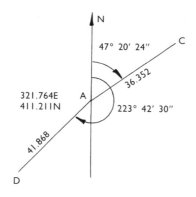

9.4 Setting out a building with known coordinates using two theodolites set up on stations with corrected coordinates_____

Where two theodolites are available it is useful to use the line between theodolite stations as a base line and to locate well conditioned points with known coordinates by turning angles with respect to the base line and locating by intersection. Checks are made on distances to ensure accuracy. The mathematics involved are illustrated in the following example.

Example 9.3

In the diagram the positions of A and B have been previously located. Illustrate the method of establishing the position of C by angle measurement and indicate a method of checking by steel taping.

$$\tan a = 60/55 \qquad a = \tan^{-1}(60/55) = 47°29'23''$$
$$\tan b = 80/30 \qquad b = \tan^{-1}(80/30) = 69°26'38''$$
$$c = 90° - b \qquad\qquad\qquad = 20°33'22''$$
$$\tan d = 20/85 \qquad d = \tan^{-1}(20/85) = 13°14'26''$$
$$\alpha_1 = 180° - a - b \qquad\qquad = 63°03'59''$$
$$\beta_1 = 90° - c - d \qquad\qquad = 56°12'12''$$
$$AC = \sqrt{55^2 + 60^2} \qquad\qquad = \mathbf{81.394\ m}$$
$$BC = \sqrt{20^2 + 85^2} \qquad\qquad = \mathbf{87.321\ m}$$

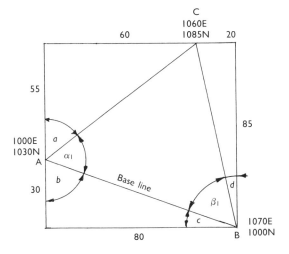

Method

1. Place a theodolite at A, zero on to B, turn through to $(360° - \alpha_1)$, i.e. $296°56'01''$ to sight C.
2. Place a second theodolite at B, zero on to A, turn through $56°12'12''$ to sight C.
3. An assistant places a ranging rod in the position which is in line from A and in line from B. Fine positioning can be completed using a driven peg and nail.
4. Distances AC and BC are checked using a horizontal tightened steel tape.

Exercise 9.3 *Setting out a building with known coordinates using two theodolites set up on stations with corrected coordinates*_____

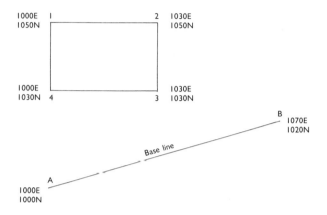

The coordinates of A, B, 1, 2, 3, 4, are as follows:

	Easting	*Northing*
A	1000	1000
B	1070	1020
1	1000	1050
2	1030	1050
3	1030	1030
4	1000	1030

Show that suitable angles to set out at A and B and zeroed with respect to the base line AB are:

Reading at A		*Reading at B*	
1	285°56′43″	1	39°08′38″
2	316°54′33″	2	52°48′55″
3	330°56′43″	3	29°58′54″
4	285°56′43″	4	24°04′32″

Show also that the check distances are:

A1 = 50.000	B1 = 76.158
A2 = 58.310	B2 = 50.000
A3 = 42.426	B3 = 41.231
A4 = 30.000	B4 = 70.711

Example 9.4 Use of the programmable calculator to establish angles of a building defined by its coordinates_____

Program	Use
2ND F	C
LRN	COMP
(	ENTER × 1
(×)	COMP
2000	ENTER × 2
	COMP
−	ENTER × 3
(×)	COMP
1000	ENTER × 4
)	COMP
÷	RESULT
(	C AGAIN
(×)	.
1500	.
−	.
(×)	
1000	
)	
=	
2ND F	
TAN^{-1}	
2ND F	
LRN	

Methods of determining θ.

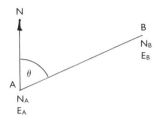

Bearing from A to B is θ

$$\theta = \tan^{-1}\left(\frac{E_B - E_A}{N_B - N_A}\right)$$

In computer program 1st X is E_B
2nd X is E_A
3rd X is N_B
4th X is N_A

Example 9.5_____

(a) Determine α_1 and β_1.
(b) Calculate α_2, α_3, α_4, β_2, β_3, β_4 and prepare the angles to set out the rectangular building 1, 2, 3 and 4 from theodolites placed at A and B.

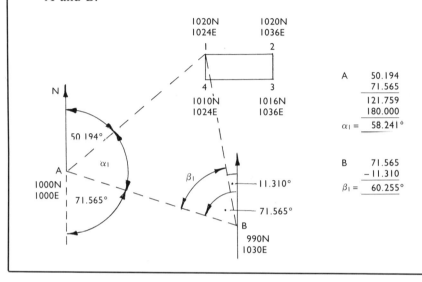

9.5 Considerations on the setting out of domestic buildings_____

Domestic buildings are normally positioned with respect to a line. The lines used are usually either a building line or a line associated with a nearby building.

On small sites the architect will relate dimensions to the corners of the existing building or, in the case of a stone-built building, will stipulate a minimum clearance distance. In order to establish the clearance distance a theodolite is place in line with two pegs 1 m away from the corner as shown in Example 9.6. A horizontal staff is read using the vertical cross hair of the theodolite at metre intervals along the wall and the minimum value obtained. Clearance will be measured from this point.

Example 9.6

Set out a rectangular building to give 3 m clearance between the buildings and a common frontage along the building line. The rear of the new building is to project 2 m beyond the existing building.

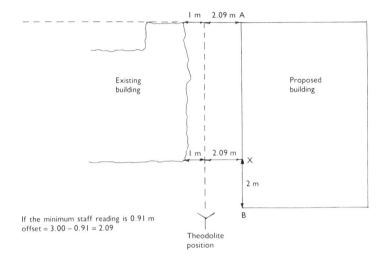

Establish pegs at A and X with nails placed 3.09 m from existing building corner in the line of the rear of the existing building. Measure the correct distance AB to establish the building base line.

9.6 Practical setting out of domestic buildings

Once the base line of a building is fixed, the positions of other pegs may be obtained by a series of means which are dependent on the size or the nature of the building.

Buildings requiring the highest accuracy, such as steel-framed buildings or buildings which must fit a strict modular system, require a theodolite. Buildings where the accuracy is not paramount can be set out by levels fitted with horizontal angles, or site squares may be used if available.

A flexible glass fibre tape using the 3:4:5 method would normally be sufficiently accurate for an extension to existing property.

The theodolite

Here the instrument is set up above the nail of one peg of the base line and the instrument zeroed and then sighted on the nail of the other peg. The instrument is carefully turned to read exactly 90° or 270° and the new peg and nail are set out using a tightened steel tape.

The sightsquare

This is an instrument which has two telescopes perpendicular to each other in a horizontal direction.

To set out at right angles the sightsquare is erected above the nail of one peg on the base line and the upper telescope is used to sight the nail on the other peg on the base line. Sights taken through the lower telescope are at 90° and enable pegs to be set out perpendicular to the base line. Measure using tapes and place nails at the required distances.

The 3:4:5 method

This is an approximate method in which a tape is set out for 4 units in the direction of the base line. A second tape is set out for 3 units approximately at right angles and a 3:4:5 triangle is completed using a diagonal of 5 units. This should set out a very reasonable value of 90°.

Checks

- Check the accuracy of the rectangular shapes by measuring the diagonals. They should be exactly equal.
- Check the drawings with the setting out and ensure that all lines and dimensions are correct.

*9.7 Use of profiles for control of domestic buildings*_____

When all of the corners of a building have been set out and the top soil removed, goal post profiles are set up as shown in Figures 9.4(a) and (b) perpendicular to the face lines and offset from the corners 1–2 m for hand diggers and 5–7 m for a machine dig. Ideally, the offset should be kept at a constant figure.

Notes on profiles

Check profiles to see if there has been movement before use. Face lines are indicated by means of nails or saw cuts and string lines. Profiles are placed at levels simply related to the finished floor level or to the damp proof course.

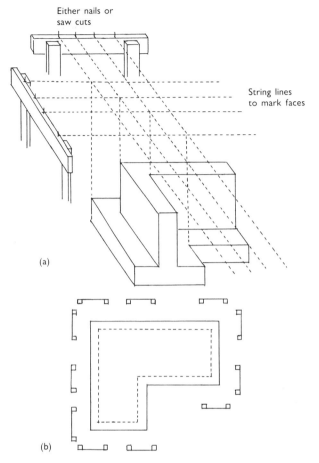

Either nails or saw cuts

String lines to mark faces

(a)

(b)

Figure 9.4 (a) Profile boards. (b) Plan of profiles.

9.8 Practical setting out of modular prefabricated building

When a construction relies on prefabricated units the specified tolerances are normally severe and accurate setting out is essential at all stages as illustrated in Figure 9.5. In order to meet the more rigorous specifications the following techniques are employed.

1. The profiles are constructed as a continuous board offset around the full perimeter of the building. The main grid lines can be set in the normal standard pattern and other lines can be introduced to locate service entry points and other special features.

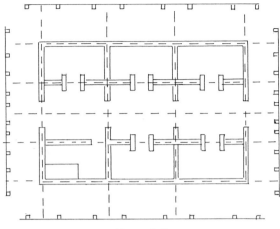

Figure 9.5

2. Theodolites should be used for setting out the main grid lines.
3. Templates should be used for repetitive dimensions which occur in modular construction to reduce the possibility of error.
4. Work below ground is normally cast *in situ* and it is extremely important that the setting out at ground level is as good as possible because all the subsequent measurements will depend on its accuracy.
5. Work up to first floor level should be set out on the ground floor slab using the theodolite and plumbed up using the plumb bob, theodolite or auto plumb.
6. At each subsequent level the dimensions and levels should be carefully checked.

9.9 The control of holding down bolts for steel structures___

The great advantage of steel structures is that they can be erected quickly. To facilitate this process the holding down bolts must be correctly set out for level, line, distance and verticality.

Control

Level
A temporary bench mark set in concrete is positioned where it will suffer little disturbance and be close to the workings. The level at the TBM is established making use of two neighbouring bench marks.

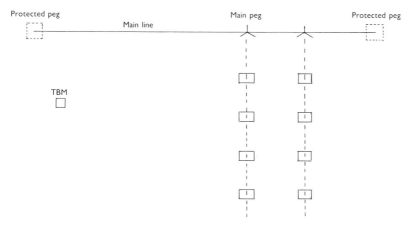

Figure 9.6

Line

A main peg is set up outside the main grid lines. From the main peg a target peg is erected which is in the distance, well protected, outside the general site traffic and parallel to the main grid lines. A secondary peg is placed at the other end of the line also in a protected position to check for movements of any of the pegs on this main line.

Grid lines are set out perpendicular or parallel to the main line as shown in Figure 9.6.

Distances

All distances are measured with a horizontal tightened steel tape. For shorter distances a cumulative measurement is taken allowing, say, 5 mm for the hooking over the nail. Larger distances can disturb the peg or the nail and when this is considered a possibility intermediate pegs must be used.

Verticality

Holding down bolts must be checked for verticality soon after the concrete is poured and if necessary rectified.

9.10 The positioning of holding down bolts for steel structures

Use of templates

A group of four or six bolts is normally required at specified spacings at each stanchion or column. In order to ensure that they are in the correct

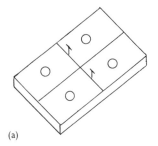 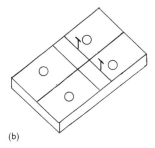

(a)   (b)

Figure 9.7

relative positions 20 mm thick rectangular plywood templates are made with holes bored out in these positions. The centre line is indicated in both directions. In most cases the grid line coincides with the centre line of the bolt group and this is indicated by nails on the template as shown in Figure 9.7(a).

If the bolts are to be offset by say 100 mm to the left of the grid line a secondary line is drawn on the template 100 mm to the right of the centre line and the nails placed on the new line as shown in Figure 9.7(b).

Bolts attached to template

The polystyrene cases shown in Figure 9.8 allow a little movement in the bolts. The bolts should be tapped with a rubber mallet within 24 hours of pour to ensure this free movement.

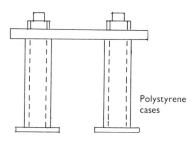

Polystyrene cases

Figure 9.8

Stretchers and bearers

In order to suspend the template and bolt assembly across the dug out base two stretchers are utilized to support each side of the template. The stretchers are normally substantial pieces of timber which allow little deflection.

The stretchers are supported by bearers which lie at right angles to the stretchers at the edge of the base.

9.11 Procedures for the positioning of holding down bolts___

The basic procedures are illustrated in Figure 9.9.

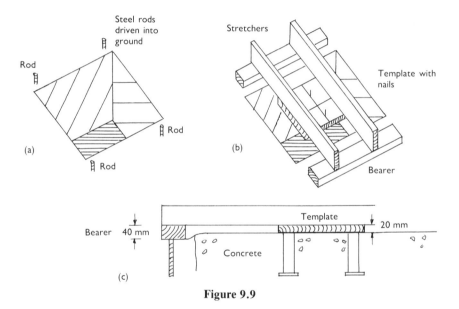

Figure 9.9

Methods of setting out the bolts in the correct position

1. Drive 300 mm steel rods into the ground at the excavation.
2. Find the level on top of each of the rods and drive them down to approximately 20 mm below the final concrete level if 40 mm bearers are used.
3. Dig out the ground to this level and fix bearer on top of the steel rods.
4. Attach the template beneath the stretcher and lay the stretcher across the bearers.
5. Adjust the bearers to give the correct level for the upper template which is to lie 20 mm above finished floor level.

6. Using the theodolite sight the protected peg and turn through 90° very accurately. Ensure that both nails in turn are in line.
7. Measure the distance from the theodolite station using a horizontal tightened steel tape.
8. Allow the pour of the concrete to achieve the level of the template which should be at ground floor level.
9. Check the template for level, line, direction and distance before the concrete has had time to harden and if necessary make any minor adjustments.
10. Check the bolts for verticality and one day later ensure there is a little movement in the bolts by tapping with a rubber hammer.

9.12 Practical setting out of sewers

The traditional method of setting out sewer trenches and pipe runs is to determine suitable sight rail levels and by using a traveller establish the levels at the bottom of the trench and the invert levels for the pipe. This method relies heavily on the ability of the workforce to line and level the pipe correctly.

In recent years the laser has been introduced which enables the pipe run to be set out more quickly and accurately. It is now common to use sight rails to cut out approximately a section of trench and to use the laser to sight the inverts of the pipe run accurately.

Setting out the trench

Generally:

Site rail level = Level at outfall + Horizontal distance from outfall
× Slope of pipe + Length of traveller

Example 9.7

- Level of the outfall is 149.36 m AOD.
- Slope of the pipe is 1 in 60.
- Length of the traveller is 2.5 m.

Determine the level of the sight rails at 27 m, 54 m and 75 m from the outfall.

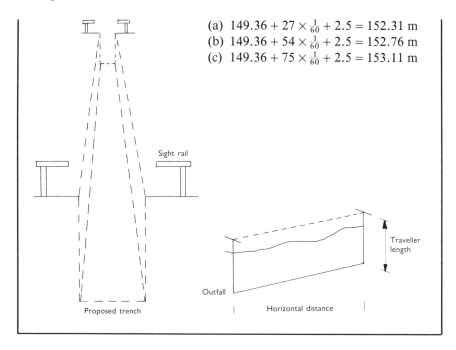

(a) $149.36 + 27 \times \frac{1}{60} + 2.5 = 152.31$ m
(b) $149.36 + 54 \times \frac{1}{60} + 2.5 = 152.76$ m
(c) $149.36 + 75 \times \frac{1}{60} + 2.5 = 153.11$ m

9.13 Setting out of pipes using the laser

The trench shown in Figure 9.10 is normally set out using sight rails and a traveller and excavated using a back actor. A 200 mm deep granular bedding is introduced into the trench to support the sewer pipes. The first pipe is lowered so that the outfall is at the correct reduced level.

The use of the laser

The laser is set up just inside the pipe near the outfall. Approximate levelling will trigger automatic levelling and the completion will be indicated by the lighting of a green bulb. A target is erected at the other end of the pipe.

Buttons are pressed on the laser until the desired gradient is indicated. When the laser beam is switched on a red spot is seen on the target. Normally the spot is off-centre and the pipe must be moved by crow bars until the spot is centralized.

Gravel is placed around the pipe in this position to achieve final stability. A second pipe is lowered and fitted into the socket of the first.

The target is placed at the end of the second pipe and the pipe is adjusted laterally and vertically until the red spot is centralized. Gravel is placed around the pipe in this position.

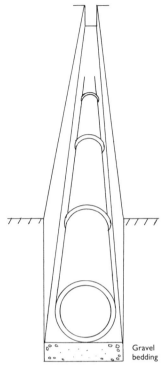

Gravel
bedding

Figure 9.10

This is repeated until the end of the run is reached.

This method of setting out is accurate, quick and can be completed with semi-skilled workers needing minimum supervision.

9.14 Difficulties experienced when setting out piles_____

The nature of the piling operation creates a series of problems for the person responsible for setting out the positions of piles:

- The heavy piling rig and the manner of its operation disturbs the ground for several metres around and existing pegs are likely to have been moved out of position.
- Vibrations from the pile rig are liable to affect the surveying equipment making readings unrealiable.
- Visibility is severely curtailed by the size of the piling equipment, the spoil heaps and the site traffic.

■ Piling is an expensive operation and the engineer must be constantly available and be able to establish accurately the new position shortly before the rig moves into place.

Methods employed to overcome the difficulties

On a small site the positions can be located by steel pins using a bricklayer's line stretching between profiles with distances measured accurately using steel tapes.

The distances from each end of a base line which is away from the site activity to the steel pin is noted before the piling rig arrives. When the rig is in place these distances are again checked and, if necessary, corrected.

On larger sites a base line is set up remote from site activities, where sights and measurements may be taken without hindrance. Bearings and distances are calculated from the known coordinates of the pile positions.

A theodolite is set up at each end of the base line and one theodolite sets out the bearing. Using EDM equipment or a horizontal tightened steel tape, it measures the distance to the pile position. The second theodolite is used mainly as a check, but where there is a visibility problem the second theodolite may set out the bearing and measure the distance while the first gives the checks.

In a very congested site a secondary base line may be set up at the other side of the site enabling four possible readings to be taken.

Example 9.8 *Setting out piles using coordinates*_____

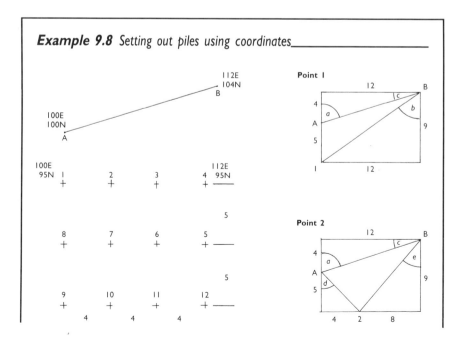

Determine:

(a) The angles to set out at A and B to set out at 1 and 2.
(b) The distances A1, B1, A2 and B2.

Solution

$\tan a = \frac{12}{4} = 3 \qquad a = 71°33'54'' \qquad c = 18°26'06''$
$\tan b = \frac{12}{9} = \frac{4}{3} \qquad b = 53°07'48''$
Angle at A $= 108°26'06''$
Angle at B $= 90° - 53°07'48'' - 18°26'06''$
$\qquad\qquad = 90° - 53.13 - 18.435 = 18°26'06''$
A1 $=$ **4.00 m**
B1 $=$ **15.00 m**
$\tan d = \frac{4}{5} \qquad d = 38°39'35''$
$\tan e = \frac{8}{9} \qquad e = 41°38'01''$
Angle at A $= 180° - 71°33'54'' - 38°39'35''$
$\qquad\qquad = 180° - 71.565 - 38.65972$
$\qquad\qquad = 69°46'31''$
Angle at B $= 90° - 18°26'06'' - 41°38'01''$
$\qquad\qquad = 90° - 18.435 - 41.63361$
$\qquad\qquad = 29°55'53''$
A2 $= \sqrt{25 + 16} =$ **6.4031 m**
B2 $= \sqrt{81 + 64} =$ **12.0415 m**

Ten

Curve ranging

10.1 Circular curves: basic geometry and definitions_____

When designing a road or railway between two points it is customary to consider initially the most appropriate route as a series of straight lines. Curves are introduced to smooth out the changes in direction or grade. The simplest curve to consider is the circular curve, indicated in Figure 10.1.

The basic geometry of the circular curve is as follows:

$$
\begin{aligned}
\text{Angles IAC} = \text{IBC} &= 90° \\
\Phi + \text{BIA} &= 180° \\
\text{ACB} + \text{BIA} &= 180° \\
\text{ACB} &= \Phi \\
\text{ACI} = \text{ICB} &= \Phi/2 \quad \text{(symmetry)} \\
\text{CDA} = \text{CDB} &= 90° \quad \text{(symmetry)}
\end{aligned}
$$

From right angle triangles:

$$
\begin{aligned}
\text{AI} = \text{BI} &= R \tan \Phi/2 \\
x &= R \sin \Phi/2 \\
\text{IC} &= R \sec \Phi/2
\end{aligned}
$$

where I is the intersection point between two straights.

Φ is the intersection angle between the first straight produced and the second straight. This angle is also known as the deflection angle or the total deflection angle.

AI and BI are tangent lengths and both equal $R \tan(\Phi/2)$.

AB direct is major chord and equals $2x$ or $2R \sin(\Phi/2)$.

AB round curve is equal to $\Phi/360 \times 2\pi R$.

IE is the apex length and equals $\text{IC} - R = R(\sec(\Phi/2) - 1)$.

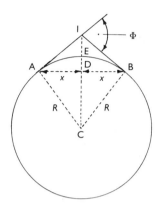

Figure 10.1

Degree of curvature

A circular curve is defined either by radius or by degree of curvature. The degree of curvature of a circular curve is the angle subtended at the centre by a 100 m arc.

*10.2 Setting out circular curves using one theodolite*_____

Consider the geometry shown in Figure 10.2:

$$IAC = A1F = 90°$$

Let $IA1 = \alpha_1$ and $FA1 = \beta_1$:

$$\alpha_1 + \beta_1 = 90°$$
$$AF1 + \beta_1 = 90°$$
$$AF1 = \alpha_1$$
$$CF1 = \alpha_1$$
$$AC1 = 2\alpha_1$$

Considering triangle FA1:

$$\sin \alpha_1 = \frac{A1}{2R}$$

Considering segment AC1:

$$2\alpha_1 \text{ radians} = \frac{\text{arc}(A1)}{R}$$

$$\alpha_1 \text{ minutes} = \frac{1718.9 \ \text{arc}(A1)}{R}$$

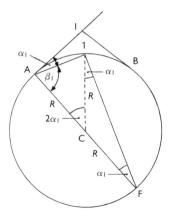

Figure 10.2

Setting out with one theodolite

1. Establish points A and B using $IA = IB = R \tan(\Phi/2)$.
2. Set up theodolite at A pointing to I with zero on horizontal circle.
3. Turn through α_1 from AI and measure the distance A1.

For normal work

Where the radius is more than twenty times chord length A1, the length A1 direct can be assumed to be the same as arc length A1. Here the same tape reading is taken from A to 1, 1 to 2, 2 to 3, etc. Angles are found using:

$$\alpha \text{ minutes} = \frac{1718.9 \times \text{Total of lengths taped}}{R}$$

For precise work

Here a correction is made for the fact that the distance round the curve is not equal to chord length. Here instead of using, say, 10 m for chord length a value of $10 \text{ m} \times [\sin \alpha_1/(\alpha_1 \text{ in radians})]$ is used and this will give a true length of curve of 10 m.

Alternative for precise work

If an EDM is used at A, measure all distances direct from A and establish the values of α for differing distances from A using $\sin \alpha = \text{Distance measured from A} \div 2R$.

Example 10.1 Setting out circular curves using one theodolite_____

Determine the tangent lengths, the curve length and the major chord length of a 400 m radius curve between straights at 90°.

Calculate the first three points on the curve using the following assumptions:

(a) That 20 m chords are used and considered to have the same length as the arc length.
(b) That the 20 m chord lengths are amended to give the length around the curve arc a length of 20 m.
(c) That electromagnetic distance measurement readings are taken from the start of the curve at 20 m intervals.

Assume:

206 265 seconds = 1 radian

Tangent length = $R \tan(\Phi/2) = 400 \tan 45° = 400$ m

$$\text{Curve length} = \frac{\Phi}{360} \times 2\pi R = \frac{90}{360} \times 2\pi 400 = 628.319 \text{ m}$$

Major chord length
$$= 2R \sin(\Phi/2) = 2 \times 400 \times 0.7071 = 565.685 \text{ m}$$

(a) α min $= \dfrac{1718.9}{R} \times \text{arc(A1)}$

$$\alpha_{20} = \frac{1718.9}{400} \times 20 = 1°25'57''$$

$$\alpha_{40} = \frac{1718.9}{400} \times 40 = 2°51'53''$$

$$\alpha_{60} = \frac{1718.9}{400} \times 60 = 4°12'50''$$

(b) Chord (A1) $= \dfrac{(A1)\sin \alpha_1}{\alpha_1 \text{ in radians}} = \dfrac{20 \sin 1°25'56''}{1°25'56'' \text{ in radians}}$

$$= \frac{20 \times 0.02499429}{5156/206\,265} = \frac{20 \times 0.02499429}{0.02499697} = 19.998$$

$$\alpha_{20} = \frac{1718.9}{400} \times 19.998 = 1°25'56''$$

$$\alpha_{40} = \frac{1718.9}{400} \times 19.998 \times 2 = 2°51'52''$$

$$\alpha_{60} = \frac{1718.9}{400} \times 19.998 \times 3 = 4°18'04''$$

(c) $\sin \alpha = \dfrac{l}{2R}$ $\qquad \sin \alpha_{20} = \dfrac{20}{2 \times 400}$ $\qquad \alpha_{20} = 1°25'57''$

$$\sin \alpha_{40} = \frac{40}{2 \times 400} \qquad \alpha_{40} = 2°51'57''$$

$$\sin \alpha_{60} = \frac{60}{2 \times 400} \qquad \alpha_{60} = 4°18'04''$$

10.3 Other methods of setting out circular curves_____

Two theodolites

Consider Figure 10.3. The angle between tangent and chord is equal to the angle on the perimeter subtended by the chord. In this case, angle IA1 = angle AB1 = α_1.

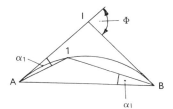

Figure 10.3

A theodolite is placed at A and a zero horizontal circle reading is set when the pointing is directed towards I. A second theodolite is placed at B and a zero horizontal circle reading is set when the pointing is directed towards A.

If an angle of, say, 5° is set on each theodolite the located intersection point lies on the circle. This can be repeated for a range of angles and the curve set out.

Offsets from chords

If the position of the major chord C is known a circular curve radius R can be established by using the coordinates x and y with the origin at the centre of the chord. Consider Figure 10.4.

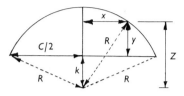

Figure 10.4

$$Z = \sqrt{R^2 - x^2}$$

$$k = \sqrt{R^2 - \left(\frac{C}{2}\right)^2}$$

$$y = Z - k$$

Polar coordinates

The use of computer and electronic distance measurement has made it a practical proposition to set out the curve from a control point with known coordinates away from the curve. The rectangular coordinates of the curve must be calculated from data supplied using the theodolite and tape method. The coordinate differences between curve and control points enable the polar coordinate method to be used to establish each point in turn (see Example 9.4).

Halving and quartering

Consider Figure 10.5.

$$D = R - \sqrt{R^2 - \left(\frac{C}{2}\right)^2} \qquad (1)$$

$$D \times (2R - D) = \frac{C}{2} \times \frac{C}{2} \qquad (2)$$

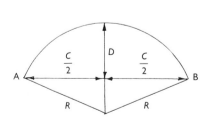

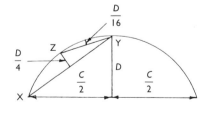

Figure 10.5

A circular curve may be set out by using central offsets to chords as shown in the figure. The central offset to chord C is D given by equation (1).

The central offset to chord XY is $D/4$ and the central offset to YZ is $D/16$.

The radius of an existing railway line or any other circular curve may be checked by measuring the central offset D to a chord C and substituting into equation (2).

Using offsets

Consider Figure 10.6:

$$l^2 = x(2R + x)$$
$$l \times 2l = y(2R + y)$$

When x and y are small compared with $2R$:

$$x = l^2/2R \qquad y = l^2/R$$

Note that on large radius curves the values of l would be equal and the angles indicated at $90°$ would be very close to $90°$.

The basic method is to measure along the tangent line a distance l then measure x at right angles to establish 1. Range through A1 produced a distance l and then measure y at right angles to establish 2.

Range through 1,2 produced and at l measure y at right angles to establish 3. Repeat the procedure until B.

An alternative for short curves is to measure values of x as perpendiculars for differing values of l measured along the tangent line.

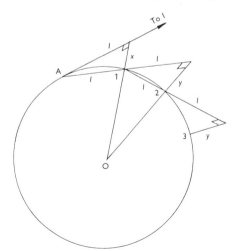

Figure 10.6

10.4 Practical problems in setting out circular curves_____

Inaccessible intersection stations

In Figure 10.7 the intersection point is inaccessible and difficulties are experienced in establishing the value of Φ and locating tangent points A and B.

The solution is to choose points X and Y lying on the tangent lines giving intervisibility and convenience for measurement. Place theodolites at X and Y to determine α and β:

$\Phi = \alpha + \beta$

Measure distance XY and using the sine rule establish distances IX and IY.

$$XA = R \tan\left(\frac{\Phi}{2}\right) - IX \quad YB = R \tan\left(\frac{\Phi}{2}\right) - IY$$

Obstacles to sighting

In Figure 10.8 the obstruction prevents sights to 3 and 4.

The solution is to set out a new tangent at one of the points already set out. Here points 1 and 2 have been set out. Place theodolite at 2 and set

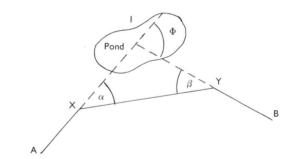

Figure 10.7

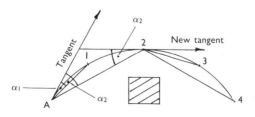

Figure 10.8

a horizontal circle reading of $(180° - \alpha_2)$ when the pointing is directly at A. When the reading is $180°$ the new tangent line will occur but in the wrong direction for progress. When the reading is zero this is the correct direction and establishes the new tangent line where point 3 will be established by α_1, and point 4 will be established by α_2, etc.

---

*Circular curves which pass through specified points*_____

Example 10.2_____

A curve has an intersection angle of $55°$ and must pass through a point P which is a minimum distance from I and has a value of 25.5 m. Establish:

(a) The value of R.
(b) The tangent length.
(c) The direct distance between tangent points.
(d) The distance around the curve.

Solution

$$\cos 27.5° = \frac{R}{R + 25.5}$$

$0.887R = 22.61877 = R = \textbf{200.166 m}$

Tangent length $= 200.166 \times \tan 27.5° = \textbf{104.200 m}$

Direct distance $= 400.322 \times \sin 27.5° = \textbf{184.852 m}$

Distance around the curve $= \dfrac{55}{360} \times \dfrac{2\pi}{1} \times 200.116$

$\qquad\qquad = \textbf{192.146 m}$

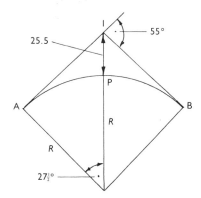

Example 10.3

A curve has an intersection angle of $68°$ and must pass through a point which is 20 m from I and 5 m from tangent AI. Establish the value of its radius.

$$IO = R \sec 34°$$
$$IO = 1.2062R$$

$$\sin a = \frac{5}{20} \quad a = 14°28'39''$$

$$2a + 2b = 180° - 68°$$
$$a + b = 56°$$
$$b = 41°31'21''$$

$$\frac{R}{\sin 41°31'21''} = \frac{1.2062R}{\sin c}$$

$$\sin c = 1.2062 \sin 41°31'21''$$
$$c = 53°5'33'' \text{ or } 126°54'26''$$
Here $d = 11°34'13''$ as $b + c + d = 180°$

$$\frac{R}{\sin 41°31'21''} = \frac{20}{\sin 11°34'13''}$$

$$R = \frac{20 \sin 41°31'21''}{\sin 11°34'13''} = \mathbf{66.10 \ m}$$

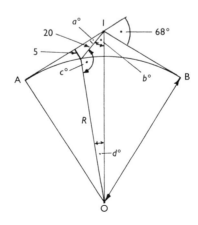

10.5 Superelevation design for highway curves_____

The design of highways takes into account geometric considerations, comfort factors and safety on the roads. In the United Kingdom, to meet these conditions the design should be carried out in accordance with the Department of Transport Standard TA43/84 'Road Layout and Geometry: Highway Link Design'.

Forces acting on vehicles on curves

Consider Figure 10.9.

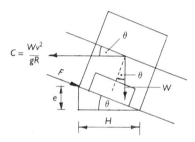

Figure 10.9

Force acting up the slope: $F = C \cos \theta - W \sin \theta$
Force normal to the slope: $N = C \sin \theta + W \cos \theta$
Friction between road and tyres: F/N

$$\frac{F}{N} = \frac{C \cos \theta - W \sin \theta}{C \sin \theta + W \cos \theta} = \frac{v^2/gR - \tan \theta}{(v^2/gR)(\tan \theta) + 1}$$

$= 0.15$ for normal conditions

TA/43/84 limits θ to $7°$ which makes the denominator approximately equal to 1. Therefore:

$$\frac{F}{N} \simeq \frac{v^2}{gR} - \tan \theta \qquad (1)$$

$$\therefore \frac{v^2}{gR} = 0.15 + 0.07 \simeq 0.22$$

TA/43/84 suggests that $v^2/gR = 0.22$ for minimum radius but recommends that a larger radius should be used.

Superelevation

From equation (1) when $F = 0$

$$\frac{v^2}{gR} = \tan \theta = \frac{e}{H}$$

$\therefore e = Hv^2/gR$.

TA 43–84 considers that the maximum superelevation should be 45% of e to minimize discomfort for drivers and recommends that:

$$\frac{e}{H} = \frac{0.45v^2}{gR} \text{ in m/s or slope } \% = \frac{v^2}{2.82R} \text{ where } v \text{ is kph.}$$

*10.6 Academic theory leading to transitional curve design*___

When a vehicle progresses from a straight to a circular curve there is a sudden application of lateral force creating a tendency for the vehicle to leave the road. To counteract this effect a curve should be introduced which gradually exerts centrifugal force and allows the superelevation to balance the forces. This curve is a transition curve.

Basic requirements of a transition curve

1. It must introduce centrifugal force directly as the length along the curve.

2. It must introduce superelevation directly as the length along the curve.

3. $\dfrac{Wv^2}{g} \dfrac{1}{r} \propto l$

$e \propto l$

$K = lr = LR$ (1)

where l is the length from the origin and r the corresponding radius, and L is the final length from the origin and R the final radius.

Academic curve to satisfy both conditions
Consider Figure 10.10. From (1) above:

$$r = K/l \text{ and } K = RL$$

From sector:

$$\Delta\phi = \frac{\mathrm{d}l}{r} = \frac{l\,\mathrm{d}l}{K}$$

$$\phi = \frac{l^2}{2K} + A \text{ (by integration of both sides)}$$

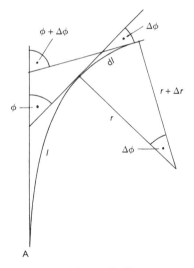

Figure 10.10

When $l = 0$ and $\phi = 0$, then $A = 0$.

$$\phi = \frac{l^2}{2K} = \frac{l^2}{2RL}$$

The equation is a **clothoid**. The clothoid cannot be used directly for practical setting out but it is used as a base for the Highway Transition Curve tables prepared by the County Surveyors' Society.

10.7 Practical setting out of curves derived from academic theory

The setting out of transition curves normally involves small offsets and small angles. Practical setting out equations can be derived by assuming a series of approximations which are valid when ϕ is small.

Consider Figure 10.11:

$$dy = dl \, \cos\left(\phi + \frac{\Delta\phi}{2}\right)$$

$$dx = dl \, \sin\left(\phi + \frac{\Delta\phi}{2}\right)$$

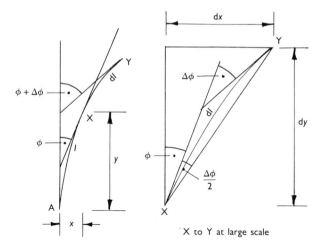

Figure 10.11

For very small values of ϕ:

$$\cos\left(\phi + \frac{\Delta\phi}{2}\right) = 1$$

$$\sin\left(\phi + \frac{\Delta\phi}{2}\right) = \phi$$

$$dy = dl\left(\cos\phi + \frac{\Delta\phi}{2}\right) = dl$$

By integration, $y = l$.

$$dx = dl\left(\sin\phi + \frac{\Delta\phi}{2}\right) = dl \times \phi = dl\,\frac{(l^2)}{(2RL)}$$

By integration

$$x = \frac{l^3}{3 \times 2RL} + A$$

When $x = 0$ and $l = 0$, then $A = 0$ and:

$$x = \frac{l^3}{6RL}$$

For small values of φ and δ

Consider Figure 10.12.

$$x = \frac{l^3}{6RL} = \frac{y^3}{6RL}$$

$$y = l$$

$$\tan \delta = \frac{x}{y} = \frac{l^2}{6RL}$$

$$\delta = \frac{l^2}{6RL} \text{ radians}$$

$$\delta = l^2 \times \frac{206\,265}{6RL \times 60} \text{ min}$$

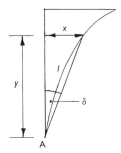

Figure 10.12

For small values of φ the above cubic equation can be used for setting out curves by offsets and by angles taken from the tangent point.

10.8 Factors governing the length of a transition curve_____

A transition curve is normally inserted between a straight and a circular curve in order to:

1. Introduce superelevation at a constant rate from the normal crossfall to that required for the circular arc.
2. Reduce the radius from infinity to that of the circular curve in order gradually to introduce radial acceleration.

The radius of the circular arc should be greater than the value given by TA/43/84 Highway Link Design.

$$\frac{v^2}{gR} = 0.22 \quad \text{or} \quad R = \frac{v^2}{g \times 0.22}$$

The length of the transition curve depends on:

1. The allowable rate of change of acceleration.
2. The radius.
3. The shift required.

$$\text{Radial acceleration on circular arc} = v^2/R$$
$$\text{Time to travel on transition } t = L/v$$
$$\text{Rate of change of radial acceleration } a = v^2/R \div L/v$$
$$a = v^3/RL$$

where L = length of transition (m), v = speed of vehicle (m/s) R = radius (m) and a = rate of change of radial acceleration (m/s^3). Note that a is normally in the range 0.3 to 0.6 m/s^3 and $L = v^3/Ra$.

The method of designing the length of a transition curve is largely dependent on the radius of the curve it introduces. Generally:

■ Curves with radii less than 998 m are normally dependent on the rate of change of radial acceleration and the minimum length of transition curve designed using $L = v^3/Ra$.
■ Curves with radii between 998 and 4860 m are designed with a transition curve length of $R/9$. This satisfies the normal rate of change of radial acceleration requirement and introduces a curve with a smooth visual effect.
■ Curves with radii in excess of 4860 m need no superelevation and are given a transition curve length of $\sqrt{60R}$ which has the advantage of giving a constant shift of 2.5 m.

10.9 Shift and its effects on transition curves

To allow the insertion of entry and exit transition curves the circular arc must be moved inwards away from the tangents by a distance known as **shift**. In the shifted position the circular arc is $R + S$.

The academic value for ϕ is $l^2/2RL$:

$$\phi_L = \frac{L^2}{2RL} = \frac{L}{2R}$$

Generally:

$$\cos \phi = 1 - \frac{\phi^2}{2!} + \frac{\phi^4}{4!} - \frac{\phi^6}{6!} + \frac{\phi^8}{8!} \cdots$$

Here:

$$\cos \phi_L = 1 - \frac{\left(\frac{L}{2R}\right)^2}{2 \times 1} + \cdots = 1 - \frac{L^2}{8R^2}$$

From Figure 10.13, $T_3Y = R\phi_L = L/2$. Now T_3Y, T_3X, AX, AT_1 are all approximately equal to $L/2$ for small angles, so:

$$T_1O = R + S = R \cos \phi_L + T_2T_3$$

$$R + S = R\left(1 - \frac{L^2}{8R^2}\cdots\right) + \frac{L^2}{6RL}$$

$$S = \frac{L^2}{24R}$$

From Figure 10.14:

$$T_1I = (R + S)\tan \frac{\Phi}{2}$$

$$AI = (R + S)\tan \frac{\Phi}{2} + \frac{L}{2}$$

$$LM = R\Phi \quad (\Phi \text{ in radians})$$

$$AB = R\Phi + L$$

$$CD = R\Phi - L$$

$$IO = (R + S)\sec \frac{\Phi}{2}$$

$$IQ = (R + S)\sec \frac{\Phi}{2} - R$$

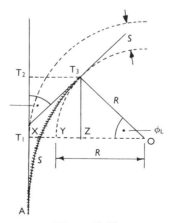

Figure 10.13

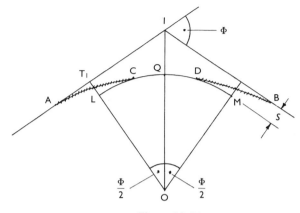

Figure 10.14

10.10 Angles consumed by a circular curve with transitions___

Consider Figure 10.15.
   Academic equation:

$$\phi = \frac{l^2}{2RL} \qquad \therefore \phi_L = \frac{L^3}{2RL} = \frac{L}{2R}$$

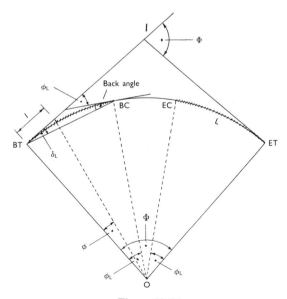

Figure 10.15

Angles consumed

1. The angle consumed by a length l of a transition curve is $\phi = l^2/2RL$.
2. The angle consumed by a length L of a transition curve is $\phi_L = L/2R$.
3. The angle consumed by both Ls of curve is $2\phi_L = L/R$.

Note:

- If Φ is less than $2\phi_L$ the transition lengths cannot be accommodated.
- If Φ is equal to $2\phi_L$ the curve is wholly transitional.
- If Φ is greater than $2\phi_L$ a circular curve must be inserted.
- Length of circular curve $= (\Phi - 2\phi_L)R = [(\Phi - 2\phi_L)/D] \times 100$
- Total length of curve $= 2L + [(\Phi - 2\phi_L)/D] \times 100$
- D is the degree of curve based on 100 m arc.

Back angle

$$\text{Back angle} = \phi_L - \delta_L = \frac{L^2}{2RL} - \frac{L^2}{6RL} = \frac{L}{3R}$$

10.11 Simplified method of designing circular curves with transitions

This method makes two assumptions:

1. The angles on the transitional curve are small.
2. Factorial expressions beyond the first two terms are sufficiently small to be ignored.

Basic method

1. The value of R is assessed using a minimum value of R given by $v^2/(g \times 0.22)$ where v is the velocity of vehicle in m/s. The value 0.22 is given by TA/43/84 Highway Link Design. This is the balancing effect due to the thrust of centripetal force offered by superelevation (maximum value 0.07) and road friction (0.15).
2. L is determined by:
   - v^3/Ra where R is less than 998 m, a is the rate of change of acceleration m/s^3.
   - $R/9$ where R is between 998 and 4860 m.
   - $\sqrt{60R}$ where R is above 4360 m.
3. Establish shift using $S = L^2/24R$.
4. The tangent length is $(R + S)\tan(\Phi/2) + L/2$.
5. Deduce the chainage at the start of the curve.

6. Determine the angles needed to set out the transition curves using:

$$\delta = \frac{l^2}{6RL} \times \frac{206\,265}{60} \text{ minutes}$$

7. At the end of the transition curves use the back angles to establish the tangent to the circular curve by setting the horizontal angle to $(180^\circ - \text{Back angle})$ when pointing from BC to BT. Use $(180^\circ + \text{Back angle})$ from EC to ET.
8. Set out the circular curve using $\alpha = (l/R)1819.9$ minutes.
9. Repeat the procedure from the far tangent point but here the angles will be set out as $(360^\circ - \text{Calculated angle})$.
10. Establish the control points such as tangent points, curve ends and centre points. Check these in the field by:
    - Comparing actual and theoretical chainage points.
    - Setting up at tangent points and noting whether the other peg can be seen at $\Phi/2$.
    - Noting whether the centre point lies on the curve and measures $(R + S)\sec(\Phi/2) - R$ from I.
    - Measuring maximum offsets of transition curve and comparing with $L/2R$.

Example 10.4 Establishing the position of control points on a circular curve with transitions_____

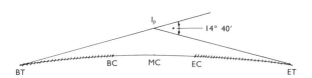

A circular curve with transitions is to be designed to meet the following conditions:

1. The deflection angle between the straights is $14^\circ40'$.
2. The design speed of the road is 90 km/h.
3. The radius must be at least 640 m and must provide for the thrust due to centripetal force where maximum permitted value of superelevation and friction are 0.07 and 0.15 respectively.
4. The maximum rate of change of acceleration is 0.3 m/s.

Design the following:

1. A suitable radius for the curve.
2. A suitable transition curve length.

3. From the diagram determine the positions of the control points at the beginning and ending of the transition curve, namely BT, BC, EC and ET and MC the middle position of the circular curve all with respect to the intersection point I_p.

Solution

1. $R = \dfrac{v^2}{g \times 0.22} = \dfrac{\left(\dfrac{90\,000}{60 \times 60}\right)^2}{9.81 \times 0.22} = 289.6$ m minimum

This value will cope with centripetal force but 640 m has been stipulated, so use $R = \mathbf{640}$ **m**.

2. $L = \dfrac{v^3}{Ra}$, $L = \dfrac{(25)^3}{640 \times 0.3} = 81.38$, say **82 m.**

3. $S = \dfrac{L^2}{24R} = \dfrac{82^2}{24 \times 640} = \mathbf{0.438}$ **m**

Tangent length $= (R + S)\tan\left(\dfrac{\Phi}{2}\right) + \dfrac{L}{2}$

$\qquad\qquad = (640.438)\tan 7°20' + 41 = \mathbf{123.421}$ **m**

$(I_p$ to MC$) = (R + S)\sec\left(\dfrac{\Phi}{2}\right) - R$

$\qquad\qquad = 645.720 - 640 = \mathbf{5.720}$ **m**

Example 10.5 *Establishing the chainage of control points on a circular curve with transitions*_____

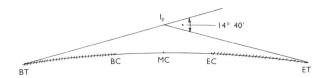

Assuming:

1. The radius is 640 m and the transitions are 82 m.
2. The tangent length is equal to 123.421 m.
3. The chainage at I_p is 527 km 540 m.

Determine the lengths between control points and hence the chainages at BT, BC, MC, EC and ET shown in the diagram.

Solution

The length around the whole curve is $R\Phi + L$ where Φ is in radians.

$$R\Phi + L = 640 \times \frac{14°40'}{180°} \times \pi + 82$$

$$= 163.828 \text{ m} + 82 = \mathbf{245.828 \text{ m}}$$

The angle consumed by transition curves is:

$$2\phi_L = \frac{L}{R} \text{ radians}$$

The length consumed by transition curves is

$$\frac{L}{R} \times \frac{R}{1} = L$$

The length of circular arc is:

$$163.828 - 82 = \mathbf{81.828 \text{ m}}$$

Chainage at I_p = 527 km 540 m
Chainage at BT = 527 km 540 m − 123.421
              = 527 km 416.579 m
Chainage at BC = 527 km 416.579 m + 82.000
              = 527 km 498.579 m
Chainage at MC = 527 km 498.579 m + 40.914
              = 527 km 539.493 m
Chainage at EC = 527 km 498.579 m + 81.828
              = 527 km 580.407 m
Chainage at ET = 527 km 580.407 m + 82.000
              = 527 km 662.407 m

Check chainage at ET = Chainage of BT + Length of curve
                    = 527 km 416.579 + 245.828
                    = 527 km 662.407

Example 10.6 *Back angles to set out tangents for circular curves*_____

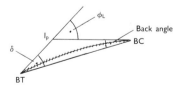
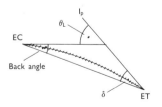

$$\text{Back angles} = \phi_L - \delta_L = \frac{L^2}{2RL} - \frac{L^2}{6RL} = \frac{L}{3R}$$

$$= 0.04270833 \text{ radians, i.e. } 2°24'49''$$

At BC sight BT with angle set $(180° - \text{Back angle}) = 177°33'11''$.
At EC sight ET with angle set $(180° + \text{Back angle}) = 182°26'49''$.

Example 10.7 *The angles to set out between the control points on a circular curve with transitions*_____

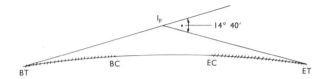

Assume:

1. The radius is 640 m and the transitions are both 82 m.
2. The chainages of the control point are:
     BT 527 km 416.579
     BC 527 km 498.579
     EC 527 km 580.407
     ET 527 km 662.407, as shown in the diagram.

Determine the angles to set out the following curves:

(a) The transition curve between BT and BC and circular curve between BC and EC.
(b) The transition curve between ET and EC and circular curve between EC and BC.

Solution

The transition angles are set out using:

$$\delta = \frac{l^2}{6RL} \times \frac{206\,265}{60} \text{ minutes}$$

The circular curve angles using:

$$\alpha = \frac{l}{R} \times 1718.9 \text{ minutes}$$

Instrument at BT			Instrument at BC		
Chainage	Length from BT	δ angle	Chainage	Length from BC	α angle
527 km 420	3.421	8″	527 km 500	1.421	3′49″
527 km 430	13.421	1′58″	527 km 510	11.421	30′40″
527 km 440	23.421	5′59″	527 km 520	21.421	57′32″
527 km 450	33.421	12′12″	527 km 530	31.421	1°24′23″
527 km 460	43.421	20′35″	527 km 540	41.421	1°51′15″
527 km 470	53.421	31′09″	527 km 550	51.421	2°18′06″
527 km 480	63.421	43′55″	527 km 560	61.421	2°44′56″
527 km 490	73.421	58′51″	527 km 570	71.421	3°11′49″
527 km 498.579	82.000	1°13′25″	527 km 580	81.421	3°38′41″
			527 km 580.407	81.828	3°39′46″

Instrument at ET			Instrument at EC		
Chainage	Length from ET	360° − δ angle	Chainage	Length from EC	360° − α angle
527 km 660	2.407	359°59′57″	527 km 580	0.407	359°58′54″
527 km 650	12.407	359°58′19″	527 km 570	10.407	359°32′02″
527 km 640	22.407	359°54′31″	527 km 560	20.407	359°05′12″
527 km 630	32.407	359°48′32″	527 km 550	30.407	358°38′20″
527 km 620	42.407	359°40′22″	527 km 540	40.407	358°11′29″
527 km 610	52.407	359°30′01″	527 km 530	50.407	357°44′37″
527 km 600	62.407	359°17′26″	527 km 520	60.407	357°17′46″
527 km 590	72.407	359°02′10″	527 km 510	70.407	356°50′54″
527 km 580.407	82.000	358°46′35″	527 km 500	80.407	356°24′03″
			527 km 498.578	81.828	356°20′14″

10.12 The method of calculation for circular curves with transitions for larger values of ϕ

The clothoid curve

For angles of ϕ between $7°$ and $80°$ the clothoid curve is normally the preferred method of setting out the transition curve. The expressions used for the basic terms are more complex than the cubic parabolic curve but the results are more precise for the larger angles.

Basic terms

$$\text{Shift } S = \frac{L^2}{24R} - \frac{L^4}{2688R^3} + \frac{L^6}{506\,880R^5} \cdots$$

$$\text{Tangent length} = (R + S)\tan\left(\frac{\Phi}{2}\right) + C$$

where C is the increase in apex distance:

$$C = \frac{L}{2} - \frac{L^3}{240R^2} + \frac{L^5}{34\,560R^4} \cdots$$

Rectangular coordinates

$$x = l - \frac{l^5}{40(RL)^2} + \frac{l^9}{3\,456(RL)^4} - \frac{l^{13}}{599\,040(RL)^6} \cdots$$

$$y = \frac{l^3}{6RL} - \frac{l^7}{336(RL)^3} + \frac{l^{11}}{42\,240(RL)^5} \cdots$$

Deflection angles

$$\tan \delta = \frac{\phi}{3} + \frac{\phi^3}{105} + \frac{\phi^5}{5997} - \frac{\phi^7}{198\,700} \cdots$$

Back angles

$$\text{Back angle} = \frac{l^2}{3RL} \times 57.2958° + \text{Correcting term}$$

Method of solution of the above terms

Criswell derived basic tables giving information on spirals for nominal speeds in imperial units.

The County Surveyors Society has computed twenty-six tables in SI units which cover a comprehensive range of speeds and incorporate a choice of three rates of change of acceleration.

Computer programs derived from the above equations are now available.

Table 11 of the County Surveyors Society's 26 tables is used in Example 10.8 to compare a non-tabular method with a tabular method of transition curve design.

Example 10.8 Design of the position of the main control points for a circular curve with transitions using a non-tabular method_____

A circular curve with transitions is to be designed for a speed of 74 km/h and a rate of change of acceleration of 0.3 m/s³. If the deflection angle for the curve is 60°, determine using the cubic parabola method:

(a) A suitable radius for the circular curve and length for the transitions.

(b) The tangent lengths.
(c) The length of the circular curve.
(d) The maximum deflection angle and backing angles.

Solution

$$\text{Velocity } v = \frac{74 \times 1000}{60 \times 60} = 20.555 \text{ m/s}$$

Minimum radius to resist centripetal force:

$$R = \frac{v^2}{0.22g} = \frac{20.555^2}{0.22 \times 9.81} = 195.8 \text{ m}$$

Check that superelevation does not exceed 7%:

$$\text{Superelevation} = \frac{0.45v^2}{gR} = \frac{0.45 \times 20.555^2}{9.81 \times 195.8} - 9.9\% \quad \text{Not okay}$$

Try $R = 290$ mm:

$$\text{Superelevation} = \frac{0.45 \times 20.555^2}{9.81 \times 290} = 6.7\% \quad \text{Okay}$$

Length of curve for rate of change of acceleration:

$$\frac{v^3}{aR} = \frac{20.555^3}{0.3 \times 290} = 99.82 \text{ m (say 100 m)}$$

$$\text{Shift} = \frac{L^2}{24R} = \frac{100^2}{24 \times 290} = 1.437 \text{ m}$$

$$\text{Tangent length} = (R + S)\tan\left(\frac{\Phi}{2}\right) + \frac{L}{2} = 291.437 \tan 30° + 50 \text{ m}$$

$$= 218.261 \text{ m}$$

$$\text{Angle consumed by } \phi = \frac{L}{2R}\frac{(180)°}{(\pi)} = \frac{100}{2 \times 290} \times \frac{180}{\pi} = 9°52'43''$$

Angle consumed by circular curve $= 60° - 2\phi = 40°14'34''$

$$\text{Length of circular curve} = \frac{\pi \times 290 \times 40°14'34''}{100} = 366.637 \text{ m}$$

$$\text{Maximum deflection} = \frac{L^2}{6RL} = \frac{L}{6R} = \frac{100}{6 \times 290} = 3°17'34''$$

Maximum backing angle $= \frac{2}{3}\phi_L = 9°52'43'' \times \frac{2}{3} = 6°35'09''$

'Table 11' of the County Surveyors Society transition curve tables

Gain of accn. m/s³	0.30	0.45	0.60	Increase in degree of curve per metre = D/L = 0°12′0.0″
Speed value km/h	73.7	84.4	92.9	RL constant = 28647.890

Degree of curvature based on 100 m standard arc

Radius R (metres)	Degree of curve D (° ′ ″)	Spiral length L (metres)	Angle consumed ϕ (° ′ ″)	Shift S (metres)	$R+S$ R (metres)	C (metres)	Long chord (metres)	Coordinates X (metres)	Coordinates Y (metres)	Deflection angle from origin (° ′ ″)	Back angle to origin (° ′ ″)
5729.5780	1 0 0.0	5.00	0 1 30.0	0.0002	5729.5781	2.5000	5.0000	5.0000	0.0007	0 0 30.0	0 1 0.0
2864.7890	2 0 0.0	10.00	0 6 0.0	0.0015	2864.7904	5.0000	10.0000	10.0000	0.0058	0 2 0.0	0 4 0.0
1909.8593	3 0 0.0	15.00	0 13 30.0	0.0040	1909.8642	7.5000	15.0000	15.0000	0.0196	0 4 30.0	0 9 0.0
1432.3945	4 0 0.0	20.00	0 24 0.0	0.0116	1432.4061	10.0000	20.0000	19.9999	0.0465	0 8 0.0	0 16 0.0
1145.9156	5 0 0.0	25.00	0 37 30.0	0.0227	1145.9383	12.5000	24.9999	24.9997	0.0909	0 12 30.0	0 25 0.0
954.9297	6 0 0.0	30.00	0 54 0.0	0.0393	954.9689	14.9999	29.9997	29.9993	0.1571	0 18 0.0	0 36 0.0
818.5111	7 0 0.0	35.00	1 13 30.0	0.0624	818.5735	17.4997	34.9993	34.9984	0.2494	0 24 30.0	0 49 0.0
716.1972	8 0 0.0	40.00	1 36 0.0	0.0931	716.2903	19.9993	39.9986	39.9969	0.3723	0 32 0.0	1 4 0.0
636.6198	9 0 0.0	45.00	2 1 30.0	0.1325	636.7523	22.4991	44.9975	44.9944	0.5301	0 40 30.0	1 21 0.0
572.9578	10 0 0.0	50.00	2 30 0.0	0.1818	573.1396	24.9984	49.9958	49.9905	0.7271	0 50 0.0	1 40 0.0
520.8707	11 0 0.0	55.00	3 1 30.0	0.2420	521.1127	27.4974	54.9932	54.9847	0.9677	1 0 29.9	2 1 0.1
477.4648	12 0 0.0	60.00	3 36 0.0	0.3141	477.7789	29.9961	59.9895	59.9763	1.2563	1 11 59.9	2 24 0.1
440.7368	13 0 0.0	65.00	4 13 30.0	0.3993	441.1361	32.4941	64.9843	64.9647	1.5971	1 24 29.8	2 49 0.2
409.2556	14 0 0.0	70.00	4 54 0.0	0.4987	409.7543	34.9915	69.9772	69.9488	1.9945	1 37 59.6	3 16 0.4
381.9719	15 0 0.0	75.00	5 37 30.0	0.6134	382.5852	37.4880	74.9679	74.9277	2.4527	1 52 29.4	3 45 0.6
358.0986	16 0 0.0	80.00	6 24 0.0	0.7443	358.8430	39.9834	79.9556	79.9002	2.9760	2 7 59.2	4 16 0.8
337.0340	17 0 0.0	85.00	7 13 30.0	0.8927	337.9267	42.4775	84.9399	84.8649	3.5688	2 24 28.8	4 49 1.2
318.3099	18 0 0.0	90.00	8 6 0.0	1.0595	319.3694	44.9700	89.9201	89.8203	4.2351	2 41 58.4	5 24 1.6
301.5567	19 0 0.0	95.00	9 1 30.0	1.2459	302.8026	47.4607	94.8953	94.7646	4.9792	3 0 27.7	6 1 2.3
286.4789	20 0 0.0	100.00	10 0 0.0	1.4529	287.9318	49.9493	99.8647	99.6958	5.8051	3 19 56.9	6 40 3.1

272.8370	21	0	0.0	105.00	11	1	30.0	1.6815	274.5185	52.4353	104.8273	104.6119	6.7170	3	40	25.8	7	21	4.2
260.4354	22	0	0.0	110.00	12	6	0.0	1.9328	262.3681	54.9183	109.7821	109.5104	7.7188	4	1	54.5	8	4	5.5
249.1121	23	0	0.0	115.00	13	13	30.0	2.2078	251.3199	57.3980	114.7279	114.3888	8.8145	4	24	22.8	8	49	7.2
238.7324	24	0	0.0	120.00	14	24	0.0	2.5076	241.2400	59.8739	119.6635	119.2442	10.0078	4	47	50.7	9	36	9.3
229.1831	25	0	0.0	125.00	15	37	30.0	2.8332	232.0163	62.3454	124.5873	124.0736	11.3026	5	12	18.2	10	25	11.8
220.3684	26	0	0.0	130.00	16	54	0.0	3.1855	223.5539	64.8120	129.4980	128.8735	12.7024	5	37	45.0	11	16	15.0
212.2066	27	0	0.0	135.00	18	13	30.0	3.5656	215.7722	67.2730	134.3939	133.6405	14.2108	6	4	11.2	12	9	18.8
204.6278	28	0	0.0	140.00	19	36	0.0	3.9743	208.6021	69.7278	139.2732	138.3705	15.8310	6	31	36.6	13	4	23.4
197.5717	29	0	0.0	145.00	21	1	30.0	4.4128	201.9844	72.1758	144.1341	143.0596	17.5663	7	0	1.1	14	1	28.9
190.9859	30	0	0.0	150.00	22	30	0.0	4.8818	195.8677	74.6161	148.9744	147.7033	19.4197	7	29	24.6	15	0	35.4
184.8251	31	0	0.0	155.00	24	1	30.0	5.3823	190.2074	77.0480	153.7921	152.2968	21.3941	7	59	46.9	16	1	43.1
179.0493	32	0	0.0	160.00	25	36	0.0	5.9151	184.9644	79.4706	158.5849	156.8352	23.4919	8	31	7.8	17	4	52.2
173.6236	33	0	0.0	165.00	27	13	30.0	6.4811	180.1047	81.8830	163.3502	161.3133	25.7157	9	3	27.2	18	10	2.8
168.5170	34	0	0.0	170.00	28	54	0.0	7.0811	175.5981	84.2842	168.0855	165.7255	28.0674	9	36	44.8	19	17	15.2
163.7022	35	0	0.0	175.00	30	37	30.0	7.7158	171.4181	86.6733	172.7880	170.0660	30.5491	10	11	0.5	20	26	29.3
159.1549	36	0	0.0	180.00	32	24	0.0	8.3861	167.5410	89.0492	177.4548	174.3286	33.1621	10	46	13.9	21	37	46.1
154.8535	37	0	0.0	185.00	34	13	30.0	9.0925	163.9460	91.4107	182.5071	178.5071	35.9077	11	22	24.9	22	51	5.1
150.7784	38	0	0.0	190.00	36	6	0.0	9.8358	160.6141	93.7567	186.6688	182.3947	38.7867	11	59	33.0	24	6	27.0
146.9123	39	0	0.0	195.00	38	1	30.0	10.6164	157.5287	96.0859	191.2094	186.5847	41.7997	12	37	38.0	25	23	52.0
143.2394	40	0	0.0	200.00	40	0	0.0	11.4351	154.6745	98.3972	195.7011	190.4697	44.9467	13	16	39.6	26	43	20.4
139.7458	41	0	0.0	205.00	42	1	30.0	12.2922	152.0380	100.6891	200.1401	194.2426	48.2274	13	56	37.3	28	4	52.7
136.4185	42	0	0.0	210.00	44	6	0.0	13.1881	149.6067	102.9603	204.5226	197.8957	51.6409	14	37	30.7	29	28	29.3
133.2460	43	0	0.0	215.00	46	13	30.0	14.1234	147.3694	105.2094	208.8445	201.4213	55.1860	15	19	19.5	30	54	10.5
103.2177	44	0	0.0	220.00	48	24	0.0	15.0981	145.3158	107.4348	213.1016	204.8113	58.8609	16	2	3.0	32	21	57.0
127.3240	45	0	0.0	225.00	50	37	30.0	16.1126	143.4366	109.6350	217.2895	208.0578	62.6631	16	45	40.8	33	51	49.2
124.5560	46	0	0.0	230.00	52	54	0.0	17.1671	141.7231	111.8086	221.4037	211.1525	66.5899	17	30	12.2	35	23	47.8

Highway transition curve tables (metric).
Reproduced by permission of the County Surveyors Society.

The remaining sections of the chapter are concerned with **transition curves**.

10.13 The procedures adopted for setting out a circular curve with transitions employing the tabular method_____

On site it is essential to establish the true value of the intersection angle by direct observation or calculation. Values given on drawings or computer printouts rely on previous practical work which is often slightly in error.

In the office the most appropriate spiral table is chosen to meet the design requirements for speed and rate of change of acceleration. A radius is chosen which meets the centrifugal force requirements and the superelevation conditions.

From the table in section 10.12 a transitional length is selected which has a corresponding radius slightly above the radius chosen. The new radius is the design radius R.

Using the table it is possible to read off the values of D, S, $(R + S)$, C, ϕ, the angle consumed, the long chord length and corresponding deflection angle, and the final back angle. From these results the following can be obtained:

$$\text{Tangent length} = (R + S)\tan\left(\frac{\Phi}{2}\right) + C$$

$$\text{MC to } I_p = (R + S)\sec\left(\frac{\Phi}{2}\right) - R$$

$$\text{Circular curve length} = \frac{\Phi - 2\phi}{D} \times 200$$

$$\text{Total curve length} = 2L + \frac{\Phi - 2\phi}{D} \times 100$$

These may be used to derive the chainages at BT, BC, MC, EC and ET.

In the field measure from I_p, the tangent length to establish both BT and ET. Check that the angles between each and I_p equal $\Phi/2$. Establish BC and EC from tangent point using the chord and deflection angles.

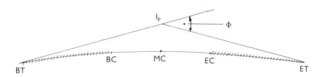

Figure 10.16

Infill the transition curve using $\phi = (l^2/6RL) \times (206\,265/60)$ min and check that the control points lie on the curve. Set up the instrument at BC and EC and use back angles to obtain tangents to the circular curve.

Infill the circular curve using $\alpha = (l/R)1718.9$ min and check that the curve passes through MC and that both curves truly overlap.

Example 10.9 Design of the position of the main control points for a circular curve with transitions using a tabular method_____

A circular curve with transitions is to be designed for a speed of 74 km/h and a rate of change of acceleration of 0.3 m/s³. If the deflection angle for the curve is 60° determine, using the tables compiled by the County Surveyors' Society:

(a) A suitable radius for the circular curve and length for the transitions.
(b) The tangent lengths.
(c) The length of the circular curve.
(d) The maximum deflection angle and the backing angles.

Solution

Velocity V is in m/s. The curves which are closest to 74 km/h with a rate of change of acceleration of 0.3 m/s³ are on Table 11, i.e. 73.7 km/h.

$$\text{Velocity}\,V = \frac{73.7 \times 1000}{60 \times 60} = 20.472 \text{ m/s}$$

$$R = \frac{V^2}{0.22g} = \frac{20.472^2}{0.22 \times 9.81} = 194.19 \text{ m minimum}$$

Check that superelevation does not exceed 7%:

$$\text{Superelevation} = \frac{0.45V^2}{gR} = \frac{0.45 \times 20.472^3}{9.81 \times 194.19} = 9.9\% \qquad \text{Not okay}$$

Try $R = 290$ m:

$$\text{Superelevation} = \frac{0.45 \times 20.472^3}{9.81 \times 290} = 6.6\% \qquad \text{Okay}$$

$$\text{Length of curve for } L = \frac{V^3}{aL} = \frac{20.472^3}{0.3 \times 290} = 98.62 \text{ m (say 100 m)}$$

From Table 11, when $l = 100$, $R = 286.479$.

Shift = 1.453 m

Tangent length = $(R + S)\tan 30° + C = 287.932 \tan 30° + 49.949$
$$= \mathbf{216.187 \ m}$$

$\phi = 10°00'00''$

Angle consumed by circular curve = $60° - 2 \times 10°00'00'' = 40°$

Curve length $= \dfrac{\pi 290 \times 40}{100} = 364.424$ m

Maximum deflection angle = $3°19'57''$

Maximum back angle = $6°40'03''$

The main reason for the differences in results between tabular and non-tabular methods is the difference in R, which is in turn due to the speeds being a little different.

10.14 Simple parabolic vertical curve design

The aim of a vertical curve is to provide the smoothing of the intersection of gradients to give passenger comfort, and adequate visibility for the driver. The most convenient curve to use is the simple parabola.

Basic assumptions

1. The vertical curve is a parabola $y = kx^2$.
2. The length of curve each side of the gradient intersection is $L/2$.
3. Horizontal, sloping, and curve distances between points on the curve are all assumed equal.
4. Vertical ordinates on the first diagram may be transferred to the verticals on the second diagram.
5. The gradients expressed in percentages indicate the change in level over a 100 m horizontal length.

Gradient sign convention

From intersection point:

- Grade falling as chainage increases is positive.
- Grade falling as chainage decreases is positive.

Any confusion regarding sign convention is best solved by means of a sketch.

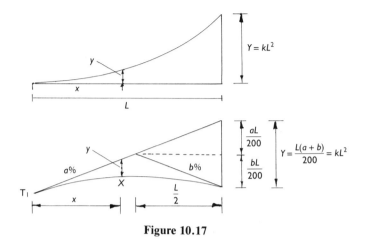

Figure 10.17

Consider Figure 10.17:

General level at x $\qquad$ $(H) = T_1 + \dfrac{a}{100}\,x - y$

$$(H) = T_1 + \dfrac{a}{100}\,x - kx^2$$

Slope at x $\qquad$ $\dfrac{(dH)}{(dx)} = \dfrac{a}{100} - 2kx$

Rate of change of slope $\dfrac{(d_2H)}{(dx^2)} = -2k$

Note that when slope $= 0$ a maximum or minimum level occurs, i.e. $0 = (a/100) - 2kx$, therefore $x = a/200k$ gives a maximum or minimum value.

Example 10.10 *Vertical curves I* _____

Design a vertical curve 800 m long to connect a rising gradient of 1.5% and a fall of 2.5% which meet at a summit with a reduced level of 152.24 m AOD.

(a) Give the levels at 100 m intervals.
(b) Determine the value of maximum level on the curve.
(c) Establish the rate of change of gradient for the curve.

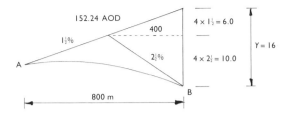

Solution

$$Y = kL^2, \quad 16 = k \times 800^2 \qquad k = \frac{16}{800^2} = \frac{0.25}{100^2}$$

$$\text{Level at } A = 152.24 - 400 \times \frac{1.5}{100} = 146.24$$

$$\text{Level at } B = 152.24 - 400 \times \frac{2.5}{100} = 142.24$$

$$\text{Level at } X = 146.24 + x \times \frac{1.5}{100} - \frac{0.25x^2}{100^2}$$

$$
\begin{aligned}
x &= 100 &\quad H &= 146.24 + 1.5 - 0.25 = 147.49 \text{ m AOD} \\
x &= 200 &\quad H &= 146.24 + 3.0 - 1.00 = 148.24 \\
x &= 300 &\quad H &= 146.24 + 4.5 - 2.25 = 148.46 \\
x &= 400 &\quad H &= 146.24 + 6.0 - 4.00 = 148.24 \\
x &= 500 &\quad H &= 146.24 + 7.5 - 6.25 = 147.49 \\
x &= 600 &\quad H &= 146.24 + 9.0 - 9.00 = 146.24 \\
x &= 700 &\quad H &= 146.24 + 10.5 - 12.25 = 144.49 \\
x &= 800 &\quad H &= 146.24 + 12.0 - 16.00 = 142.24
\end{aligned}
$$

$$\text{Slope at } x = \frac{(\mathrm{d}H)}{(\mathrm{d}x)} = \frac{a}{100} - 2kx = 0$$

$$\therefore x = \frac{a}{200k} \text{ gives a maximum or minimum value}$$

$$x = \frac{1.5}{200} \times \frac{100^2}{0.25} = 300$$

Maximum level = 148.46 m AOD

$$\text{Rate of change of acceleration} = 2k = \frac{2 \times 0.25}{100^2}$$

i.e. 0.5% per 100 m

Exercise 10.1_____

A vertical curve 500 m long connects rising gradients of 0.8% and 1.2% which meet a summit with a reduced level of 100 mm AOD. Show that:

(a) The levels at 100 m intervals are 98, 98.6, 98.8, 98.6, 98.0 and 97.0 m respectively.
(b) The slope at 300 m is -0.4%.

Example 10.11 *Vertical curves II* _____

A vertical curve is used to connect a falling gradient of 1% to a rising gradient of 2% which meet at a valley intersection point with a value of 100 m AOD. If the curve is to pass through a level of 101.7 m AOD at a chainage 50 m short of the intersection point, determine:

(a) The length of the parabolic connecting curve.
(b) The minimum level of the curve.

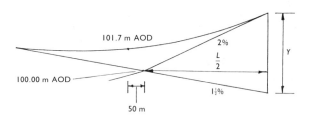

Solution

$$Y = kL^2 = \frac{L}{2}\left(\frac{2}{100} + \frac{1}{100}\right)$$

$$k = 3/200L$$

Level at 50 m from intersection point $= \dfrac{1}{100} \times \dfrac{50}{1} = 0.5$

$$y = 1.7 - 0.5 = 1.2$$

$$y = kx^2 \qquad 1.2 = \left(\frac{3}{200L}\right)\left(\frac{L}{2} - 50\right)^2$$

$$\frac{240L}{3} = \frac{L^2}{2^2} - 100\,\frac{L}{2} + 2500$$

$$\therefore \frac{L^2}{4} - 130L + 2500 = 0$$

$$L = +130 \pm \frac{\sqrt{130^2 - 4 \times \dfrac{1 \times 2500}{4}}}{\frac{1}{2}} = 260 \pm 2\sqrt{130^2 - 2500}$$

$$= \mathbf{500\ m}$$

Level at $T_1 = 100 + \dfrac{1}{100} \times 250 = 102.5$ m AOD

$$H = 102.5 - x \times \frac{1}{100} + \frac{3}{200 \times 500}\, x^2$$

$$\frac{dH}{dx} = -\frac{1}{100} + \frac{6x}{200 \times 500}$$

$$\therefore x = +\frac{1000}{6} = \mathbf{166.666}\ \text{when slope is zero}$$

$$H_x = 102.5 - 166.666x\,\frac{1}{100} + \frac{3}{200 \times 500} \times \frac{166.666^2}{1}$$

$$= 102.5 - 1.666 + 0.833 = 101.667\ \text{m AOD is minimum level}$$

Exercise 10.2

A vertical curve is used to connect a falling gradient of 1.5% to a rising gradient of 2.5% which meets at a valley intersection point 152.34 m AOD. If the curve is to pass through a level of 154.715 m AOD at a chainage 50 m beyond the intersection point show that:

(a) The length of the parabolic curve is 400 m.
(b) The minimum level on the curve is 154.215 m AOD

10.15 Mathematical formula for the lengths of vertical curves

Consider Figures 10.18(a)–(d). Assumptions:

1. Vertical parabolic and circular curves almost coincide.
2. Intersect of chords theories are acceptable.
3. Velocity in m/s = Velocity/3.6 kph.

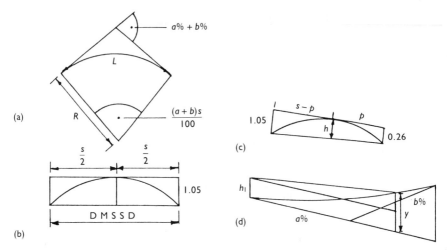

Figure 10.18

4. Grade difference $= (a + b)/100$

$$L = R\left(\frac{a+b}{100}\right) \tag{a}$$

Desirable minimum stopping sight distance

$$\frac{s}{2} \times \frac{s}{2} = h(2R)$$

$$R = s^2/8.4 \tag{b}$$

$$L = \left(\frac{a+b}{840}\right)s^2 \tag{1}$$

Absolute minimum stopping sight distance

$$1.05 = K(s - p)^2$$
$$0.26 = K(p)^2$$

$$\sqrt{\frac{1.05}{0.26}} = \frac{s-p}{p} \qquad 3p = s$$

$$h = 0.26 + \tfrac{1}{3}(1.05 - 0.26) = 0.523$$

$$\tfrac{2}{3}s \times \tfrac{1}{3}s = h(2R) \qquad R = \frac{s^2}{4.71} \tag{c}$$

$$L = \left(\frac{a+b}{471}\right)s^2 \tag{2}$$

Comfort

$$V^2/R = 0.3 \text{ m/s}^2$$

$$\therefore R = \frac{V^2}{0.3} \tag{d}$$

$$L = \left(\frac{a+b}{389}\right)V^2 \qquad (V \text{ is in kpm}) \tag{3}$$

Sag curves

Assume headlights tilted upwards $\theta°$ and height of headlamps is h_1:

$$y = s \sin \theta + h_1$$
$$y = Ks^2$$

$$Y = KL^2 = \left(\frac{a+b}{200}\right)L$$

$$K = \left(\frac{a+b}{200L}\right)$$

$$s \sin \theta + h_1 = \left(\frac{a+b}{200L}\right)s^2$$

when $\theta = 1°$ and $h_1 = 0.6$ m:

$$L = \frac{(a+b)s^2}{3.49s + 120} \tag{4}$$

10.16 Use of road data in DTp 'Highway Link Design' Standard TA/43/84 for the design of vertical curves_____

Table 5

This table is used for dual carriageway design where the stopping distance is the most important consideration.

TA/43/84 defines the desirable minimum stopping sight distance as the minimum sight distance between two points each 1.05 m above road level but on opposite sides of the summit of a crest curve.

TA/43/84 defines the absolute minimum stopping sight distance as the minimum sight distance between two points, one 1.05 m above road level and the other on the opposite side of the summit at 0.26 m above the road level.

The values for desirable minimum stopping sight distance can be taken directly from Table 5.

The values for absolute minimum stopping sight distance are one design step below. For example: design speed of 85 kph gives desirable minimum stopping sight distance 160 m, and absolute minimum stopping sight distance 120 m.

Table 6
This table is used for single carriageway design where overtaking is the main consideration.

If two cars travel close at a speed, two design steps below design speed, and the rear car accelerates to design speed, it will take a certain distance to overtake the constant speed car. This is the full overtaking sight distance (FOSD).

Drivers naturally take different distances to complete this manoeuvre. Table 6 indicates that 50% of drivers will complete the manoeuvre in x metres and 99% in $2x$ metres.

Table 11
Here the table indicates the K values for differing criteria to be considered for a crest curve or summit curve.

Table 12
This table is used for design and appreciates that for speeds above 50 kph visibility criteria take precedence over comfort considerations, and below 50 kph comfort usually takes precedence.

Table 13
Here the table indicates the K values for differing criteria to be considered for a sag curve.

Table 14
This table is used for design and appreciates that for speeds above 70 kph comfort is critical, but below 70 kph in unlit areas headlamp visibility takes precedence.

Design of the lengths of vertical curves

For values of K given by Tables 11, 12, 13 and 14:

$L = KA$ where A is grade difference, i.e. $(a + b)$
For desirable minimum $K = s^2/840$
For absolute minimum $K = s^2/471$
For comfort $K = V^2/389$
For headlight visibility on sag curves $L = s^2/(3.49s + 120)$

Road curve data in DTp 'Highway Link Design' Standard TA/43/84

Values of sight distance

Table 5 Desirable minimum stopping sight distance (SSD)

Design speed (kph)	120	100	85	70	60	50
Desirable minimum SSD(m)	295	215	160	120	90	70

Table 6 Full overtaking sight distance (FOSD)

Design speed (kph)	120	100	85	70	60	50
FOSD 99%ile	960	820	690	580	490	410
85%ile	690	580	490	410	345	290
50%ile	490	410	345	290	245	205

Values of K

Table 11 K values for different criteria of crest curve

Design speed (kph)	120	100	85	70	60	50
Visibility criteria						
Desirable minimum K	182.4	99.2	54.6	30.4	17.2	9.8
Absolute minimum K	99.2	54.6	30.4	17.2	9.8	5.7
Comfort criteria						
Minimum K		37.0	26.2	18.5	13.1	9.3	6.5

Table 12 K values for the design of crest curves

Design speed (kph)	120	100	85	70	60	50
Desirable minimum K	182	100	55	30	17	10
Absolute minimum K	100	55	30	17	10	6.5

Table 13 K values for the different criteria in the design of sag curves

Design speed (kph)	120	100	85	70	60	50
Headlamp visibility						
Desirable K	75.0	53.3	37.8	26.6	18.6	12.9
Absolute K	53.3	37.8	26.6	18.6	12.9	8.9
Comfort K	37.0	26.2	18.5	13.1	9.3	6.5

Table 14 Minimum K values to be used for sag curves

Design speed (kph)	120	100	85	70	60	50
Minimum sag K value	37	26	20	20	13	9

Tables reproduced with the permission of the Controller of Her Majesty's Stationery Office.

Eleven

Tunnelling

11.1 Lining in a tunnel at surface level

A tunnel is best defined as an artificial underground passage. When a tunnel is driven, accurate setting out is critical to the success of the operation. Even small errors are difficult to rectify which makes it essential that adequate care be taken over the whole surveying operation. At all sections the centre of the tunnel face should be on line, at the correct level and at the specified distance.

Establishing the line of the tunnel

Headings for road and railway tunnels
In these cases a long base line can be provided outside the tunnel at each end and the section within the tunnel is a continuation of this line.

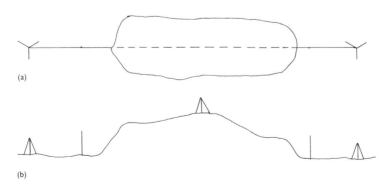

(a)

(b)

Figure 11.1 (a) Plan. (b) Elevation.

Figure 11.2

Figure 11.1 shows a plan and elevation for a situation where there is **intervisibility** between the central instrument position and the base line provided at each end. If a straight line is established between all five positions then the tunnel must follow this line.

In the situation shown in Figure 11.2 a very accurate open traverse must be run between each end. A secondary traverse should be used to check that the direction of the base lines are correct.

11.2 Establishing the line of the tunnel at a lower level_____

Headings which provide sewers and pipe lines at a much lower level than the natural ground are set out from the bottom of a shaft at each end.

Here the base lines are restricted to less than the diameter of the shaft

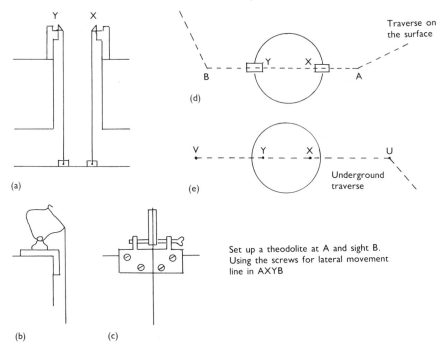

Figure 11.3 (a) Section. (b) Details at Y. (c) Screw for lateral movement. (d) Plan on surface. (e) Plan on underground.

and are related to a ground surface traverse by means of two plumb lines hanging close to each side of the shaft. Details are given in Figure 11.3.

Factors affecting the connection between surface and underground traverses

The plumb bobs tend to behave as pendulums, and in order to prevent this the plumb bobs are placed in buckets of water or light oil.

Ventilation currents in the shaft causes movement of the wires. While readings are being taken the forced ventilation should be switched off and the natural ventilation reduced by shielding the wires.

Spiral deformation of the wires cause twisting. This can be neutralized by using heavy plumb bobs.

11.3 Methods used in transferring traverses at the surface to traverses down the shaft

Method 1: coplanning

Place the instrument approximately in the line YXW shown in Figure 11.4. Taking special care that the tripod head is level, focus first on the front wire and then on the rear wire. If the two are not in line use lateral adjustment until at one focus position the front wire can be seen on the vertical hair and at the second focus position the rear wire can be seen on the vertical hair. YX and W will then be truly in line.

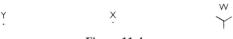

Figure 11.4

Method 2: the Weisbach triangle

Place Z in a position shown in Figure 11.5 so that angle XZY is less than 20 minutes and note its value. Measure the horizontal distances YZ, XZ and YX. Next calculate the value of angle XYZ and hence determine WXZ.

$$d = XZ \sin WXZ$$

With the zero position on X, turn through $(90° - WXZ)$ and measure the distance d. This will lie on the line YXW extended.

With zero position on X, turn through $(180° - WXZ)$ and this will give a line parallel to YXW extended with the distance d being the distance between the parallels.

Figure 11.5

Method 3: the Weiss quadrilateral

This method, shown in Figure 11.6, is used when it is not possible to set up the instrument close to the line YXW extended.

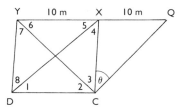

Figure 11.6

Here the instrument is set up at C and D and the angles 1, 2, 3 and 8 are measured. Angles 4 and 7 are deduced.

$$5 + 6 = 1 + 2 = y \qquad 5 = (y - 6)$$

$$\frac{\sin 1 \times \sin 3 \times \sin 6 \times \sin 7}{\sin 2 \times \sin 4 \times \sin 6 \times \sin 8} = 1$$

$$\frac{\sin 5}{\sin 6} = \frac{\sin 2 \times \sin 4 \times \sin 8}{\sin 1 \times \sin 3 \times \sin 7} = x$$

$$\frac{\sin(y - 6)}{\sin 6} = x$$

$$\frac{\sin y \cos 6 - \cos y \sin 6}{\sin 6} = x$$

$$\therefore \cot 6 = \frac{x + \cos y}{\sin y}$$

Example 11.1 *The Weisbach triangle*_____

Plumb bobs Y and X are 5 m apart and the measurements taken from instrument position Z are distance ZX = 2.5 m, distance ZY = 7.5 m and angle XZY = 12 minutes. Determine:

(a) The angle XZY which sets out a line parallel to YXW and the distance between the parallel lines.

(b) The distance ZW and the angle XZW if W lies on the straight line YXW is 8 m from X.

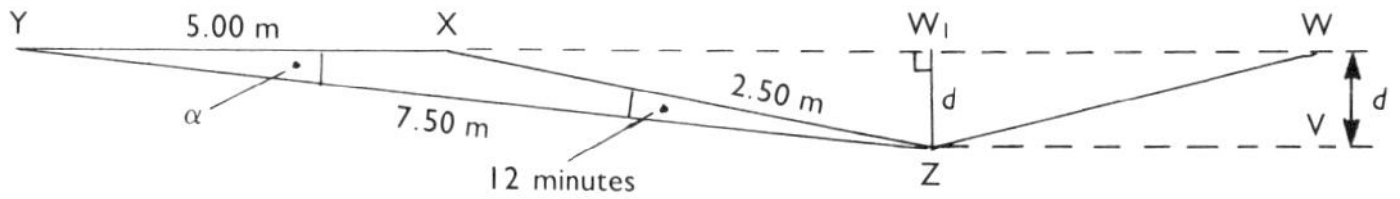

$$\frac{5}{\sin(12\text{ mins})} = \frac{2.5}{\sin\alpha} \qquad \sin\alpha = \sin(12\text{ min}) \times \frac{2.5}{5}$$

$$\alpha = 5.99999 = 6\text{ min}$$

$$WXZ = 18\text{ min} \qquad d = 2.5\text{ m}\sin 18\text{ min} = \mathbf{13.1\ mm}$$

$$XW_1 = 2.5\text{ m}\cos 18\text{ min} = \mathbf{2.49997\ m}$$

$$\text{angle } XZW_1 = 90^\circ - 18' = 89^\circ 42' 00''$$

$$\text{Angle } W_1ZW = \tan^{-1}\left(\frac{8 - 2.49997}{13.1/1000}\right) = 89^\circ 51' 49''$$

$$\sin 89^\circ 51' 49'' = \frac{8 - 2.49997}{ZW}$$

$$ZW = \mathbf{5.500\ m}$$

$$d = 13.1\text{ mm}$$

$$\text{Angle } XZV = 89^\circ 42' 00'' + 90^\circ = 179^\circ 42' 00''$$

$$\text{Angle } XZW = 89^\circ 42' 00'' + 89^\circ 51' 49'' = 179^\circ 33' 49''$$

Exercise 11.1 *The Weisbach triangle*

If plumb bobs Y and X are 4.5 m apart and the measurements taken from the instrument at Z are distance ZX = 3.87 m and the angle ZXY = $6^\circ 27' 39''$, show that:

(a) The angle XZV which sets out a line parallel to YXW is $167^\circ 59' 09''$ and the distance between the parallel lines is 0.8055 m.
(b) The distance ZW is 6.2667 m and angle XZW is $160^\circ 36' 01''$ if W lies on the straight line YXW 10 m from X.

Example 11.2 *The Weiss quadrilateral*

Plumb bob Y and X were hanging 5 m apart. Instruments were placed at C and D and the following angles were taken:

$1 = 45^\circ 20' 20''$ $\quad 2 = 49^\circ 58' 40''$
$3 = 39^\circ 16' 30''$ $\quad 8 = 55^\circ 08' 12''$

YXQ is a straight line with YX = XQ = 5 m. Determine:

(a) The angles of the quadrilateral.
(b) The angle and distance to be set out from D in order to establish position Q.

Solution

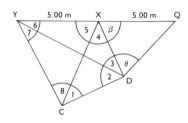

$4 = 180° - (1 + 2 + 3) = 45°24'30''$
$7 = 180° - (1 + 2 + 8) = 29°32'48''$
$1 + 2 = 5 + 6 = 95°19' \qquad 5 = (95°19' - 6)$

$$\frac{\sin 1 \cdot \sin 3 \cdot \sin 5 \cdot \sin 7}{\sin 2 \cdot \sin 4 \cdot \sin 6 \cdot \sin 8} = 1$$

$$\frac{\sin 5}{\sin 6} = \frac{\sin 45°24'30'' \cdot \sin 49°58'40'' \cdot \sin 55°08'12''}{\sin 45°20'20'' \cdot \sin 39°16'30'' \cdot \sin 29°32'48''} = 2.01522$$

$$\frac{\sin 95°19' - 6}{\sin 6} = \frac{\sin 95°19' \cdot \cos 6 - \cos 95°19' \sin 6}{\sin 6} = 2.01522$$

$$\sin 95°19' \cot 6 - \cos 95°19' = 2.01522$$

$\cot 6 = \dfrac{1.922566}{0.9956977} \qquad 6 = 27°22'47''$
$\qquad\qquad\qquad\qquad\quad 5 = 67°56'13''$
$\qquad\qquad\qquad\qquad\quad 4 = 45°24'30''$
$\beta = 180° - (5 + 4) = 66°39'17''$

$$\frac{5}{\sin 39°16'30''} = \frac{XD}{\sin 27°22'47''}$$

$$XD = \frac{5 \times 0.4598855}{0.633043} = 3.63234$$

$DQ^2 = 5^2 + (3.63234)^2 - 2 \times 5 \times 3.63234 \cos 66°39'17''$
$DQ^2 = 25 + 13.193887 - 14.3939 = 23.7999$
$DQ = 4.8785 \text{ m}$

$$\frac{5}{\sin \theta} = \frac{4.878}{\sin 66°39'17''} \qquad \sin \theta = \frac{5 \times \sin 66°39'17''}{4.8785}$$

$$\theta = 70°13'13''$$

11.4 Setting out within the tunnel_____

Tunnel section

A tunnel section is shown in Figure 11.7. In order to set out tunnels, the line and level above and below ground should be accurately related. An

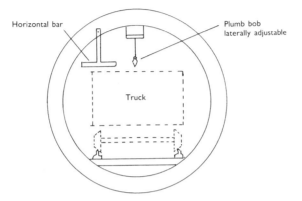

Figure 11.7 Tunnel section.

accurate line is achieved by employing plumb bobs and the use of one of the following theodolite operations:

Coplanning
Weisbach triangle
Weiss quadrilateral.

   The line is transferred to a number of plumb bobs which hang from the roof of the tunnel. The general line of the tunnel is achieved by lining in plumb bobs at intervals and carefully checking some of these by theodolite to ensure accuracy.

Lining plumb bobs in sequence

The level underground is found by attaching a standard weight to a steel tape and measuring the depth of the shaft. The level is transferred to a

Figure 11.8 Lining plumb bobs in sequence.

series of horizontal bars hanging from the roof of the tunnel making use
of a small inverted staff.

Levels from soffit

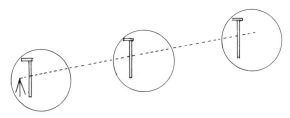

Figure 11.9 Levels from soffit.

11.5 Setting out of tunnels using lasers_____

In recent years lasers have been extensively used in tunnels, particularly in
conjunction with tunnelling machines.

The laser beam is extremely useful in that it provides a ray giving a distinct red spot which, when aimed in the direction of the tunnel, can be
easily interpreted by both engineers and semi-skilled operatives. It must be
remembered that the accuracy of the direction of the laser beam is dependent on normal base lines and theodolite and level work. The beam may
be disturbed by tunnel traffic and consequently must be checked regularly
for line and level.

Although the centre of the tunnel would be the most appropriate direction for the laser to be aimed, in fact this is rarely possible due to tunnel

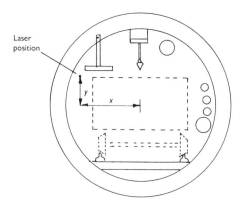

Figure 11.10

traffic. It is normal to offset the laser position in both x and y directions to a position which allows a continuous path of light. A series of brackets is attached to the tunnel walls and holes drilled allowing the beam to pass through. Failure of the beam to pass through the holes is a clear indication of disturbance of the laser instrument or one of the brackets.

In some of the tunnelling machines, a white beam of light is directed at points x and y when the machine is correctly placed. This means that if the tunnelling operators find that the red spot does not appear in the centre of the white circle of light the machine needs adjustment until they coincide.

Twelve

Setting out of roads

12.1 Main line setting out

In this type of work the surveyor is normally provided with a setting out folder and a computer printout.

The setting out folder details, to a scale of 1 : 500, chainage intervals, road and verge widths, transition points and other information such as access roads, bridge crossings, etc.

The computer printout indicates the coordinates of the main line at 5 m chainages.

Horizontal alignment

The main line may take the form of a centre line or the left-hand channel of a 7.3 m wide carriageway at one of the two inner channels of a dual carriageway as shown in Figure 12.1.

Objectives of main line setting out

1. To define the proposed road position.
2. To allow a means of checking from existing features to reveal irregularities in setting out and in computer printouts.
3. To provide a base from which boundaries, fence positions and batter rails may be positioned.

Practical methods for setting out the main line

The main line may be set out using either the traditional method or the

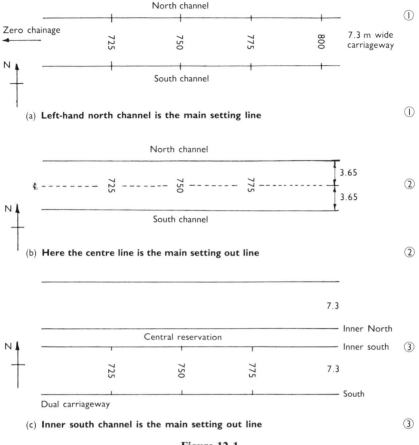

(a) **Left-hand north channel is the main setting line**   ①

(b) **Here the centre line is the main setting out line**   ②

(c) **Inner south channel is the main setting out line**   ③

Figure 12.1

modern (coordinate) method. Both require the same equipment, namely a theodolite with an EDM attachment and a three tripod traverse set. These are dealt with in the following sections.

12.2 Traditional method

This method requires that the position of the transition points be determined in order to define the limits of an element prior to 'filling' in the line from the transition points.

1. Establish the transition point A, making use of distances and bearings from stations 1 and 2 (i.e. stn 1 and stn 2).
2. Set up the instrument over the peg established at point A.
3. Sight and set back bearing onto RO stn 1.

4. Unclamp upper plate, rotate instrument and set forward bearing of target stn 3. If A is correctly placed, stn 3 should be bisected.
5. Set out points B, C, D, E, etc. using the derived curve expressions for the angles as shown in Figure 12.2.

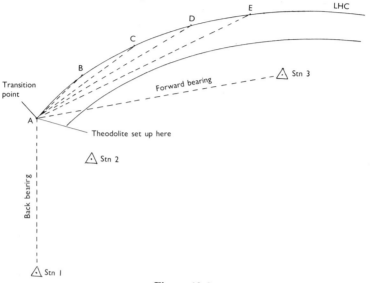

Figure 12.2

12.3 Coordinate method

Knowing the coordinates of the traverse stations and the points on the curve, the distances and bearings from the traverse station to the individual points can be established. In the situation shown in Figure 12.3:

1. Set up the instrument at stn 2. Sight and set back bearing on reference object RO stn 1.
2. Unclamp upper plate, rotate instrument and set forward bearing of target stn 3. The vertical hair of the telescope should now bisect target stn 3.
3. Set out pegs at chainages A, B, C, D and E from stn 2. Check distances from stn 3.

Note: F.A. Shepherd describes in detail two methods of establishing coordinates on road curves in his book *Advanced Engineering Surveying* published by Edward Arnold.

The advantages of the coordinate setting out system

In this method there is no need to establish the transition point and deduce the curve from there. The use of coordinates reduces the problem to a

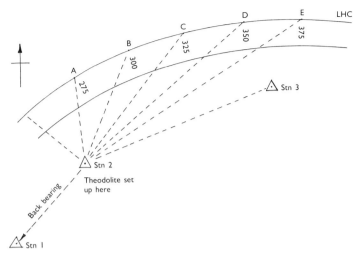

Figure 12.3

simple trigonometrical relationship between any two selected points. For this reason it is possible to start setting out in the middle of one element and finish in the middle of the next element.

The method is much more flexible and problems on the route can be temporarily left aside until conditions improve.

When using this method it is valuable to know the coordinates of the tangent points so that they can be used, if necessary, for checking or establishing the position of long straights.

12.4 Setting out boundaries and fences

When the main line control has been set out the next operation is to set out boundaries to define the limits of the site.

The positional details of the boundary are usually indicated on the accommodation works drawings. Care must be taken where both hedges and fences are indicated. In such cases the boundary lines of the plan usually correspond to the hedge centre line. Fence lines are offset from the main line control at the same chain intervals as the main line. The offset distances are shown on the cross-sectional drawing.

Methods of setting out

Ranging poles, fibron tapes and optical squares are considered sufficiently accurate for this type of work. Step taping is employed for steeper cross gradients. See Figures 12.4–12.6.

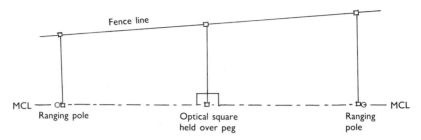

Figure 12.4 Setting out from straights.

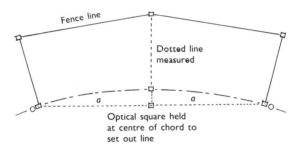

Figure 12.5 Setting out from curves.

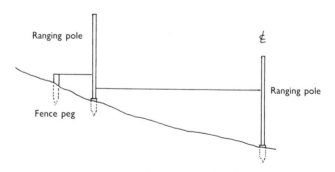

Figure 12.6 Step taping.

12.5 Controlling earth moving operations

Batter rails are placed to indicate the line of cut or line of fill for a cutting or embankment (Figures 12.7 and 12.8.).

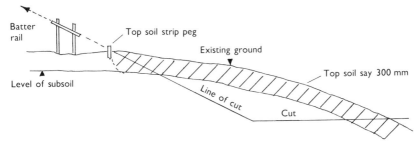

Figure 12.7 Line of cut.

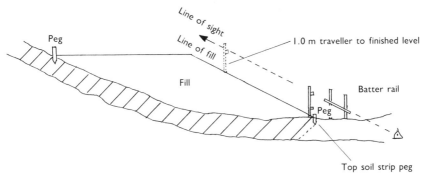

Figure 12.8 Line of fill.

Setting out strip pegs

Method of using cut rails to define top-soil strip
View along the top edge of the board and where the line of sight intersects the ground drive in a peg.

Method of using fill rails to define top-soil strip
Fill rails should be used in conjunction with a 1 m traveller to control the finished level of the embankment. View along the top edge of the board and sight in the 1 m traveller. Holding the traveller upright, move down the line of sight towards the observer until the base of the traveller strikes the existing ground. At this point, drive in the peg.

Other methods of setting out strip pegs
When the proposed road level coincides with the existing ground level and cross fall is negligible it is possible to position the strip pegs directly. However, when differences in level occur and the cross fall is not negligible an adjustment process is necessary which is best done by the batter rails.

Exercise 12.1 Cutting cross-sectional details_____

Chainage	C F	Verge level	Verge O/S	Batter O/S + 1 m	Slope of cutting	Width L_1 or L_2	Calc. level + 1 m trav. for fill	Slope length S_1 or S_2
L 2 350	C	37.984	3.5	23	1 : 2	18.5	47.234	20.7
R	C	37.890	13.5	23	1 : 2	9.5	42.640	10.6

Road width = 7.3 m
C is cut, F is fill.
O/S distance is on site measurement from O.

Side slopes of road = $\dfrac{1}{36.5}$ Side slopes on pavement = $\dfrac{1}{28.7}$

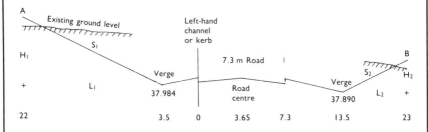

The main line control for this example is the left-hand channel peg on a line perpendicular to the alignment.

$L_1 = 22.0 - 3.5 = 18.5$ m
$H_1 = 18.5 \times 1/2 = 9.25$ m
$S_1 = L_1 \sec \theta = 18.5 \times 1.118 = 20.68$ m

Show that $L_2 = 9.5$ m, $H_2 = 4.75$ m and $S_2 = 10.62$ m.

Level at A = 37.984 + 9.25 = 47.234 m AOD
Level at B = 42.640 m AOD

Assuming the road and path slopes are as indicated and that the road kerbs are 115 mm high:

Level at left-hand upper kerb = $37.984 + 3.5 \times \dfrac{1}{28.7}$

= 38.106 m AOD

Level at left-hand lower kerb = 38.106 − 0.115
= 37.991 m AOD

$$\text{Level at centre of road} = 37.991 + 3.65 \times \frac{1}{36.5}$$

$$= 38.091 \text{ m AOD}$$

Show that:

(a) Level at right-hand upper kerb = 38.106 m AOD
(b) Level at right-hand lower kerb = 37.991 m AOD
(c) Level at centre of road = 38.091 m AOD

12.6 Setting out of batter rails for cuttings where stake and line of cut coincide

Field procedure

The main line control for the example shown in Figure 12.9 is the left-hand channel. A stake is driven in at 22 m left of the left-hand channel peg on a line perpendicular to the alignment. This stake position corresponds to the 'batter O/S + 1.0 m' or 1 m beyond sight intersection point for the left-hand side.

A further stake is driven at 23 m right of the left-hand channel peg on line perpendicular to the alignment. This stake position corresponds to the 'batter O/S + 1.0 m' for the right-hand side.

The two stakes are then levelled. A comparison is made between the top of stake reduced level and the calculated level of the line of cut at the stake position. On the assumption that horizontal adjustment is not necessary, the calculated level is subtracted from the top of stake reduced level to give the measurement down. This point is marked on the face, it corresponds to the intersection point with the proposed line of cut. A second stake is knocked in approximately 0.5 m away from the leading stake. The board

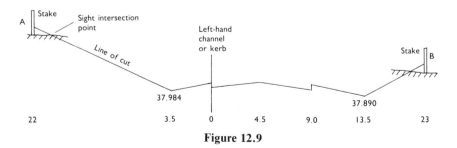

Figure 12.9

level on the second stake is set out using a wooden 1 in 2 triangular template with a spirit level or an Abney level adjusted to 26.5°. The rail is then positioned and nailed to coincide with the marks to complete the batter rail as shown in Figure 12.7.

A nail at the front edge of the leading stake is left protruding from the face of the rail in order to hook on the end of a tape to allow slope distance checks to be carried out during the course of the earthworks. Slope measurements are taken to the nearest 100 mm. Chainage O/S distance, slope distance and depth of top-soil reinstatement should be marked on the leading stake.

12.7 Setting out of batter rails for cuttings where stake and line of cut do not coincide

Stake below line of cut

In Figure 12.10 the stake top is below the level of the line of cut. For a 1 in 2 cutting the stake must be moved towards the proposed excavation by twice the difference in level. In the new position, if the ground is level, the stake and line of cut will coincide, enabling the batter rails to be established as before.

Minor adjustments to the stake position may be required to ensure the batter rail is at a convenient height. Note that adjusted slope distances must be calculated based on the new stake position.

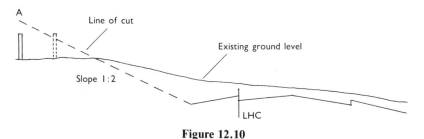

Figure 12.10

Stake above line of cut

In Figure 12.11 the stake top is above the line of cut. For a 1 in 2 cutting the stake must be moved away from the proposed excavation by twice the difference in level.

As before, minor adjustments will ensure the batter rail is at a convenient height. Note again that adjusted slope distances must be calculated based on the new stake position.

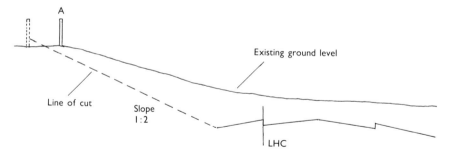

Figure 12.11

Exercise 12.2 *Embankment cross-sectional details*_____

	Chainage	C F	Verge level	Verge O/S	Batter O/S + 1 m	Slope of cutting	Width L_1 or L_2	Calc. level + 1 m trav. for fill	Slope length S_1 or S_2
L	2650	F	28.430	4.5	20	1 : 2	15.5	20.680	17.3
R		F	28.457	10.8	26	1 : 2	15.2	20.857	17.0

C is cut, F is fill
O/S distance is on site measurement from 0
Road width = 7.3 m
Side slopes of road and pavement = 1/37

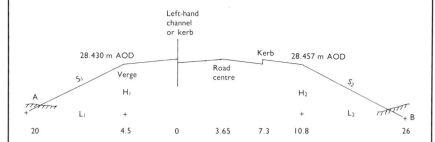

$L_1 = 20 - 4.5 = 15.5$ m
$H_1 = 15.5 \times 1/2 = 7.75$ m
$S_1 = L_1 \sec \theta = 15.5 \times 1.118 = 17.33$ m

Show that $L_2 = 15.2$ m, $H_2 = 7.6$ m and $S_2 = 17.0$ m.

Level at A = 28.430 − 7.75 = 20.68 m AOD
Level at B = 20.857 m AOD

Assuming the road and path slopes are as indicated and that the road kerbs are 115 mm high:

$$\text{Level at left-hand upper kerb} = 28.430 + 4.5 \times \frac{1}{37}$$

$$= 28.552 \text{ m AOD}$$

$$\text{Level at left-hand lower kerb} = 28.552 - 0.115$$
$$= 28.437 \text{ m AOD}$$

$$\text{Level at centre of road} = 28.437 + \frac{3.65}{37}$$

$$= 28.537 \text{ m AOD}$$

Show that:

(a) Level at right-hand upper kerb = 28.552 m AOD
(b) Level at right-hand lower kerb = 28.437 m AOD
(c) Level at centre of road = 28.537 m AOD

12.8 Setting out of batter rails for embankments

Consider the situation illustrated in Figure 12.12.

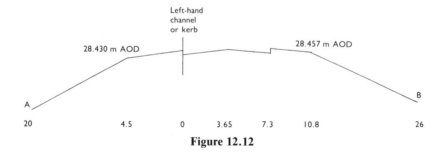

Figure 12.12

Field procedure

It is not practical to set out the line of fill directly from a batter rail. It is usual to erect batter rails at 1 m above the line of fill and to employ a 1 m traveller as shown in Figure 12.13.

The main line control for this example is the left-hand channel. A stake is driven in at 20 m left of the left-hand channel peg on a line perpendicular to the alignment. This stake position corresponds to the 'batter O/S + 1.0 m'. Another stake is driven at 26 m right of the datum.

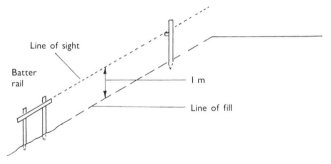

Figure 12.13

The two stakes are then levelled. A comparison is made between the top of stake reduced level and the level of the line of sight calculated by adding 1 m for the traveller to the calculated level of the line of fill. If the stake and line of sight coincide then this point should be marked on the face. A second stake is knocked in approximately 0.5 m away. The board level on the second stake is set using a 1 in 2 triangle template with a spirit level and nailed to coincide with the marks.

The line of sight from the batter rail should be parallel to and 1 m above the line of fill.

12.9 Setting out of batter rails for embankments where stake and line of sight do not coincide

Stake below line of sight

Consider the situation illustrated in Figure 12.14.

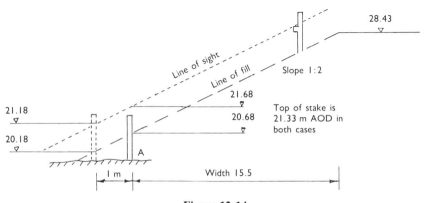

Figure 12.14

- Calculated values for A:

    Width = 15.5 m
    Line of fill level = 20.68 m AOD
    Line of sight level = 21.68 m AOD
    Slope length = 17.33 m

- Site values. Level at top of stake is 21.33 (this is below line of sight).
- Calculated values for (A + 1 m):

    Width = 16.5 m
    Line of fill level = 20.18 AOD
    Line of sight level = 21.18 m AOD
    New slope length = L_1 sec θ = (21 − 4.5)1.118 = 18.45 m

If top of peg is 21.33 the line of sight will be (21.33 − 21.18) = 0.15 m from the top of the peg, an ideal position for a batter rail.

Stake above line of sight

Consider the situation illustrated in Figure 12.15.

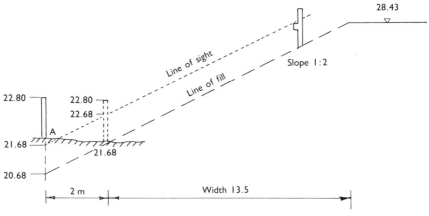

Figure 12.15

- Calculated values for (A − 2 m):

    Width = 13.5 m
    Line of fill level = 21.68 m AOD
    Line of sight level = 22.68 m AOD
    New slope length = (13.5)1.118 = 15.09 m

If top of peg is 22.80 the line of sight will be (22.80 − 22.68) = 0.12 m from the top of the peg, an ideal position for a batter rail.

12.10 Vertical control of road works_____

Profile rods

The purpose of the profile rod shown in Figure 12.16(a) is to provide permanent on-site control for level and occasionally for line of excavation.

A sight line is established at a constant height above, and sometimes offset at a constant distance from, the proposed line of working. The cross pieces of successive profile rods give a line of reference when aligned by eye. The movable traveller shown in Figure 12.16(b) transfers the line of reference to line of work.

Guidelines for use of profile rods

1. Profile rods should be established at proposed changes in gradient so that the slope between successive rods is constant.
2. Offsets should be used where plant is likely to disturb the rod. The offset distance should be written on the stakes.
3. The proposed level of the works at the point where the stake is to be established must be found.
4. The cross piece must be set horizontally by spirit level at a suitable constant height above this proposed level. The constant height should be written on the stake.
5. The cross pieces should be painted in distinguishing colours, particularly if profiles have been established to control more than one operation.
6. Stakes must be driven firmly in position at the calculated offset distances from the main line control (centre line or channel). Offsetting is to be carried out using tape and optical squares to ensure the stakes lie on perpendiculars to the main line chainage.

Method of employing profile rods

The top of each stake is levelled and a comparison of the stake reduced level with that proposed for the cross pieces gives the amount to be taped up or down from the stake top. When the measurement is above the stake top an extension piece has to be made.

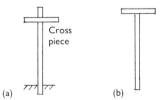

Figure 12.16 (a) Profile rod. (b) Traveller.

12.11 Sequence of setting out cut locations_____

1. **Monitor slope distances**. The engineer must monitor earthworks from batter rails until slope distances are achieved as shown in Figure 12.17.
2. **Monitor main line**. Fix profiles at A and B as shown in Figure 12.18 and set out main line.
3. **Monitor muck foundation and capping layer**. Fix profiles at C and D to control muck foundation, capping layer and drainage as illustrated in Figure 12.19.

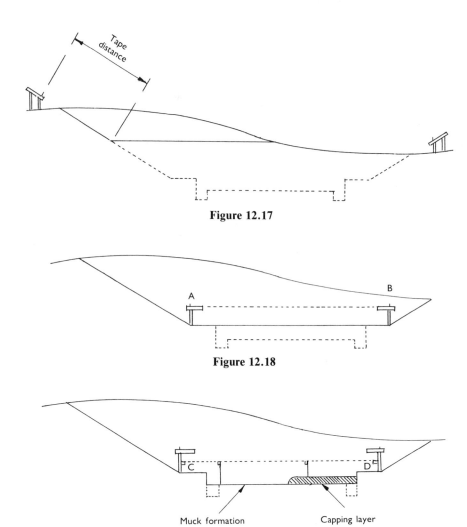

Figure 12.17

Figure 12.18

Figure 12.19

12.12 Sequence of setting out fill locations_____

1. **Monitor slope distances**. Measure from the batter rails the revised slope distance to establish the muck foundation level as shown in Figure 12.20.
2. **Monitor main line**. Fix profiles at both verge positions and set out main line control as shown in Figure 12.21.
3. **Monitor the various surfaces of the pavement construction**. Level stakes and fix profile boards according to calculated levels as shown in Figure 12.22.

Typical pavement construction is as follows:

40 mm	Wearing course ⎫	
60 mm	Base course ⎬ Black top	
200 mm	Road base ⎭	
250 mm	Type 1 sub-base material	
350 mm	Capping layer	
900 mm	Total pavement construction	

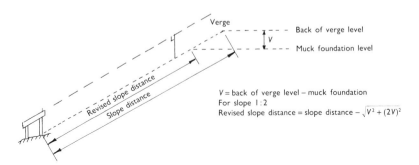

V = back of verge level – muck foundation
For slope 1 : 2
Revised slope distance = slope distance $- \sqrt{V^2 + (2V)^2}$

Figure 12.20

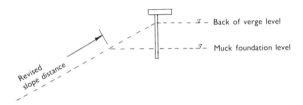

Figure 12.21

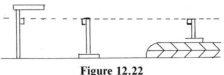

Figure 12.22

12.13 Second stage profiles_____

The cross-fall of the finished road is matched by that of the sub-base. Thus it is important to shape the sub-base accurately which normally means controlling at 10 m intervals.

The sub-base level is 50 mm lower than the proposed finished level and the traveller is designed to set out this lower level. The outstanding 50 mm rip is placed and compacted after kerbs are laid.

Typical sections

Equal or balanced cross-fall is shown in Figure 12.23; pitched cross-fall developing superelevation is shown in Figure 12.24, and cross-fall (superelevation fully developed) in Figure 12.25.

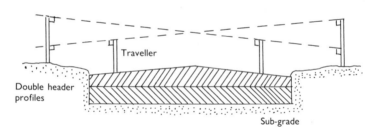

Figure 12.23 Equal or balanced cross-fall.

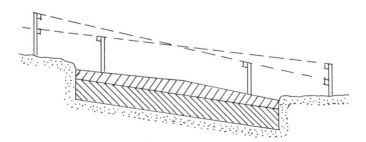

Figure 12.24 Pitched cross-fall developing superelevation.

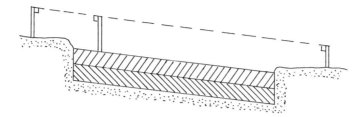

Figure 12.25 Cross-fall (superelevation fully developed).

Example 12.1 *Typical calculations for second stage profiles*_____

Consider a road section whose left-hand and right-hand channel levels are as shown in the diagram. This is commonly referred to as a balanced road section.

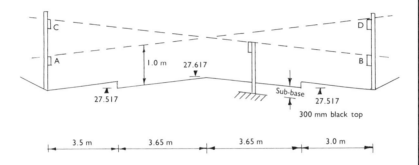

Difference between crown and channel
$$= 27.617 - 27.517 = 0.100 \text{ m}$$

$$\text{Gradient} = \frac{0.100}{3.65} = 0.02739$$

Assuming a sight line 1 m above the final finished surface:

Level of sight line above crown $= 27.617 + 1.00 = 28.617$ m AOD
Reduced level at C $= 28.617 + 0.02739 \times (3.65 + 3.50)$
$= 28.617 + 0.196$
$= 28.813$ m AOD
Reduced level at A $= 28.617 - 0.196$
$= 28.421$ m AOD
Block up A to C $= 0.392$ m
Reduced level at D $= 28.617 + 0.02739 \times (3.65 + 3.00)$
$= 28.617 + 0.182$
$= 28.799$ m AOD

Reduced level at B = 28.617 − 0.182
                  = 28.435 m AOD
Block up B to D   = 0.364 m
Traveller lengths: 1.00 m to surface
                    1.30 m to sub-base
                    1.35 m to underside of kerb race

12.14 Setting out drainage for roads

Information

The engineer is given information regarding the drainage on site in many forms.

Working drawings
These drawings normally indicate:

1. The direction and diameter of the pipe.
2. The backfill material.
3. The position of manholes and catchpits.
4. The type of run.

Standard detail
This gives specific information on:

1. Construction of manholes and catchpits.
2. Trench widths relative to pipe diameter and depth.
3. Backfill material and pipe bedding.
4. Gully details and connections.
5. Pipe connection details.
6. Special requirements regarding the runs which pass beneath the carriageway.

Specification
This indicates the quality of work expected and gives information such as:

1. Pipe strengths
2. Test requirements.
3. Dimensional information.

Control

Horizontal control
The line of the run may be fixed by direct measurement from first stage

profile stakes. In cases where back of verge control is non-existent the main line horizontal control will have to be re-established. The drainage along the alignment will be fixed dimensionally from the kerb face which itself may be the main line control.

Vertical control
Drainage profiles may be fixed to the first stage profile stakes following relevelling.

12.15 Setting out sequence for profiling a filter/carrier drain

Horizontal control

The existing first stage profiles are used to establish the offset distance to the centre of the pipe run as shown in Figure 12.26. Pegs are normally at, say, 20 m intervals with extra pegs placed on the external bends.

Vertical control

Place profile board on the stake at a level 2.5 m (say) above the level of the invert of the pipe at the sections as shown in Figure 12.27.

Typical completed section

Shown in Figure 12.28.

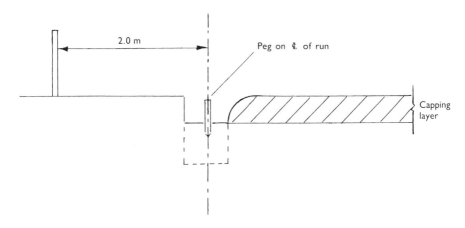

2.0 m

Peg on ℄ of run

Capping layer

Figure 12.26

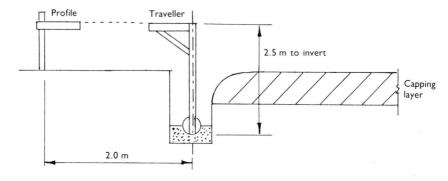

Figure 12.27

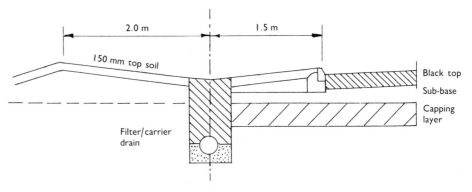

Figure 12.28

Example 12.2 Typical calculations for setting out of profile heights_____

Consider the section of road shown in Example 12.2.

Invert position	Distances from D_1	Level above D_1		Level at invert
D_1	0		0.000	56.740
D_2	16	$\frac{16}{86}(58.02 - 56.74) =$	0.238	56.978
D_3	36	$36(0.01488)$	$= 0.536$	57.276
D_4	56	$56(0.01488)$	$= 0.833$	57.573
D_5	76	$76(0.01488)$	$= 1.131$	57.871
D_6	86	$86(0.01488)$	$= 1.280$	58.020

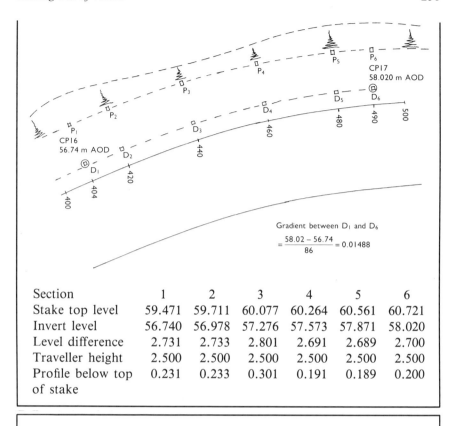

Gradient between D_1 and D_6

$$= \frac{58.02 - 56.74}{86} = 0.01488$$

Section	1	2	3	4	5	6
Stake top level	59.471	59.711	60.077	60.264	60.561	60.721
Invert level	56.740	56.978	57.276	57.573	57.871	58.020
Level difference	2.731	2.733	2.801	2.691	2.689	2.700
Traveller height	2.500	2.500	2.500	2.500	2.500	2.500
Profile below top of stake	0.231	0.233	0.301	0.191	0.189	0.200

Exercise 12.3 Setting out of a filter/carrier drain

For the section of road shown in the diagram:

(a) Show that the level for the inverts are as follows:

Chainage	490	500	520	540	560	574
Invert level	58.020	58.187	58.520	58.853	59.187	59.420

(b) Show that level differences between top of stake and reduced level of invert at the chainage are given by:

Chainage	490	500	520	540	560	574
Level difference	2.243	2.245	2.303	2.137	2.111	2.210

(c) Using a 2 m traveller show that the profile should be nailed below the top of the peg by the following values:

Chainage	490	500	520	540	560	574
Profile below top of stake	0.243	0.245	0.303	0.137	0.111	0.210

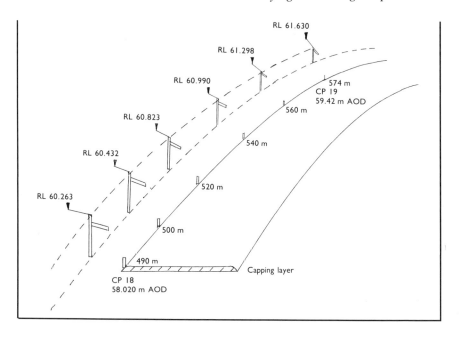

RL 61.630

RL 61.298

RL 60.990

574 m
CP 19
59.42 m AOD

RL 60.823

560 m

540 m

RL 60.432

520 m

RL 60.263

500 m

490 m

Capping layer

CP 18
58.020 m AOD

12.16 Drainage connections and other considerations_____

Connecting into existing services

If the new run is to discharge into an existing manhole or outfall, check physically on site that the level shown on the drawings is accurate. This is vital as errors may require redesign of part or whole of the system.

Gully connections

Check that the invert of the surface water drain is such that connections from road gullies can be made. The distance below the top of the cast iron gully grate to the invert of the outlet pipe from the gully pot will be up to 750 mm.

Control of manhole position

Since the drains running alongside the alignment are usually filter carriers, catchpits are specified in preference to manholes. The usual method of construction is to place a 300 mm deep ring on E mix concrete to act as the sediment retaining sump.

The pipes are then laid on top of this ring. The line and level of the ring are therefore controlled by the line and level of the incoming and outgoing pipes. Extra excavation at the catchpit may be accommodated by extending the traveller by 450 mm to invert. This distance makes allowance for the 300 mm sump ring and 150 mm base concrete.

Adjacent and crossing existing services

Consult Public Utilities' drawings of mains and cables to ensure that proposed sewers and manholes do not conflict with these services. If in doubt, dig trial holes. Do not assume that an existing sewer follows a uniform gradient or straight line between manholes. Do not forget to take into account pipe thickness and collars or patent joints.

Mark up drawings with all available information and confirm these with the statutory undertakers. Check that the distance between new and existing services will be sufficient for excavation, trench support and working space including construction of manholes.

Remember: record drawings of existing services are frequently inaccurate.

12.17 Setting out kerb lines

Basic control

The road engineer is supplied with the coordinates of a series of pegged stations which lie close to the road. These coordinates have previously been established by engineers using 1 second theodolites with electromagnetic distance measurement equipment on a traverse between two nearby triangulation stations. Corrections have been applied for small closure errors and for scale factor. The coordinates of significant positions on the kerb must be known and these are usually supplied in the form of a computer printout.

Basic method

Two 20 second theodolites placed on adjacent known stations are used to establish the extreme chainage points on the north (left-hand) channel by adopting the intersection method. Infilling is usually completed using angle and distance measurement.

Setting-out work sequence

1. Visit site, judge the approximate end chainage positions on the channel, make sure two selected stations are intervisible from these points.
2. Consult drawings and computer printout, calculate the 'whole circle bearings'.
3. Set up theodolites on stations and set out extreme chainages on channel using intersection method.
4. Set up on first intersection point, sight through to second intersection point, set out north channel.
5. Offset to south channel.

6. Offset kerb pins at chainage points to back of kerb.
7. Level pins, consult longitudinal sections or additional printout information to determine channel levels. (Remember that face of kerb is 115–125 mm deep: this measurement must be added to channel level to give top of kerb level.)
8. Mark top of kerb level on pins using adhesive tape.
9. Mark gully chainages and changes in kerb type on the sub-base using spray paint. (Kerb types include full batter, half batter, transition and droppers.)
10. Sights along the line of pins, make sure the finished setting out 'looks' right.

Example 12.3 Setting out kerb lines

Calculation establishing the horizontal angular relationships between stn 14, stn 15, ch. 950 and ch. 1050.

Coordinates

Stn 14	7657.603 E	8699.749 N
Stn 15	7761.285 E	8685.363 N
Ch. 950	7660.277 E	8667.444 N
Ch. 1050	7758.534 E	8649.257 N

Sign convention

To first	From last		Quadrant bearing	
−E +N	+E +N	(4th quad.) $360° -$ WCB	WCB	(1st quad.)
−E −N	+E −N	(3rd quad.) WCB $- 180°$	$180° -$ WCB (2nd quad.)	

Determine WCB from stn 14 to stn 15:

		E	N	
(to)	stn 15	7761.285	8685.365	+E
(from)	stn 14	7657.603	8699.749	−N ∴2nd quadrant
		+103.682	−14.386	

$$\frac{E}{N} = \frac{103.682}{14.386} = 7.20714 \quad \text{inv(tan)} = 82°06'02''$$

$$180° - \text{WCB} = 82°06'02'' \quad \therefore \text{WCB} = 97°53'58''$$

Determine WCB from stn 15 to stn 14:

		E	N		
(to)	stn 14	7657.603	8699.749	$-$ E	
(from)	stn 15	7761.285	8685.365	$+$ N	$\therefore$ 4th quadrant
		$-$ 103.682	$+$ 14.386		

$$\frac{E}{N} = \frac{103.682}{14.386} = 7.20714 \quad \text{inv(tan)} = 82°06'02''$$

$$360° - \text{WCB} = 82°06'02'' \quad \therefore \text{WCB} = 277°53'50''$$

Determine WCB from stn 14 to ch. 950:

		E	N		
(to)	ch. 950	7660.277	8667.444	$+$ E	
(from)	stn 14	7657.603	8699.749	$-$ N	$\therefore$ 2nd quadrant
		$+$ 2.674	$-$ 32.305		

$$\frac{E}{N} = \frac{2.674}{32.305} = 0.08277 \quad \text{inv(tan)} = 4°43'54''$$

$$180° - \text{WCB} = 4°43'54'' \quad \therefore \text{WCB} = 175°16'06''$$

Exercise 12.4

Using the information in Example 12.3, show that:

(a) WCB from stn 14 to ch. 1050 is $116°34'38''$.
(b) WCB from stn 15 to ch. 1050 is $184°21'25''$.
(c) WCB from stn 15 to ch. 950 is $259°56'25''$.

Total length	277.395				
Right-hand curve	Radius	Coordinates of centre		Degree of curvature	Chord
	750.000	7573.206	7922.515	7 38 22	5.000
	Chainage	X	Y	Bearing of tangent	
TP	920.647	7631.063	8670.280	94 25 28	
	925.000	7635.402	8669.932	94 45 25	
	930.000	7640.383	8669.501	95 8 20	
	935.000	7645.362	8669.036	95 31 15	
	940.000	7650.337	8668.539	95 54 10	
	945.000	7655.309	8668.008	96 17 5	
	950.000	7660.277	8667.444	96 40 0	
	955.000	7665.241	8666.847	97 2 55	

	960.000	7670.201	8666.217	97	25 51
	965.000	7675.157	8665.554	97	48 46
	970.000	7685.055	8664.128	98	34 36
	975.000	7685.055	8664.128	98	34 36
	980.000	7689.996	8663.366	98	57 31
	985.000	7694.933	8662.571	99	20 26
	990.000	7699.863	8661.743	99	43 21
	995.000	7704.789	8660.882	100	6 16
	1000.000	7709.708	8659.989	100	29 11
	1005.000	7714.622	8659.062	100	52 6
	1010.000	7719.529	8658.103	101	15 2
	1015.000	7724.429	8657.111	101	37 57
	1020.000	7729.323	8656.087	102	0 52
	1025.000	7734.210	8655.030	102	23 47
	1030.000	7739.090	8653.940	102	46 42
	1035.000	7743.963	8652.818	103	9 37
	1040.000	7748.827	8651.663	103	32 32
	1045.000	7753.685	8650.476	103	55 27
	1050.000	7758.534	8649.257	104	18 22
	1055.000	7763.374	8648.005	104	41 17
	1060.000	7768.207	8646.722	105	4 13
	1065.000	7773.030	8645.405	105	27 8
	1070.000	7777.845	8644.057	105	50 3
	1075.000	7782.651	8642.677	106	12 58
	1080.000	7787.447	8641.265	106	35 53
	1085.000	7792.234	8639.820	106	58 48
	1090.000	7797.011	8638.344	107	21 43
	1095.000	7801.778	8638.836	107	44 38
	1100.000	7806.535	8635.297	108	7 33
	1105.000	7811.282	8633.725	108	30 28
	1100.000	7816.118	8632.122	108	53 24
	1115.000	7820.743	8630.488	109	16 19
	1120.000	7825.458	8628.822	109	39 14
	1125.000	7830.161	8627.124	110	2 9
	1130.000	7834.852	8625.396	110	25 4
	1135.000	7839.532	8623.636	110	47 59
	1140.000	7844.201	8621.845	111	10 54
	1145.000	7848.857	8620.823	111	33 49
	1150.000	7853.501	8618.169	111	56 44
	1155.000	7858.132	8616.285	112	19 39
	1160.000	7862.751	8614.370	112	42 34
	1165.000	7867.357	8612.425	113	5 30
	1170.000	7871.950	8610.449	113	28 25
	1175.000	7876.529	8608.442	113	51 20
	1180.000	7881.095	8606.404	114	14 15
	1185.000	7885.648	8604.336	114	37 10
	1190.000	7890.186	8602.238	115	0 5
	1195.000	7894.711	8600.110	115	23 0
TP	1198.042	7897.456	8598.801	115	36 57
Long chord	275.816				

Figure 12.29

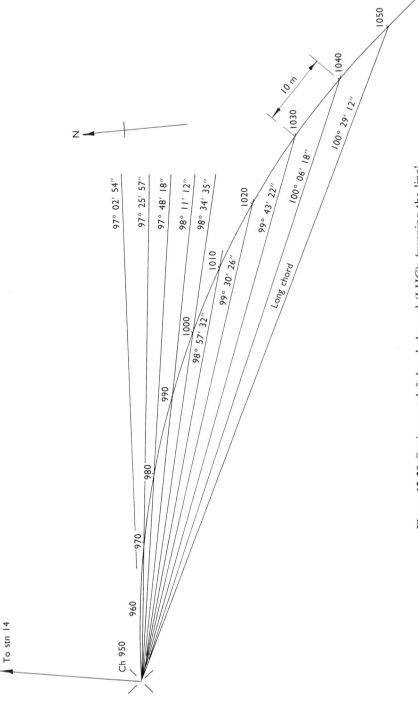

Figure 12.30 Setting out left-hand channel (LHC): 'running the line'.

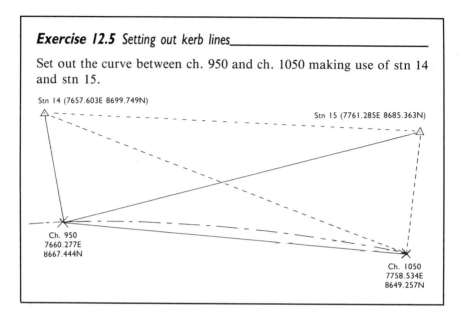

Exercise 12.5 Setting out kerb lines_____

Set out the curve between ch. 950 and ch. 1050 making use of stn 14 and stn 15.

Figure 12.29 shows a representation of a computer printout for the horizontal alignment of a 7.3 m wide standard carriageway. The relevant coordinates have been extracted and are shown below with calculated bearings to be taken with instrument at ch. 950. Figure 12.30 shows the situation to which the coordinates relate.

Ch.	E	N	Diff. E	Diff. N	Bearing	Chord length
950	7660.277	8667.444				
960	7670.201	8666.217	− 9.924	+ 1.227	97°02′54″	10.000
970	7680.108	8664.857	− 19.831	+ 2.587	97°25′57″	10.000
980	7689.996	8663.366	− 29.719	+ 4.078	97°48′48″	10.000
990	7699.863	8661.743	− 39.586	+ 5.701	98°11′42″	10.000
1000	7709.708	8659.909	− 49.431	+ 7.455	98°34′35″	10.000
1010	7719.529	8658.103	− 59.252	+ 9.341	98°57′32″	10.000
1020	7729.323	8656.087	− 69.046	+ 11.357	99°20′26″	10.000
1030	7739.090	8653.940	− 78.813	+ 13.504	99°43′22″	10.000
1040	7748.827	8651.663	− 88.550	+ 15.781	100°06′18″	10.000
1050	7758.534	8649.257	− 98.257	+ 18.187	100°29′12″	10.000

*12.18 Practical setting out from traverse stations*_____

Setting out of chainage 950 north channel from stations 14 and 15

In Figure 12.31, two 20 second optical microptic theodolites are set up: one at station 14 and the other at station 15. Engineer 1 is positioned at station 14 and engineer 2 at station 15. A chainman is nearby at ch. 950.

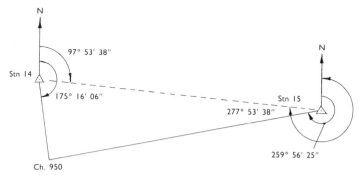

Figure 12.31

Operation carried out by engineer 1
1. Sets up and levels over stn 14.
2. Sets optical micrometer to 13′58″.
3. Slackens the upper clamp and rotates instrument until it is near to 98°.
4. Clamps and then sets precisely to 97°40′ giving a complete angle reading of 97°53′58″.
5. The lower clamp is slackened and the instrument rotated until it points near to target of stn 15.
6. The instrument is clamped and the target bisected using the lower tangent screw.
7. The instrument now points to stn 15 and reads 97°53′58″.
8. The optical micrometer is set to 16′06″.
9. The upper clamp is released and 175° is approximately set on the instrument.
10. The upper clamp is clamped 175° is set precisely using upper tangent screw and the instruments points 175°16′06″ towards ch. 950 north channel.

Operation carried out by engineer 2
This engineer repeats the process, establishing the angle to stn 14 to be 277°53′38″ and turning through to 259°56′25″ to point directly to ch. 950 north channel.

The intersection of both pointings will be the precise position of ch. 950 north channel.

12.19 Establishing the precise position of intersection at ch. 950 north channel_____

1. Both engineers line in a ranging rod as shown in Figure 12.32.
2. At the point of intersection, place a 300 mm square hard board. Secure the board using 150 mm long nails driven on the skew.
3. Mark front face and rear face of board along the line of sight from both theodolite positions, join successive lines and mark intersection with a 50 mm round head nail.

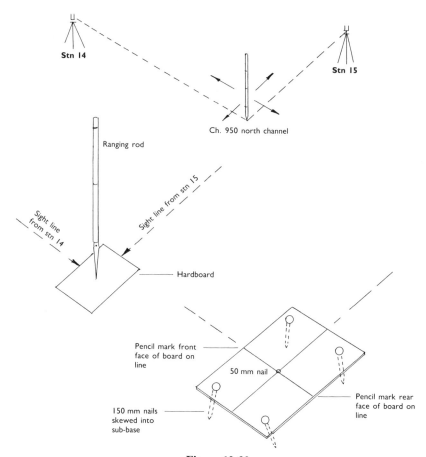

Figure 12.32

12.20 Setting out procedure: running the line

Establish the position of ch. 1050 from stn 14 and stn 15 in the same manner as ch. 950 was previously fixed.

One instrument is moved to ch. 950 north channel and the following procedure carried out using the information given by Figure 12.30:

1. Set up over nail ch. 950, set angle to $100°29'12''$ and sight nail at ch. 1050.
2. Set the optical micrometer to $2'54''$.
3. Slacken the upper clamp and rotate the instrument until it is set near to $97°$. Tighten the upper clamp and set the reading exactly to $97°$ by means of the upper tangent screw. The instrument now reads $97°02'42''$ and points along the first deflection angle (the WCBs used to run the line may be considered as deflection angles whose base line is grid north) for ch. 960.
4. Measure 10 m from ch. 950 and hammer in a 150 mm nail tagged with fluorescent tape along the line of sight.
5. The process is continued through for successive angles. However, the tape is always held at the previously established chainage to keep distance measurement to a fixed 10 m interval. Any error incurred in distance measurement between ch. 1040 and ch. 1050 should be proportioned out over several nails. Chainage errors up to 50 mm are acceptable providing the rate of change of the vertical alignment is not too great.

Offsetting the south channel

The chainage on the south channel must be fixed perpendicular to its corresponding nail on the north channel. This is achieved by spraying arcs at a measured distance from adjacent nails as shown in Figure 12.33. The 7.3 m measurement may then be pulled through each intersection mark to fix the south channel nail.

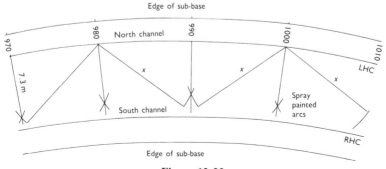

Figure 12.33

*12.21 Setting out procedure: pinning the line*_____

Kerb pins are set at the back of a 125 mm wide kerb as shown in Figure 12.34. Use a measurement of 130 mm from the edge of the nail, this ensures that the minimum 7.3 m carriageway width is achieved.

Following pinning, the tops of the pins are levelled in the usual way. Adhesive tape, fixed at the measured distance down the pin, is used to control the top of kerb level. The levels set out are derived from the slopes of the gradients or from the results of vertical curve calculations.

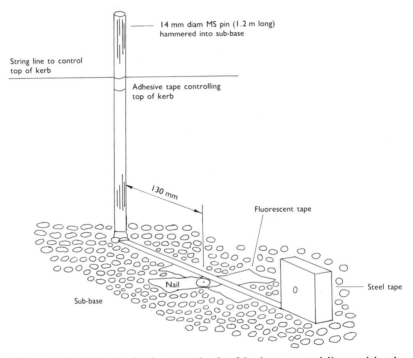

Figure 12.34 Offset kerb pin set at back of kerb to control line and level.

*12.22 'Tie ins'*_____

When setting out the terminating chainages the proposed line should tie in with the existing face of the kerb. In practice, due to traverse survey adjustment and permitted setting out variance this does not occur.

Errors up to 500 mm horizontal alignment and 100 mm in vertical alignment are typical. If the values fall within the limits indicated practical procedures are adopted to spread the error.

Horizontal alignment

The final chainage point should be set out and compared with the existing local position before local setting out begins. This will establish the value of the error. The resident staff should be notified of the discrepancies and confirmation given in writing.

The error perpendicular to the existing kerb must be corrected and the chainage value at this position noted. To correct the perpendicular discrepancy, the final chainage angle is turned on the existing kerb position and the last length is set out again repeating the same angles.

Having completed this horizontal setting out operation look at the finished line to make sure it looks right. If the line does not appear smooth the angular error should be shared in proportion to the distance from the theodolite.

Vertical alignment

Level the existing kerb at the terminating chainages and assess the difference between actual and specified levels. The resident staff should be notified of the discrepancy and confirmation given in writing.

To correct the level difference adjust the difference equally over several pins. For example, 30 mm difference may be 'taken out' at a rate of 5 mm per pin over six pins set out at 5 m intervals.

Having completed the setting out operation look at the finished line, make sure it looks right. Submit an 'inspection request form' detailing the adjustment and ask for verification of procedure and acceptance of the completed setting out.

12.23 Constructing the footway

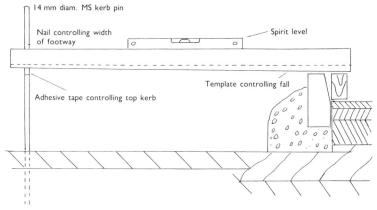

Figure 12.35

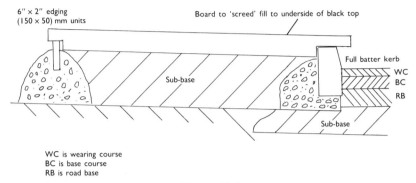

Figure 12.36

Cross-fall and width of footway can be controlled by positioning kerb pins using a template as shown in Figure 12.35.

The fill to underside of blacktop is controlled in a similar manner using kerb and edging to regulate the surface level as shown in Figure 12.36.

12.24 Simple block ups with straight cross-fall

When the kerbs have been laid, block ups are used to control the final trim of the sub-base and the black-top operation. Nylon lines pulled across the carriageway at specific chainages control cross-fall relative to the top of the kerb.

Figure 12.37 shows the method of 'dipping' to regulate the thickness of the various layers which make a typical pavement section.

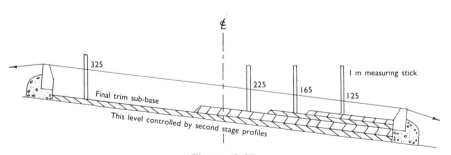

Figure 12.37

Simple crown

In Figure 12.38 the block ups are equal.

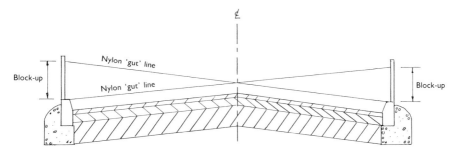

Figure 12.38 Blocking-up to form a crown.

12.25 Complex block ups

In locations where a crown is present, it is necessary to block up the lines to form the shape. Calculations similar to these used to establish the double header second stage profiles are employed. However, a formula may be used which simplifies the procedure as shown in Figure 12.39.

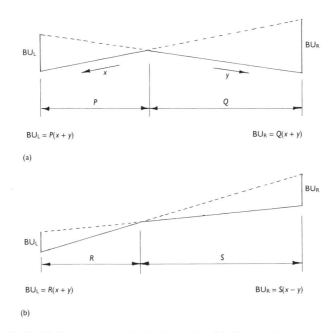

Figure 12.39 (a) Crown above both channels. (b) Crown above one channel.

Example 12.4 Crown above both channels_____

$P = 3.0$ m, $Q = 4.3$ m
Level left = 86.532 m
Level crown = 86.556 m
Level right = 86.519 m

$$x = \frac{86.556 - 86.532}{3.00} = 0.008$$

$$y = \frac{86.556 - 86.519}{4.30} = 0.0086$$

$BU_L = (0.008 + 0.0086)3 = \textbf{49.8 mm}$
$BU_R = (0.008 + 0.0086)4.3 = \textbf{71.4 mm}$

Example 12.5 Crown above one channel_____

$R = 3.2$ m, $S = 4.1$ m
Level left = 103.538 m
Level crown = 103.586 m
Level right = 103.622 m

$$x = \frac{103.586 - 103.538}{3.2} = 0.015$$

$$y = \frac{103.662 - 103.586}{4.1} = 0.00878$$

$BU_L = (0.015 + 0.00878)3.2 = \textbf{76.0 mm}$
$BU_R = (0.015 - 0.00878)4.1 = \textbf{25.5 mm}$

12.26 Block ups at roundabout locations_____

In these situations, sections are chosen as far as practicable to be square
to the channel lines. Block up values are calculated and marked together
with the chainage top of the kerb, preferably prior to the black toppers
visiting the site so that traffic management and construction joint positions
may be discussed. This is particularly relevant when dealing with live
roundabout locations.

Figure 12.40 indicates a roundabout site with scale 1 : 500 where a series
of sections has been selected.

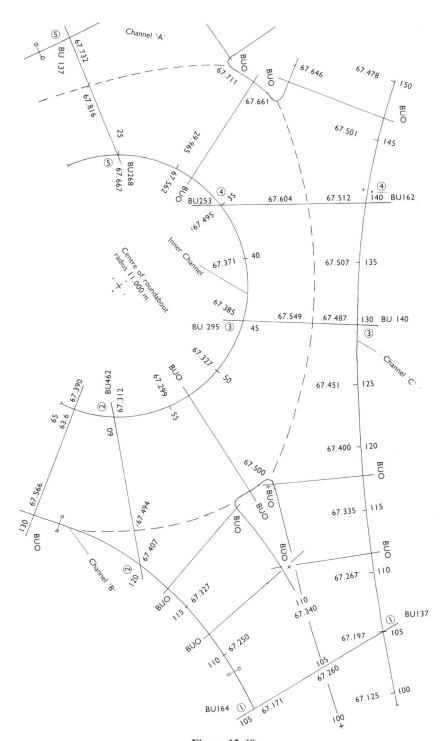

Figure 12.40

Exercise 12.6

For the sections indicated, show that the following results are correct:

Section 1 1

$P = 6.7$ m, $Q = 5.6$ m, $x = 0.01328$, $y = 0.01125$
$BU_L = 164$ mm, $BU_R = 137$ mm

Section 2 2

$P = 2.8$ m, $Q = 9.6$ m, $x = 0.03107$, $y = 0.01896$
$BU_L = 140$ mm, $BU_R = 480$ mm

Section 3 3

$P = 5.9$ m, $Q = 3.6$ m, $x = 0.02779$, $y = 0.01722$
$BU_L = 265$ mm, $BU_R = 162$ mm

Section 4 4

$P = 7.4$ m, $Q = 4.8$ m, $x = 0.0126$, $y = 0.01917$
$BU_L = 235$ mm, $BU_R = 152$ mm

Section 5 5

$P = 4.20$ m, $Q = 6.2$ m, $x = 0.020$, $y = 0.0240$
$BU_L = 185$ mm, $BU_R = 273$ mm

Recommended further reading

Bannister, A. and Raymond, S. 1984. *Surveying*. Pitman.

Barnes, W. M. 1988. *Basic Surveying*. Butterworth.

Bird, E. A. 1978. *Electronic Data Processing and Computers for Commercial Students*. Heinemann.

Brighty, S. G. 1989. *Setting Out: A Guide for Site Engineers*. BSP Professional Books.

Burnside, C. D. 1982. *Electromagnetic Distance Measurement*. Granada.

Milne, P. H. 1987. *Computer Graphics for Surveying*. E&FN Spon.

Muskett, J. 1988. *Site Surveying*. BSP Professional Books.

Sadgrove, B. M. 1988. *Setting Out Procedures*. Ciria.

Schofield, W. 1984. *Engineering Surveying*, vols 1 and 2. Butterworth.

Uren, J. and Price, W. F. 1985. *Surveying for Engineers*. Macmillan.

Wilson, R. J. P. 1983. *Land Surveying*. M&E Handbook Series.

Index